DATE DUE

AP 9 '93		
MY 13 '94		
JY 6 '95		
MR 8 '96		
MY 26 '98		
NO '0?		
FE 12 04		
DE '03		

Black Men: Obsolete, Single, Dangerous?

**Afrikan American Families in Transition:
Essays in Discovery, Solution and Hope**

Also By Haki R. Madhubuti (Don L. Lee)

Poetry

Think Black
Black Pride
Don't Cry, Scream
We Walk the Way of the New World
Directionscore: Selected and New Poems
Book of Life
Earthquakes and Sunrise Missions
Killing Memory, Seeking Ancestors

Criticism

Dynamite Voices: Black Poets of the 1960s

Anthologies

Say That The River Turns: The Impact of Gwendolyn Brooks
To Gwen, With Love
    (co-edited with Pat Brown and Francis Ward)

Essays

Enemies: The Clash of Races
From Plan to Planet, Life Studies: The Need for Black Minds
    and Institutions
A Capsule Course in Black Poetry Writing
    (co-authored with Gwendolyn Brooks, Keorapetse
    Kgositsile and Dudley Randall)
Black Men: Obsolete, Single, Dangerous? Afrikan American
    Families in Transition

Records/Tapes

Rappin and Readin
Rise Vision Coming
   (with the Afrikan Liberation Arts Ensemble)
Mandisa
   (with the Afrikan Liberation Arts Ensemble)

Black Men: Obsolete, Single, Dangerous?

**Afrikan American Families in Transition:
Essays in Discovery, Solution and Hope**

By Haki R. Madhubuti

THIRD WORLD PRESS • Chicago

First edition
Fourth printing

ISBN: 0-88378-135-2 (paper)
ISBN: 0-88378-134-4 (cloth)

Library of Congress catalog card number: 89-051325

Manufactured in the United States of America

Third World Press
7524 South Cottage Grove Avenue
Chicago, IL 60619

Cover illustration by Calvin Jones
Cover concept and design by Gina Minor

Dedication

Malcolm X
(El-Hajj Malik El-Shabazz)

Hoyt W. Fuller

Two mountains who left fertile valleys

and

*The millions of Black people who have given their lives in our struggle
for liberation.*

and

Black women

In memory of

James Baldwin   *M. Carl Holman*   *John O. Killens*

Mickey Leland   *Harold Washington*   *Bob Marley*

Max Robinson

**For the example of the brothers of the
National Black Wholistic Retreat Society**

Jesse Carter   *Chester Grundy*   *David Hall*

John Howell   *Kamau Jawara*   *Jack Thomas*

and

Nelson Mandela

Bob Law   *Lu Palmer*   *Don Johnson*

Acknowledgments

This book could not have been completed without the ground-breaking works of Robert Staples, Marcus Garvey, Hoyt W. Fuller, Bobby Wright, Gwendolyn Brooks, Frances Cress-Welsing, Neely Fuller, James E. Blackwell, Charles V. Willie, E. Franklin Frazier, W.E.B. Du Bois, Vivian Gordon, Nathan and Julia Hare, Wade Nobles, Maulana Karenga, Chancellor Williams, Ayi Kwei Armah, Harold Cruse, Cheikh Anta Diop, Jeff Donaldson, Abena Joan Brown, Margaret Burroughs, Hannibal Afrik, Murray DePillars, Harriette Pipes McAdoo, Useni Eugene Perkins, Na'im Akbar, Conrad Worrill, Kalamu ya Salaam, Gil Scott-Heron, Barbara Sizemore, Olomenji, David Lemieux, Richard Wright, Malcolm X, Asa Hilliard, Jacob Carruthers, Imari A. Obadele, Carter G. Woodson and others. Their research and/or actions helped to shape my thesis. However, I am totally responsible for any misinterpretation of their works or errors that may appear in this book.

I must also give a sincere thanks to my editor Christine Minor. Her help has been invaluable and her eye keen. Thanks also to Gina Minor (marketing & production), Tonya Thompson (typesetting) and Kelvin Dance (editing).

H.R.M.

Note:

I used a capital "B" when referring to Black people. The word "Black" is descriptive, but also it is a political and cultural term that identifies people of Afrikan descent at a world level. See the chapter "Nothing Black But a Cadillac."

In spelling Afrika I use "k" rather than "c" because for many activists the "k" represents an acknowledgment that "Africa" is not the true name of that vast continent. When I speak of Afrika, I'm bringing an Afrikan-centered view to my meaning. Therefore, the Afrika spelled with a "k" represents a redefined and potentially different Afrika, and also it symbolizes for me a coming back together of Afrikan people worldwide. Let it be understood that when I speak of Afrika and when most whites think of "Africa," we are coming from two different worldviews.

"A well-educated Black has a tremendous advantage over a well-educated white in terms of the job market. And, I think sometimes a Black may think that they don't really have the advantage...but I've said on occasion — even about myself — If I were starting off today, I would love to be a well-educated Black because I really believe they do have an actual advantage today."

Donald Trump
on R.A.C.E. (an NBC special)

"This is a very dangerous statement, especially since it wasn't challenged by anyone."

Haki R. Madhubuti

"A rich white boy can say anything he wants to in this world — no matter how ignorant it is."

A Black Female Student

The pain is in the eyes. Young Black men in their late twenties or early thirties living in urban America, lost and abandoned, aimlessly walking and hawking the streets with nothing behind their eyes but anger, confusion, disappointment and pain. These men, running the streets, occupying corners, often are beaten beyond recognition, with scars both visible and internal. These men, Black men — sons of Afrika, once strong and full of the hope that America lied about — are now knee-less, voice-broken, homeless, forgotten and terrorized into becoming beggars, thieves or ultra-dependents on a system that considers them less than human and treats them with less dignity and respect than dead dogs. I am among these men. I will *never* forgive white people for what they have done to Afrikan-American men, women and children. This is our story, and this time *we are not asking for* or waiting on *apologies* and *handouts*.

H.R.M.
1990

Contents

Introduction
A View from the Second Sunset

Why this Book

I consider myself primarily a poet. I'm a poet in the Afrikan griot tradition, a keeper of the culture's secrets, history, short and tall tales, a rememberer. As a Black poet, I have a certain sense for language, both its beneficial and destructive powers. Therefore, as a writer who is well aware of his own cultural heritage, I am extremely affected by anything that alters that heritage.

In America, not only has my Afrikan heritage been altered (a polite description), but also Afrikan American people have been mentally (and in many cases physically) disfigured. We are not who we used to be. I am keenly aware that all people change. However, we've been transfixed, made motionless by others, transformed into people who are often unrecognizable from our original Afrikan selves. We are people who, by and large, have been taught to deny reality as we hurriedly try to fit into somebody else's worldview.

I wrote this book because I sensed a need in the United States for a new truth — a truth not based on false histories, false assumptions, false arguments or false realities. In a *Newsweek* essay (1-21-80), the scientist/writer Isaac Asimov wrote about the "cult of ignorance" in this country. He said, "The strain of anti-intellectualism has been a constant threat winding its way through our political and cultural life, nurtured by the false notion that democracy means that 'my ignorance is just as good as your knowledge.'"

Ignorance about the state of Black people in America is appalling. However, what is even more appalling is that few people in the dominant culture even give a damn, and too many Afrikan American leaders have no idea how to improve the lives of their people.

This book is the result of a certain amount of frustration. I had grown tired of reading sociological and political reports alleging to address the Black condition. Most of these books, which were published by large trade or university presses and written by whites or negroes, contain only analysis without offering workable solutions for improving the status of

i

Black people. If explanation or examination was enough, after the tens of thousands of pages published over the last thirty years on the problems of Black people, Black families, Black women and Black men, we should be a free, conscious and developing people. This is not the case. It's like saying that the air is clean and the water is drinkable in Los Angeles.

Lack of Consciousness

One of the tragedies of Black life in America is that too many Black people never acquire insight into their own existence. *They just do not know who they are.* And, this confusion about *identity* and *source* is at the core of our ignorance. The Afrikans have a saying: "If you don't know who you are, any history will do." Welcome to America. This is the land where genocide was committed against nations of indigenous people; where New York was purchased with beads; where the abnormal defines normality; and where young people live and breathe on the words of burnt-out rock stars with their noses cut off.

Afrikan American people have little knowledge of themselves. We are products of a slave history, a Eurocentric worldview, that by definition cannot be developmental or inspirational. This history, for the most part, has been written, disseminated and taught by the sons and daughters of the people who raped Afrika of its people and wealth and literally sprinkled Afrikans around the world. They, while doing this, developed (created) in their politics, science, arts, economics, education and religion a rationale for Black destruction. This Eurocentric rationale provided the "intellectual and moral" basis for their taking of the world. Thereafter the world was divided into colors — Black, white and others.

Not Knowing and Not Wanting to Know

The education I received in the Black community was entirely different — in content and context — from that of whites. Not only was my "training" not a challenge, it was discouraging. The major piece of information I absorbed after twelve years of public education was that I was a problem, inferior, ineducable and a victim. And, as a victim, I began to see the world through the eyes of a victim.

I'll never forget how hard my mother worked to make ends meet for my sister and me. Our material lives were impoverished; we didn't have a television, record player, car, telephone or too much food. We acquired much of our clothing from secondhand stores, and I learned to work the streets very early. My life began to change when I was introduced to other worlds.

One year on my birthday, my mother took me to a five-and-dime store to buy me a gift. She bought me a blue plastic airplane with blue wheels, a blue propeller and a blue string on the front of the plane so that one could pull it across the floor. I was happy. That following week she took me and my sister to Dearborn, Michigan where she occasionally did "day work." Day work, for the uninformed, means Black women cleaning up white folks' homes. Dearborn, Michigan is where many of the movers and shakers who controlled the automobile industry lived. What I quickly noticed was that they lived differently. There were no five-and-dime stores in Dearborn at this time; there were craft shops. This is where the white mothers and fathers bought their children airplanes in boxes. In the boxes were wooden parts, directions for assembly, glue and small engines. Generally, the son would assemble the plane (which might take a day or two) and then take the plane outside and — guess what — it would fly.

This small slice of life is an example of the development — quite early — of two different consciousnesses. In my case and that of other poor youths, we would buy the plane already assembled, take it home and hope it rolled on the floor as if it was a car or truck rather than a plane. In Dearborn, the family would *invest* in a learning toy, and the child would put it together. Through this process, the child would learn work ethics and science and math principles. And, as a result of all that, the plane would *fly*. I was learning to be a consumer who depended on others to build the plane for me. The child in Dearborn made an investment, worked on it and, through his labor and brain power, produced a plane that flew. Translating this to the larger world, I was being taught to buy and to use my body from the neck down, while the white upper class boy was being taught, very early, to prepare himself to build things and run things, using the neck up. Two different worlds: my world — depending on and working for others, and his world — controlling his own destiny.

Economics and the Black Community

We have three billion-dollar businesses in the Black community: the church, drugs and consumerism. The Black church, basically, is the main spiritual, moral and cultural institution. It is not viewed as a business and, therefore, its economic benefit to the Afrikan American community is somewhat dubious. Drugs represent the backbone of the underground economy. Drug profits ($45 million last year in New York City) support a large chain of growers, suppliers, pushers and their families. However, the damage of the drug business to the Black community is disastrous, and it hovers over our community like a white plague. Obviously, consumerism is not a business. But, the extent to which Afrikan American consumers support businesses outside of their community as well as businesses located within but not of their community makes a profound economic statement.

A *people* cannot develop into a serious "autonomous" community without a financial base that initiates and provides for the community's creativity and resources.

White business since 1968 has been moving rapidly out of the inner cities as well as the country. Such exclusion of Blacks from available work, along with poor education, leads to a drop-out and give-up mentality. This country was built upon the backs of slave laborers. In the 20th century, America grew to its present state due to the development of small and medium-sized businesses. Today, according to the Small Business Administration, there are 19 million small businesses, and over one-half of them are family owned and operated. SBA has projected that over one-third of the new jobs created between the years 1990 and 2005 will require a college education; one-half of the jobs will require a minimum of 13.5 years of education.

Where does that leave Afrikan American people? Less than half of the Black students in the high school class of 1990 will finish; and of those who do, most will be under-educated. Couple this with the "outlawism" of big business and the 8.5 million unemployed white people, and it looks as though Black people will continue to be blamed for being lazy and not wanting to work. With Black male unemployment approaching 48%, the future doesn't look too inviting. Less than 4% of the jobs in the United States are manned by Black men. I'm not an economist, but I'm intel-

iv

ligent, and after reading *The Great Depression of 1990* by Ravi Batra, I think we are headed for a fall worse than that of 1929.

The destruction of Black men starts at birth, intensifies during boyhood, accelerates during the teen years and finalizes in early adulthood. I fear white people. This fear is based upon my interaction with them as well as my ongoing study of them, their history, psychology, politics, economics and culture. This fear comes from the experiences that Black people and other people of color have encountered in their contact with whites. Even the most naive understanding of European-American history should lead one to the conclusion that white people, as a collective body, have left huge scars of death and destruction on *all* of the people of the world whom they have "visited." Herein lies my fear: the one "creative act" at which few people have been able to beat white people is that of producing large death. We live among the chief killers in the world; I tried to document this in my last book of essays *Enemies: the Clash of Races*.

The world has gotten worse for Black men. A young Black man, according to the U.S. Census Bureau, has a 1-in-21 chance of being murdered as compared to a 1-in-333 chance for a white man of the same age. One out of two Black young people lives in poverty. The Black male prison population is over 50%, whereas our population in the country is around 13%. Of the six leading causes of death among the adult population, Black men lead the list in each category: homicide, heart attacks, cancer, suicide, strokes and accidents. The status of Black males in America is beyond the endangered species category.

At War?

A common saying among conscious Black men in regards to our current political, social and economic status in America is, "We are at war." I used to subscribe to such a theory myself. However, after many years of front-line activity in Black struggle and eleven years of research for this book, I've come to the conclusion that the relationship that Black and white men have is worse than war.

Nations fight wars. Nations prepare, execute and win or lose wars. Professional fighters fight personal wars. They prepare, execute and either win or lose. Even though we like to call ourselves the "Black nation," in fact, we are a heterogeneous body of Afrikan American men, women and

v

children searching for a better life. And, we are about as prepared to fight a war as we are to educate our children.

I think the best word to accurately describe the impact that the white nation is having upon Black people is *terror*. The Black community is being terrorized by whites at all levels of human involvement. The question that usually surfaces when I make this point is, "Are all white people terrorizing Black people?" It doesn't matter. What does matter is that the terror that is being inflicted upon the Black community is effective and has stopped most serious development.

Racism is not only alive and well in America, it is a growth industry. We need to understand that white world supremacy (racism) is a *given* fact of life in the world and is not vanishing. Therefore, we cannot, if we are intelligent, continue to use racism as an excuse to not execute our worldview. If this is clear, we will save a lot of hearts and minds that think we can change white people with conversation, spiritual sharing, money or astronomy.

White men and their women kick ass and dig graves all over the world. Mass media in the United States consistently portray Black men as the chief villains in this country. The best example of this portrayal is the last Presidential election. The fear of two Black men, Jesse Jackson and Willie Horton, helped to elect George Bush. America is drowning in drugs, and Congress and the President give $150 billion to the savings and loan industry and $8 billion to fight drugs. Evidently, the savings and loan industry's lobby is more effective than millions of ordinary lives being destroyed daily by drugs. The Black men murdered in Howard Beach and Bensonhurst are only very small examples of racially motivated crimes against Black people. Where is the lobby for the disenfranchised Blacks of America?

This book is not a cry for white help, white pity or even white understanding. Literally hundreds of books do that. After thirty years of active participation in the Black liberation movement in this country and the world, I'm convinced, without doubt or hesitation, that white world supremacy (racism) has to be seen as an organized and deliberated attack on all people of color. And, an effective defense against it must be incorporated into the teaching of every Black youth in the world.

John Kenneth Gallbrath in his book *The Nature of Mass Poverty* talks about people accommodating themselves to their condition. Poverty exacts its own reality. A poor person, like a poor family has to make his or her life out of what is available or what is left over from the well-to-do. This is, in part, the sort of terrorism about which I write. Often the only thing that can come from nothing is less than nothing. Poverty is, indeed, slavery.

As I was completing this book, the National Research Council issued its report *A Common Destiny: Blacks and American Society.* Here are some of its findings:

Economic Status: In income and earnings, Blacks gained fairly steadily relative to whites from 1939 to 1969. The percentage of people living in households with incomes below the poverty line has risen for both Blacks and whites in the past decade. Black poverty rates have been two to three times higher than those of whites at all times.

Residential Segregation: Residential separation of Blacks and whites has remained practically unchanged since the 1960s. The report notes that discrimination against Blacks currently seeking housing "has been conclusively demonstrated."

Education: "Segregation and differential treatment of blacks continue to be widespread in the elementary and secondary schools," the committee reported. College enrollment rates of all high school graduates declined sharply after 1977; while white rates have recovered, Black rates remain significantly lower than those of the 1970s. The odds of a Black student entering college within a year of graduating from high school are less than one-half the odds for a white student.

Political Participation: The proportion of Black federal, state and local public administrators rose from less than 1% in 1940 to 8% in 1980, but this figure is still less than Blacks' current 13% proportion of the U.S. population. Blacks still make up only about 1% of all elected officials.

Crime: "Black Americans are disproportionately victims of crime," the committee found. Blacks are twice as likely to be victims of robbery, vehicle theft and aggravated assault. "As long as there are great disparities in the socioeconomic status of blacks and whites, blacks will continue to be over-represented in the criminal justice system as victims and offenders," the committee stated.

Health: There are wide gaps in the mortality and morbidity of Blacks compared to whites at all ages except for individuals 85 and older. The odds that a Black baby will die shortly after birth are consistently twice as high as those for a white baby.

Child and Family Issues: The majority of Black children under the age of 18 live in families that include their mothers but not their fathers, while one in every five white children lives with just his or her mother. These figures are particularly significant considering the fact that female-headed families were 50% of all Black families with children in 1985, but they received only 25% of total Black family income. During the 1970s, one in every three Black children lived in poverty for at least seven of those 10 years; for white children the figure was one in 33.

I've tried to speak to all of these issues in this book. In the chapter "Never Without a Book," I write about the importance of literature. However, there are three books of which most people may not be aware; these books should be on every Afrikan American adult's "must study" list: *The Isis Papers* by Dr. Frances Cress-Welsing; T*he United Independent Compensatory Code/System/Concept* by Neely Fuller, Jr.; and *The Destruction of Black Civilization* by Chancellor Williams.

This book is a call for serious Afrikan American men to
stand tall and dare to be great,
dare to move beyond the limited ideas of others,
dare to think for yourselves,
for the future.
dare to conceive a world where you
are more than a consumer,
a buyer,
a clown in purple
wearing odd clothes finding glory in not being
Black.
dare to stretch your imagination to where
beauty is the norm
rather than an ignorant accident
stomped upon in the stupor of quick
highs and lies masquerading as

truth.
dare to be beauty,
dare to be creative fire,
dare to be fathers, husbands,
dare to be quiet life fighters with a smile
dare...

H.R.M.

I. Changing Seasons

"It is always easier to proclaim rejection than actually to reject."

Frantz Fanon
The Wretched of the Earth

The B Network

brothers bop & pop and be-bop in cities locked up
and chained insane by crack and other acts
of desperation computerized in pentagon cellars producing
boppin brothers boastin of being better, best & beautiful.

if the boppin brothers are beautiful where are the sisters
who seek brotherman with a drugless head unbossed or beaten
by the bodacious West?

in a time of big wind being blown by boastful brothers,
will other brothers beat back backwardness to better & best
without braggart bosses beatin butts,
takin names and diggin graves?

beatin badness into bad may be urban but is it beautiful & serious?
or is it betrayal in an era of prepared easy death hangin on corners
trappin young brothers before they know the difference between
big death and big life?

brothers bop & pop and be-bop in cities locked up
and chained insane by crack and other acts
of desperation computerized in pentagon cellars producing
boppin brothers boastin of being better, best, beautiful
and definitely not *Black*.

the critical best is that
brothers better be the best if they are to avoid backwardness
brothers better be the best if they are to conquer beautiful bigness
Comprehend that bad is only *bad* if it's big, Black and better than
boastful braggarts belittling our best and brightest
with bosses seeking inches when miles are better.

1

brothers need to bop to being Black & bright & above board
the black train of beautiful wisdom that is bending this bind
toward a new & knowledgeable beginning that is
bountiful & bountiful & beautiful
While be-bopin to be
better than the test,
brotherman.

better yet write the exam.

Were Corners Made for
Black Men to Stand On?

The larger question is what do a people do when the social, political and economic conditions under which they live are not only designed to limit their intellectual and material development, but are structured ultimately to kill them?

Every day, books, magazines, and newspaper articles are published with information detailing the "Decline of the Black Family," "The Crisis of Black Teenage Pregnancy, " "The Vanishing Black Male," "Brothers," and on and on. In much of the material published, the information is either rehashed sociological theories, excerpts from recent Ph.D. theses or articles from young hot-shot reporters looking for front-page bylines.

Black misery has always made good copy, yet there is much missing in this approach. There are answers, lies, music and many complexities in the lives of Afrikan Americans. However, the great majority of our people are not able to hear the survival songs.

Black people are not listening to the correct songs and their dance is increasingly becoming that of a beginner willing to accept "solutions" from the false musicians. It is not that Afrikan American people are inherently negligent in their search for life-giving and life-saving answers. The problem is the context and content of the answers that are presented. Social-political theory is passed off as "objective wisdom," as the worldview of Euro-Americans permeates Black life in ways that inhibit the majority of Blacks from functioning in their own best interests.

Cultural Absolutions

There are certain cultural resolutions that should be non-negotiable as a people pursues beauty and power. At the top of such a list is the necessity for the members of a people to know and be themselves (i.e., Afrikan Americans or Black people, all 30 million plus, must have a common and individual understanding of their history, traditions, accomplishments and mistakes).

Secondly, it is crucial that a people develop and listen first to its own "experts," seers and wise women and men. A people's worldview can be a major detriment in the construction of possibilities and future.

Thirdly, in the construction of a future, a people needs, as clearly as possible, to define and understand its enemy(ies).

Finally, a people needs to develop its own workable worldview (of all areas of human activity). In doing so, that people brings forth a leadership that is dedicated and willing to work incessantly to fulfill the constituents' wishes. Afrikan Americans at the national level do not have these cultural resolutions.

America 1989 is where millions of homeless people are dismissed with, "They are lazy and have too many babies;" where AIDS is the new megadeath, and its origin is falsely and maliciously placed in the Afrikan community. America is where most problems are treated by either taking drugs, over-eating, exercising, having sex, spending money, committing raw violence, reciting Sunday morning prayers, or staring at 110-channel television sets.

Material Value

Young unwed Black girls who give birth are no longer the exception, and young Black fathers have no idea of the "destruction" they bring forth with each of their seeds that matures to birth without proper nurturing. The U.S. is a country in which an educated person is measured by degrees, letters of reference and who one knows, rather than products produced. Value is determined by what one wears, where one lives, what one drives, where one parties and the type of employment one has.

America's trillion dollar budget supports an antiquated defense structure, while the poor of the land are redefined and ridiculed as their benefits are legislated downward. America's 36 % Black unemployment rate is considered tolerable as the Black underground economy expands and consumes those who least need it.

The West is canned food, processed knowledge, imitation grass and an economic system that rewards few. It also includes fake art, overly amplified "music," oppressive architecture, plastic shoes and a political system that operates for the wealthy. Many people endure 25-floor public housing, pencil-less classrooms, junk "food" and inadequate medical care. Malnourished children, material-minded adults, addictive religions and

4

political ideologies that condone a "Killing Field" attitude toward the unbelievers are viewed as normal. Black life is affected by overcrowded prisons, too few homes, over-stressed minds, fat bodies and a communicative network that legitimizes the easy, the quick and 30-second answers. America's context and content is built upon a subtle and effective ideology of White World Supremacy that few people understand. For those who do, many are unwilling to voice the call to resist.

Culture

As a people, our understanding of culture is severely limited. Black culture, as a force for survival and development, is given very little attention in the education of our young. However, the education that is transmitted (or not transmitted) is a product of the dominant white culture.

The politics and the economics that a people experience do not just appear, but are the unique results of that people's or somebody else's culture. The language, science and technology that bring meaning (or control) to a people's existence are also cultural.

One problem, of course, is that to most of us culture, as a concept, is abstract — that is, one does not actually observe culture. Yet, we all experience its manifestations, such as clothing, art, music, housing, weapons, films, literature, language, food, political, educational and social organizations and economic structures. Anthropologist Laura Thompson sees culture as

> ...the supreme creation of a human community, the product of its deep-seated urge to fulfill and perpetuate itself...it is primarily a group problem-solving device instituted by a human community to cope with its basic practical problems.

Aspects Of Culture

Dr. Thompson places great emphasis on the coping and problem-solving aspects of culture. However, it must be noted that among anthropologists and sociologists, there are differences of opinions as to conclusive definitions of culture. Edward T. Hall, in his *Beyond Culture*, states that most serious students of culture, however,

...do agree in three characteristics of culture: it is not innate, but learned; the various facets of culture are interrelated — you touch a culture in one place and everything else is shared and in effect defines the boundaries of different groups.

Hall goes on to point out that:

...Culture is man's medium; there is not one aspect of human life that is not touched and altered by culture. This means personality, how people express themselves (including shows of emotion), the way they think, how they move, how problems are solved, how their cities are planned and laid out, how transportation systems function and are organized, as well as how economic and government systems are put together and function.

Misconceptions

My focus on culture is to clear the air of serious misconceptions regarding cultural influence and hopefully to move our analysis beyond the trap of looking at race, politics and economics as isolated and unrelated entities. The way people view themselves and the extent to which they rise up out of any situation and decide their own course is a serious cultural question.

Culture, "shared understanding," is that medium in which values are transmitted from generation to generation. It is generally accepted that human behavior can be and is systematically observed, and that the variability of individuals is a result of inherited characteristics (biology) and life experience (culture).

A people's consciousness, the way they view and operate in the world, is shaped by their (or another's) culture. All of the answers are not certain, but it seems that culture can disable and kill as well as develop and give life.

The most prevailing consciousness among Black people today is one of survival. And this survival is not of a collective nature, in which individuals, communities and institutes work together to solve problems. Black survival, especially in the urban areas, is more Darwinian, a "survival of the fittest" attitude. Its proponents will use whatever means at their disposal to achieve their ends, regardless of the cost and pain to others.

6

It has often been stated that Black people in America represent the revolutionary vanguard. Indeed, we may be a vanguard, but revolutionary we are not — that is, if I understand the concept of revolutionary vanguard: a people who are bold and sophisticatedly violent while actively involved in replacing an unjust, corrupt system with one that is just and incorruptible.

De-revolution

The evidence does not support this concept, no matter how we wish to romanticize today's "revolutionary climate." If any climate exists, it is one of de-revolution. The political, educational, military and financial organizations of the U.S. have been actively involved — especially in the last twenty years, through the use of mass media, politics, sports and entertainment — in depoliticizing millions of Black people.

Ask the average Black person to articulate what he or she wants out of life, and you will get about the same answers the white middle class would give. However, the great majority of Blacks, who are not able to move to the middle class, end up settling for what they can get. Therefore, we have been forced into and have helped develop a culture of survival and/or dependency, not one of development.

The survival/dependent culture deals more with immediate needs rather than long-term needs. The ongoing search for food, shelter, clothing, sex, material artifacts, social status and fast weekends are what direct us and absorb our energies on a day-to-day basis. As a result, there exists very little time for serious development. Yet, the most hurting aspects of this is that if the time existed, there would still be few examples of genuine development.

Cultural Mentalities

The culture of survival/dependency breeds people who riot rather than plan progressive change or revolution. It develops people who react rather than act, beg rather than take, play rather than study and follow rather than lead. Let's take a closer look at these two cultural mentalities: 1) the revolutionary or progressive mentality is one that creates, builds and works for the long term; 2) the riot mentality is one that seeks instant gratification and is more destructive than constructive. The revolutionary would

7

take over a school system or build a school, while the rioter would burn the school down and give little thought to the results of that action.

The charts below are designed to more clearly characterize these two mentalities as they affect our development as a people. This comparison is not scientific. But it represents my conception of the highest and the most destructive responses of two opposing cultural orientations.

MAXIMUM CULTURAL DEVELOPMENT
Revolutionary Mentality

1. Study-oriented: reads, evaluates and debates books, newspapers, magazines and scholarly journals. Accepts the challenge of education.
2. Worker: looks for ways in which to actively work for self; may hold a job outside in order to sustain self and family. Self-reliant.
3. Organized and systematic. Efficient and diligent.
4. Progressively collective; conscious of others; cooperative.
5. Family-oriented: regards mate as partner in struggle; loves children. Values trust in relationships.
6. Land conscious: realizes that the only thing that nobody is making any more of is land.
7. Disciplined; strong, unyielding and energetic.
8. Serious. Practices fair play, order and punctuality. Honest and dependable.
9. Analytical and critical.
10. Frugal: buys mainly on need basis; saves.
11. Social life is developmental and involves children.
12. Creatively aggressive: will dare the impossible if it is possible.
13. Respects elders.
14. Dislikes incompetence and mediocrity.
15. Fights against Black-on-Black crime and understands that its root is white-on-Black crime.
16. Loves Black art, music and literature.
17. Can give and follow instructions. Encourages experimentation and criticism.
18. Committed to Black liberation, local, national and international.
19. Does not use drugs.
20. Politically active. Not crisis-oriented; acts on information rather

8

than reacts. Plans for the long term; alert; prepared for change.
21. Self-confident. Respects others regardless of race or culture.
22. Understands the economic forces that control our lives on a local, national and international level.
23. Rational in decisions and actions.
24. Rewards merit and achievement.

SURVIVAL CULTURAL EXISTENCE
Accommodationist/Riot Mentality

1. Does not read or study after "formal" education. Buys few books; reads mainly newspapers, sports pages or popular novels and magazines.
2. Works eight hours a day for someone else. Welfare conscious, get-it-for-nothing attitude.
3. Unsystematic and definitely not organized unless it is for someone else.
4. Backwardly individualistic: I, me, mine mentality.
5. Not family-oriented: regards mate as property; rates children low; generally single-minded; does not want children or responsibility of home life.
6. Not land conscious.
7. Actively fights against discipline.
8. Non-serious majority of time.
9. Not critical or analytical; prefers not to think for self.
10. Consumer junkie; if it's advertised, he's got it. Cannot distinguish wants from needs.
11. Loves social and night life (i.e., lives for the weekend, loves sexual conquests).
12. A defeatist; has few goals other than acquisition of material artifacts.
13. Puts elders in nursing homes and forgets them.
14. Gravitates towards incompetence and mediocrity.
15. Involved in Black-on-Black crime or is apathetic about the issue.
16. Loves any kind of music of the new generation.
17. Can give instructions but not follow them; avoids/rejects criticism.
18. Committed to self-liberation only.
19. Drug dependent — cigarettes, alcohol, hard drugs, etc.

20. Politically inactive; crisis-oriented; reacts.
21. Egotistical, ignorantly arrogant, has little concept of culture; feels he will be forever the racial underclass.
22. Naive about economics; unaware of the international nature of capitalism that touches all of our lives.
23. Rewards "yes" people.

Revolutionary Culture

It is obvious that there cannot be progress without a progressive and revolutionary culture working at its highest level. The rebellions of the sixties were both reactive and proactive. Much of the destruction that took place in the sixties was in the Black community. There are concrete reasons for this and if we are to move forward, we have to confront the truth. As I see it, these are the reasons that most Blacks don't struggle at a political level:

- Many Black people are satisfied with the way their lives are and fear radical change from any segment of society.

- Of those Black people who believe change is necessary, many don't know what to do about it and feel that their individual efforts are not worth much. Therefore, they do nothing but talk.

- Just about every Black family in the country has one or more personal traumas that consume their quality time (e.g., a son or husband in prison; a mother or family member seriously ill; basic economic survival, etc.).

- In most Black families, members can point to at least one family member, no matter how remote, who has "made it" in America and that person(s) is constantly used as the example of what we all can do with hard work, fortitude and initiative. This implies that Black failure is always individually instituted.

- A great many young Black adults are interacting on a day-to-day basis with white people either at school, work or play and find it difficult to separate the evils that the white race has perpetuated against Blacks from their new found friendships. Somehow, the one or two white friends or mates exonerate the crimes of their people. Therefore, to many Blacks "people are just people," and organized white death squads fall in the category of unbelievable. A historical perspective of Black/white confrontations is generally unknown or dismissed.

• There is a failure of Black leadership to accurately inform.

Historical Perspective

It is clear that our cultural models must be sophisticated as well as revolutionary. The culture of accommodation, submission and riot is encouraged and glorified in the United States. The culture of material acquisition is normal and those that reject such obvious nonsense are regarded as abnormal. We are encouraged and, indeed, rewarded with trinkets and positions of pseudo-responsibility if we seek the "American dream" through the avenues of a survival culture.

The unplanned and "matter of fact" misuse and abuse of women exists in most cultures. The relegation women to procreation and housework is a universal practice. The West has sought to answer the question by providing an economy that demands that all work if they are to eat.

The white female's entrance into the economy, according to Marvin Harris' "America Now," displaced Black male and female workers and, in effect, hurt the Black family economically. Most Black women, however, have had to work; as a result, their relationships with Black men have been somewhat different. Some of the problems in stable Black homes begin to surface when the men lose their jobs and cannot find new employment.

It is axiomatic that a sexist culture will produce a sexist mind. To deny that sexism exists is to deny we breathe. No matter how enlightened one thinks he or she is, this sexism seeps into our actions daily.

Cultural Imposition

However, it is obvious to the enlightened that there are few jobs men do that women cannot. Cross-cultural studies have indicated time and

11

time again that work women perform is not necessarily their choice but is culturally imposed. In most cultures, males dominate the process of defining cultural norms.

As we move into the 21st century, especially in a highly scientific and technological society that has changed from a labor intensified economy to one that functions with computers and technology, the distinctions between men's and women's work will evaporate. If the workplace is able to move to an enlightened state, perhaps similar actions will prevail in the home.

While spending three years in the United States Army, I learned a great lesson. I, like all the other men, had to make my bed, clean my work and sleep areas, do kitchen duty and perform other acts that had been defined by U.S. culture as women's work. It seems to me that if we could do so-called "women's work" in the Army, then we can do it in civilian life, especially if our mates are working full-time jobs also.

It is insensitive and callous for men to expect their wives or mates, who often work eight hours, to come home and cook the food, clean the apartment, feed their children and husbands, do the dishes, mop the floors, wash the clothes and perform other household chores. If Black women are to advance and develop, they need time for self-realization. The sharing of housework does not diminish a man's masculinity; rather, it affirms a man's sense of fairness, love and security.

Gender Distinctions

The bottom line is this: if we are to develop as people, enlightened education requires that gender distinctions be minimized to those areas where such distinctions are vital and necessary. Understand that I am not pushing for a gender-free society but a society where one is not oppressed due to sex, race, religion, etc.

It is obvious that women cannot be replaced as mothers, nor men as fathers, without serious and often detrimental disruptions of the family. The family is a priority, and one must be clear that the ideal family structure is one where partners (men and women) communicate. Parenting and home duties are not pre-defined as something only women do. Serious development is a family activity that must include all members of the family.

12

1. We need an immediate halt to the destruction of Black families. This means that: a) examples of stable families have to exist; b) family-making has to be taught; c) young people should be discouraged from getting married at an early age; d) all our institutions should stress the emotional, economic and political benefits of strong Black families; e) Black families currently in difficulty should seek adequate family counseling; f) family support networks (indigenous and state-supplied) need development.

2. Black families should be nonviolent. Domestic violence, whatever the reason, should be outlawed. The increasing problems of battered Black women, as well as all forms of rape that often go unreported, must be addressed: a) conscious men need to help unconscious men (e.g., workshops, sports outings, clubs); b) shelters for battered women and children need to be supported; c) help for Black men unable to control their aggression towards mates and children is needed.

3. The great majority of our art and creative production must stress: a) strong families; b) self-respect, self-reliance and self-protection; c) the love of self and one's people; d) the need for functional education at all ages; e) strong political involvement; and f) institutional development (e.g., schools, churches, political clubs, social clubs and self-defense units). It is clear that we must create a mass Black media that can turn the negative tide of the mass white media.

4. We have to organize and demand full employment, better housing and quality education that will prepare us for the 21st century. It is also clear that we cannot be totally dependent upon the state for all of our needs. We must always seek alternatives to what is "given" to us.

5. Strong, innovative young adult programs need to be instituted immediately. Our youth are forever looking for productive programs, but there are very few. Structured youth development in an atmosphere of love and discipline is urgently needed.

6. The adult and juvenile justice systems need a complete overhaul.

National Problem

Youthful aggression and violence are learned behavior, and cannot be blamed totally on "female-headed households" or the lack of male presence. What is missing is an all-encompassing developmental environment where adequate support systems exist. This is a national problem, and it is the federal government's responsibility to aid in the development of social policies and intervention procedures that will support current and new family structures.

Effective political and social organizing is all but impossible if we do not rebuild from the inside. Strong families are key to fighting crime as well as building a strong people.

The answers are not as difficult as we expect them to be; much work has already been produced in this area. It is imperative that the national associations of Black social workers and Black psychologists join hands and minds and design programs that will positively impact our people.

Our approach to knowledge, especially the written word, should be at as serious a level as our approaches to lovemaking and war. Remember that the only places in the Western world where large quantities of "pertinent" knowledge (information) are stored are in government, educational, military and corporate computerized data banks and libraries (books).

Black people, en masse, do not have free and unlimited access to the data banks, and our accessibility to libraries and books is automatically and seriously curtailed as young Blacks become increasingly disrespectful of the written word. The old saying, "The best way to hide something from black people is to put it in a book," is quickly becoming reality. We are fighting for the minds of our people as well as the just development of the world.

High School Reading

Think of the possibilities, if before graduation, all Black high school students had to study and digest the works of Richard Wright, Gwendolyn Brooks, Sterling Brown, Chester Himes, Margaret Walker Alexander, Langston Hughes, Maulana Karenga, Sonia Sanchez, Lerone Bennett,

14

Harold Cruse, Sam Yette, Chancellor Williams, Mari Evans, W.E.B. Du Bois and others. What would be the results of that?

That's our mission if we believe in the future of Black people. We must develop not only a literate generation but one which also is politically and culturally aware. Reading is a major life developing requirement.

General knowledge doubles itself about every six years, and scientific knowledge doubles every two to three years. There are approximately 56,000 books published in the U.S. each year and an unbelievable number of specialized magazines, scholarly journals and monographs. Newsletters and special interest papers also flood the market.

The U.S. may not be the most literate nation in the world, but it certainly has more information available to the general public than any other nation. The great majority of information that is freely circulated goes untouched by the Black community, either because of ignorance or non-concern. The need for a highly literate and analytical mind to deal with today's world is not considered as important as basketball or hairstyles. Until our priorities change, we will not be able to compete or complete our task.

Education Of Children

Mothers and fathers, on special days (and not so special days), buy your child a book instead of candy or toys. When birthdays come around, introduce your children to the beauty of words. Limit television and comic books. To do less speaks of death in its most lasting form — the slow but efficient erosion of the mind.

A mindless people is a people that joins rather than initiates, obeys rather than questions, follows rather than leads, begs rather than takes. To allow this state of affairs to continue is, indeed, a serious and profound comment on the state of our literacy. Let's move the brothers off the corners, put them back into serious learning situations, and introduce them to new definitions. A good place to begin is with a re-evaluation of what it means to be a Black man in this world. Therefore, a working definition of Black manhood is needed:

15

your people first. a quiet strength. the positioning of oneself so that observation comes before reaction, where study is preferred to night life, where emotion is not seen as a weakness. love for self, family, children, and extensions of self is beyond the verbal.

making your life accessible to children in meaningful ways. able to recognize the war we are in and doing anything to take care of family so long as it doesn't harm or negatively affect other Black people. willing to share resources to the maximum. willing to struggle unrelentingly against the evils of this world, especially evils that directly threaten the development of our people.

to seek and be that which is just, good and correct. properly positioning oneself in the context of our people. a listener, a student, a historian seeking hidden truths. one who develops leadership qualities and demands the same qualities of those who have been chosen to lead. sees material rewards as means toward an end and not an end in themselves. clean — mentally, spiritually and physically. protector of Black weak. one who respects elders. practical idealist, questioner of the universe and spiritually in tune with the best of the universe. honest and trusting, your word is your connector.

direction giver. husband. sensitive to Black women's needs and aspirations, realizing that it is not necessary for them to completely absorb themselves into us but that nothing separates the communication between us. a seeker of truth. a worker of the first order. teacher. example of what is to be. fighter. a builder with vision. connects land to liberation. a student of peace and war. statesman and warrior. one who is able to provide as well as receive. culturally sound. creative. a motivator and stimulator of others.

a lover of life and all that is beautiful. one who is constantly growing and who learns from mistakes. a challenger of the known and the unknown. the first to admit that he does not know as he seeks to find out. able to solicit the best out of self and others. soft. strong. not afraid to take the lead. creative father. organized and organizer. a brother to brothers. a brother to sisters. understanding. patient. a winner. maintainer of the i can, i must, i will attitude toward Black struggle and life. a builder of the necessary. always and always in a process of growth and without a doubt believes that our values and traditions are not negotiable.

REFERENCES

Hall, Edward T. *Beyond Culture*. Garden City: Doubleday, 1977.

Harris, Marvin. *America Now*. New York: Touchstone Books, 1982.

Thompson, Laura. *The Secret of Culture*. New York: Random House, 1969.

Greed is Only the Beginning:
Leadership, Money, Persona and Hypocrisy

On the streets the word is "Greed is not enough." In fact, among the junior players, it's "Greed plus anything else you can get," or "Enough is never too much." Hopefully, these sentiments are shared by only a few people. But if one is to measure the greed factor by the judges, lawyers, stock brokers, politicians, and junior Black players that populate the state and federal prisons, it would seem that "we've only just begun."

I

Part of the problem in Black communities is that too many talented, gifted, professional, artistic and wealthy persons leave. Not only do many of these people seldom return, for the most part they do not make significant contributions (financial or otherwise) to their people.

A lifetime membership in the NAACP or $1,000 donation to the local Afrikan American museum, Black theatre or Black charity is not really a significant contribution if a person is truly well off. If we survey the number of Black doctors, lawyers, professionals, entertainers, sports figures and business persons whose yearly net worth is beyond $100,000, it becomes a national shame to view the demise of Black communities across America.

I get tired of reading each week or month in *Ebony, Jet* and *Black Enterprise* about the latest Black millionaire, or the newest negro to close the multi-billion dollar deal for white people. I've had enough of reading and hearing about Reggie Jackson's cars, Wilt Chamberlain's beds, Diana Ross' houses (and marriages to white men), Sydney Portier's Caribbean paradise, Eddie Murphy's parties, Walter Payton's guns, and Oprah Winfrey's diet. Where are the serious rich among our people who are concerned about the vast majority of Black people — those who are poor, ignorant and see no hope of advancement or improvement in their future?

Yes, we do have some exceptional Black people with money. Ed and Bettiann Gardner of Soft Sheen restored the Regal Theatre (a theatre in the Black community) and are known for aiding the Black arts. Bill and Camille Cosby ran to aid Fisk University and are out front making significant contributions to their people ($20 million to Spelman College). Ossie Davis and Ruby Dee have always been at the starting line of giving back to the "roots" of their beginnings. However, it is sad to say there are tens of thousands of Black people in the United States with serious money, skills and talent who do nothing except talk bad about their own people and compete in the Western race for conspicuous consumption champions.

The real dilemma among most Blacks with money is that of *values*. Really, how many houses does one need; how many cars can one drive; how many vacations to Europe and the Caribbean in a year are needed; how many closets of clothes can one wear; how much money must one accumulate to be successful or prove a point; and how much jewelry is necessary to make a statement of *wealth*? The Black poor and middle class, by comparison, give more to the less fortunate of our people than the Black rich. Many will observe, "That's why they are rich." Don't buy into that answer. The Black rich and the white rich are different and respond differently to their respective communities. The two groups also view their responsibilities to their people differently.

The white rich start foundations, build art centers, finance new wings for museums and libraries, endow university chairs and create scholarships for the less fortunate of their people and others. The white rich finance all types of summer camps, help keep white businesses viable, start independent think tanks, support their writers, artists and musicians and buy sports franchises. The major business of the white rich is world control and dominance while legitimizing the white way of life. The white rich hide their money and entrust their futures to lawyers, bankers, accountants, stock brokers and a highly trained and professional armed forces.

II

I've listened to revolutionary rhetoric for thirty years, and I've been accused of leaving a little of such rhetoric around myself. I've heard some of our most progressive "seers" talk about the new brotherhood and sisterhood of Blackness. I've been involved in and sat through heated debates in Tanzania and Algeria, in Washington, D.C. and Los Angeles, in smoke-filled rooms at retreats in North Carolina and Chicago, deciding the fate of the Black race as if the "seers" had that power. We've talked about the important issues of our people while our respect and love for each other slowly faded with the sunset, being replaced with the big "revolutionary" picture.

I now know that not only is it possible to smile and lie at the same time, but many of us have been convinced that it's *logical*. Somehow, I think that in fighting our "enemies" we've created new "enemies." For example, at many predominantly "Black" or "historically Black" universities, the "New Negro" administrators run their institutions like 16th century plantations, as if the faculty are children and the students are babies. I worry about the current and next generation of Afrikan American students. For many of them to *think* for more than thirty seconds is a probable cause for brain damage. Yet, their examples (us) are often men and women (mainly men) who talk a good game and invent the "right" words, but whose day-to-day actions — private and public — would, in a head-to-head competition, put most soap operas out of business.

This issue of the private and the public persona needs to be examined because we know, *we really do know*, that Mayor Getup, in fact, is a confirmed drug addict or alcoholic behind closed doors. However, his public pronouncements against drugs and alcohol put him to the right of Nancy Reagan. Publicly, Attorney Smith is at the forefront of advocating the rights of women and children, but back on the ranch he physically and verbally abuses his family and female associates; and most brothers encourage such actions by saying or doing nothing. Each Sunday morning Rev. Dr. So-And-So shouts eloquently about the need for morality, but privately he chases little boys and can't keep his hands off of his stepdaughter. Dr. Akhtar is quick to preach honesty among the people, but under the covers he sells his people bogus insurance and vacations to whore houses in Europe and the Caribbean. In the public's eye Mayor The-Buck-Stops-Here presents himself as a serious stand up politician who can't be be bought, but he allows bombs to be dropped on Black people. And finally, Dr. Such-And-Such raves abundantly across the country about how egalitarian his business or department runs, but privately his people can't take a decent bowel movement without his permission in writing. This is the point: the persons we often see in leadership positions are not the real men or women we think they are, but are studied creations of *false and disguised images* which, more often than not, take advantage of and will pimp off Blackness as quickly as they buy weekly lottery tickets. In fact, Black people are to this leadership a private lottery to be played whenever they wish — generally, every Sunday morning or around election time. *Integrity* has become a noun that is missing from our vocabulary, and the only *honor* that exists is among thieves and an incestuous leadership that has lost touch with reality. *And*, it must be made very clear that this leadership is made up of 98% Afrikan American men. Nationally, Black women are still tokens in Black leadership positions, and they are nonexistent at the international level.

The money that Black people earn in the U.S. (and most of our money comes from wages) stays in the Black community for about four hours. Again, it's a question of *values, beliefs* and *knowledge*. However, one should not be too critical of the Black poor and middle class when they see the Black "well off" with afterburners on escaping to live, work, shop and play with whites. The $200 billion Afrikan American economy that Black leaders so often brag about is not an economy based upon Afrikan Americans' production of goods, or the distribution of indigenous products or services. The $200 billion Black economy is based upon Black people working for white people. Such an "economy" would end if white people ceased to employ Afrikan Americans. The major "businesses' in the Black community are the *church*, drugs and crippling consumerism. However, this does not mean that such an economy cannot be improved upon and transformed to aid in our own rebuilding.

III

There are *two* types of Afrikan American people that make it "big" in the Western world. The first is the *thief* in $2000 suits, with an idea, a lot of get-up-and-go and a Ph.D. in street smarts. This person has a frontier mentality of shoot first and answer questions if caught. Many politicians, business persons and big time preachers would fall into this category. This Type I person is a born and cultivated hustler and is often highly intelligent; he or she understands the psychology of the oppressed and the needs of former slaves, negroes, coloreds, Blacks, Afrikans and new slaves and will take advantage of all of them if given the opportunity or, better yet, the opening. Life to him or her is a poker game.

Type I hustler's belief in himself or herself boarders on the psychotic. His or her ego far surpasses anything that the artist, musician, actor, writer or performer needs to be successful. Self adulation and the need to be surrounded with yes people is crucial to the success of this person. This person has the style of a Duke Ellington without the substance, the ambition of an Oprah Winfrey without the backing and the mind of a petty criminal that got lucky. His or her working belief is "catch a sucker, bump his head," and the motto of this hustler is "find the weakness, exploit the need; if possible, avoid checks — cash only."

The other person that generally makes it in the West is the true visionary that plows ahead against tremendous odds to bring beauty into this world. Such persons fall into several categories, but I will highlight only two.

Visionary A is the man or woman with talent who has had the good fortune of living in an environment where such talent is encouraged and cultivated. This person is generally very creative and gifted and shares his or her gift with others. This person may create as a writer, visual artist, dancer, actor, musician, inventor or designer. Persons in this group spend most of their time creating and working at their art, designs or inventions; most of them are successful in their creating. However, they give away too much, and it is far too easy to get to their *hearts*. They are loving and caring people, and if they do not come in contact with serious and fair minded business people, they may work themselves into an early grave — primarily because most of them have to work "outside" jobs in order to live and are "single" focused. They do not take care of their bodies. And their families are generally "second" to their creative work.

Visionary B is the same as Visionary A with one big exception. He or she has the added insight of understanding that talent and creative genius in America are like intelligent Presidential candidates, neither will make it without proper packaging, management and serious resources. Visionary B is the creative person who takes the arts one step further; she or he makes it possible for the art form or product to get to the people or consumer. These are the people who often sacrifice their own personal creative years for the big picture. Hoyt W. Fuller in his cultivation of young writers; Dudley Randall in his founding of Broadside Press; Naomi Long Madgett through her Lotus Press; Abena Joan Brown in her ETA Creative Arts Foundation; Safisha Madhubuti through New Concept Development Center (a school for children); Ossie Davis and Ruby Dee in their cultivation of young actors; Margaret and Charles Burroughs and the groundbreaking Du Sable Museum of African American History; and Maulana

Karenga in his creation of Kwanzaa, Kawaida theory and the Nguzo Saba (the seven principles of Blackness). These are just a few cultural stabilizers who need to be identified, listened to, supported, highlighted and honored.

Visionary B people understand the limitations America puts on the artist and serious thinker. They have a burning desire to create institutions and structural support for Afrikan Americans. Many of these visionaries came out of the heat of the Black Power/Civil Rights movement of the sixties. Most of them have defined their needs carefully so as not to find themselves in conflicts of interest between their own work and the works of the artists they support and promote. Most of them have confronted struggle in America on many levels and will not allow their principles to be compromised by short-sighted clowns disguised as concerned Black people. Most Visionary B people live a comfortable "middle class" life but are without serious money. This brings me to the real concern that confronts us: it's not that we don't have leadership; we have the wrong leadership. It's a leadership devoid of ideas, resources or consistent following. It's a leadership that has been consumed by its own greed, its own ego, its own limitations. It's a leadership that ceases to be bold and, worse yet, ceases to listen to bold and creative people who are within their culture but outside of their cult.

IV

I am deeply concerned about the corruption, cynicism, dishonesty, power abuses, sexism and incompetence in our own ranks. I am concerned about our leaders looking evil in the eye and smiling with palms up. I'm concerned about our tendency to tap dance rather than take moral and ethical positions because it means that we must act morally and ethically. I am concerned about Afrikan American people who control large, urban school systems and who have proven beyond a doubt that things *can* get worse. I am concerned about Afrikan American people who have serious personal assets and don't share resources or knowledge with the less fortunate of our people. I am frightened by the "deals" and "treaties" we make — in the name of the people — with the enemies of the world, as we lie to our children about possibilities and future.

But what really digs into my gut is how we lie to each other. The 1989 versions of negroes are much bolder than they've ever been, and they are

24

taking over Black Studies departments, Black universities, Black businesses, Black politics, Black organizations, Black media and Afrikan nations. Things are not right in the Black world. Show me two progressive Afrikan nations, and I'll show you ten that are an embarrassment to the memory of Nkrumah, Du Bois and Queen Ann Nzinga. The political and economic status in most Afrikan nations borders on lunacy. Show me two conscious Black Studies departments, and I'll show you five that are a joke; and if they were not our joke, they would not exist at any serious university. For example, there are people seeking employment in Black Studies who have *never* been involved in serious research of the Afrikan world community. Most of these people got into Black Studies as the last possibility for a university position, and while there they work their behinds off trying to get into other departments. For every three committed Black politicians I can name twenty who will sell their mommas if the deal is right. (Look at the 1989 Mayoral election in Chicago.) Show me an honest politician, and I'll show you someone who is unelectable because honesty, integrity, virtue, goodness, rightness and other ingredients of a *whole* people are quickly fading from our lives. They have been replaced with an arrogant pimpism that has aided in the subtle, but effective, destruction of our community.

What I'm trying to make clear to others and myself is that serious, honest, incorruptible, ethical and competent men and women are in the clear minority in Black America. Such people need to be identified, encouraged, supported, rewarded and protected. Black thinkers are constantly caught between a hurricane and a volcano. For example, to constructively question or criticize Afrikan American leaders like Jesse Jackson, Louis Farrakhan, Coretta Scott King, Benjamin Hooks or the *Big Black* in any city is not looked upon by this leadership or the majority of Black people as the responsibility or duty of serious thinkers and activists. Rather, such actions often are reduced to a *betrayal of the race*. Black people who think or, more accurately, those who think and disagree with the accepted line, no matter how inadequate a policy or program may be are always suspect and locked out. The reaction of the public to the criticism of accepted Black leadership often is personal, overlooks the possible validity of the criticism, and reduces a public problem to a personal one. As long as our condition is reduced to the egos of a few insecure men and women, there can *never* be progress or development.

Leadership by personality is cultism, and we all know where that can lead us. I hope that we've not forgotten Jonestown.

That which is missing in much of our leadership and community is a moral and rebuilding consciousness. We need a home-based regeneration. This act of re-creation must come from home-based activity in all walks of life. This will not be an easy task but one that demands that absolute best from all of us. John W. Gardner, in his important book *Morale*, states, "What makes a collection of people a society is the cohesiveness that stems out of shared values, purposes, and belief systems. When the inner cohesion dissolves, nothing remains." I contend that our "inner cohesion," or what I call *inner spirit*, has eroded with the acceptance of "integration," a national welfare system and a Euro-American worldview of success and possibilities. We have lost *our way*.

Regaining the incentive is not impossible. We need direction and a redefined purpose (i.e., focused lives that are based upon shared values, common needs, individual commitments, an understanding of the future and a willingness to accept light rather than weakening darkness). We need family, leadership and institutions. I often say that Black people in the Western Hemisphere are the real miracle on this landscape, and we need only to recapture our original music to survive this war. However, as we enter the 21st century, survival clearly is not enough. We've survived since we've been in the West. The crucial need today is for measurable progress and development for the majority of our people and not just for the talented few.

We need a new leadership that truly believes in our community and is willing to invest its time, resources and spirit in rebuilding. Again, quoting Gardner:

> There is risk for those who take the lead in rebuilding. People who act and initiate make mistakes. People seeking the path to the future often wind up in blind alleys. Those who have the confidence to act creatively to regenerate the society must also have the humility to know the danger of overestimating what they can accomplish.

However, on the brighter side, somehow I don't think Sonia Sanchez will betray thirty odd years of work, struggle and creative production for a job. It does not seem to me that Mari Evans — no matter how difficult it gets — will ever go back on forty years of Afrikan-centered work for a literary prize. For the twenty-five years that I've known Dr. Barbara Sizemore and Dr. Duke Jenkins, they have never displayed anything less than love and Afrikan-centered professionalism in their work. If Dr. James Turner and Dr. Ronald Walters give their word, it is done. It is inconceivable that Gwendolyn Brooks, after fifty years of teaching us all, would do anything to repudiate her work. Dr. Frances Cress-Welsing has lost jobs, patients, a school and her health due to the principles by which she lives. We need a whole new ethos that states, emphatically and subtly, that Afrikan American people can do whatever we need to do to advance ourselves. And like other successful cultures, our relationships with other people must be interdependent rather than dependent. If there is to be dependency, let it be within our culture.

When a community loses its foundation (philosophers, writers, poets, visual artists, skilled workers, musicians, professionals, dancers, business people, teachers), there is little left on which to build. The illusory benefits of integration and federal/state welfare, and the acceptance of both as panacea, have had disastrous effects on our people. The strength needed to wage this war is quickly fading into the moonset. There must be a renewed dedication to the values and principles that have enabled us to survive the worse holocaust ever to hit a people. Resistance must be our call, structured activism our plan, conscious sharing our method, a working presence our model — anything less is tantamount to surrender and certain death. This rebuilding must start immediately in those areas that we have the capacity to change: family, leadership and community-based institutions.

History, accurately understood, is very important in our struggle. As former chattel slaves in this country, it is absolutely foolish and stupid to turn to former slave masters for answers, serious aid or empathy in our struggle against them. Black struggle has been like trying to hold onto a slippery bottle of clear, lifesaving water; one may steal a drink or two, but in America the real requirement for liberation is the remaking of the mold in which the container was cast. Such a challenge, it seems, will take a lifetime and then some to complete. But that doesn't mean we should all go into debt, give up, and join the killers of the world.

Many of the activists who were initiated by fire into the Black movement in the sixties have only recently begun to understand the conditions for *true* and *lasting* liberation for Afrikan American people. A people is as strong as its institutions, and the primary institution of any strong people is the family.

Black people's status in the United States is worse than that of many Third World nations. We cannot continue to fool ourselves into believing that white people and others are concerned about our best interests. Two suggestions: 1) Black people in America need to elect an Afrikan American Congress. We need a new leadership that is not self-appointed or made for us by others. We need a new and bold leadership that *truly* will work in the best interests of the *majority* of Black people. Wherever Black people exist in large populations, we should elect representatives to air our views and decide our fate — similar to the function of the U.S. Congress; 2) All *aid* coming to the Black community from the white community should be looked upon and received as *foreign aid*. In 1988 Israel and Egypt received over $4 billion from the U.S. in foreign aid, and few people accused the people in those two countries of being lazy, unemployable or uneducable. Any aid — whether it's food stamps, AFDC, scholarships, grants or food — should be taken out of the category of welfare. We have *never* received our just due for contributing to the wealth of this country. All "welfare" has done is made many of our people into beggars and/or dependents. We never received the promised "40 acres and a mule;" the amount we are owed in reparations is in the trillions of dollars. The Afrikan American Congress would decide on this and other urgent matters facing our people. (Also see *Reparations Yes!* by Lumumba, Obadele and Taifa.)

Individually, we all have to become larger persons — persons who seek and demand *quality* rather than *weakening quantity*, persons who whisper good things to others rather than happy-hour gossip. We must become individuals who encourage, inquire about and, when possible, *help each other while working to eliminate dependency on other people.*

If I've read our philosophers and theologians correctly, what they are saying is, *"Do right."* If I've correctly digested the Afrikan idea, it is about the transformation of a *can't do* philosophy to a *must do* philosophy. If the work of Garvey, Du Bois, Washington, Nkrumah, Muhammad, King, and Malcolm X means anything, it means not accepting anything less than our best. If I've learned anything from Gwendolyn Brooks, Margaret Burroughs, Margaret Walker, John H. Clarke, Queen Mother Moore, Ossie Davis and Ruby Dee, it is to be progressively consistent in my politics and profoundly kind in my manners. This is what I've learned from those who have survived the sixties and who continue to labor day after day after day, without reward or thank you.

The only voice that can sustain a people is the *inner cultural wisdom* of that people. We've bought and paid doubly for the Eurocentric image; let's now try the Afrikan-centered substance and quality — bring it into our homes, jobs, campuses, prisons, pulpits, politics and institutions. Let us cease being the great waiters and make *quality* our guiding word and winning production our goal.

We must be motivated *activists*. We exist in a world that does not respect people who do not speak up and fight for what is rightfully theirs. We must be able to rejoice in the world in which we find ourselves. It may be true that we've had little voice in the making of this world, but that doesn't mean we will *not have a hand in its reconstruction.*

Fighting in the Dark:
The Negro's Philosophy of Life

1) Ignorant of self, filled with self-hatred and has no *idea* of who he or she is. Runs from knowledge that may alter such feelings.

2) Believes that white people follow their own laws, rules, ethics, pronouncements and declarations. However, the negro will follow white laws, rules, ethics, pronouncements and declarations — even to his own detriment.

3) Believes that in the United States a person's color, hair, religion, politics, wealth and the way he/she speaks English are immaterial and not important to non-Black individuals and institutions.

4) Believes that money can buy one's freedom and liberty.

5) Believes that the answer to the negro's problem is lots of prayer and "who-you-know," Chicago style. Trusts white people and believes that most of them are fair minded on the race question.

6) Believes that a job/position with a Fortune 1000 company is security and progress and that those who do not have such are either lazy, lacking ambition or living in the sixties.

7) Believes that true democracy exists in the United States and that capitalism is the best economic system.

8) Advocates capital punishment, gun control, prayer in schools, anti-quota laws and anti-abortion legislation.

9) In a world ruled by unified groups, the negro is the world's most confirmed individualist. Believes that a person will eventually come and save him.

10) Believes that the mass media (press, television, radio) are fair, unbiased and free.

On The Streets:

A Chicago Cop's Inside Voice

In writing this book, I was missing one voice. It was the voice of the men who are charged with tackling the most difficult problems confronting the Afrikan American community on a daily basis. It was the voice of the men who have to be social workers, educators, protectors, enforcers, friends, enemies, doctors and lawyers: policemen.

I know a few cops. Many of the brothers who were a part of the Civil Rights and Black Power struggle of the sixties are now in law enforcement. In fact, many of the men were responsible for starting the Chicago Afro-American Policemen's League. However, I was not only looking for a person that I had personal knowledge of, but one who was younger than I and was currently working the Chicago streets. My search was a short one; the person I decided to approach for an interview had been in and out of my life for about twenty years.

David Lemieux has been active in the Pan-Afrikanist/Black Nationalist community in Chicago for at least twenty-three years. In the early days he was immediately noticeable because of his skin color; he could almost pass for white. He was one of the few brothers in struggle who was lighter than I, and his hair was totally straight. He also reminded me of myself at his age, he's about eleven years younger than I. Also, like many other light-skinned Blacks, he was forever trying to prove to himself and others (mainly darker-skinned brothers) that he was *really* Black. He was always the first to volunteer for the most difficult tasks. He would take chances that others wouldn't even think about. He was always studying and trying to stay ahead of the "enemy."

David was into weapons. We become close by going to the range together. I was amazed at his proficiency with all types of weapons, from hand guns to assault weapons. With weapons he seemed to be in his natural element. What I had learned in the military about weapons and the "art" of war seemed to have been born in David. When David decided to become a police officer, I was one of the men he consulted. I felt then, as I do now, that he would make a fine Afrikan American police officer. After

33

seven years in the Chicago Police Department, he has thoroughly convinced me that he made a good decision.

As this interview details, he has not forgotten *who he is*, but the realities of the streets have forced him to be more serious and contemplative in his approach and response to the heterogeneous Black community. He is less romantic about being able to solve the very complex problems that Black people face in this country. As he pondered each question, I noticed that his youthful and quick responses of old had been replaced with slow and deliberate answers, more like interpretations or explanations rather than answers set in self-righteous stone.

It was clear that his seven years as a Chicago policeman had taken its toll. His growth was unmistakable, not only in terms of physically aging (strands of gray hair and lines in his face), but also in the wisdom of how he continued to approach each day with a glimmer of hope and spirited determination. He still feels that he can make a difference. Police work and social work are known for their high stress factor. The burn out rate among all police — Black and white — is very high. David had definitely become a "brother-in-blue" among the men and women who shared the uniform. However, he maintains and even nurtures his community relationships. He has not lost touch with those who taught him the way of Black manhood.

This interview was in the works for about six months. We talked at length many times, with me taking handwritten notes. In the final interview we used a tape recorder, and that is what is published here with very little editing. My gratitude to David Lemieux is unlimited.

David: My name is David Lemieux. I'm thirty-six years old. I've been a police officer in Chicago for the last seven years. Prior to becoming a police officer, I worked construction for about seven years. I've had all the miscellaneous boy jobs. I've been a file boy, stock boy, delivery boy, bus boy. I got into the construction industry because at one time I was involved with a group of Hebrews that were going back to Africa to live, and we all decided among us that we would each have some sort of trade. I chose to be a carpenter. Obviously, I never made it to Afrika.

To go back a little bit more, when I was sixteen years old, I was in the Black Panther Party. Way back then the farthest thing from my mind was being a police officer. The police were certainly considered our enemy for several reasons. First, they were the police and they represented the

34

military arm of the government, and secondly, most of them were white, and we recognized basically that Caucasians were our enemy. So, the police department was never an organization that I would consider aligning myself with. As I got older and observed the situation in the community and how the community was being destroyed from the inside out, as well as from external pressure, I wanted to do something about that. I've been involved with different people, different groups of brothers at different times, and we thought that perhaps we could move on certain problems in the community on our own and be successful. That never really worked out very well. Unfortunately, the way things are set up, when a private citizen tries to remedy some of the problems in his community, if he takes overt action, he places himself in more jeopardy than the good that he's trying to accomplish is worth. That's just the way it is right now because there's not enough support from the community; and such actions only work when the community at large is behind this sort of thing.

I'd considered becoming a police officer way back. I think that the police test was given in '76 and it cross my mind to take it, and I said, "No, that's ridiculous." The test was given again in '81. By this time I was twenty-eight or twenty-nine years old. I took the test because I've always been military in my spirit. I've always wanted to do things, put my hands on things, sometimes put my hands on people. I've considered myself a soldier or a warrior for the race since I was thirteen years old. I was not in the military. I came of age during the Vietnam years, and I certainly wasn't going to Vietnam. My politics rejected that. So, I saw the police department as possibly a vehicle that I could use to legitimize being armed. I've been armed almost all the time since I was sixteen. I figured that I could use the police department as a vehicle to legitimize that basic need, but much further than that, to give me a chance to intervene on some of the problems that are in our community. So, I took the test, and I was fortunate enough that I didn't have to wait a long time to be called. Within about a year's time I was at the academy.

Now, going to the police academy was very much like going back to high school. It involved some of the same indignation that I would have imagined they have in the military. They try to get you very involved in the group, being a member of their department brotherhood in blue and all that. Most of the stuff falls, pretty much, on deaf ears. At the age of twenty-nine, I had a realistic appraisal of where Black people stood in relation to other people and made it through the academy. I did well at some things there.

I won an award in shooting, which is no big thing to me. It was nice being in front of other people who are not accustomed to seeing Black men excel at that sort of thing. I was assigned to a district on the south-side of Chicago. I worked in uniform for a year and did some of the more mundane police work like writing reports, traffic accidents and giving out parking tickets, but also I did start to make some pretty decent arrests. I wanted to be in plain clothes from the time that I came on the job. I saw that it was something that I could do. In about a year's time, after almost daily harassing some of the people who were in charge of the plain clothes unit in the district, they finally assigned me to the tactical unit, and I've been working tact for the most part for the last six years. What we do mainly is narcotics and violent crimes. We deal with the more serious crimes that are called "part one," which are the felonies, and we deal with the narcotics and also a little gambling and prostitution.

Haki: How did becoming a police officer affect your relationship with your family? How did it affect your relationship with other brothers and friends?

David: As far as my friends were concerned, I was blessed in the fact that I did discuss my decision with people that I've known for years, people in what I would describe as the Afrikan community, people with the same politics as my own and the same philosophy that I have. I thought at first I'd meet a negative reaction, that people would say, "How can you do that?" But, the reaction that I get more often than not is, "We need more brothers like you on the force. We need people that think the way that you do because we're certainly not going to get the service that the com-munity is in bad need of from people who don't have any interest in what happens to us. At the very least, the other people will be indifferent to our needs, and at worst, they'll be hostile to our needs, which will make our existence even worse." So, for the most part, people in the community that I spoke with prior to coming on the job were supportive. Now, as far as family is concerned, they weren't thrilled about it — because of the danger of the job more so than anything else. I haven't run into any philosophical problems with anybody. It was mainly just the danger. It is dangerous — although I felt more in harm's way while working construction than I have on this job.

Haki: What is the relationship that you have with the other police officers?

David: That's a good question. I have a circle of people that I work around that I would say know me pretty well or that I have a very good rapport with. I would say that I am considered somewhat of an oddity because of the way I act and express myself and because of the way I dress. A lot of things that are taken for granted in the cultural and Pan Afrikanist community are considered odd by outsiders. We get very isolated because we only deal with people who are about the same things that we're into. Well, on this job I'm around people who are the antithesis of everything that we represent. I'm not just talking about the other police officers who may have an adversary attitude about what I believe in, but I'm also talking about the people in the community that I come in contact with. In general, I get along. I think I'm well liked, or at least I should say, "I'm well respected," even though I'm sure that those who don't like me respect me because of my work. I make a lot of arrests and I make them with a clean conscience. When I jail people, these are people that the community need not have around. I never had any problem with that. I think that in six years I've made one or two arrests that I wish that I could have gone and unarrested. Considering I've probably made a thousand arrests, that's not bad.

Haki: Out of the thousands of people that you've arrested, what percentage of them are Black men and what ages are these Black men? And what percentage are white men?

David: I work almost exclusively in the Black community. White boys don't come through our community to commit crimes. In six years, I've arrested ten white people. The reality is that the crimes in our community are committed by Black people against Black people.

I have tried to consciously observe what is happening to us as a people for at least twenty-two years. I became involved in the movement when I was thirteen; I was still in grade school. I'm thirty-six now. That's well over twenty years of Black street experience. I have observed with vested interest what's happening to our people and what's happening to our community. It would seem to me that our exposure to this alien culture in the United States has had the effect on our people that reminds me of these science fiction movies where they drop an atomic bomb somewhere and you see all these people running around with four arms and three legs — mutations. It would seem that our exposure to this constant war against our whole spirit, psyche and self-esteem has created almost generations of mutants of people. There's almost nothing else left to build on. It's like the eggs that you buy in the supermarket; a hen can sit on an egg until she dies, and no chick will ever come from it because it no longer has the necessary ingredients to promote life; it has a clear sticky fluid that looks like life fluid and a yellowish mass that looks like yoke, but it doesn't contain the genetic information to produce life. This is what I think has happened in a large degree to our community. A lot of the of the genetic information to promote life has been destroyed. There has been so much death and disease and unhealthiness. I'm not just talking about physically, mentally, spiritually, emotionally or materially, but at every possible level. There has been too much death generated in our community — in the minds of our children, elders and everybody in between. Generations of losers are created.

Many Black adults find it very difficult to locate fertile ground for creative and life-giving thoughts and actions. An example is this: I arrested a guy for burglary one time. This brother had gone downstairs to his neighbor's apartment, kicked in the door, stole his neighbor's stereo set, took it upstairs, and set it up in his house. Well, his neighbor comes home and calls the police, and after our little investigation, we were able to get inside and find out that his equipment was right at this other guy's house. Now, this was not a dope dealer gone bad. This was not, "He owes me some money." It wasn't anything like that. It was simply, "I will go downstairs and steal what's in this guy's house and take it to my house." Well, both the victim and the offender were in their early twenties. I had the offender in the room and I was talking to him, and I was pretty new on the job. As a matter of fact, I was still in uniform back then. I haven't been in uniform for about five years. And I talked to him, "Now brother, listen. Think about what you've done. You've gone downstairs, you've stolen this stuff from your neighbor. Maybe you don't understand the relationship that Black people should have to one another." Now, I'm saying all this to him. This is the police, the uniformed police standing here giving this brother a lecture on Black awareness. That's what I was doing. I said, "Even if you don't understand how we should relate to each other as a community, you should at least figure, 'Well, he's my next door neighbor. I'll watch his back, he'll watch my back.' If nothing else, there would be some kind of relationship there. You're a young brother in your twenties. He's a young brother in his twenties. I'm sure that whatever you have you had to strive for and struggle to get and he had to do the same thing." So, I'm talking to this brother like this, saying all what I consider to be the most sensible things. I talked to him for a while — fifteen, twenty minutes, and when I finally paused, he said, "Are you through?" I said, "Yeah." He said, "Let me tell you what I think about what you just said." And he spit on the floor; he actually spit on the floor. He said, "Man, fuck some Black people!" Now, see that attitude, that's not the rare attitude; that's the common attitude. It would be OK if you only ran into this now and then.

Haki: Common attitude among whom?

David: The community at large does not have race consciousness or Black consciousness. I mean, we are always aware of our Blackness in the sense that we are aware of the difference in the way we look from the way that some other group of people look, but as far as our Blackness as a positive bond to one another, no. That's not the general feeling of the community. I would say that feeling did manifest itself when Harold Washington was elected. It was because of something we could focus on as a community. Our Blackness is the most permanent circumstance to anything that happens in our life. But, it is not perceived that way by the community at large, certainly not in a positive way.

Haki: What do you think is the cause of this? Do you see any redeeming factors that could possibly turn this around?

David: What disturbs me most about my perception of other Black men across the board is that despite the movement of the '60s, despite better access to information about ourselves, it still appears to me that we do not love ourselves for what we are. Black Americans, Black people that live in the United States, people of Afrikan descent that live here still reject those things in us that are most Afrikan. We still do not like "nappy" hair, "dark" skin, "thick" lips, "broad" noses, those very essential personal traits about Blackness. Afrikan characteristics are rejected. However, most Black people have "nappy" hair, "dark" skin, "full" lips. So, those very things which are most common among us are still the most unloved.

The reason that I am mentioning this is because I don't see that as superficial; I see that as something very, very deep. You still have Black women coming up to a child saying, "Oh, you got good hair, or "Oh, you got bad hair." This is some stuff that goes all the way back to slavery, all the way back to our initial encounter with the Europeans. I think that the lack of racial self-esteem is at the core of everything. Certainly, we can speak about the historical causes of enslavement and of our presence here. I don't have to document that. The final outcome of our experience here has been this very personalized self-hatred having to do very much with the way we look. Ironically, I am very light complexioned. And, because an issue is made out of complexion in our community, I have very personal experiences with the way our people assess each other based on color. When someone tells a dark brown-skinned woman because they see her with a very light-skinned man, "Oh, you all will have pretty babies," they are not saying that because of any reason other than the fact than that if this darker-skinned person has a child with this person who is lighter than her, there's a chance that the offspring's going to be lighter at least than the woman who bares it. That's sick, that's very sick. I don't think white people do that at all. I just don't see that. There is a perception of beauty that's based on symmetry and certain things among Europeans. Maybe if two attractive white people were together perhaps someone would say to them, "Yes, you all are going to have attractive children." But, a dark-skinned brother could be with a light-skinned woman that looks like a toad and someone is gonna say to him, "You all are going to have pretty children," because that child may be lighter. Or, a dark-skinned sister could be with a light-skinned man that looks like a toad, and someone is going to say, "Ah, you all are going to have some pretty babies," simply because in his mind there is a belief that the complexion is gonna change. Well, I've never heard a white man say about a white woman, "She's too white." I've never heard that. Now, I've worked around white men. I've worked construction. I've worked around plenty of them. We use to work on job sites, and white women walked pass the job sites, and the men would stand out there and look at them and whistle at them and stuff. Not once, and I was listening to them, that's for damn sure, but not once did I hear a white man say to another white man, "Man, she's too white." Not once. But, I wish I had a dollar for each time I heard a Black man say, "She's too Black," or every time I heard a Black woman say, "He's too Black." Now, keep in mind there is a segment of our community that is not like that, obviously. But, in general, who do most Black people think are the most beautiful Black women? Jane Kennedy, yellow woman. What's this Miss America lady — Vanessa Williams, little yellow woman. I'm not faulting these sisters for their complexion; I'm light-skinned. We're not in control of how our complexions come out, but it's the way that our people approach the standards of beauty which are still white, European and anti-Black. It's not a thing of we appreciate this and we appreciate that. We appreciate this at the exclusion of that, you know, and that's not good.

Haki: Getting back to the Black men...specifically, what do you see as the major problem? What is the state of young Black men in Chicago?

David: I would say confused. No, you're only confused if you're pondering a question and you don't know what's going on. The confusion comes when you're seeking a solution without any success. So, "confused" wouldn't be a good word. It's horrible, it's horrible.

Haki: What do you mean "horrible"?

David: It's horrible in the sense...Our people, our young people don't love the things about themselves that are already there. In other words, our young Black men don't have any — you know, this sound so trite — no positive heroes, but there's really no other way to put it. I mean, money is admired. Obvious consumption is admired. It's like the dope dealers set the standards for acquisitions.

Haki: And what about a man like Jesse Jackson or Louis Farrakhan as freedom fighters?

David: Well, you know it would seem that young Black men in their late teens and early twenties don't pay a lot of attention to people like Jackson and Farrakhan. Well, to give an example, I had a button once with Farrakhan's picture on it, and I asked the guy who it was. He said,

41

"I know who that is, that's Jackie Wilson." You know, I mean I was surprised he even knew who Jackie Wilson was. We're so unaware of what we have to be proud of.

Haki: Why do you think that the unawareness exists?

David: We stopped making education that was relevant to us as a people an issue. Black history, Black culture and Black achievement ceased to be important. The information of what we have to be proud of is not getting out to our children. Consequently, they grow up not being proud of anything remotely connected to themselves.

Haki: The majority of the young men that you deal with, are they from single parent homes, foster homes or two-parent homes?

David: I'd say many of them come from single-parent homes. I deal mostly with single parents, mainly women.

Haki: What about single females?

David: Most of the unaware are single Black females although this lack of self-knowledge and this lack of self-esteem seems to be throughout the community. See, I work in the district that encompasses what we would call the low end into the high end. It encompasses Woodlawn, Park Manor, South Shore, Jackson Park, Highlands. So, the community that I work in has on one block homes that cost three hundred and fifty thousand dollars, and two blocks away there are people that are living six in one little room with rats and roaches and the whole deal. So, all the economic levels of our people are represented in the community that I work in, but this attitude or lack of understanding of who we are and what we should be about seems to run through both communities.

It is true, yes, that there's a disproportionate number of homes that are headed by single Black females, and there are a lot of Black men that grow up without fathers. I don't even like the word image — a father reality, a male, a positive male reality. I mean, that person doesn't have to be the children's biological father, just any positive male reality. This is a man; these are the expectations of the man; this is how the man should be. Well, that's just not happening enough in our community. We think we're men

42

once we start screwing. Our young men become sexually active possibly earlier than other groups of young men. I can only talk about us. I don't know what goes on in the white community, but I know in our community we become sexually active certainly earlier than we should be, and it's totally opposite of the way of traditional African culture. For example, in traditional African culture, the young men are prepared for manhood. Now, what that means is whatever responsibility that men have to fulfill in that society, whether they are hunters, or farmers whatever it is that men do in that particular society, the young men are trained for this by other older men, not just their own fathers but, groups of men, groups of elders — and the same with the women. Whatever it is that women do in the society, whether they are hunters, fisherman or farmers, they're prepared for those responsibilities by other women who have obtained status already. In our community, in general, young brothers are on their own. The major teachers are the streets.

Haki: At what age do you see young men hitting the streets on their own?

David: Well, I'm seeing a lot of fourteen-year-olds and fifteen-year-olds that are living by themselves. What I mean is fourteen-year-olds and fifteen-year-olds already, as we say, think they are grown. They feel as though they're adults. They may be responsible for some of their basic needs. Certainly, there's not great responsibility being taken for the education and protection of these young men. If their needs were being met, they wouldn't be out there roaming the streets at fourteen and fifteen years old, instead of in school where they are supposed to be.

Haki: What do you see as the major problem with Black men?

David: The drug problem is so out of control. It cuts up people coming and going. I tell these little dope dealers that I lock up all the time that I understand why anybody wants to acquire money. You need money in this society to take care of yourself. You need money to buy things with. Nothing is given away free. It's something that you want badly. They are not going to give you transportation. They are not going to give you a car. They are not going to give you decent clothing. They are not going to

43

give you decent shelter. So, if you want to elevate your life-style, you do need money.

Dope is a way to make money, make no mistake about it. But, what I tell them is, "Dope is making a few Black people rich and a whole lot of Black people miserable." Of course, keep in mind what I said earlier about the guy that spit on the floor. I still say this stuff now. I'm sure it has as about as much of an effect now as it did then. It's just that maybe these guys don't feel like my temperament is as stable as it use to be, that maybe if they spit on the floor something might happen to them. But the thing with drugs and the reason that it is drawing so many people is the lure of money. At one time you thought that the dealer was real smart, that the dope dealer did not use his product. Because cocaine is such a prestige thing, you get all these dope dealers self-destructing because they make their money, but they also start using their product, which insures the fact that they are going to go under eventually.

None of this is doing the community at large any good at all. You get the teenagers thinking this shit is great. They see these brothers in these Corvettes and Blazers, you know, nineteen, twenty years old, making several thousand dollars a day. It's very hard to explain this to a fifteen or sixteen-year-old who has never had anything and who all of a sudden has an opportunity to make a lot of money. Not only does he have an opportunity to make a lot of money, but it has been so glamorized that, of course, no one ever thinks that they are going to get caught. And see, that's another thing, we haven't even talked about the penitentiary mentality. I stopped this brother one night, and this was a narcotics investigation, which is mostly what I do. This brother told me that the penitentiary makes a man out of you. Now, this brother is like twenty-three years old. He was standing there. He had his little girlfriend with him. I was so enraged, I was trembling. "You mean to tell me that your freedom just being totally taken away from you and put in a cage is something that makes a man out of you?" The ability to endure hardship may attest to our toughness. Sometimes it just attests to our numbness.

Haki: What do you think he meant by that?

David: He meant that he thought that it was a real test to his mettle to go to the penitentiary and survive. And I said, "Man, that's ridiculous." I asked him if he had younger brothers and sisters. He said he had some

44

younger brothers. I said, "Would you want them to go to the penitentiary?" His answer was, "Well, if they did something and got caught, they could go." And he meant that. He was serious as I am.

Haki: What do you think is happening in the penitentiary?

David: Now, keep in mind I have not been inside any penal institutions. I've been locked up in some of those lock-ups overnight. I have never sat in county for weeks and months and certainly never been in Stateville. I know people who have. From what I see, from what I hear on the street, the fear of the penitentiary is no big thing because the penitentiary is *so* full of Black men, so full of people that people know, it's like a reunion. "Oh, Reggie, what's happening? That's right, you did that robbery, right? Yeah, ok." There's dope in the penitentiary. There's everything else in the penitentiary. Sometimes it becomes a blur whether the community is a extension of the penitentiary's life-style or the penitentiary is an extension of the community's life-style. That's real bad. We have come to accept enslavement as a reality of our existence and not reject it. It's like people who think they have to have bacon and eggs for breakfast every morning. They'll eat bacon and eggs even if they don't taste it. They eat it because it's just a habit. Being incarcerated has become a habit with a large segment of Black men and it's just accepted.

Haki: What group of Black men do you see that exist in our community who have any effect on young Black men? What about the preachers? Ministers are generally considered the male leaders along with the politicians. How do young street men see and deal with that?

David: I'm going to probably step on a lot of toes here, but I think at this point with the eighties attitude, ministers are starting to carry a real stigma of homosexuality. It's like no one is a man. There are churches with large followings and there are ministers that have nothing to do with any homosexuality, I'm sure.

It seems to be an older generation of people that are more involved in the church. I don't see many people flocking to the churches. Keep in mind these observations about the community are always with exception. There will always be groups of us who will go forward and not be beaten down, but I look at the community at large and I really try not to oversimplify. I really, truly believe that the worst problem in our community is a lack of self-esteem as a race. People that really care about who they are are not going to take just anything, they are not gonna take abuse from other people, and they are not going to abuse themselves.

Haki: What about the gang problem?

David: The gangs, as mentioned earlier, are men between the ages of fifteen and twenty-five. Well, it's really extended to Black men between fifteen and forty-five, but at least between fifteen and twenty-five you are in your warrior state. You are also in an immature state because you haven't been on the planet long enough to be wise and to be experienced, so you have a lot of energy that really needs someone to direct it. And that's why it is important to have a culture that's intact as opposed to one that isn't. You have this whole huge group of Black men that have no direction. I'm saying that fourteen to twenty-five-year-olds are not old enough to make quality decisions based on their own experience, and there's no one directing them and no examples for them to make quality decisions based on someone else's wisdom. The gangs are an appeal to people because they are something that someone can belong to. A gang is something that's identifiable. It's something that creates, something that has an element of danger and something that instills fear in other people. Power is an important thing to young people who have been pushed out of society.

Haki: What about this old fear factor? What do you think young men are scared of?

David: Well, I hate to say this, but it sure seems like our people fear the white man. Sometimes in the way of just doing police work...the things that Black citizens will say to Black police officers that they won't say to white police officers. It's like people in the community will treat Black police and white police very different. They fear the white police. They don't necessarily fear Black cops. There are good reasons for them to fear a whole lot of police of color, believe me. They fear the white police, I think, because they don't feel as though they have any win at all with white police, whereas with Black officers they feel they can get over. Again, this is because of our lack of self-esteem. They don't accept the fact that we will the same power. I hate to put it that way, but they sort of reject that. This is not all the time; make no mistake about it. You say, "What do our young men fear the most?" When I say, "The white man," I don't mean the white police necessarily. It just seems that our rebelliousness is directed toward each other and not toward anything else. We fear white people.

Haki: What's the feeling of male cops toward female cops? Have female cops been a force in terms of young Black males? Have they been effective?

David: That's a very relevant issue for me. I've worked with several female police officers. I worked with the first Chicago female officer to be killed in the line of duty. There is such a hellacious disrespect for Black women among Black men and especially among so called "Black" police officers. If they were really Black, they wouldn't disrespect the sisters. Negro police treat Black women horribly. They treat them terribly — sometimes, I think, even worse than the white boy because I think that the white boy has a different idea about women than we do. Not that their perception is necessarily correct, but it's just different and it may not be manifested in as harsh a matter. I think many Black men see themselves in adversary relationships with Black women. It's like a constant battle, and that will be manifested on this job. If a female officer is in an adversary relationship with a Black man, then it will undoubtedly replay itself on the job.

Haki: So, you're saying the Black female officers have the qualifications and capabilities of being a good police officers as far as you're concerned. You do not have problems with them?

David: Not at all. I could talk for a long time about the science, the logistics, or whatever of police work. It's a whole different thing; it's a whole different world, but it is our world. It's something that our community is deeply involved in. It's just like anything else. If you have someone who's a jerk, he's going to be a jerk as a police officer. If you have a nonconscious *negro* who doesn't like himself and doesn't like other Black people, then he's going to be brutal, rude, disrespectful; he's going to make all the same mistakes that the white boy makes. And he's going

47

to hurt us worse because our expectations are greater. If you have someone who's conscious, then you're going to get better service. That's with anything. If you go to the library to get a book, and the librarian doesn't like Black people, you're gonna have a problem.

Haki: What about getting back to Afrikan American men and the question about drugs and gangs?

David: Well, it always sounds like the catch all answer, but the community has to reject drugs. I do know enough about how that has worked in places where it is legal. I think England has some sort of setup where they register their heroin addicts and they go and get their treatments and medication. Something like that may reduce the crime that surrounds narcotics. I say reduce it, not eliminate it.

Haki: Is it worse than alcohol?

David: Yes, I think it's certainly worse than alcohol.

Haki: So, if you legalize marijuana, heroin and so forth, then someone is always in the laboratory making up a new drug.

David: Yes.

Haki: So, you're always going to have a drug problem unless you go to the core of the problem. And the core of the problem is poverty, lack of self-esteem, ignorance and powerlessness. You have politicians saying, "Lets get rid of drugs," etc., etc., but once they get out of the limelight, they shoot-up too. There are few serious examples.

David: Well, they are certainly not serious about drugs. I don't feel that the governmental agencies even on a local level are really serious because they are so out-of-tune with what we have to deal with. I mean, I know it's a problem. I realize that it's a big problem in the white community too. It's not like this is something that's exclusively ours. The reason why it's such a big issue now is because it's become a problem in the white community. It's getting a lot of attention, but as to them being really serious? I can't see it. I think there are some individuals that are

48

serious about it, but do I think that the nation is institutionally serious about it? No.

Haki: What about the courts? Are the defendants predominantly Black?

David: When you go in the court room you think white people don't commit crimes because you hardly see any. I mean, you do see some, but the courts, just like the jails, are full of Black men and women.

Haki: More Black men than any other group?

David: Yes, but I would say I've arrested more women in the past year than I did in the first five.

Haki: Why is that?

David: Narcotics, dope, the status. It's the good life "shit." I mean, these sisters like running with these dope dealers and riding in somebody's Corvette, and they like going to these little lounges and places, sitting up there with the guy with the gold. He'll buy them this and he'll buy them that, but also when the police pull up behind their car, they also sit and let the guys hand them the dope because they think that the police won't find it. But see, we got something for that — that's called "female officers." That doesn't mean anything. I've made some very hostile lectures to some of these young sisters. I say, "OK, y'all think this shit is cute? You'll be sitting in Dwight Penitentiary looking crazy, thinking about how you wasted your young life sitting in somebody's jail 'cause you think it's fun to ride around with this jerk here who's selling poison to the community." Then too, there are more and more women using drugs.

Haki: Any concluding remarks?

David: White people and their systems have us locked in between a rock and a hard place. We cannot depend on them to pull us out of the quick sand they put us in. Even though whites deserve most of the blame, we are not completely clean. If we are to survive, we have to dig deep, we have to take long breaths, we have to be honest around our own weaknesses and corruption. I guess what I'm trying to say is that I don't have all the answers, but I do know that if we don't care for ourselves and do not act in ways that demand respect from others, there is no hope. We've got to clean up home first, and try to understand the very complex ways of the world.

Haki: Thank you.

AIDS: The Purposeful Destruction
of the Black World?

If there was one subject I was sure that I would not write about, it was AIDS (Acquired Immune Deficiency Syndrome). Like most misinformed, confirmed heterosexuals, I was convinced that AIDS was a white middle-class homosexual disease that, at worse, would only touch Black homosexuals. I also felt that the AIDS reports coming out of Afrika were exaggerated, and that white people were doing what they normally do with things that had gotten out of hand, *blame the victim.* As the saying goes, "ignorance is bliss." Well, in this case ignorance kills; and AIDS, unlike anything else that has invaded the Black World or any world, has the potential of devastating the Afrikan population unlike any weapon we've known since the Afrikan holocaust, the enslavement of Afrikan people by Europeans.

My enlightenment occurred because of five unrelated incidents. About two years ago, Dr. Frances Welsing sent me some of her research, including the book *A Survey of Chemical and Biological Warfare* by Cookson and Nottingham, published in 1969. This text details the type of biological and chemical research and warfare being carried on in the Western world. Their work centered on chemical agents for riot control and the rise of biological agents as weapons that could be dispatched unexpectedly on the "enemy." In many ways, the book is a frightening exposé on the early genetic/biological research of mad men parading as scientists. All of this research was/is being supported by the United States, Canada, Britain and West Germany. The crucial thing is that the authors document the early experimentation with viruses that would attack the immune systems of people.

The second and most jarring incident occurred at a national conference where a dear friend admitted during a presentation that her brother had just recently died of AIDS. This friend is a very strong person, a product of the Black Liberation struggle of the sixties and one who does not weaken easily. I could only share her pain from a polite distance, but it was something that I could not forget.

In 1988, I received, by mail from the publishers, a copy of Michael Meiers' *Was Jonestown A CIA Medical Experiment?* This 575-page book is the first serious text to look at the Jonestown murders as murders, implying that they were CIA ordered. Mr. Meiers, without doubt or hesitation, theorizes that the 900 people killed (most of whom were Black) were unknowingly involved in a CIA-sponsored human behavior experiment. His documents suggest that "Jim Jones was involved with the CIA and that the medical laboratories at Jonestown were much too large to be consistent with the professed religious purpose of that group." He provides reason to believe that "the purpose of Jonestown was to establish a controlled environment in which a large number of persons could be brainwashed into the act of ultimate self-denial, mass suicide." He also points out that U.S. Representative Ryan, who was also killed at Jonestown, was an "active critic and investigator of CIA activities." Meiers raised too many questions to be ignored.

The next message of death was closer to home. Max Robinson, a friend and brother in struggle, the first Afrikan American news anchor on national network television, became very ill and was isolated in a hospital outside of Chicago. Upon seeing him, I was inwardly crushed by his loss of weight and his emaciated look. It was difficult to keep the tears back. However, Max did not tell me that he had AIDS, and he was in good spirits; according to him, he was improving quickly and would be able to go home soon. I let it go at that, and two months later — without my seeing him again — Max was dead. It was his wish that people know he died of AIDS and that he did not contract it through the *assumed avenues* of drug use or homosexual activity. Max was a woman's man to the bone (one of his problems), and he did drink a great deal. However, he wanted his death to mean something and hoped that his community would begin to respond more positively to the current crisis. He knew that the topic of AIDS was such a taboo in the Afrikan American world that even he, as strong as he was, could only share it with a few family members and trusted friends.

The final alert came Federal Express. A friend from the West Coast sent me a video tape of the work being done by Dr. Theodore A. Strecker. With the tape, he sent piles of other written documentation that convinced me that AIDS is not the next mega-killer, but is *now* ravishing the Black world from Zaire to Haiti, from Zambia to Chicago, from Uganda to Brazil, from Malawi to New York and San Francisco. Here are some of the major misconceptions about AIDS documented in Dr. Strecker's "The Strecker Memorandum" that we need to be immediately aware of:

1) AIDS is a man-made disease.
2) AIDS is not a homosexual disease.
3) AIDS is not a venereal disease.
4) AIDS can be carried by mosquitoes.
5) Condoms will not prevent AIDS.* (This goes against the findings of other research.)
6) There are at least six different AIDS viruses loose in the world.
7) There will never be a vaccine cure.
8) The AIDS virus was introduced into Afrika by the World Health Organization (WHO).
9) The AIDS virus can live outside the body.

Dr. Strecker has unearthed evidence that the AIDS virus was created in a laboratory at Fort Detrick, Maryland from smallpox and hepatitis B vaccines. It is now certain that the World Health Organization introduced the vaccine that contaminated east and central Afrika with the AIDS virus.

Dr. William Campbell Douglass, a fourth-generation physician and the National Health Federation's "Doctor of the Year" in 1987, agrees with Dr. Strecker's assertion that AIDS is man-made. In his book, AIDS: The End of Civilization, he states:

> The world was startled when the *London Times* reported on its front page, May 11, 1987, that the World Health Organization (WHO) had "triggered" the AIDS epidemic in Africa through the WHO

---

*More than one out of every 200 condoms were found to be defective in laboratory tests, a UCLA study has found. The defective condoms either allowed water or air to escape, failed strength tests or leaked the AIDS virus, the Los Angeles Times reports. Brands that allowed the virus to escape, either through pinholes, tears or pores in the rubber membrane, included the Lifestyles Conture Trojan Naturalube, Trojan Ribbed and Contracept Plus. "All condoms may not be equally effective in preventing [AIDS] transmission," the report said. Nevertheless, it's still safer to use even the worst-scoring condom than no condom at all. (Briefing, "Some condoms leak AIDS," September 17, 1989 issue of the Chicago Sun-Times)

smallpox immunization program. The only people in the free world not surprised by the *London Times* front page exposé were the Americans — because they never heard about it. It is chilling to think that our press is so controlled that the most momentous news break since the assassination of President Kennedy didn't even make the sports section, much less the front page *of any American daily paper, radio or television news.*

According to the *London Times* of May 11, 1987 in an article, "Smallpox Vaccine Triggered AIDS Virus" by Pearce Wright:

> Although no detailed figures are available, WHO information indicated that AIDS league table of Central Africa matches the concentration of vaccinations...The greatest spread of HIV infection coincides with the most intense immunization programmer, with the number of people immunized being as follows: Zaire 36,878,000; Zambia 19,060,000; Tanzania 14,972,000; Uganda 11,616,000; Malawi 8,118,000; Ruanda 3,382,000 and Burundi 3,274,000.

Pearce Wright also notes that Brazil was also "covered in the eradication campaign," and that about 14,000 Haitians on United Nations assignment to central Afrika were also infected. Mr. Pearce also states, "Charity and health workers are convinced that millions of new AIDS cases are about to hit southern Africa. After a meeting of fifty experts near Geneva this month it was revealed that up to 75,000,000, one-third of the population, could have the disease within the next five years." And, we know that due to the inhumane nature of the South Afrikan white supremacy system, the Afrikans will be "contained." This containment will "intensify its (AIDS) outbreak by confining the groups into comparatively small, highly populated towns where it will be almost impossible to contain its spread" among Afrikan people. There have been over 50,000 deaths in Afrika already and *it is conservatively believed that close to 75,000,000 Afrikan people could be infected.*

Dr. William C. Douglass, writing in the December 1987 edition of *Health Consciousness* in an article entitled "WHO Murdered Africa," states emphatically that the World Health Organization used Afrikans as the testing ground for the man-made deadly virus AIDS. He points out that this green monkey business was a lie to confuse the world and make small of the epidemic while blaming its origins on Afrikans. Nothing

54

could be further from the truth. Dr. Douglass, quoting from the World Health Organization (WHO), volume 47, pp. 251, 1972, states: "An attempt should be made to see if viruses can in fact exert selective effects on immune functions. The possibility should be looked into that the immune response to the virus itself may be impaired if the infecting virus damages more or less selectively, the cell responding to the virus." The major question being asked is, "Why should anyone want to do this?" I think that the answer is rather simple if one reads this release from Moscow, published in the *Herald Examiner*, June 6, 1987:

> Soviets Charge U.S. Has Germ Weapon To Kill Blacks MOSCOW — U.S. Information Agency director Charles Wick said he broke off talks yesterday with the chief of a Soviet news agency that claims the CIA has a biological weapon for killing blacks. Wick told a news conference at the U.S. Embassy that he received a cable from Washington on Thursday about a dispatch from the Novosti news agency that asserted the Central Intelligence Agency had developed an "ethnic weapon." Summarizing the story, Wick said it claimed that CIA agents "employ war gases in the developing countries" and that "the latest stride in this field is the ethnic weapon, morbific bacteria which is lethal for the Africans but harmless for those of European extraction."

We do know that much of this biological/chemical research re-emerged (much of it started during World War II in Germany) after the rebellions of the 1960s, when white men viewed their cities going up in flames set by Black men and could do nothing. Well, part of their answer, as always, was, "How do we *eliminate* (not solve or understand, but eliminate) the problem?" In the United States, according to these people, Black people — more specifically, Black men — are the problem.

Dr. William C. Douglass is absolutely certain that the AIDS virus did not originate in monkeys, and he states, "In fact it doesn't occur naturally in any animals...AIDS started practically *simultaneously* in the United States, Haiti, Brazil, and Central Africa. (Was the green monkey a jet pilot?) Examination of the gene structure of the green monkey cell proves that it is not genetically possible to transfer the AIDS virus from monkeys to man by natural means." Dr. Theodore Strecker's research clearly shows the connection between the National Cancer Institute (NCI) and the World Health Organization in creating the AIDS virus. Dr. Douglass states:

...they combined the deadly retroviruses, bovine leukemia virus and sheep visna virus, and injected them into human tissue cultures. The result was the AIDS virus, the first human retrovirus known to man and believed to be 100 percent fatal to those infected."

Maybe the reader has doubts about this information, and the one question that continues to tag at him or her is, "Why has AIDS been viewed as a homosexual, and now drug-user, disease when in Afrika it was obviously a heterosexual disease?" I think that the answer is not difficult; the two groups that a great many people in the population do not care about and would not be overly-concerned if they disappeared are homosexuals and drug-users. Their logic is that since AIDS is a homosexual and drug-related disease, then — because "I'm not homosexual, don't use drugs, and don't care for either group — I'm safe. Anyway, AIDS is probably the wrath of God against their evil ways." As I said earlier, such nonsense can get one killed and should be left to the mindless bigots and racists that blame the world's ills on everybody except themselves.

I could go on giving example after example about the eminent danger of AIDS, but I'm sure I made my point. Tony Brown in his syndicated column raised the question and asked another one:

> Is it a coincidence that Ft. Detrick, which is where Col. Huxsoll's biological warfare research is being done, is also the site of AIDS research? This coincidence certainly fuels the rumor, whether true or not, that the AIDS virus was genetically engineered at Ft. Detrick and aimed at the same groups that Hitler tried to exterminate in WWII: Blacks (Hitler considered Jews to be non-Whites, among other things); homosexuals; prisoners; and drug addicts. The AIDS epidemic of today is also concentrated worldwide and in the United States among the same groups — if you substitute Blacks for Jews (on whom there is ample genetic research for biological weapons). Another coincidence?

Two other recent books on this man-made disease are *AIDS: Biological Warfare* by retired Lt. Col. T.E. Bearden, and *AIDS and the Third World*, by the PANOS Institute. Also see "AIDS Update," an article by Frank Murray in the September/89 edition of *Better Nutrition*; this article explores a holistic approach to "curing" AIDS.

In the white world when it comes to warfare, there are very few *coincidences*. That is why the United States has war colleges, one of the largest standing armed forces in the world, think tanks, and thousands of secret research projects underway at universities and private companies coast to coast. There also exist in this country a spineless media system and a corporate structure that will maintain its power, "by any means necessary." I do not have an answer to this one, except — *educate* yourselves, be understanding of those that are ill and, as always, be *activists* about this and any other death that threatens our community. As we face life, we cannot let the horrors in this world stop us. *Seek preventative health and each day fight for that which is good, just and right, regardless of what others are doing.*

REFERENCES

Bearden, T.E. *AIDS: Biological Warfare.* Greenville: Telsa Book Company, 1988.

Campbell, William. *AIDS: The End of Civilization.* Clayton: Valet Publishers, 1989.

Cookson, John and Nottingham, Judith. *A Survey of Chemical and Biological Warfare.* New York: Monthly Review Press, 1969.

Douglass, William C. "WHO Murdered Africa," *Health Consciousness.* December, 1987.

Michael Meiers. *Was Jonestown A CIA Medical Experiment?* Lewiston: The Edwin Mellen Press, 1988.

The Panos Institute. *AIDS and the Third World.* Philadelphia: New Society Publishers, 1989.

"The Strecker Memorandum" by Theodore A. Strecker (tape and written documents), 1986.

"This is a Bio-Attack Alert" by Theodore A. Strecker, 1986. The Strecker Group, 1216 Wilshire Boulevard, Los Angeles, CA 90017. (213) 548-3198

Wright, Pearce. "Smallpox Vaccine Triggered AIDS Virus," *The London Times*. England. May 11, 1987.

Black Men: Obsolete, Single, Dangerous?

Where is the Future?

It was late Friday on a hot July night that the temperature rose to 101 degrees, driving mothers, fathers and children out of projects and tenements to front stoops, parks, bar stools and small back-alley crap games. Anything to deal with the heat. Johnny J., T.C. and Bigfoot were throwing sevens for small change in the back of the Godfather No. 2 lounge on Chicago's west side.

At about 1:00 a.m., lights from two directions hit their game, and they were ordered to "hug the ground" by two white male cops and one Black female cop. One of the white cops told all three to get up and spread eagle against the wall of the Godfather lounge and ordered the Black woman cop to search the Black men. As the woman went up and down Bigfoot's pants legs he moved as she touched his penis and commented "ain't that a bitch." At that moment, the Black woman cop — hearing only the word "bitch" and feeling his movement — fell backwards, pulled her 38 special, and proceeded with surgeon's accuracy to blow the right side of Bigfoot's head off. The Black woman cop was congratulated, promoted, decorated by her superiors and detailed to another Black community. All three Black men had records, and T.C. and Johnny J. were given three years for resisting arrest. What had been described as "justifiable homocide" was in the real world "one less nigger," murdered not by a white or Black male cop, but by a Black woman cop. Few saw the significance of this act.

Bigfoot, at twenty-five, was in the prime of his life and *never* had a chance. To die at such a young age and at the hands of a Black woman remains a mysterious irony that will plague us as we move into the 21st century. What may be the ultimate and most profound reality of our current situation may well be that some of the mothers that bring life may indeed be the mothers or daughters of mothers that aid Black men and white men in the removal of Black men from this part of the earth. It's a perfect situation. No voices of protest will fill the streets because it is well known that "niggers" with criminal records are fair game for anybody, especially if one has a license to carry a weapon.

Much of the current Black studies have focused on either the Black family, Black women, Afrika, the Black homosexual community or Europe's and America's influence on the Black world. Few Black scholars or activists have given serious attention to the condition of Black men. There are many reasons for this: 1) much of the published scholarly work on Black people is by Black men and many of them do not see the importance of public self-analysis; 2) it is easier to get studies on Black women or the Black family published; 3) few Black male scholars wish to "wash dirty clothes" in public — and the other side of that is if the Black male situation is accurately assessed, it also means for the intelligent scholars and activists to "clean up their own acts;" 4) many of the scholars and activists are actually functioning in their personal lives contrary to the best interests of Black people (some outright traitors) and finally; 5) studies that bring clarity and direction to the Black male situation as an integral part of the Black family/community are unpopular, not easy to get publish and very dangerous. Too many Afrikan American scholars have looked at the Black situation in America from a European sociological framework, and in doing so, their work has been instrumental in distorting reality and exists as a body of "negative ammunition" to secure faculty positions and publishing contracts, and is ego grease for their warped worldview and sense of importance.

Not Allowed To Be Lovers

The root, as well as the quality, of Black life is in the relationship established between Black men and women in a white supremacist system. Black struggle, that is the liberation of our people, starts in the home. This is not to suggest that the dominant society does not affect what happens in the home, but to a significant degree individual members of the family — regardless of the political system they endure — are still able to define relationships among themselves and the society if they are able to *divest* themselves of *role models imposed from the outside*. Indeed, this is not easy and requires an almost complete negation of present values to those that put people in relationships first and prioritize the development of children. Sound and loving relationships are the core of a sane, happy and fruitful life. This is crucial because all too often our patterns of behavior have nothing to do with the real world but are sincere imitations of white European-Amercian madness.

Black life, especially interaction between Black men and women, is perceived from the outside as being fragmented, unstable, insecure, and woman-dominated. This image is solidified by white and Negro doctoral theses and mass media nonsense. If this view of the Black situation is "the" truth (and yes there are elements of truth here), we are indeed in trouble and possibly headed for complete destruction as a people. However, if our family construction, as I believe, was/is built upon a very positive man-woman relationship, one that has enabled us to weather the most severe form of human bondage, then and only then is there hope.

Yes, there is hope, but in the last twenty-seven years or so there has been serious cultural slippage in the Black community to the point that many Black men and women are becoming antagonists, and the liberating cooperation, respect and single-mindedness of spirit and purpose that existed are being replaced with the most gross forms of competition, decadent individualism and sexual exploitation.

Black men in the United States are virtually powerless, landless and moneyless in a land where white manhood is measured by such acquisitions. Most Afrikan Americans have been unable to look at their lives in a historical-racial-political-economic context. Thereby, without the proper tools to analyze, many Black men have defined their lives as Black duplicates of the white male ethos. The problem (and there are many) is that Black men in relationship to Black women cannot, a great majority of the time, deliver the "American dream." Therefore, the dream is often translated into a Black male/female nightmare where Black men, acting out of frustration and *ignorance,* adopt attitudes that are not productive or progressive in relationship to Black women, i.e., many Black men end up treating (or trying to treat) Black women like white men treat white women. The political and sexual games that exist in most cultures of the world that are largely demeaning and disrespectful to women become, due to a lack of *self definition,* Black men's games also.

That this quality of life exists in white America is not unexpected. Alvin Toffler in his persuasive books *Future Shock* and *The Third Wave* forecasted the dismantling of the American family, a concept he called the "end of permanency." To a greater and somewhat extreme degree, other social scientists and novelists (Huxley, 1953; Orwell, 1950) have concluded that the raising of children will be completely taken out of the

61

hands of the biological parents and replaced with state farms, institutions or schools, which will program the children from birth. This, indeed, may well be the wave of the future of child rearing in the west when in reality the development of a good many of the nation's children is currently left to daycare centers, the streets, pre-schools and the favorite standby — television.

The cultural *values* that are the stabilizing ingredients of the Afrikan American family quite often are not coming to the children in a progressive manner from the parents, extended family, cultural institutions or community, but from incompetent training centers, mass media nonsense and negative peer relationships. The cultural imperatives that direct and develop a people — in this case, Black people — are being replaced with chocolate city silliness and spiderman solutions.

Young Black boys are not taught the positive aspects of Black manhood and Afrikan responsibility. And young Black girls by the age of thirteen are more concerned with hair, clothes and how to be sexually active without getting pregnant rather than understanding the life process and their special place in it. Couple this with the failure of *most* educational institutions in the Black community, the oppressive nature of the political system, the non-responsiveness of the economic sector and the killing style of the legal apparatus, and it's truly a wonder that Black people are able to function sanely at any level. The fact that today's Black children are tomorrow's adults is not cause for much jubilation if we are serious about true liberation, true wholeness and bright tomorrows for all people.

There is hope. Black people have survived the middle passage, chattle enslavement, the buffalo and little men in white robes with black books. As dim as the sun's rays are, the *will* remains to conquer this oppressive and impersonal world. In our darkest moments, we must never forget that the United States, actually the West, is not a reflection of Black people, but we, in our sleeping hours (which is sometimes twenty-four hours a day), all too frequently duplicate the negative aspects of it.

Sleeping Hours and Confusion About Existence and White World Supremacy

Of all the species that populate the earth, *homo sapiens* (human beings) are the most unpredictable and complex. A complete and working knowledge of human behavior is still being pieced together by anthropologists, archaeologists, historians, Egyptologists, theologians, ethnologists, political scientists, philosophers, psychologists and socio-biologists (social-biology — the most recent "bioscience" — examines evolution, ecology and animal behavior, as well as takes into account the subject's complete sociological and biological history).

If we can appreciate the difficulty that scientists are having trying to bring meaning, reason, and understanding to the human race, it is no small wonder that the average man or woman is often confused and downright ignorant as to why people function as they do. In terms of analyzing and codifying human behavior, most of us cannot separate *fact* from *theory* or *wishful thinking*. If one is critical, this same judgement can be applied to the social sciences (anthropology, psychology and sociology) and one would not fall too short of detecting astronomical confusion and/or disagreement among the scholars as to *why* humans behave a particular way. One can easily spend a lifetime studying the theories and counter-theories of Herbert Spencer, Max Weber, Emile Durkheim, Sigmund Freud, Karl Marx, B.F. Skinner, Jean Piaget, Carl Jung, Alfred Adler, Herbert Marcuse and others and emerge totally bedeviled and misdirected. Most of the Western World's most eminent scientists of human behavior can't seem to agree or disagree on anything. The pitiful aspect of this is when a Black social scientist absorbs much of their nonsense, accepts it as undebatable and "god-given" fact, and tries to apply it to the Black situation without question. The "educated" elite of the Western World have made a rather comfortable living out of disagreeing and openly fighting each other over the reasons why people, for example, excrete waste in a sitting position rather than standing.

The major quality that separates men and women from the rest of the animal world is the use of *language* (speech) and the invention of/and adaptation to *culture*. David Barash, in his *The Whisperings Within*, states that human beings:

> form societies in which, for example, age and power are closely al-
> lied, in which relatives are distinguished from non-relatives, in
> which men and women do predictably different things, in which ex-
> change, barter and gambling occur, and in which there is some sort
> of formalized association between men and women. Some of these
> things show our similarity to other animals, others such as our use
> of language and our ability to carry out rapid culture change, show
> our uniqueness. But any way you slice it, human nature, diverse as

63

it is, looks narrow indeed in the wider context of the diversity of living things.

Thus the nature of humans, or what is best known as *human nature,* is now an accepted description of the actions of the most distinctive and flexible animal in the world — human beings. Many take the position that human behavior is acquired through two very complex (and not completely understood) developmental avenues: 1) Biological — which is an examination of the *homo sapien's* relationship to plant and animal life. This study also takes into account evolution, ecology and environment; genes and genetic make-up is of crucial importance. I will also take the liberty to add nutrition, keeping in mind that little scientific work has been done in this area by biological or social scientists; and 2) Culture — the act of developing intellectual and moral (ethical) faculties; integrated patterns of human behavior that include thought, language, action and invention. A culture, if it is to survive and develop, depends upon a people's capacity for learning and transmitting knowledge to succeeding generations. The development of family, institutions and governing bodies are examples of cultural entities. Ideologies, philosophies and political thought emanate from cultures working to perpetuate themselves (Mead, 1949; Tiger, 1969; Freedman, 1979).

For instance, the philosophy of White World Supremacy or white racism is both biological and cultural (Diop, 1959; Wobogo, 1976; Bradley, 1981; Welsing, 1989; Fuller, 1986). Europeans (the white race), upon discovering that other people and cultures existed and flourished independently of Europe and realizing that they (Europeans) were/are indeed a numerical minority, developed a system of thought and action that would help to guarantee white survival and development and at the same time put white people at the *center of the world, indeed the universe.* This system of thought essentially stated that white (Western-European) thought and action was right, necessary, best, the only way, correct, powerful, godly, clean, efficient, beautiful, etc. From the prehistory of the white race, all of their support systems began to confirm that white (European) is the past, present and future. The scholars, religious leaders, politicians, scientists, educators, military and business men of the white race took this message, in book and gun powder, to all parts of the earth and physically and mentally forced the "inferiors" to accept it (Bradley, 1981; Wright, 1986).

Therefore, this European frame of reference, which is diametrically opposed to most things not white (or European), spelled the near death of many non-white people and cultures worldwide (Fanon, 1967). White World Supremacy (white racism) emerged as an effective survival and defense mechanism for the development, perpetuation and maintenance of white political, philosophical, scientific and military thought on an international level. All the people who had the misfortune of being conquered and absorbed by the culture of Europeans (or their children, the Americans) have for thousands of years been reacting to white supremacy, the extreme survival expression of a people who are less than eleven percent of the world's population. The works of Chancellor Williams, John G. Jackson, Yosef ben-Jochannan, Frances Welsing, Neely Fuller, Cheikh A. Diop, John H. Clarke, Harold Cruse, Shawna Maglangbayam, James G. Spady, Anderson Thompson, Jacob Carruthers, Asa Hilliard, Na'im Akbar, Vivian Gordon, LeGrand Clegg II, Maulana Karenga, Molefi Asante, Michael Bradley and others have documented the most ancient as well as current racism. (Also see Madhubuti's *Enemies: The Clash of Races*, 1978.) Any meaningful discussion of the Black situation in the United States must not only understand this systematic pattern of thought and action, but must be sensitive to how it (white supremacy or racism) has been integrated into the entire life of Afrikan American people and has intimately affected Black peoples' interaction among themselves as well as with other cultures and races (Greer and Cobbs, 1968; Wright, 1986). Few state it better than Michael Bradley in his important book, *The Iceman Inheritance*:

> Racism itself is a predisposition of but one race of mankind — the white race...Nuclear war, environmental pollution, resource rape...all are primary threats to our survival and all are the result of peculiarly Caucasoid behavior, Caucasoid values, Caucasoid psychology... There is no way to avoid the truth. The problem with the world is white men. (Bradley, 1981)

Misinformation

That there are more televisions, radios, record players, tape recorders and VCR's in the average Black home than books[*] or computers has a great deal to do with where our information-gathering priorities are. It is now an accepted fact that the public school system, for the majority of Black people in most urban areas, is a dismal failure and will continue to be a failure. Not only cannot a great number of our young people read, write, compute or articulate their thoughts (Copperman, 1979; Shneour, 1974), there exists in many of them a severe dislike and fear of the written word, language (Madhubuti, 1984). And, since there are only a few places where large quantities of lifegiving and lifesaving information is available[**] to the majority of Black people, we now are finding that most Black people rely heavily and almost exclusively on mass media — television, radio, newspapers, magazines — and each other (Mander, 1978; Mankiewiez and Swerlow, 1978).

The fact that many Black people have bought into white America's gigantic melting pot lie is directly related to white seasoning, acculturation, the breakdown of the Black family, the weakness of Black social and business institutions and the sophisticated influence of other outside forces (i.e., integration has not worked). One cannot speak too loudly of the effects television and mass media have played in programming Black families for failure. If *Dallas* and *Dynasty* are the most successful white shows and *The Cosby Show* and *Amen* are their counterparts, one can easily understand why many Black families, as a unit, may have difficulty deciphering the real world. The traditional institutions that have held the Black community together, such as the church and the family, are current-

---

[*]I am mainly talking about books that provide information, knowledge, skills and inspiration that enable people to effectively deal with the real world.

[**]Information — that is, *working knowledge* that is current, accurate and functional can be found in computerized data banks which are controlled by the federal government, the military, private corporations and large universities. The other area that quantities of information can be found is in *written materials*, mainly *books*, scholarly, theoretical and professional journals, etc. Therefore, libraries, schools, universities and bookstores are a functional part of a community that is aware of its own intellectual needs.

ly not as effective as they should be in this highly racist, capitalist, scientific, technological and white male-centered world.

For example, rather than taking the lead in our struggle, a significant number of the Black churches have acted as interpreter and mediator with death; many church leaders have insulated themselves in medieval rhetoric and hidden behind black books that have little meaning to fourteen-year-old junkies or young men and women who seek answers to negative peer pressures and awsome world realities. Many churches practice outdated "traditions" and support outmoded practices of male chauvinism and unquestioned male dominance that have little to do with today's reality. It is important that we understand that many Black ministers in their pseudo-positions of power and influence are not necessarily the best examples of strong Black male leadership. This is especially sad in many Black churches where Black women, in terms of membership, far outnumber Black men. Indeed, the Black church would not exist as such a force if it were not for Black women who have, by and large, financed "modern" Black churches. This male leadership is, for the most part, patronizing and backwards (yet loving and considerate) in relationship to Black women, and is a profound statement on Black leadership. Indeed, if one seriously studies Judaism, Christianity and Islam (the so-called western religions), one will understand why in the actual world women are relegated to a position of polite tolerance. Religious symbolism for God in all three religions is masculine and very seldom do women share in decision-making or power-yielding positions in the sacred text or the hierachy of the church, synagogue or mosque. This sad state of affairs not only applies to the church, but sadly has filtered down throughout most of the world's religious, social and political structures.

War on Black Men

First, for the conscious observer, it should be quite obvious that this society is bent on destroying Black people, specifically Black men, as quietly and efficiently as possible (Obadele, 1968; Yette, 1971; Willhelm, 1971; Pinkney, 1984). What is not talked about is the ability *of great numbers of Black men to survive America's worst conditions, and their potential for revolutionary and progressive organization, which remains the greatest threat to white male rule.* This is why *most* of the Euro-American systems and sub-systems are structured to systematically keep *conscious*

Black men out. However, if Black men wish to become imitation white men, there exist within the political-industrial-military complex significant token positions (Gibson, 1978) — which are used to legitimize the system and to cloud its true relationship to Black people, a relationship of slavemaster to slave. In fact, the "slave" position is the major rank that Black men, regardless of title and income, are allowed to occupy.

The Kerner report, issued over twenty-one years ago, stated that the nation was moving toward two societies, one Black, one white — separate and unequal; and ten years later a major investigation by the *New York Times* (Herbers, 1978) confirms the accuracy of the report. In reference to the Kerner report, Robert Blauner, in his book *Racial Oppression in America*, states:

> Despite the Kerner Report, it is still difficult for most whites to accept the unpleasant fact that America remains a racist society. Such an awareness is further obscured by the fact that more sophisticated, subtle, and indirect forms, which might better be termed neo-racism, tend to replace the traditional, open forms that were most highly elaborated in the old South. The centrality of racism is manifest in two key characteristics of our social structure. First, the division based upon color is the single most important split within the society, the body politic, and the national psyche. Second, various processes and practices of exclusion, rejection, and subjection based on color are built into the major public institutions (labor market, education, politics, and law enforcement), with the effects of maintaining special privileges, power, and values for the benefit of the white majority.

Simply put, Black people in the United States are *powerless*. I define power in terms of the ability to make *life-giving and life-saving decisions*, as well as the ability (knowledge, resources and desire) to deliver on the decisions made. As a part of the political body, Black men do not have much, if any, power to speak of; as a cultural unit, Black men do not make important life-giving or life-saving decisions about Black life on a local, national or international level. Black men are not able on a national or mass level to protect Black women, educate Black children, employ Black youth, clothe Black families or house Black communities. Our input into a national Black domestic policy is laughable; our involvement in a "Black" foreign policy is minor. Our relationship to Black women is quickly approaching the point of disaster. Black economic-political clout on the world level is miniscule, and our understanding of the forces that regulate our lives is embarrasing — especially since we are supposed to be the most "educated" and the most "creative and talented" community of Black men in the world.

Black Men/White Men: White on Black Crime

For the 15.5 million Black men in the United States,* life expectancy is 62.9 years compared to 68.9 for white men; infant mortality is 27.6 per 1000 for Black people compared to 14.1 for whites; and Black male infant mortality exceeds that of Black females. Admission rates to mental clinics and hospitals is 998 per 100,000 for Black male in-patients (whites 642.1) and 873.4 per 100,000 for Black male out-patients (whites 599.4). The 1976 death figures for Black men are staggering: heart attacks 176.5 per 100,000; cancer 179.2 per 100,000; accidents, strokes and hemorrhages 79.3 per 100,000 and homicide 55.8 per 100,000 — bringing the total to 590.8 deaths per 100,000. These figures do not include drug related deaths or suicides, which are extremely high and far out of proportion for the Black male population. Other statistics in the areas of employment, education, under-employment, male heads of households are also discouraging.

Therefore, in the United States Black men are still involved in the establishment of significant firsts, such as: first jailed, first killed in the streets, first under-employed, first fired, first confined to mental institutions, first imprisoned, first lynched, first involved with drugs and alcohol, first mis-educated, first denied medical treatment, first in suicide, first to be divorced, first denied normal benefits of this country, first to be blamed for "Black" problems — indeed, Black men are the *first* victims (Boskin, 1976; Weisbord, 1975; Fedo, 1979; Ginzburg, 1969).

The concept of Black men being the first victims (Ginzburg, 1969) is not to set in motion the argument of who is oppressed the greatest, Black

---

*This data was compiled by Howard University Institute for Urban Affairs and published in their *Urban Research Review,* Vol. 6, No. 1, 1980. This entire issue of the *Urban Research Review* is devoted to the study of the Black male and is highly recommended. Much of the work was done by Dr. Leo Hendricks. In reviewing more current data, it is clear that these figures are, indeed, conservative.

men or Black women. Oppression is oppression, and to quibble over degrees of oppression, more often than not, is an accurate measure of the effectiveness of white oppression. However, there are some basic male dynamics that need to be understood: men run the world; this is not a sexist statement but one of fact. Also, men fight men (and women) to maintain control of "their" part of the world. There may be women in leadership positions (elected and appointed), but they are there because men see such concessions as politically wise and in their best interest. White men control most of the world — economically, politically, and miltarily — and undoubtedly control all of the Western /Northern World.

Other facts are: 1) White men *do not fear* white women; they are concerned, yes, but fearful, no; white men and women are partners, be it senior and junior partners; 2) White men do not fear Black women. The white man's relationship to Black women traditionally has been one of use, sexually and otherwise; the wide spread of color that exists among Black people proves this point — it was white men raping Black women that produced the mixed race Black person worldwide (Weisbord, 1975; Day, 1972; Stember, 1976; Hernton, 1965); 3) White men *do fear Black men*. This fear may not be spoken and obvious to many Black people, but if one understands the history of white male/Black male relationships, it is quite evident that it is a history of war, with the horrid and severe physical and psychological enslavement and elimination of Black men by white men (Ginzburg, 1969; Williams, 1974). Sterling Brown's classic words are instructive when he says of white men venturing into the Black community, "they don't come by ones, they don't come by twos, they come by tens."

The Black male/white male confrontation is not only racial and cultural, it is also a serious question of what group of men is going to "rule" the world. The concept of *shared* power has always been a major question within the white male ethos, especially if it involves the inclusion of men outside their racial or cultural grouping (Tiger, 1969). However, it must be understood that white men actually don't like or trust each other. Their cultural, religious and nationalist wars are legendary. Any serious study of European wars will validate this point. When one analyzes the war-like nature white men exhibit among each other, only the naive and severely mentally handicapped would expect white male attitudes towards Black males to be any different than they are. These attitudes are historical and cultural and, therefore, psychological (Bradley, 1981; Wright,

70

1986; Akbar, 1984; Welsing, 1989) and intimate. To change such negative and "natural" attitudes would require a revolution of the most profound kind. Michael Bradley in his important book *The Iceman Inheritance* carefully documents the white race's war on the non-western world, and clearly gives reasons for western man's racism, sexism, and killing aggression.

The Black male/white male dynamic can be best described as one of continued and unrelenting *war*, with Black males being consistently on the losing end of most battles (Williams, 1974; Martinez and Guinther, 1988). One of the major problems is that most Black men in the United States are fighting the wrong war — that is, many are fighting to get a "piece of the pie," therefore not understanding the "bio-social" nature of white males, which is that of conquest, domination and self-development, not one of sharing (Storr, 1972; Lorenz, 1962) power or decision-making with the vanquished (i.e., former slaves). The best that most Black men can hope and work for within this society is a "job" which, indeed, has been defined by many disillusioned Blacks as "a piece of the pie."

It is true that the future of any people can be measured by its cultural sophistication and the political, economic and military success of its male population in dealing with its natural and unnatural enemies. However, when that male population can't or doesn't *clearly* and *definitively* identify the *enemy*, it *cannot*, on a continuous basis, develop effective means and methods of neutralizing or eliminating said enemy. If this is the case, the future of that people can only be one of doubt and continued subjugation; and subtle, yet effective, elimination and/or subjugation is all but guaranteed in any white-American "multi-racial" situation, especially when the racial minority in that culture is economically obsolete (Willhelm, 1971; Yette, 1971) and Black. When a people does not have strong, resourceful, energetic, honest, serious, intelligent, committed, incorruptible, fearless, innovative and fighting men in a world ruled by the force of men, then that people is in serious trouble. When a people does not have men of integrity and vision, long term and lasting development is just about impossible.

The internal direction of Black people to a large degree is destructively influenced by the ongoing Black male/white male conflict. White men in the United States control everything of material value; this is true in all of the life-giving areas such as economics, entertainment, politics, science, sports, education, law, communication, real estate and the military.

71

If Black men want to be a part of the Euro-American structure in an "intimate and non-superficial" way, they will have to give up the most important aspect of their being, their Blackness. And in thought and actions they will have to become *white*; a transformation that is ultimately impossible but tempting enough to unconscious Black men that millions in this country on a daily basis unknowingly betray their people, themselves and the future of their children.

The history of Black/white racial interaction demonstrates that even if Blacks were allowed into the white infra-structure at important levels, they still would not have access to "ultimate and decisive" information or binding decision-making powers. The reason is quite obvious. Information is power (Brucker, 1973); and if it is translated and used in a self-protective manner, its value is of critical importance to those who have exclusive and first use of it. Generally, the information that the Black community organizes around is at best second-hand and is often of minimal value, having been filtered through the white screening systems before Blacks are able to see or use it. When any people (especially if it is *landless* and *defenseless*) loses its men in a world ruled by men, that people ceases to be a threat to anybody. The loss of Black men between the ages of thirteen and twenty-nine, which is the warrior class, represents a danger of genocidal proportions. To destroy or neutralize Black men creates a critical void in the Black family structure and forces Black women (without men) to assume the role of women (mothers) as well as men (fathers). About sixty percent of current "heads" of households in the Black community are women. This unusual condition has created some obvious readjustments, mostly negative:

1) The present generation of Afrikan American children is, by and large, being raised by Black women and their extended family network. The strain on single mothers is unduly harsh and often unreal. This condition influences the mothers' activities with their children as well as how they approach future relationships with Black men.

2) Black men have ceased to have a major influence on the development of their children, therefore leaving the "education" of the children to their mothers and other outside forces.

3) It is quite obvious now that single mothers without the proper male support are having serious difficulty raising sons. By the time most young boys reach the age of thirteen, the negative options that are available are overwhelming, especially from their peers.

4) The socialization of Black males without conscious and caring Black men around is, more often than not, replaced with gangs or other negative groups.

The U.S. white supremacy system works overtime to disrupt Black families and neutralize Black men. The most prevalent tactics used are these:

1) Create Black men who will *be* and *act white* in thought, actions and image (i.e., acculturation or seasoning). This produces Black men who consciously work in the best interest of their teachers. *Therefore, no serious definition of Black manhood is ever contemplated.* The call from white people is to always to rise above one's culture, tradition and history — if you are Afrikan American.

2) Drive Black men out of the economic sector, thereby making it impossible for them to take care of themselves and their families in "the American way." If fruitful work is not available, most men will seek other avenues of employment. A life of "crime" or the underground economy is the next step for many of them.

3) Use the prison system as a breeding ground for hard, non-political Black men who, for the most part, will return and prey on their own communities. (There are exceptions.)

4) Supply Black men with unlimited negative options (incorrectly defined as freedoms) such as drugs, night life, alcohol and unrestricted sex. The use of drugs and other stimulants has seriously affected the Black community in a destructive manner. The constant search for "fun," "pleasure," or the next "high" is the best example of an immature, enslaved mind.

5) Drive Afrikan American men *crazy* so that they turn against themselves and the Black community. Then the only recourse left will be a) mental hospitals or homelessness, b) suicide or c) Black on Black destruction.

6) Make them into so-called "women," in which case homosexual and bisexual activity becomes the norm rather than the exception. Men of other cultures do not fear the so-called "woman-like" men of any race.

7) Teach Black men to believe in a force(s) greater than their own people, their own culture, their own destiny. Afrikan American men's internal monitors (i.e., gut feelings and gut reactions, their spiritual connectors to reality and their sense of self) have been destroyed spiritually and culturally. Their moves toward self-determination and self-reliance are always questioned and put down as unimportant or meaningless.

8) Kill them — not just mentally, but physically, and do it in a way that strikes fear into the hearts of other Black men. This fear of death and/or imprisonment has been an important hindrance in keeping Black struggle "legal" and above ground. The killing of Martin L. King, Malcolm X, Fred Hampton, Mark Essex and others influenced the actions and non-actions of an entire generation of Black men.

Locking Black people (especially the men) into a legal process *that by definition doesn't work for them* has effectively set the Black struggle back years (Wright, 1988; Spence, 1989). *The freedom of Black people* cannot be won in the United States through legal means or *on a part time basis only*. The negative politization of Black men has effectively wiped out many serious *full-time* Black male freedom fighters. *Making it* in America to a great many Black men today means *how much money they can make in the shortest amount of time*, doing the least amount of work. Family Building, Nation Building, sincere deep Black male/female partnerships, are literary and academic verbage for the most part among Black men. The *vision* to see beyond the crippling mentality of sophisticated beggars is clearly on the decline among Black men.

Even though there exists much in-fighting among white male leadership, there does exist structured maximum and effective information flow. Contrary to popular belief, leadership in the United States is "shared" and decisions are "collective" (Green, Fallows & Zwick, 1972). However, within the Black community ultimate leadership is in the hands of one group, Black male ministers, and these men, by and large, are not "political" in a self-developing or self-protective manner for the Black majority. (See chart).

White Western Leadership	Black Western Leadership
(information is shared and decisions are collective)	(information is limited and decisions are inclusive)
1. Businessmen and industrialists; economic support systems	1. Male religious communities
	********************
2. Politicians and diplomats	2.
	A. Politicians
	B. Educators
3. Military: Armed Forces; CIA; FBI; state and local law enforcement	C. Businessmen
	3. & 4.
	There is *no* working Black military or scientific community; if they exist, they are not effective
4. Scientific and technological community	
	********************
********************	Support System
Support System	
A. Educators	A. White people
B. Religion	
C. Entertainment	
D. Communication	
E. Sports	

Black male Christian ministers, whose theological training, for the most part, is based on a deep "moral and spiritual" commitment to a white Supreme Being, find it extremely difficult to separate that Supreme Being from the white male image (Welsing, 1979; Akbar, 1984). But to bring the argument back to earth, this male leadership, due to training, acculturation, seasoning and desire is not equipped intellectually or in any other way to deal effectively with white politicians, who will kiss Black babies at Sunday morning service and arrange the death of Black men and women who they are dissatisfied with at night. The Black leadership's understanding of and opposition to white international corporations and their concept of a one world economy made in their own image is, for the most part, nonexistent. The white military structure (U.S. Armed Forces, CIA, FBI and local, state and federal "law" agencies) spends a great deal of time laughing at Black impotence in the area of self-defense (Blackstock, 1975). The question of a Black defensive or offensive force has definitely taken a back seat in most areas of the Black community. Ever since the "set up" and total disruption of the Black Panther Party and Black Liberation Army, the Black Liberation movement has moved the question of a Black self-defense to the back burner. One must understand that the U.S. military apparatus is trained to *kill* and *not negotiate*, and the moral and spiritual values that Afrikan American leadership represents play no part in their worldview (Marchetti and Marks, 1974; Agee, 1975; Janowitz, 1971).

Finally, the key to continued Euro-American development and expansionism has been its ability to actively and "successfully" challenge and regulate not only the *known*, but also the *unknown* of the physical, material and spiritual world. This challenge, for the most part, has been overseen by the scientific and technological communities, whereas in our community no such apparatus exists — unless one includes the Black steps made in the area of hair style arrangement and disfiguration. However, the killing point of our leadership is that their worldview does not allow or encourage them to challenge the *known* or the *unknown*. If the information needed is not in the Bible, the Holy Koran or some other spiritual or holy book, then that information is generally considered of little value and is often disregarded and ridiculed. The position of Black male leadership is, at best, weak, unorganized and ineffectual (See "Greed..."). It is said that when a people has more religious leaders than business and military men in a world ruled by business and military men, that people is in *serious trouble.*

Black Men Need Family: Functional and Extended

As Black families in America are being effectively dismantled and destroyed, their male members often confusingly seek other alternatives — e.g., bacherlorhood, gangs (*Ebony*, 1980, Perkins, 1987). The white and negro destroyers of Afrikan American families know that deep in the heart and meaning of *any* people the one real barometer of a people's strength is loving, strong, productive, creative, and unified families, which when connected become communities.

The Black family, beyond the individual, represents the smallest unit of organization among Black people and is reponsible for the first line development of future generations. Properly functioning Black families will produce healthy male-female relationships; create sane, healthy and energetic youth; provide basic life-giving and life-saving support systems (economic, social, educational, health, military, etc.); and clearly define, in a programatically and progressive manner, the roles of men, women and children. Doctrines of right and wrong, concepts of love and caring are family-centered. Human values (spiritual and material) are first practiced and taught at a functional level by the family. The major social agency that any Black progressive movement (or Nation) cannot do without is *family.* Generally, when the family structure is seriously altered or ceases to function at a loving, political and cultural level, the effects of such a weakness will greatly determine the future development of that people.

There are within the Black community several family arrangements, but the two basic family types are 1) *monogamous* or nuclear — man, woman and children; and 2) *extended* — a) an extension of the nuclear, to include grandparents, aunts, uncles, and close neighbors and/or ; b) single- parent family (mainly women), to include children, male friends, brothers, sisters, aunts, uncles, grandparents and friends; c) poly-nuclear family, to include man, two or more mates, children, aunts, uncles, grandparents and friends. In the Western world, monogamy is the accepted and often the only legal form of male/female bonds. The much discussed nuclear family is monogamous-based and has the sanction of and is pushed by the state, church and other institutions. The extended family in its various forms — mainly the single-parent (mother headed) household — is becoming the most prevalent alternative to monogamy. Traditional family structures (extended family) and knowledge of such quickly are fading from certain sections of our community, and the role of Black men is rapidly becoming "whatever it takes," regardless of how it affects Black life.

Many Black men and boys twelve years and older now realize that they are, indeed, marginal to this economy, and that as technology advances and job requirements become more technical, their chances of "good" employment are just about negligible. *Black young men are quickly becoming an illiterate, non-verbal, directionless, unattached, non-responsive, uncreative, jobless problem.* Those of you who don't believe this and wish to continue to color-coat our situation, come walk with me. White on Black crime has taken a disastrous toll on the warriors of our people. It has not always been this way.

In the tradition of our people the men were intimately involved in the raising of children, especially the male children. The Afrikan way was one where fathers passed their skills on to their sons. The arts of food gathering (hunting and agriculture), medicine, building (housing and public dwellings), military science and other skills were not skills that the sons of the nation acquired accidentally (Kenyatta, 1938). The young men were not only taught to be providers and protectors of their families and nations, they also were instructed in the art of healthy love-making, and knowledgeable sexual development was not relegated to the cult of the misinformed. Therefore, the elder men, whether they were biological fathers or not, played key roles in the development of the young Afrikan males into warriors, husbands, fathers, statesmen, artisans, leaders, etc. This carefully structured guide into Black manhood does not exist in the United States today at a mass level, and young Black male development is left to Black women, peer association, white men or *chance* (Perkins, 1975, 1987).

The models of Black manhood for most Black males today are very negative and anti-Black women. The mass media, again, has been instrumental in portraying Black men as studs, pimps, super-detectives or imitation white men (Bogle, 1973). Films such as *Superfly*, *The Mack*, *Shaft*, *Sweet Sweetback's Badass Song*, *The Great White Hope*, *Blackula*, *Legend of Nigger Charley*, *Slaughter*, *Watermelon Man*, *A Soldiers Story*, *The Color Purple*, *Native Son*, *Colors* and others represent a profound comment on the type of popular miseducation that a majority of Black youth continue to receive on a daily basis in the Black community. Without permanent and structured positive male education, young Afrikan American males have been left to themselves and the streets.

The most important example of young Black male/female relationships can be seen in the astronomical rate of Black babies born out of wedlock. In 1979, 62% of Black babies in Chicago were of unmarried Black women (DeVise, 1979); and in 1978, half of all Black children born in the United States were to single Black women (Feinberg, 1978). This high birth rate is mainly among Black teenagers between the ages of fourteen and sixteen (Scott, 1979). These fatherless homes lower the chances of the children developing into productive Black men or women, and the economic and social strain on the mothers will undoubtedly have an effect on their continued development. Hannibal Tirus Afrik has stated most forcefully in an analysis of the Black male problem:

> the glorification of the "phallic power," hustling, conning and strong-arm techniques against our own people is rewarded with materialistic trinkets and false ego-tripping. The best way to build a 'rep' in the neighborhood is through getting over on Black folks.

I might add that the impregnation of sisters adds "positively" to the "reputation" of young Black men. Of course, this has little to do with assuming responsibility for the children's development and well-being. Young Black males' attitude towards family and Black women today is such that familyhood is the lowest priority in their fight for survival. The most dominant characteristic of Black males' non-caring attitude toward their community is the recent epidemic of Black on Black rape (ya Salaam, 1978; Douglass, 1978). This forceful intrusion into the most intimate aspect of Black womanhood is without precedent in Black history and familyhood. However, its appearance in the Black community is cause for immediate action on the part of conscious Black men. Sexual assaults on Black women are probably double that which are reported, and in many cases rapes "involve close friends or acquaintances of the women involved" (Staples, 1973). Black women have come together to try to protect themselves, but unless Black men step forward and actively deal with each other, little will be done about this most serious of problems.

Indeed, it is now an accepted fact that when a society does not provide healthy releases for its male population's more aggressive, competitive, risk-taking and combative nature, that male population will release itself whenever it finds the opportune time, even if its negatives act against its own people. Black men's sexual aggression against Black women is an extension of a very serious cultural, economic, political and biological dilemma. Carol Jacklin and Eleanor Maccoby have documented important biological differences between the sexes:

1) Males are more aggressive than females in most human societies for which evidence is available.

2) The sex differences are realized early in life, at a time when there is no evidence that differential socialization pressures have been brought to bear by adults to "shape" aggression differently in the two sexes.

3) Similar sex differences are found in man and subhuman primates.

4) Aggression is related to levels of sex hormones and can be changed by experimental administration of these hormones (Gilder, 1979).

These findings have been confirmed by other behavioral scientists (Tiger, 1969; Freedman, 1979; and Lorenz, 1974). That Black men are obsolete as a labor force in this country ultimately means that the frustrations and energy within are denied normal releases; and when normal avenues are removed, self-destruction cannot be far away, especially in a society where the total livelihood of Black men is dependent on what white men do.

In Richard Gilder's *Naked Nomads: Unmarried Men in America,* he writes about the "naturalness" of male aggression and its intimate affect upon men:

> The denial of aggression or the attempt to abolish the impulse in men may well create a more threatening and exploitative society in which the Louies and other psychopaths, from high government offices to the streets, ride roughshod over everyone else...We are not

allowed to suppose that male aggression will inevitably lead to male dominance in most competitive activities. We assume instead that the successful man is a product of discrimination against women. We fail to recognize that the absence of arenas for aggressive male groups will lead to the eruptions of such aggressions against the society itself, or the festering of them in the mind of the men. And as in Victorian England, when suppression of sex led to an epidemic of perversity — all kinds of lurid flowers in the secret gardens of society, so the denial of male affirmation in modern life leads to pervasive distortions and perversions of healthy masculine aggression — to violence and pornograpy, to fear and exploitation of women, to the quest for potency through drugs and alcohol, to punch-drunk music and to fighting at sports events. Millions of reckless men feed on the masculinity of a few heroes — boxers, football players, politicians, rock stars...Male aggression and violence animate our movies, T.V. shows, magazines, newspapers, politics, culture. Our city streets are guiled by it. Our city schools are terrorized by it. "Liberated" women are obsessed by it — laboring through hours of karate, palavering endlessly through rap sessions on rape. It would be better to confront the reality and address the real problem, which is the lack of ways for men to achieve sexual identity and express aggression.

The killing point of Black life in America is that the racial and cultural aggression by whites has effectively moved Black people closer to *total* extinction in the United States. Konrad Lorenz in his important book *On Aggression* states:

> The balanced interaction between all the single norms of social behavior characteristic of a culture accounts for the fact that it usually proves highly dangerous to mix cultures. To kill a culture, it is often sufficient to bring it into contact with another, particularly if the latter is higher, or is at least regarded as higher, as the culture of a conquering nation usually is. The people of the subdued side then tend to look down upon everything they previously held sacred and to ape the customs which they regard as superior. As the system of social norms and rites characteristic of a culture is always adapted, in many particular ways, to the special conditions of its environment, this unquestioning acceptance of foreign custom almost invariably leads to maladaptation. Colonial history offers abundant examples of its causing the destrucion not only of cultures but also of peoples and races. Even in the less tragic case of rather closely

related and roughly equivalent cultures mixing, there usually are some undesirable results, because each finds it easier to imitate the most superficial, least valuable customs of the other.

Conscious Black men realize that they control insignificant amounts of land, produce few needed goods, and provide little independent lifegiving or lifesaving services for their communities; they also realize that they are *totally dependent* on the national socio-economic system for survival. Some would call this slavery, not freedom; the name has changed, but the game remains the same. Black men in America *do not make any earth-changing decisions about anything that concerns the well-being or future of Afrikan American people.*

Many Black men know this and have developed a comfortable compromise. Some feel that money and/or political clout within the system is the road to manhood. Others think that "education" or some special talent is the way out. However, most Black men by the age of thirty-five understand such powerlessness and establish a "working" existence. However, a significant number have said that enough is enough and have begun to struggle against what they see as certain death if there is not movement.

Many see that the first line of this struggle is a complete redefinition of Black male/female relationships. Maleness and femaleness are biological facts. That is, one's gender is generally an absolute (except in the West, where sex change operations are being considered and performed) and stay with one for life. The definitions of what a man or a woman is or should be are both cultural and biological. That is, there are many universal traits that men and women share worldwide, but so too are there differences that are culturally local and significant. The core of much of the Black male/female problem lies in incorrect definitions. In redefining Black men and women, several areas of study should be undertaken and understood first: 1) Afrikan and Afrikan American history; 2) European, Asian and Euro-American history; 3) White Supremacy (racism); 4) the dynamics of culture and biology; 5) the misuse of religions in defining male/female roles; 6) modern economic and political systems; and 7) psychology, especially the psychology of the oppressed as well as the psychology of the liberated. Actually, a cleansing of incorrect attitudes and actions is beginning to come about in parts of the Black community, and Black women continue to play a partnership role in the new definitions.

War on Black Women

That Black women have been a major and positive historical force in the Black struggle is undeniable. The works of Joyce Ladner (*Tomorrow's Tomorrow*), Robert Staples (*The Black Woman in America*), Inez Smith Reid (*Together Black Women*), Andrew Billingsley (*Black Families in White America*), Toni Cade Bambara (*The Black Woman*), Jeanne Noble (*Beautiful Also Are the Souls of My Black Sisters*), Paula Giddings (*When and Where I Enter*) and other writers — like Alice Walker, Gwendolyn Brooks, Toni Morrison, Vivian Gordon, Sonia Sanchez, June Jordan, Mari Evans and Assata Shakur — attest to this. The works of Gwendoloyn Brooks and Toni Morrison are must reading. The poetry of Mari Evans and Sonia Sanchez is direction for young women seeking their way. Black women sit on corporate boards and run their own companies. Black women head civil rights organizations and are invited to international conferences. Rosa Parks is credited for igniting the Civil Rights Movement of the sixties. In our women is the legacy of Queen Ann Nzinga, Harriet Tubman and Fannie Lou Hamer. Above all, Black women are visible. Yet, with all of this visibility and much, much more, Black women are considered in this society to be, in some minds, not quite as low as Black men in America but certainly in the running.

The struggle against white supremacy has been unrelentingly waged by Black women. Zora Neale Hurston's *Dust Tracks on a Road* and Angela Davis' *Women, Race and Class* speak eloquently of Black women fighting the real fight. From the works of Chancellor Williams (*The Destruction of Black Civilization*), Cheikh Anta Diop (*The Cultural Unity of Black Africa*), and Paula Giddings (*When and Where I Enter*), we see firsthand the role Black women have played in the liberation struggle. Assata Shakur's most recent autobiography *Assata* puts Black women in the front ranks of serious Black struggle in the world. Indeed, Black women have been the stabilizers of the race. Jorja Palmer confirms this in a strong rebuttal to narrow anti-man Black feminism when she suggested that Black women are...

...the transmitter of culture...the keeper of the cultural flame...the nourisher, comforter and anchor in all matters of life and death of that culture...It is not by chance, no accident, no false appeal to our senses when it is said, the world over, that the hand that rocks the cradle rules the world.

Sociologist Joyce Ladner seconds this when she states in *Tomorrow's Tomorrow*:

> In many ways the Black woman is the "carrier of culture" because it has been she who has epitomized what it meant to be Black, oppressed, and yet given some small opportunity to negotiate the different demands which the society placed upon all Black people. Thus, she can be considered an amalgam of the diverse components which comprise Black culture: the pains and sorrows as well as the joys and successes. Most of all, it was she who survived in a country where survival was not always considered possible.

There is a saying in the Black community: "When you educate the woman, you the educate the race."

As white men have focused on keeping Black men in their "place," not allowing them to take care of their families or protect the most precious parts of them ("their women" and their children), Black women have *had* to be strong and resourceful in untold ways. In fact, Joyce Ladner feels that Black women are the only women in this society who have forged their own definition of womanhood:

> By this I simply mean that much of the current focus on being liberated from the constraints and protectiveness of the society which is proposed by Women's Liberation groups has never applied to Black women, and in that sense, we have always been "free," and able to develop as individuals even under the most harsh circumstances. This freedom, as well as the tremendous hardships from which Black women suffered, allowed for the development of a female personality that is rarely described in the scholarly journals for its obstinate strength and ability to survive. Neither is its peculiar humanistic character and quiet courage viewed as the epitome of what the American model of feminity should be.

The sophisticated use of racism and capitalism has placed unconscious Black women in the positon of being a major competitor of Black men for jobs, education, housing and other services and necessary resources.

Black women did not place themselves in this delicate position; as wards of this system, they have been maneuvered and strategically used for the benefit of the white majority just as Black men have. Since there are so few jobs available, few openings for quality education and little housing that is habitable in the Black community, both Black men and women quite naturally try to acquire the best available for themselves and their families. Dr. Phyllis A. Wallace, a Black economist at the Massachusetts Institute of Technology (MIT), in an interview in *Black Enterprise* stated that 38% of all Black families are headed by women. Also, 44% of all Black children live in female-headed families and one in five of the mothers have never been married. Dr. Wallace also points out that the median income of Black female-headed families is $5,900. Black male median income is $9,420, whereas the median income of Black two-parent families is $15,700. Keep in mind that the poverty line is $6,700 for a family of four (Wallace, 1979). Therefore, the majority of the Black female-headed families live below the poverty level, and the majority of the never-married female family-heads are dependent upon the poverty-breeding welfare system. These are 1979 statistics and considered very conservative today.

The Black two-parent household is rapidly becoming a vanishing breed in the United States (U.S. Government Report on Black People in U.S. 1979). Many Black fathers who leave the family situation very seldom contribute to the upkeep of their children at the same level they would if they were there. Therefore, unskilled Black mothers, who comprise the the majority of heads of households, are unable to prepare their children for the highly scientific and technological labor market of the 21st century. When one sees that more than 40% of Black families headed by single Black women (Wallace, 1979) are responsible for almost half of the next generation of adult Black men and women, one can easily understand the frustration and downright anger many Black women expressed toward Black men. According to Dr. Wallace, these women are the least educated and the most lacking in marketable skills; they have children as dependents without child support, and they have little upward mobility.

The disruption of the Black family has come partially through the elimination, displacement, assimilition and/or co-opting of Black men.

The Black male on a day-to-day basis finds himself in an insecure and hostile world where his presence commands little, if any, respect; where his marketability as worker and provider is slowly eroded by unemployment, underemployment and hyper-inflation; and where his association with Black women and children is often frustrating and non-developmental. The entire Black community is jeopardized, and its survival and development at a healthly level is seriously threatened by this erosion.

It must be understood that biological and sexual roles within the human species are not interchangeable. The paralyzing damage done to many Black men, as a result of not having *positive Black male role models* to emulate and surpass, has been devastating. Black males' warped understanding of their roles as warriors, providers, husbands, fathers is superceded by the street pimp mentality (Hare, 1977, 1984). Long term sexual commitments are becoming increasingly rare, and Black women are left on their own to be both mother and father; a role that is just about impossible to perform. The sexual deficiencies and needs of men and women are, indeed, different and correlate along biological and cultural lines (Gilder, 1973; Stassinopoulus, 1973; Mead, 1949).

Developing in the Black community are short-term sexual patterns, where responsibility to sexual partners is shorter than the sex act itself. However, stable and developmental societies are based on long-term sex patterns and the birth of children represent committments made and kept (Gilder, 1973; Hare, 1984). Irresponsibility in regards to who a Black woman lets make love to her is recent. We must understand that generally women and many men have a sense of completion and value through the act of reproduction. The nine month carrying period, the delivery, the nursing all are uniquely feminine and not understood by the average man. Therefore, it is not unusual that women, on the whole, have been more discriminating in choosing their mates. Their investment in the birth process is much greater than the men's and, quite naturally, women are in a better position to seek and to bring into the world "superior" children who are both mentally and physically strong and able to cope.

The concept of hypergamy ("to marry upward") is widespread among many people but is especially a strategy of women (Barash, 1979). Very seldom today (this was not the case forty years ago) do we see a Black professional woman in a long-term relationship with a Black man not of her educational, economic or professional level. The reverse is more common — a Black professional man with a non-professional Black wife.

Black women teachers, doctors, lawyers, etc. are therefore placed in a very difficult position in terms of developing long-term relationships with Black men since more and more Black men are being forcefully excluded from "upward" mobility. Another side of this question is that it takes a Black man with an *exceptionally strong ego and enlightened worldview* to seriously, on a long-term basis, deal with a Black woman who is educationally, financially and professionally his superior. Few of these relationships work.

The idea of sex must again be put into the family context. Short-term sexual encounters or "conquests," especially in the age of AIDS, must be discouraged. This is not to suggest that *all or most* male/female sexual activity must lead to procreation, but if the family is to be the major entity for socialization, *children* must cease being accidents and again be seen as priority. When sex is easy, quick and involves many partners, its meaning is surely to diminish, developing a "get it while its hot" or "pussy is a penny a pound" mentality; and the proponents of this approach cannot possibly be serious about anything or anyone other than *themselves.* According to Gilder:

> ...the women's attitude, which devalues the procreative symbolism of intercourse, encourages the man to abandon the long-term sexual commitments that are the basis of his marriage and his role in civilized society. For if sex is not profoundly important — if the woman treats it as a perfunctory pleasure, a matter of tension and release like unsocialized male eroticism — then the structure of male socialization itself is imperiled. The man is subtly pushed towards the uncivilized patterns that come so naturally to him and that are insistently propogandized in the society.

The socialization of Black males is by no means an easy task. Too much of this socialization is left to forces that are unable to effectively direct the bio-sexual energies of young Black males. Most young Black men do not want to be seen as "Mama's boys" and therefore are left to their own and their peer group's inventiveness to prove that they are "men." The *rites of passage* that institutionalize a boy's movement from boyhood to manhood are now left to failed schools, pool halls, street gangs, armed forces and other negative influences (Perkins, 1987). It is now obvious that manhood and womanhood carry two separate but complimentary meanings. And it seems necessary that the "first" teachers of our people — Black mothers — be aware of the positives and negatives of both. Too many Black women consistently are associating their oppression with Black maleness. This is a difficult question because Black men *do* abuse Black women and children. Therefore, many Black women's fears, concerns and indictments of Black men are correct. However, Black women must understand that the positive masculine releases that white men have are not functioning within the Black community for Black men. White men in this world build cities, run countries, develop businesses, start political parties, maintain armies, develop technology, run universities, go to the moon and live in and on the ocean. Most Black men generally watch white men do these things, play a supporting role, or clean up after them. Normal outlets for Black aggression among many Black men do not exist, and Black men too often turn such aggression inward or towards those they "love" the most. The *quality* of the home life, where Black women have traditionally had a very secure and demanding voice, must return; and Black men must again assume a position of responsibility in the home. This is not going to be easy, but it is definitely necessary if we are to move into the 21st century with any hope of survival and development.

Misdirected Warriors

A profile of the average Black person that took part in the rebellions of the 1980s in Miami is a 27.8 year-old (warrior class) male, unmarried, high school dropout before completing his senior year. He is dissatisfied with his neighborhood and home, unemployed and of the opinion that the criminal justice system discriminates against Blacks. He is angry and bitter, and he "believes America is not worth fighting for" (Morin, 1980). There is more, but the key element here is that young, single Black men can either represent a positive progressive force or one that just continues to react to crisis after crisis.

It is also true that single Black males are committing most of the Black on Black rapes and crimes in our communities. These individuals represents a *real* danger, and their energies need to be channeled into functional work and struggle. There is very little that Black women can do for men in this state of mind other than organize into self-defense units, lock their doors, stay off unknown streets after dark and buy weapons. The *negative politicization* of Black men by this white supremacist society may be the final step in dismantling and destroying the Black world in the United States (i.e., let Black men destroy and disrupt their own communities).

For thousands of years men have been patriarchal and have sought male dominance and attainment (Goldberg, 1974). Thus, male dominance has been a practically universal law. This is *not to suggest that it is correct* but *only reality, a fact*. There are only a few societies where this has not been the case — up until today in America, where Black women, rather than Black men, are now the primary decision-makers in the family. Male dominance is on the decline in the Black community (due to white on Black crime), which places that community in jeopardy. *Unwarranted* competition between Black men and women for jobs, housing, health care, education, political positions, etc. only leads to further erosion of Black male/female relationships. Understand what I'm saying: under "normal" conditions this unusual competition may not exist, for there are *natural* ways to solve these problems when a people controls its *own* land, means of production and distribution, and support systems. White men have boxed Black men into a corner ("contained") with only one option — to come out fighting, regardless of who they destroy. Without question, those closest to them will be destroyed first — mates, sisters, daughters, sons, brothers and others of their community. This is a no-win situation for Black men, especially when most don't realize that they've been "set up" and that the biological/cultural and sexual differences and needs that normally exist between Black men and women are not being allowed to develop and express themselves in a healthy and productive manner.

Black male patriarchy, dominance and attainment are not being realized among most Black men, and many *incorrectly* feel that this is because Black women have written them off as serious providers, partners, lovers or protectors. This is not the whole truth. Often Black women understand Black men at a greater level than the men understand themselves. Many Afrikan American women realize that if Black men are going to rise to meet the real needs of the Black world, they have got to stop "mothering" them and really work for partnerships in struggle and life. Black men as a collective body have not been able to get our act together, and it is not accurate or in our best interest to blame Black women for our current condition. In this war situation that we are in, our women can not effectively deal with white men; they need us — *that's our job*.

We, Black men, have to stop and take a close look at ourselves and ask two important and penetrating questions:

1) Why are Black women, by and large, more responsible than we? (One reason is that many go through a birthing process. (However, there are exceptions.) Carrying a child for nine months, breastfeeding and actively rearing that child — 75% of the time, makes most Black women more responsible. Men, for many reasons, need to be a part of the whole birth and parenting process. It will give them a new understanding of life and a new sensitivity in understanding Black women and children, and will bring a much more functional definition to parenthood.

2) Is life worth living as wards of the state, wards of our women and without the ability to *actively* determine our own destiny?

It is now clear that politically conscious Black men can influence unconscious Black men under the right conditions. Black women who are conscious generally will not be listened to, and white men and white women who can influence Black men will do so only in the best interest of the white race. The best way to effectively influence other Afrikan American men is to 1) be an example of what a real Black man is and should be; 2) be able, in an organized manner, to offer a bright and practical future to Black men, even if that future is difficult and dangerous to obtain; and 3) provide brothers with a purpose and vision of life that is beyond the syndrome of "making it" in white America.

The family still represents the basic and best learning institution. Families give Black men purpose and reason to fight and build. Parenthood in the proper context (family) bestows on men a new urgency around life and future. It slows them down and dictates that they not only care about tomorrow, but that they also must prepare to take it because tomorrow will affect their offspring in crucial ways.

Male Patriarchy* and Misconceptions of Black Female Matriarchy**

The current American family pattern, which is patriarchal, is designed to maximize the influence of males over females and children. In fact, the status of women within such family arrangements can be directly traced to the "white constitution for the institution of marriage anywhere in Western civilization," and that constitution is the Bible (Baker, 1979). This well may be a misinterpretation of the Bible; however, few men, Black or white, have come forth to challenge such an interpretation. The family arrangement of the West, for the most part, is not working within the Black community and is experiencing serious difficulty in the white community (Metrus, 1979; Gardner, 1978) as well.

The biblical family structure is closely examined in David Dakan's *And They Took Themselves Wives*, where he states the common ideal of family that is associated with the Bible:

> Sexually, the norm is virginity prior to marriage, with all sexual relations limited to married heterosexual couples. Great significance is assigned to the female's virginity prior to marriage and to her fidelity after marriage. Fundamental authority within the family resides in the husband-father. Children are expected to be deferent to their parents, and the wife-mother is expected to be deferent to the husband-father. Social status and material inheritance from parents to children are usually transmitted patrilineally. Parents are obliged to provide maintenance, protection, and education for the children. The husband-father is primarily responsible for bringing outside resources into the household and to toil and sweat for food (Genesis 3:17-19). The wife-mother is responsible for production of in-house resources, and the appropriate use of resources in housekeeping and nursing. Physical nurturance and protection against everyday dangers rests primarily with the wife-mother. Protection against outside dangers, such as marauders and predators, is largely the responsibility of the husband-father. Early education of the children

---

*Social organization marked by the supremacy of the father in the clan or family, the legal dependence of wives and children, and the reckoning of descent and inheritance in the male line (Webster, 1979).

**A system of social organization in which descent and inheritance are traced through the female line.

91

rests with the wife-mother; while later education, particularly of the male children, is the obligation of the husband-father.

However, today this biological-social organization clearly works against the development of Black people in the United States. Why is this so? The authority of the husband-father role goes hand in hand with the ability of the husband-father to provide for his family's basic needs such as food, education, housing, clothing, a measurement of security and material well-being. Also, in today's consumer-oriented society, wives, husbands and children are looking for a certain amount of consumer goods and entertainment that may or may not be of any real value but are viewed as measurements of a family's success by family, friends and others.

Most secure employment opportunities in the white economic sector, for the most part, are closed to the average Black man. This precipitates a situation that forces many Black men to develop a *hustler-survival mentality* that eventually is manifested at the most destructive level, that of interpersonal relationships between Black men and women and Black men and children. It is obvious that when the Black man cannot effectively negotiate a life for himself and his family within the existing structure, he will *go outside* of it and do whatever is necessary to maintain himself and those he has assumed responsibility for. To many Black people, this type of action is viewed as *failure,* and very subtle spoken and unspoken attitudes develop within the family and community to accent such "failure." Black men react in a variety of ways:

1) Some become introverts, and their actions are only shared with a few male partners. They are loners in relationship to their families and the "legitimate" Black community.

2) Some move to lives of "crime," which definitely is psychologically damaging because their culture does not condone such actions, and neither do their families.

3) Most Black men in America have never been very communicative with their women, and when friction develops, it often becomes "easier" for the men just to leave home since a great deal of street education is grounded in avoiding social responsibility.

4) Many Black men find other women and develop relationships in keeping with current realities (difficulties). Therefore, explanations for why things are so bad will not have to be made in the future. However, this is not to suggest that intimate and sexual contact is not maintained with the first family.

5) Other Black men resort to *suicide* — that is, self-destruction through drugs (i.e., alcohol, cocaine or other stimulants that are openly available in the Black community) (Hendin, 1969).

6) Some become immersed in self-pity and the destruction of self-worth. A begging dependency on the welfare system which fosters in Black males a beggar mentality and the loss of self-esteem.

7) Others exploit their own people. Black on Black crime. This avenue is quite prevalent among former prisoners who when released cannot find adequate employment and turn to the streets again. The great equalizer has been misdirected violence. Many men engage in very serious wife/woman beating. Other than rape, the ultimate act of powerlessness and worthlessness is the rise of child molestation in the Black family; this is of critical concern.

8) A few Black men have been turned into revolutionaries, sought other men of like values, and begun to organize in many ways. These men have also redefined their relationships with their women and made new and more meaningful lives for themselves and their families. This group of men is small and can be considered the exception.

The Black family is in a serious period of disintegration. With fathers absent, Black women have had to assume dual roles that few, if any, have been prepared for. The impotence of the Black male population has forced Black women to be *strong* and resourceful in unusual ways. Many outside the Black community confuse this *strength* with *dominance* and, thus, conclude that the two-parent Black family is basically matriarchal, which is definitely not true (Staples, 1976).

Black female "matriarchal" actions have been complimentary, moving in concert with Black men. That Black women on many occasions have had to make and act upon their own decisions only points out the high level of non-involvement of Black men in the family structure and the independent nature that Black women have had to assume in the United States. We must keep in mind that more often than not the decisions made singly by Black women do not affect Black men but are generally directed towards making their lives and those of their children liveable. More often than not, when there is a man in the house he is the "head," and the Black woman recognizes this and negotiates her life so that conflicts are kept to a minimum. However, many of today's Black women, who currently are single family heads, refuse to enter relationships that do not give them a certain amount of mobility and decision-making power; this is correct. Afrikan American men and women must be partners.

Monogamy, Omnigamy, Illegany and Polygyny: Where Are We Going?

Where are we going as a people when we allow a great many Black families to become non-functional units or units composed of only single adults and children without support? It should be obvious that monogamy as the "only" way towards happiness and development has its limitations and hazards (Goldberg, 1976). It should also be obvious that as the sex ratio now stands, it is impossible for "every" Black woman to have a monogamous relationship with a Black man (Staples, 1978; Madhubuti, 1978; Scott, 1977). And, unless Black people boldly and consciously tighten up *their* family arrangements, their future will continue to be uncertain. As stated earlier, all social, political, economic and military movement against an enemy is deterred when a people's internal operation is weak and non-functional. If Black men and Black women can transcend Western cultural influences and openly and honestly face themselves, while continuously questioning the functionability and legitimacy of their family arrangements, without a doubt they can recapture their rightful place in this world.

As a start, let's critically but briefly look at some current Black male-female social arrangements and try to understand the positives and negatives of each.

As European Christians took the world, the one man/one woman form of male/female relationships became dominant (Awoonor, 1975; Leith-Ross, 1965; Beidelman, 1971). The Catholics were especially forceful in this regard, preaching that polygynous arrangements were pagan and tools of the devil (Beidelman, 1971). In fact, until the spread of Western ways, 70% to 75% of the world's people were polygynous (Wilson, 1978; Freedman, 1979; Barash, 1979). Monogamy as a social arrangement has not been able to meet the needs of a great many of those who believed in it; marriages fail because after the basic needs of food, shelter, and clothing are met partners are also looking for intellectual stimulation, shared values, "romantic love," continued sexual pleasure, high levels of intimacy, economic security, commonality of vision and moments of deep personal completion. To say that this is not working among many Black people is an understatement. However, in white America the traditional family — husband at work, wife at home and two children — now makes up only 7% to 10% (Selson,1979) of existing households.

According to Lionel Tiger (1978), the divorce rate has jumped 250% in the past twenty-one years. The number of single-person households is increasing within the society, especially in the Black community. From the most current information available (CPS,* 1978), over one-fifth of all American households in 1978 consisted of persons living alone, and 62% of these single-person households were maintained by women. The number of Black women maintaining single households since 1970 has just about doubled due to five factors: 1) Black women not getting married; 2) married men leaving home; 3) Black women widowed; 4) divorce; and 5) the non-availability of marriageable Black men. According to CPS data, there are approximately 2.5 million Black single female-headed households.

Monogamy in this country is certainly having its ups and downs; when you couple this with the mid-eighties mentality held by many Black men and women that "single is best," the future seems in trouble. However, it must be understood that not *everybody* needs to be married or is capable

---

*Current Population Survey (CPS) — Marital Status and Living Arrangements: 1978.

of marriage; yet, if a people are to develop and expand their positions in the world, it is absolutely certain that this cannot be done without procreation. This cult of the singles goes hand in hand with white Western education that pushed the ultra-individuality rather than community, and many Afrikan American men and women see no need for long or short term commitments of any kind that are not immediately financially and sexually rewarding. Another reason that many young Black professional men don't marry is that marriage would cut off their *sexual exploration and, thus, confine their sex drive to the pattern of one woman.*

Monogamy as an institution has, to a degree, been a stabilizing force in most societies. However, people must realize the inherent limitations of monogamy and make internal adjustments if it is to work on a developmental level. The larger question is, can one person (male or female) supply another with all his/her needs for life? These needs are not only sexual but material, emotional, social and intellectual. Men and women have allowed and encouraged *prostitution* (Winick and Kinsie, 1971) because most people recognize that monogamy, especially for men (and this is cultural), has not worked (Wilson, 1978); and many women will endure their men having brief sexual encounters as long as they do not threaten or impinge on the emotional, financial, etc. security of their relationships. However, many women have not accepted the fact that the sexual patterns of men and women are extremely different (Freedman, 1979; Wilson, 1978; Barash, 1979) and that monogamy as an institution has attempted to contain the male's "natural" behavior, binding his sexual urges to the one-woman pattern (Gilder, 1973, 1987). This has not been successful and more men and women are making their commitments to monogamy later in life, if at all (CPS, 1988).

Omnigamy (Serial Marriages)

Omnigamy, or serial marriages, has been the West's answer to polygyny (Tiger, 1978). Lionel Tiger has pointed out that this society, which was once based on the principle of solid monogamy "until death do we part," has shifted toward a pattern of serial marriages, in which people experience more than one spouse — if only one at a time. Tiger states that a "third to a half" of the marriages formed in this decade will end in divorce. This failure is astonishing when you consider that if anything else failed at such a rate it would be abolished or seriously altered.

Black participation in omnigamy is not as extensive as that of whites. The trend, it seems, is that if the first one doesn't work, be extremely careful about the second. And since Black professional women have entered the job market and are closer to surpassing Black men in terms of positions of responsibility and money (O'Connell, 1979), they have definitely become a part of the growing single-parent households in the country.

Omnigamy is statistically the most prevalent alternative white social arrangement because it is *legal*. However, there will continue to be some doubt on the parts of persons moving towards marriage again, as they ask themselves, "Will it work?"

Illegany (The Ball Game)

The male is on home plate and has women on first, second, and third. This is, in reality, nickle and dime pimping and whoring that lonely and insecure women allow into their lives. The male in this arrangement is busy running bases trying to service and control as many women as he can, and responsiblity to the "real" needs of these women and their children is not even a part of the equation.

Illegany, or the ball game, is what I feel is becoming the dominant Black male/female social arrangement in the country. This Afrikan American form of polygany is closer to pimpism than anything else, depending on the line that the male is running to the female(s) involved. Generally one will find a single, married, divorced or separated male dealing with two or more women. And the women more than likely have some knowledge of the other women but never discuss them due to deep patriarchal holds most men have on their mates. Here are some of the most prevalent elements of illegany:

1) It's underground. Knowledge of affairs is restricted to a few friends or running buddies.

2) Women are generally supporting themselves (jobs, welfare, etc.) and may be contributing to the males' support.

3) If children are involved, the male may act mainly as disciplinarian — especially if the children are not biologically his.

4) These relationships are short-term unless children are involved.

5) Children are considered illegitmate by the society, and the father does little to invalidate this nonsense.

6) Male has irregular visiting schedule, but shows up at least once a week. Mostly unexpected, this is to keep the women off guard.

7) Time male spends with female is basically sexual; there is little verbal communication.

8) The pressures on the female are very great, many of her friends (who may be involved in similar situations) think she is a fool to put up with his "shit."

9) Very seldom do females visit males without invitation.

10) Relationships are male-centered.

11) Women in all economic levels engage in this type of arrangement.

12) Males contribute little, if any, financial help to females.

13) There are few, if any, social pressures on males to become more responsible.

There is more to this. However, these are the most outstanding characteristics of illegany. This type of misuse of Black women needs to be cut into and cleaned up. However, this will not happen unless people are willing and able to openly and honestly make major adjustments in their lives and actively seek developmental alternatives. Audrey B. Chapman in her book *Man Sharing* has tackled this problem head on and has come up with some very practical and innovative solutions. And because of this, she has suffered much abuse and criticism from other Black women — much of it undeserved and highly insensitive to the larger problem of Afrikan American family life.

The question may arise as to whether or not there is ever a situation where Black women take advantage of Black men; the answer is yes. Scott and Stewart (1979) speak of the *Pimp-Whore Complex in everyday life* and illustrate how Black men and women play games with each other daily. However, in the final analysis, males have an upper hand in the category of *emotional and physical abuse*.

Polygyny (Many wives)

As mentioned earlier, up until the spread of Western culture, the great majority of the world was *polygynous*; multiple mating among males and females existed. *Polygyny* (many wives), the most prevalent form of multiple mating, covered much of Africa and the world before the intrusion of Christians or Muslims (Awooner, 1975). *Polyandry* (many husbands) also existed but to a much lesser degree. *Polygyny* for much of Afrika was/is patriarchal, and women were virtually the property of males. One other form of marriage called *levirate*, where a man inherits his brother's widow (Ayisi, 1979), also existed.

Western culture, particularly Christianity, to a large degree has altered traditional polygynous societies (Racliffe-Brown and Forde, 1970; Leith-Ross, 1965). But where these societies still exist, some things are very striking. All of the women are under the protection of the men. Prostitution is not as prevalent because *all* women must marry in their teens from fifteen to twenty (Kenyatta, 1938). In the Gikuyu culture, there is no term for "prostitution," "unmarried" or "old maids" (Kenyatta, 1938). However, this does not mean that "prostitution" does not exist.

Before European intervention in Afrika the female children were seen as "connecting links" between generations and from clan to clan. Through marriages the clans were bound and the communality of the females were accented. In fact, Kenyatta states:

> ...the tribal customary law recognized the freeedom and independence of every member of the tribe. At the same time all were bound up together socially, politically, economically, and religiously by a system of collective activities and mutual help, extending from the family group to the tribe. The Weltanschauung of Gikuyu people is: 'Kanya gatuune ne mwamokanero' ("Give and take").

This philosophy of "Give and Take" is in concert with Ayi Kwei Armah's description of the Afrikan Way (1979), a state of *reciprocity* or mutual exchange. Children in Afrikan society are seen as rewards and are also evidence of a woman's and man's well-being. Therefore, the more wives, the more children. In the Gikuyu tribe, the wife initiates the question of another wife after a year or so, especially if she is with child:

> My husband, don't you think it is wise for you to get me a companion (moiru)? Look at our position now. I am sure you will realize how God has been good to us to give us a nice and healthy baby. For the first few days I must devote all my attention to nursing our baby. I am weak...I can't go to the river to bring water nor to the field to bring some food, nor to weed our gardens. You have no one to cook for you. When strangers come you have no one to entertain them. I have no doubt that you realize the seriousness of the matter. What do you think of the daughter of So-and-so? She is beautiful and industrious and people speak highly about her and her family. Do not fail me, my husband. Try and win her love. I have spoken to her and found that she is very interested in our homestead. In anything that I can do to help you I am at your service, my husband.

> Even if we have not enough sheep and goats for the dowry our relatives and friends will help you so that you can get her into our family. You are young and healthy and this is the best time for us to have healthy children and to enlarge our family group, and thereby perpetuate our family name after you and I have gone. My husband please act quickly as you know the Gikuyu saying: 'Mae megotherera matietagerera mondo onyotie' ('The flowing water of the river does not wait for a thirsty man').

However, one doesn't want to leave the impression that polygyny was restricted to Afrika. One of the best examples of Euro-American polygany was the Mormons (O'Dea, 1957). Plural marriages, as they were called, were essential to the early development of the Mormons. In fact, due to their plural relationships, the Mormons literally were forced out of Illinois — only to eventually take up settlement in the Great Salt Lake (Utah) area. "Women were not allowed to remain single in Mormon land and virgins were presumed to be barred from heaven — therefore, no prostitutes and no spinsters. Every plural wife had or was supposed to have a house of her own and became a sister to the other wives of their single husband; they all felt much freer than single wives in that they were liberated from excessive male lust and free to raise smaller families" (de-

Riencourt, 1974). Due to an aroused public and severe problems with the federal government, the Mormons discarded polygyny in the 1890s.

Polygyny has survived in Afrika even though its forms may have altered to a degree due to the Christian and Muslim (who allowed up to four wives) onslaught. It has been noted that Islam had an "easier" time in Afrika because it did not disrupt the multi-wife tradition (Awoonor,1975). As young Afrikan men absorbed themselves in Western education, they too took on the culture of the West. Among the Western "educated" young Afrikan men and women monogymy is now the prevalent form (Sithole, 1972). However, we must not give the impression that polygyny was/is all peaches and cream. Women did and do have problems (Achebe, 1959), and there are avenues that they are able to take to get out of undesirable relationships. However, on the whole, monogamy (which has always existed in Afrika) and polygany seem to have found their mutual places in Afrika.

Black people in the United States, for the most part, have walked a thin line between monogamy and illegany, and the results have not always been healthy. Prevailing cultural moods restrict innovative and creative thinking or actions in regards to personal realtionships and most Black people continue to stay underground with relationships outside the traditionally accepted form. The inability of monogamy to accomodate the total needs of Black people is often spoken to, but little has been done to suggest other alternatives that might accomodate Black people's needs. The exceptions are most notably men (Semaj, 1980; Obadele, 1975; Scott, 1976; and Madhubuti, 1978). Whatever is ultimately decided upon, Black women will have to play a *paramount role in its design and execution*. I think that Audrey B. Chapman has taken a big step in this direction.

New Lives

Research over the last twenty years has confirmed a fact of which few people were in doubt: men and women are uniquely and complimentarily different in the ways their brains function — i.e., their thinking patterns (Restak, 1979; Goleman, 1978); in their actions (Mead, 1949; Hall, 1979; Harris, 1975); and in their genetic and biological make-up (Wilson, 1978; Farb, 1978; Tiger, 1971; and Freedman, 1979). These differences are complimentary, positive and functional when a people realize and carry out their "proper" roles within that society. Our capacity for change is unlimited if we recognize the importance of change. My contention is that in the United States Black people are on a collision course with certain death. And, the only way we can avert it is by shifting gears and *totally redefining, from our own experiences and world realities, what is best for us at all levels of human involvement*. The redefinition most immediately needed is one for the family because we are losing our children.

Children

A people's offspring are priority. When a people does not place the development of its children as foremost on its list of priorities, that people is killing itself internally. All serious nation-builders think in *generations* and often in *centuries* and therefore the children are *automatically an integral part of the future*. Currently, Black children are in serious trouble due to the disintegration of the Black family, where we have an abundance of single-parents, working mothers, unsupportive fathers and insensitive people in day-care and home-centers as our children's first-line teachers. My focus is on the children because the children's development is key to the success of any social arrangement ultimately adopted by Black people. Congruently, if Black adults develop, the children will develop. If the quality of adult relationships are loving, productive and secure, the chances increase that the children's will be also.

Extended Families, Functional Communities

Margaret Mead noted as early as 1949 that "In modern societies where polygany is no longer sanctioned and women are no longer cloistered, there is now a new problem to be met, the competition of females for males" (Mead, 1949). Attempts at solving this problem in the Black community through illegany or other variations of it has made conditions much worse.

Extended families are biological and/or social groupings of men, women and children that have banded together to share resources, ideas, politics and love. An extended family is *not* meant to replace monogamy but supplement it. However, the extended family is meant to replace *illegany*. Yet, it must be noted that *no* family arrangement will succeed if the partners involved are not mature and willing to compromise and make adjustments in their own lives. The extended family could be either sexual or non-sexual. A person's sexual needs should *not* be the major deciding factor for such an arrangement.

The central question should not be, *"Does a man need more than one woman or a woman more than one man?"* Rather, it should be, *"Can a mature single Black man or woman fulfill the emotional, economic, sexual, intellectual, spiritual and security needs of more than one partner?"* These questions would have to be answered on an individual basis, but let's generally look at a few absolutes that brothers should consider:

1) A Black man who has not exhibited responsibility in monogymous relationships probably will have difficulty maintaing relationships with two or more Black women.

2) A Black man who has not achieved a "responsible" level of economic stability probably will have trouble handling more than one relationship.

3) A Black man who has not developed himself intellectually and culturally probably will not be able to satisfy such needs in two or more Black women.

4) A Black man who has had difficulty relating to and developing long-term relationships (friendships, work relations, social relations, etc.) with one woman probably will not be able to meet the emotional needs of two or more Black women.

5) A Black man who has exhibited sexual insecurity and spiritual vacantness undoubtedly will experience these same problems with one or more Black women.

6) A Black man who does not or has not related to children (his or others) on a high level definitely will have to prepare himself, and monogamy is the best start.

This is my way of stating that for the vast majority of Black men in the United States the extended famly that includes more than one mate is *not* the solution. However, for the others, such a family structure *may* be a serious option, and consideration of it should be undertaken. However, it must be understood that it is much easier to *collect* sisters and have babies than to build businesses, schools, institutions and nurture children to adulthood. It is said that white men collect nations, while brothers collect sisters.

Young Women for Young Men

The suggestion to study and consider the extended family is not a subtle or sociological maneuver to provide Black men with many women or vice versa. In fact, I feel that this type of family arrangement should only be for mature adults; and mainly for single, divorced or widowed women with children. The ideal age — in terms of experience and maturity — should be thirty-five and over. For men, the suggested age is forty and older.

Also, rather than men seeking to add to their families, the best situation would be a wife inviting a "single," divorced or widowed "sisterfriend" into her family. In the age of liberated women, one can also imagine two or three women (friends-sisters) coming together and approaching a brother with the idea of an extended family, making him an offer. Again, I must stress that the man be forty or older because most serious men should have defined themselves intellectually and financially by that age. Obviously, men without serious means of support cannot hope to develop and sustain one-on-one relationships and, therefore, the extended formation would not be a serious option.

Another important point is that *young women should be left for young men.* Young Black men have enough to deal with without worrying about losing their mates to older, more "experienced," financially secure Black men. It is extremely difficult and nearly impossible for a young, inexperienced (sexually and otherwise), poor Black man to compete with a more "worldly" older brother who has resources.

Sex — The 10% Solution

Throughout history, males have been more sexually active than women; this is both in frequency and number of partners (Wallace, 1979; Gilder, 1973; Tiger, 1969; Freedman, 1979). This was by design and is cultural. In the West, male and female sexuality has been suppressed by Christian thought. Sexual pleasure in the past has been condemned as a sin, and its suppression has aided men and women in developing new forms of perversion and neurosis. The emergence of rape, pornography and incest (Butler, 1979) is closely related to psycho-sexual problems. The most sought after experience by humans, after eating, is sex, and to continuously keep it in the closet will undoubtedly cause serious problems for future generations.

The key to healthy, enjoyable sex is to understand that a person should study ways to sexually satisfy a partner — and communication (which is crucial to good sex) is primary. The first reason for sex is reproduction, and this must never be forgotten. Most sexual encounters are for pleasure and not reproduction, but that is not an adequate reason to lose sight of the primary purpose of sexual activity. According to Donald Symms in the *Evolution of Human Sexuality*, the male and female have two different sexual strategies. Whereas the male strives toward multiple sexual partners, the female — who can only bring a limited number of children into the world (while the male's capacity for reproduction is almost unlimited) — seeks a permanent relationship with a good provider to help guarantee the survival of her children. However, *the proliferation of birth control in the United States has dramatically altered the strategies of both males and females.* The use of birth control has had a liberating as well as destructive effect on relationships. A significant book that brings clarity to this important subject is *Crisis in Black Sexual Politics*, edited by Nathan and Julia Hare.

It is clear that sex is integral to any loving relationship. The individual sex drive among women and men — according to Dr. Samuel Okpaku — is a "powerful force that permeates consciously and subconsciously every phase of her or his activities and interactions with others." (Okpaku, 1984). However, it is also clear that in most serious relationships sex takes up less than 10% of a couple's quality time — *be it an important 10%*. Yet, the crucial point is that 90% of a couple's time is used in other family and related activities. The emphasis in enlightened relationships will revolve around those activities that happen outside of the bedroom. Those activities — work, study, entertainment, spiritual development, eating, institution building, etc., will take up about 60% of a couple's quality time with the remaining 30% used for sleeping.

As important as sex is, much more is needed for couples to build and sustain a relationship. A new relationship that is highly sexual will not grow or develop if it cannot move beyond the bedroom to the mind-room.

Traditional Black families have always been extended, where members represented two and sometimes three generations. In fact, it was not uncommon in the south to see father, mother, children, grandparents and a great grandparent under one roof. The value of this type of living arrangement is that the art of familihood is experienced and learned simultaneously. All the rites of passage from birth to death are expressed in an atmosphere of respect.

The extended families also included same sex communal households. This is where grandmother, mother and daughter lived and shared experiences and life together. The call is to build family networks that work. Same sex male and female households are generally temporary but can be a fruitful starting point. This arrangement is most often seen when two women or two men share an apartment and expenses until they decide to marry or live alone.

Cultural Change is Not Easy, but it is Necessary

If most Afrikan American people were financially secure, educated, lived in clean neighborhoods, had good jobs, controlled their communities and felt protected, both physically and mentally, from harm's way, there would still be problems. No community, no matter how well off materially or spiritually, is insulated from *white world supremacy* (racism). Also, Black people are not perfect, even under ideal conditions. However, one must remember that the *seasoning* that Black people underwent during the long period of enslavement has left negative physical and psychological scars. Therefore, transformation will be difficult and will require a commitment of the most profound kind. Throughout this book I make suggestions; here are a few with which to start:

1) *Accurate Definitions are Needed.* In the chapter "Were Corners Made for Black Men to Stand On?" I give a beginning definition of Black manhood. This definition is only a starting point, but I think it should be incorporated in all early learning situations for Black boys. What it means to be a Black man starts with understanding the transition from boy to man. Those *rites of passage* that define us, such as birth, naming, birthdays, formal schooling, graduations, age groupings, sexual activity, high school education, military and/or college, marriage and other cultural forces,

106

are *crucial* in stabilizing and giving direction to young Black boys and girls.

2) *Examples* of what is right and what is workable. Black boys, like others need possibilities. They need to know that there is a beneficial tomorrow for them. This means that they need to be around "successful" and "caring" men — men who are not caught up into themselves, but Black men who have made an impact in the world and will not lie to young men about the sacrifices necessary for "success." Young men and women need examples of successful Afrikan Americans in all of the lifegiving and lifesaving areas. These examples are not to be paraded out as showcases once or twice a year, but must somehow be "programmed" into the lives of our children. Examples of right and wrong, good and bad, positive and negative are value-based and often involve moral decisions. Knowing what is best under many different situations requires critical thinking and a great deal of knowledge and self-confidence. This is why child-rearing or parenting should be taught and not left to the whims of the misinformed.

3) *Study* (individual, family and group) — Serious study should be like eating. Our homes should be mini-learning institutions. A people "may" achieve liberation through sheer physical force, but they cannot maintain that liberty without intelligent and wise men and women. If our children see us studying everyday, they will too. *Turn the television off* — and if you watch it, do so with discretion. One of the reasons that our analysis is faulty is because our information is faulty. Study should be both practical and theoretical. However, the greater focus must be in that area that you plan to be most active. We must become "specialists" as well as men and women who possess a good "general knowledge" about the forces that move the world. However, it is imperative that all Afrikan American people have more than a working knowledge of their own people's contribution to civilization. I am not talking about a "slave" history but a history that accurately states the Afrikans' contributions to science, religion, health, art, humanities, mathematics, etc.

4) *Love* of self and people is one of our highest principles. Rather than "falling in love" — *learn to love*. Grow into love. Sometimes it is an easy process; often it's difficult. The *Afrikan* way is to give as well as receive. Caring beyond the normal is normal for our new direction. Be willing to share self and material possessions beyond the expected.

5) *Family Development*. First-line struggle. If you and your partner cannot communicate, check yourself out first. Make sure that you are aware of her needs and your "shortcomings" before "jumping" into her chest. The key to family is shared values and communication. *Family-making* is a teaching and "being taught" proposition. The key is always "progressive compromise" around principles and values that work for us rather than against us. Open up to your woman; let her share your pain and joy; do not hide special weaknesses or strengths. Remember, being strong is not a macho character or expensive makeup. Strength is positive decision-making and living up to responsibilities, whatever they may be.
   A. Every serious Black man should be relating positively to a Black woman.
   B. Relationships should be nonviolent and proactive.
   C. Try not to send children to be taught by people who do not care for them.

6) *Activist for life*. Progressive activity in an organized manner in all areas of human activity. This is important because of this system of corporate capitalism where money or profits are valued over people. Therefore, people have to organize and be prepared to do battle in many areas at any given time to combat evil corporations and any other entities. Also, organized struggle will generally move people past pure theory. Struggle is not impressing others with your ability to quote revolutionaries. Struggle, in the first analysis, is *work* and the ability to function productively with other Black people in an organized manner. The building of institutions, parties and nations depends first on effective building of Black individuals and families.

A. Each family needs to start a defense fund. The money will be used to acquire "materials" that will aid in the defense of the family in times of emergency.

7) *Afrikan American Cultural Boot Camps.* Fathers *must* become involved in parenting. Men must form men's groups to aid in the development of conscious young people. Due to the lack of functioning families, we must, in the meantime, develop alternatives. Year-round "boys and girls" camps or clubs functioning out of churches or other Afrikan American cultural institutions are needed. An experience that I'll never forget is my U.S. Army boot camp training. I think that such a concept is now needed in most Black communities. The Afrikan American Cultural Boot Camps would be an educational system that would immerse young people in a total cultural, physical and academic learning experience away from their homes. They would operate on a "boot camp" philosophy but out of an Afrikan American philosophical frame of reference.

These camps would be operated by Afrikan American people and would solicit the services of retired and active high school and college coaches, retired and active military drill sergeants, university professors and parents interested in a complete and radical change in the education of their children. Such cultural camps should ideally be located in rural areas. They would be run during the summer from one to four weeks and on the weekends year-round. "Support camps" would be set up in most Black urban communities. The type of losses we experience each day only means one thing — *we are at war.* Our young people must learn this before we lose them. Each sizable community would develop "100 Black men" groups to give financial, emotional and ideological guidance to the Afrikan American Cultural Boot Camps.

8) *National Afrikan American Think Tank and Leadership Council.* A national group of Black men and women who have proven beyond a doubt their commitment to Black people. Their charge is to think about the future and to begin charting a course of direc-

tion for Afrikan American people. This think tank/leadership council would include: parents, public and private school teachers, university professors, business leaders, religious leaders and representatives from major national organizations, such as National Council of Black Studies, National Association of Black Psychologists, African Heritage Association, NAACP, Operation PUSH, National Urban League, National Black United Front, Nation of Islam, etc. This group must not be made up of the same tired old guard.

9) *Become responsible men and stand up.* Stop crying on wives/lovers breasts about how the "man" treats you on the job, in the streets, at school and elsewhere. It is not that we need to present a false picture of our lives, but sisters are under enough weight themselves and do not need their men's false tears. That is how our women lose respect for us. They are actually waiting on us to do something about the "man" if we are going to continue to call ourselves men. If Black women can't occasionally lean on the shoulders of Afrikan American men, who can they lean on? We are incomplete without each other.

10) Develop a *work* attitude about the world. Nobody is giving anything of value away, and if someone does, you can be sure that he or she can take it back. We must become *business-oriented.* The real economic base of the United States is small and medium size businesses. We must teach our children early the *neces-*sity of starting *their* own businesses, and I'm not talking about franchising McDonald's or Wendy's. Living in a multi-cultural and multi-racial world controlled by white people is not easy. When Afrikan Americans begin to take control of their own lives, then they will become a serious threat to white control. The two best ways to relate to white people during this time of war are...
   A. Business only. Work with them, study with and under them, but do not allow them into your institutions at a decision-making level.
   B. *Never* let them into your heart or mind. *Stop* confessing inner secrets to them.

11) *The search for truth* should always be our guiding force. Times and situations change. Just because something was correct in the sixties, seventies and eighties doesn't mean that it can be used in the 21st century. Always be willing to question past actions as well as accept constructive criticism. Advocating an Afrikan American cultural movement doesn't mean being dogmatic and insensitive to other positions. Good is good, no matter where it comes from.

Struggle in the United States is extremely dangerous. However, our very lives depend on an ongoing conscious movement for liberation. The goal is development and bright tomorrows for all people.

We All Hurt But Most of Us Can Be Healed

People involved in serious day to day struggle of survival are not about to get involved in cultural nonsense that they feel is going nowhere. It is enough just to be able to clothe, house and feed ourselves. The *personal* side of struggle is often overlooked, but mothers and fathers who maintain their families, raise their children into productive adults are to be congratulated and supported. It is clear that we cannot build and sustain a "nation" if we cannot develop families that are culturally stable, physically strong, creative and ready to defend their people.

People endure through the power of their minds and the strength of their vision. A people's culture, if it is functioning properly, will supply the vision. Our supreme capacity to adapt has allowed Black people worldwide, but especially in America, to continue to change and grow. Whether our adaptability is in our best interest will be answered, most certainly, in the next decade. However, it is evident to those who wish to notice it that Black people are reshaping their lives according to what they think is best and, in the long run, beneficial to them and their loved ones.

As some Black women join white men and Negro men as part of the occupying force, we must certainly realize that people — all of us — *do what we have been taught to do.* Black women and men, just as most people, move out of self-interest and self-protection; that some of them are being positioned as legal killers against their people speaks to the weakness of Black people and their misunderstanding of Afrikan American political, racial and economic status. If the men do not step forward to take control and /or give leadership, the women have only one option — to do it themselves. Black women are doing the best that they can do. Black men need to come forward in force.

As mentioned earlier, it is no accident that our leadership largely comes from the ministry. When a people has more preachers than military men in leadership positions in a world ruled by scientists, politicians, industrialists, and military men, without a doubt that people is in trouble. Contrary to popular belief, *we are not our own worst enemy*. Our national Black male leadership has not exhibited any semblance of consistent and noncontradictory examples of Black manhood. This must be corrected, for in this world it is us (Black men and women) and them (white men and women), and we must make sure our backs are covered.

It is time for Black people to retake the responsibility of Afrikan American cultural design. We have the capacity and the resources (mental and economic) to do what we want to do. We need to rearrange our lives around values and principles that are best for Black people. The *family* and close communities remain the foundation of all nations, and the protection and intimacy that they provide for their members is irreplaceable. The family is, without a doubt, the best institution in which to raise our children, and when it wavers so does everything else. If we are truly working for a collective and sharing society, the quality of the persons involved in that society depends on the quality of the families. And the ultimate quality of the family depends upon the beauty of interpersonal relationships:

> There is no beauty but in relationships. Nothing cut off by itself is beautiful. Never can things in destructive relationships be beautiful. All beauty is in the creative purpose of our relationships; all ugliness is in the destructive aims of the destroyers' arrangements. The mind that knows this, the destroyers will set traps for it, but the destroyers' traps will never hold that mind. The group itself is a work of beauty, creation's work. Against such a group the destroyers will set traps for the body, traps for the heart, traps to destroy the mind. Such a group none of the destroyers' traps can hold (Armah, 1979).

If we are to move toward maximum development, Black men and women are the key elements in such movement. Many Black people in the United States, for better or worse, move on the solutions to their problems and needs without discussion. That is real. The starting point is already over when comunication begins.

Black men and women must move toward a more meaningful partnership where their complimentary elements become the defining rather than the negative aspects of each. Consciously try to make each other happy. Communicate at the highest level possible on all subjects, no matter how small or large. Recognize each others' weaknesses and strengths, and forever reach into the soul of the other. Compliment the good, correct the bad and draw strength from the positive. Question the world and be ready to implement the answers. Create a life-style of seriousness and you can be sure that the world will look at us differently. Our vision is clear, and our children demand that we reach for the best. Again, meet as lovers and do not be afraid to say, "*I care.*"

REFERENCES

Achebe, Chinua. *Things Fall Apart.* New York: Astor-Honor, 1959.

Akbar, Na'im, *Chains and Images of Psychological Slavery.* Jersey City: Mind Productions, 1984.

Armah, Ayi Kwei. *Two Thousand Seasons.* Chicago: Third World Press, 1979.

———. *The Healers.* London: Heinemann International, 1989.

Awooner, Kofi. *The Breast of the Earth.* New York: Doubleday, 1975.

Ayisi, Eric O. *An Introduction to the Study of African Culture.* London: Heinemann, 1979.

Bambara, Toni Cade. *The Black Woman.* New York: Signet, 1970.

Beidelman, T.O. *The Kaguru: A Matrilineal People of East Africa.* New York: Holt, Rinehart & Winston, Inc., 1971.

Billingsley, Andrew. *Black Families in White America.* Englewood Cliffs: Prentice-Hall, Inc., 1968.

Blackwell, James E. *The Black Community: Diversity and Unity.* New York: Harper & Row, 1985.

Blauner, Robert. *Racial Oppression in America.* New York: Harper & Row, 1972.

Bogle, Donald. *Toms, Coons, Mulattoes, Mammies and Bucks.* New York: The Viking Press, Inc., 1973.

Boskin, Joseph, ed. *Urban Racial Violence.* Beverly Hills: Glencoe Press, 1976.

Bradley, Michael. *The Iceman Inheritance.* New York: Warner Books, 1981.

Bronfenbrenner, Urie. *The Ecology of Human Development.* Cambridge: Harvard, 1979.

Brucker, Herbert. *Communication is Power.* New York: Oxford University Press, 1973.

Butler, Sandra. *Conspiracy of Silence: The Trauma of Incest.* New York: Bantam, 1979.

Chapman, Audrey B. *Man Sharing.* New York: Morrow, 1986.

Cress-Welsing, Frances. *The Cress Theory of Color-Confrontation and Racism (White Supremacy).* Washington, D.C.: published by author, 1970.

_____. *The Isis Papers: The Keys to the Colors.* Chicago: Third World Press, 1990.

Day, Beth. *Sexual Life Between Blacks and Whites.* New York: World Publishing, 1972.

Davis, Angela Y. *Women, Race and Class*. New York: Vintage, 1983.

de Riencount, Amaury. *Sex and Power in History*. New York: David McKay Co., Inc., 1974.

Diop, Cheikh Anta. *The Cultural Unity of Black Africa*. Chicago: Third World Press, 1978.

Douglas, Grace. *Rape: Taking by Force*. Rumble, 1978.

Edelman, Marian Wright. *Families in Peril*. Cambridge: Harvard, 1987.

Esfandiary, F.M. *Optimism One*. New York: W.W. Norton & Col., Inc., 1970.

_____. *Up-wingers*. New York: The John Day Co., 1973.

Fanon, Frantz. *Black Skin, White Masks*. New York: Grove Press, 1967.

Farb, Peter. *Humankind*. Boston: Houghton Miffln, 1978.

Fedo, Michael. *They Was Just Niggers*. Ontario: Brasch and Brasch, Publishers, 1979.

Feinberg, Lawrence. "Half of Black Children Born to Unmarried Women." *Washington Post*. (5-4-78).

Gardner, John W. *Morale*. New York: W.W. Norton & Co., Inc., 1978.

Gibson, D. Drake. *70 Billion in the Black*. New York: Macmillan Publishing Co., Inc., 1978.

Giddings, Paula. *When and Where I Enter: The Impact of Black Women on Race & Sex in America*. New York: Bantam, 1985.

Gilder, George. *Sexual Suicide*. New York: Quadrangle, 1973.

_____. "Can Women Fight?" *Chicago Tribune,* (2-18-79).

Ginzburg, Ralph. *100 Years of Lynchings.* New York: Lancer Books, Inc., 1969.

Goleman, Daniel. Special Abilities of the Sexes: "Do They Begin in the Brain?" *Psychology Today.* November, 1978.

Green, Mark J., Fallows, John M. and Zwek, David R. *Who Runs Congress?* New York: Bantam, 1972.

Grier, William H. and Cobbs, Price M. *Black Rage.* New York: Basic Books, Inc., 1968.

Guinther, Jon and Thomas Martinez. *Brotherhood of Murder.* New York: McGraw-Hill, 1988.

Guttentag, Marcia and Secord, Paul F. *Too Many Women?* Beverly Hills: Sage, 1983.

Hall, Edward T. *Beyond Culture.* New York: Doubleday, 1976.

Hare, Nathan. "Street Pimp," *First World.* Vol. 1 Nol. 4. 1977.

Hare, Nathan and Julia. *Bringing the Black Boy to Manhood: The Passage.* San Francisco: The Black Think Tank, 1985.

_____,eds. *Crisis in Black Sexual Politics.* San Francisco: The Black Think Tank, 1989.

_____. *The Endangered Black Family.* San Francisco: The Black Think Tank, 1984.

Harvey, Aminifu R. *The Black Family: An Afro-Centric Perspective.* New York:UCCRJ, 1984.

Hendin, Herbert. *Black Suicide.* New York: Basic Books, Inc., 1969.

Herbers, John. "Two Societies: America Since the Kerner Report." *New York Times.* (three part series), 1978.

Hernton, Calvin. *Sex and Racism.* New York: Doubleday, 1965.

Hilts, Philip. *Behavior Modification.* New York: Harper's Magazine Press, 1974.

Hurston, Zora Neale. *Dust Tracks on a Road.* 2nd Ed. Urbana: Universtiy of Illinois, 1984.

Huxley, Aldous. *Brave New World.* New York: Bantam Books, Inc., 1953.

Kenyatta, Jomo. *Facing Mt. Kenya.* London: Secker & Warburg, 1938.

Ladner, Joyce. *Tomorrow's Tomorrow.* New York: Doubleday, 1971.

Leith-Ross. *African Women.* New York: Praeger, 1965.

Lorenz, Konrad. *On Aggression.* New York: Bantam, 1967.

McAdoo, Harriette Pipes, ed. *Black Families.* Beverly Hills: Sage, 1988.

Madhubuti, Haki. *Enemies: The Clash of Races.* Chicago: Third World Press, 1978.

_____. "Black Writers and Critics: Developing a Critical Process Without Leaders," *The Black Scholar,* 1978.

_____. *From Plan to Planet: Life Studies: The Need for Afrikan Minds and Institutions.* Chicago: Third World Press, 1983.

_____. *Earthquakes and Sunrise Missions.* Chicago: Third World Press, 1984.

Mander, Jerry. *Four Arguments for the Elimination of Television.* New York: William Morrow and Co., Inc., 1978.

Mankiewics, Frank and Swerdlow, Joel. *Remote Control.* New York: New York Times Books, 1978.

Marvin, Harris. *Cows, Pigs, Wars and Witches.* New York: Vintage Books, 1975.

Mead, Margaret. *Male and Female.* New York: Morrow, 1949.

Metraux, Rhoda. *Margaret Mead: Some Personal Views.* New York: Wallace and Co., 1979.

Noble, Jeanne. *Beautiful Also Are the Souls of My Black Sisters.* Englewood Cliffs: Prentice-Hall, Inc., 1978.

Obadele, Imari A. *War in America: The Malcolm X Doctrine.* Chicago: Ujamaa Distributors, 1968.

_____. *Foundation of the Black Nation.* Detroit: Home of Songhay, 1975.

O'Connell, Brian J. *Blacks in White-Collar Jobs.* New York: Universe Books, 1979.

O'Dea, Thomas F. *The Mormons.* Chicago: University of Chicago Press, 1957.

Okpaku, Samuel O. *Sex, Orgasm and Depression.* Chrisolith Books, 1984.

Orwell, George. *1984.* New York: The New American Library, 1950.

Perkins, Useni Eugene. *Home is a Dirty Street: The Social Oppression of Black Children.* Chicago: Third World Press, 1975.

Pinkney, Alphonso. *The Myth of Black Progress*. New York: Cambridge University Press, 1984.

Radcliffe-Brower, A.R. and Forde, Daryll, eds. *African Systems of Kinship and Marriage*. Chicago: Third World Press, 1975.

Restak, Richard M. *The Last Frontier*. New York: Doubleday, 1979.

Robinson, Lovie. "The Case For Staying Single," *Ebony*, 1979.

Scott, Joseph. "School Age Mothers," *Black Books Bulletin*, 1979.

_____. "Polygyny: A Futuristic Family Arrangement for African-Americans," *Black Books Bulletin*, Summer 1976.

Semaj, Leahcim Tufani. *Black Books Bulletin*. 1980.

Shakur, Assata. *Assata: An Autobiography*. Westport: Lawrence Hill, 1987.

Sithole, Ndabaningi. *The Polygamist*. New York: The Third Press, 1972.

Slesin, Suzanne. "Changing Housing as Families Change," *New York Times*, (11-22-79).

Spence, Gerry. *With Justice for None*. New York: New York Times Books, 1989.

Staples, Robert. *The Black Woman in America*. Chicago: Nelson Hall, 1973.

_____, ed. *The Black Family: Essay and Studies*. Belmont: Wadsworth Publishing Co., 1986.

_____. *Introduction to Black Sociology*. New York: McGraw-Hill Book Co., 1976.

_____. "The Myth of Black Sexual Superiority: A Reexamination," *The Black Scholar,* April, 1978.

Stassinopoulos, Arianna. *The Female Woman.* New York: Random House, 1973.

Stember, Charles Herbert. *Sexual Racism.* New York: Harper Colophon Books, 1976.

Stewart, James and Scott, Joseph. "The Pimp-Whore Complex in Everyday Life," *Black Male/Female Relationships,* Vol. 1, No. 2. 1979.

Storr, Anthony. *Human Destructiveness.* New York: Basic Books, 1972.

Symons, Donald. *The Evolution of Human Sexuality.* London: Oxford University Press, 1979.

Tiger, Lionel. *Men in Groups.* New York: Random House, 1969.

_____. "Omnigamy: The New Kinship System," *Psychology Today.* 1978.

Wallace, Robert A. *The Genesis Factor.* New York: Morrow, 1979.

Weisbord, Robert G. *Genocide?* New York: Greenwood Press and the Two Continents Publishing Group, 1975.

"Where Are the Eligible Men?" *Ebony,* 1980.

Willhelm, Sidney M. *Who Needs the Negro?* New York: Anchor Books, 1971.

Williams, Chancellor. *The Destruction of Black Civilization.* Chicago: Third World Press, 1974.

Wilson, Edward O. *On Human Nature.* Cambridge: Harvard University Press, 1978.

Wilson, William J. *The Truly Disadvantaged*. Chicago: University of Chicago Press, 1987.

Winick, Charles and Kinsie, Paul M. *The Lively Commerce: Prostitution in the United States*. Chicago: Quadrangle.

Wobogo, Vulindlela. "Diop's Two Cradle Theory and the Origin of White Racism," *Black Books Bulletin,* Vol. 4, No. 4. 1976.

Wright, Bobby. *The Psychopathic Racial Personality*. Chicago: Third World Press, 1986.

Wright, Bruce. Black Robes, White Justice. New Jersey: Lyle Stuart, Inc., 1988.

ya Salaam, Kalamu. "Rape: A Racial Analysis," *Black Books Bulletin*, 1980.

Yette, Samuel F. *The Choice: The Issue of Black Survival in America*. New York: G.P. Putnam's Sons, 1971.

II. Missions and Visions

"You watch. I will be labeled as, at best, an 'irresponsible' black man. I have always felt about this accusation that the black 'leader' whom white men consider to be 'responsible' is invariably the black 'leader' who never gets any results. You only get action as a black man if you are regarded by the white man as 'irresponsible.' In fact, this much I had learned when I was just a little boy. And since I have been some kind of a 'leader' of black people here in the racist society of America, I have been more reassured each time the white man resisted me, or attacked me harder — because each time made me more certain that I was on the right track in the American black man's best interests. The racist white man's opposition automatically made me know that I did offer the black man something worthwhile."

Malcolm X
The Autobiography of Malcolm X

The Question

Question: What is the greatest challenge you face as a Black man?

Answer: My continued quest is to be a responsible, loving and effective Black man, husband, father, writer, educator and publisher in this ocean of *white world supremacy* (racism), and not to allow *white supremacy* to alter or destroy my memory, spirit, drive, integrity, worldview, convictions and values, which are the results of twenty-five years of work, excruciating pain, serious study, critical thinking, actions and organized struggle.

Also, with my wife, my challenge is to pass on to our children positive Afrikan (Black) values, which demand the maintenance and development of our family, extended family, community and people, by highlighting and pushing progressive ideas as well as historical examples of Harriet Tubman, Nat Turner, Martin R. Delaney, Marcus Garvey, Mary McLeod Bethune, Fannie Lou Hamer, Martin Luther King, Malcolm X and others.

My fight is to be an inspired example of a caring, healthy, intelligent and hard-working brother who understands this *war* and works daily for the development of our brothers into multi-talented, family-based, conscientious Black men who will not settle for anything less than self-determination and beauty for all people.

Never Without A Book:

Educating the poor and rich:
Two hundred plus books every
conscious Afrikan American should study

I

From the age of thirteen, after my mother introduced me to *Black Boy* by Richard Wright, seldom has there been a day that I've been without a book. For a poor boy coming from the lower east side of Detroit by way of Little Rock, Arkansas, books at such a *late* age represented *revelation* and *intellectual liberation.*

I grew up in the Black church (Baptist) and the unforgiving urban streets. The three "skills" I learned very early were how to pray, rap and lie to white people; without them one could not survive in Black Town, U.S.A. Books revealed to me other *possibilities*, introduced me to poverty greater than my own and wealth that was unimaginable. In books I discovered that Black women and men could not only write and publish, but that words — combined in a certain way, somewhat like a musician combines notes into music — *could make a difference.* I learned that, if used wisely, language (written and spoken) distinguished and freed a person, if only temporarily, from the awesome weight of race, gender, class and poverty in America.

Books taught me a new language, a new music. I had been exposed to the melodic lines of Black song writers. Growing up in Detroit in the late fifties, one could not escape the profound influence of the Motown sound. Little Stevie Wonder was approaching genius, while the Four Tops and the Miracles filled the streets with love songs. The tempting Temptations and the Supremes had not gone crazy yet. And writing poetry was something that was *just not done* by "real men." The creative atmosphere was different. So, if I was caught writing poetry, I generally said that I was writing lyrics for Little Anthony and the Imperials.

I became aware of the liberating force of literature very early. Like most young Black men, as a teenager I met each day with a certain amount of fear. This fear was both physical and intellectual. Being tall, thin, light-skinned and about the size and weight of a 6'1" skeleton didn't help my stature among the local brothers. Also, going to a high school out of my neighborhood was a daily exercise in avoiding a beating and/or intellectual embarrassment. Learning how to fight, run and rap at the earliest sign of danger got me through school with only a small razor cut and a mind that was not beyond repair. Conquering the written word made high school something to look forward to each day. I knew how brothers fought in the streets, but I had no idea of the extent to which we were being annihilated intellectually in the class room and elsewhere where language and cultural knowledge were the weapons of power and destruction.

Among the Black writers that I read during this period (1955-1959) was Chester Himes — *Cast the First Stone, The Lonely Crusade, Third Generation,* and *If He Hollers, Let Him Go*; these four novels exposed me to the complexity of Black involvement within the problem of white supremacy (racism). I continued with Richard Wright and consumed *Native Son, Lawd Today, Uncle Tom's Children, Black Power, Eight Men, White Men, Listen, The Color Curtain, 12 Million Black Voices* and *The Outsider.* Through Richard Wright and Chester Himes, I received a beginning in literary and political education. Frederick Douglass' *My Bondage and My Freedom* incited me to think, at a new and more questioning level, about the issue of slavery and Black people in the United States. However, it was Booker T. Washington's *Up From Slavery* that signaled in me other possibilities for Black people who had functional skills. None of these books were assigned in school; nor was there *ever* an Afrikan American writer discussed or even mentioned during my early formal education. The Detroit Public Library became my second home, and along with Black music, I began collecting Black literature.

My mother was killed in 1959; my sister was fifteen, unmarried and with her first child. I had become a disillusioned firebrand with a basketball court full of unanswered questions, trying to understand Carter G. Woodson's *The Miseducation of the Negro.* After my mother's death, I Greyhounded it to Chicago, lived with an aunt for a while, and ended up with a room at the YMCA. I completed high school and, in between the few "boy" jobs that existed at that time, continued my adventure into books. Margaret Walker, Sterling Brown and Claude McKay were the poets I was reading. Also, I had become aware of the "negro" political struggle and began seeking materials that would shed light on it. I was glad to leave the fifties but did not realize how the sixties would change me, my people and America.

II

By 1960, the paperback revolution was changing the *entire publishing industry*, and books written by Blacks were becoming the "in" thing. By this time, I had discovered the "Chicago" writers Frank London Brown (*Trumbull Park*), Lerone Bennett, Jr. (*Before the Mayflower*) and Gwendolyn Brooks (*A Street in Bronzeville*, *Annie Allen* and *Maud Martha*). The works of Langston Hughes entered my world with his *The Langston Hughes Reader*. The "boy" jobs were unstable and didn't pay enough to meet my major expenses of food and housing, so I decided to leave Chicago.

The year 1960 was to be a pivotal one for a number of reasons. I discovered that the needs and problems of what little family I had were so great that they could not help me. I also learned that life's options for a young Black man ranged from few to almost none. The only value a high school diploma had was that, for one who could read, it would facilitate entrance into the armed forces. However, due to a minor heart problem, I couldn't pass the physical and was rejected by the Air Force.

After being rejected by the military (the poor boy's answer to the future and full employment) I did not see too much of a bright tomorrow. I joined a Black magazine selling caravan that traveled throughout downstate Illinois. We stopped in small towns — going from door to door — hawking the popular magazines of the day. There was little money or enjoyment in this work, but it was a way to get out of Chicago. I traveled with an all Black group of young women and men in a caravan of four cars. My second "skill" came into use because the selling pitch was "We are working our way through college." The interesting thing about this slice of life is that this was the first time college *ever entered my mind at a serious level*. I did not think that a university education was possible for poor Black people in America.

Anyway, my travels with these young "entrepreneurs" ended in St. Louis where they left me in a two-dollar-a-day hotel with a serious virus that would not allow food or liquid to remain in my body. Upon recovery, I did "boy" work to survive and spent my evenings in the public library of St. Louis. By that time I had discovered Carter G. Woodson's *The Negro in Our History*; W.E.B. Du Bois' *Souls of Black Folks, Black Reconstruction in America, Dust of Dawn, The Suppression of the African Slave-Trade to the United States*; and *Crisis* magazine. However, the work that was to cause me much conflict and inner searching was the *Philosophy and Opinions of Marcus Garvey*. I was becoming more and more aware of the issue of *color*, and these books gave me the historical and political foundation that would lead me to a realistic and deadly understanding of *white world supremacy*.

In October of 1960, without funds or the possibility of a job in a city that was less friendly than Detroit or Chicago, I tried to join the military again. This time it was to be the U.S. Army. Because of my "heart" condition, I knew that the physical exam could be a repeat of my Air Force experience. Therefore, when I walked into the examining room, which was a large, wide open area, I looked for the youngest doctor. They were all white males. During my examination, he caught an irregular heartbeat and asked if I had a heart problem. I promply said, "No. This is the first time that I've been away from home. I've never been around this many white people before, and I'm a bit nervous." I got in and was shipped to Fort Leonard Wood, Missouri for basic training.

On the bus to basic training, I was reading Paul Robeson's *Here I Stand*. The book, according to the drill sergeant that welcomed us to the camp, was written by a Black communist (the word "Black" was just as negative as "communist" in 1960) and would only confuse and corrupt my negro mind. He took the book, held it high above his head as an example of "forbidden fruit," and — in between gutter room invectives — tore the pages from the book, distributing them to the new male recruits and instructing the "ladies" to use the pages as toilet paper. I will not go into this in any more depth except to say that, for me, the military was a blessing in disguise, even though it was there that I had put my life in the hands of men less intelligent than I.

By this time, I was reading E. Franklin Frazier's *Black Bourgeoisie* and Drake's and Clayton's *Black Metropolis*. Race-politics in the United States was heating up, and upon completion of basic training, I was shipped south to Fort Bliss, Texas for advanced training in military mediocrity. In Texas, partially because there was little to do, I made a decision that would change my life. I took a speed reading course that enabled me to increase my reading speed greatly. I decided that I would become as knowledgeable as possible about Afrikan and Afrikan American people. I was nineteen, and I consciously stopped apologizing for being Black and went on the offense.

III

My study regiment for the next five years (1961-1966) was to read *a book a day* and write a 150 to 200-word review of the book. The reading went close to schedule, but the review writing revealed another inadequacy— that of my putting words on paper to convey critical meaning. Also, the task of critically analyzing what I read presented a problem. I was not prepared to do either well. But, I was in the military; I had learned discipline, and I had plenty of time. In fact, at that time the U.S. Army's unofficial motto was "hurry up and wait."

John O. Killens' *And Then We Heard The Thunder* gave me insight on Black men fighting in a racist military. It also gave me the confidence I needed to take the balance of my military time and use it to my advantage. I learned from Killens to get good yardage out of a bad situation. I realized the full range and scope of Black writing by reading anthologies and the collected works of authors. Books like James Weldon Johnson's *The Book of American Negro Poetry*; Sterling Brown's, Arthur P. Davis' and Ulysses Lee's *Negro Caravan*; and Arna Bontemps' and Langston Hughes' *The Poetry of the Negro* made it clear to me that writing as a profession was not only possible but necessary. The ignorance that Black people lived with spoke directly to their station in life. However, the lack of self-knowledge displayed among many Black people convinced me that, if nothing else, I must never put myself in the position where my ignorance would embarrass me. The study of Black people became as important to me as love-making. Therefore, reading was not only developmental, it was pleasurable; it was food and new life.

My favorite spots for acquiring Afrikan American literature — at that time it was still "negro literature" — were the Salvation Army used clothing stores and used book stores. I remember the ultimate joy of finding a mint condition, first edition copy of Richard Wright's *Native Son* for 25¢. From that day on, I was in first gear about books. Since 1961, every trip I've taken has included visits to local book stores. I found copies of Alain Locke's *The New Negro* and *The Negro in American Culture* — completed after his death by Margaret Just Butcher. Julian Mayfield's *The Hit*,

Wright's *Color Curtain*, and Saunders Redding's *The Lonesome Road* were all found in mint condition at used book stores.

The first time I encountered the term "Afro-American" was in the title of an anthology of short stories edited by Nick Aaron Ford and H.L. Faggett, *Best Short Stories by Afro-American Writers*. Up until that point (1962), the term "Negro" — capitalized due to the Garvey movement — was the "correct and accepted" designation for people of Afrikan descent in America. Ford and Faggett's title forced me to reassess what we called ourselves. Lights began to click in my mind. In contemplating this question, the crucial issue of self-definition and self-reliance took on a larger meaning. The key to any people's liberation quite logically starts with that people defining itself. As long as a people accepts the conqueror's definitions, it will be *impossible* to imagine other worlds.

Two other points need to be made about my reading. Most of the authors who influenced me were Black men, and in much of their literature they displayed the sexist attitudes and beliefs of the culture. By this time, I was reading James Baldwin's *Go Tell It On the Mountain* and *Notes of a Native Son*; Ralph Ellison's *Invisible Man*; William Gardner Smith's *Last of the Conquerors*; Ann Petry's *The Street*; Claude McKay's *Selected Poems*; Paule Marshall's *Brown Girl, Brownstones*; LeRoi Jones' *Preface to a 20 Volume Suicide Note*; John A. Williams' *Night Song*; William Melvin Kelly's *A Different Drummer;* and Lewis Lomax's *The Negro Revolt*.

The two writers who signaled to me the possibilities of poetry were Margaret Walker and Gwendolyn Brooks. Walker's *For My People* gave me fighting poetry in free and unclustered form. However, it was Gwendolyn Brooks who gave me the greatest gift — the gift of *time, caring* and *example*. This woman is as close as anybody can be to existing without *hypocrisy*.

It was the serious examples of Gwendolyn Brooks, Dudley Randall and Margaret Burroughs that pushed me to start Third World Press, the Institute of Positive Education, *Black Books Bulletin* and the African American Book Center. Because of the influence of Gwendolyn Brooks, Margaret Burroughs, Hoyt W. Fuller, Dudley Randall and Malcolm X, I am the man that I am today. I learned from them that one must *never give up in the right fight*. Yet, one must always be prepared to carry the battle to a more effective level. I may be one of the few writers of Afrikan descent who do not have to give credit or thanks to white people for our development or "success" as writers or publishers. My books have sold a million plus copies not because of white publishers, but due to the fact that Dudley Randall's Broadside Press, Chicago's Third World Press and our readers never gave up on us. That is truly progressive and revolutionary.

I left the military in September of 1963, just as four little girls were being bombed in Birmingham, Alabama. To a young man with a warrior's attitude, this state of affairs was unacceptable. I also left the military with an unofficial Ph.D. in Afrikan American literature and the words of Robert Hayden ringing in my ears, "Mean, mean, mean to be free."

IV

There are literally thousands of books that should be read by people who are truly trying to bring beauty into this world. In the United States in 1988, over 56,000 books were published. Therefore, a reader needs to be selective in her or his reading. Readers need to understand that the *introduction* to knowledge does not mean the acceptance of knowledge. There is a wealth of armchair intellectuals in the West, and the damage they do — as far as I know — has never been accurately calculated. Knowledge, if it is indeed useful, must lead one to an active consciousness; a creative and productive mind-set; a *doing* and problem-solving life-style; an environmentally conservative approach to nature; a sharing and loving presence among children and others; and the *will* to find and be an example of an enlightened person who is seeking wisdom.

The books listed here are not all-encompassing. I chose the books that I think provide a good starting point for a person seeking wholeness. I tried to divide the selection evenly between women and men. I *strongly* support the position that reading *must* become like eating — done daily and consuming the best.

Libraries are the one true gift for poor people in America. However, most poor people don't take full advantage of public libraries. We pay for libraries through our tax dollars. A well-stocked and well-staffed library is a blessing. I would not have gotten hooked on books if it wasn't for the Detroit Public Library. The free library system in this country is still an undiscovered secret.

Finally, a few tips: 1) if parents read, chances are children will read; 2) develop reading time for the home — a time when television and radio are off and books are on; 3) try to visit the library weekly as a family; 4) take children to bookstores (new and used) and encourage them to spend their own money on the books they want; 5) each home should have a library (i.e., a collection of best-loved books to be read often and shared with others); 6) parents should read to young children; 7) self-discipline is the key to a life of reading pleasure — read for information and fun; and 8) remember, books are like good fruit — rare and precious and healthy.

The first list of books is comprised of writers of Afrikan descent: Afrikan, Afrikan American, Afrikan Caribbean, etc. The second list is of non-Afrikan writers; books that I feel will bring another, yet important, perspective to international understanding. Finally, those persons who have first use of knowledge and use it in a way that advances world development are to be congratulated and rewarded. Look for them, and join their ranks; they are truly in the minority and know something the rest of us don't.

Black Writers

Achebe, Chinua
Things Fall Apart
Anthills of the Savannah
The Trouble with Nigeria

Akbar, Na'im
Chains and Images of Psychological Slavery
From Miseducation to Education

Alexander, Margaret Walker
Jubilee
Richard Wright: Daemonic Genius
This is my Century: New and Collected Poems

Angelou, Maya
I Know Why the Caged Bird Sings

Armah, Ayi Kwei
Two Thousand Seasons
The Healers
The Beautiful Ones Are Not Yet Born
Fragments

Asante, Molefi Kete
Afrocentricity
The Afrocentric Idea

Baldwin, James
The Fire Next Time
The Evidence of Things Not Seen
Another Country
Price of the Ticket

Bambara, Toni Cade
The Sea Birds Are Still Alive

The Salt Eaters
The Black Woman (ed.)

Baraka, Amiri
Black Magic Poetry 1961-1967
Home: Social Essays
In Our Terribleness (With Billy Abernathy)
Black Music
Blues People

Beason, Jake Patton
Why We Lose

Bell, Derrick
And We Are Not Saved: The Elusive Quest for Racial Reform

Ben-Jochannan, Yosef
Black Man of Nile
African Origins of the Major "Western Religions"

Bennett, Jr., Lerone
Before The Mayflower
The Shaping of Black America

Biko, Steve
I Write What I Like

Blackwell, James E.
The Black Community: Diversity and Unity

Bontemps, Arna
Black Thunder

Brathwaite, Edward Kamau
Islands
Masks
Rights of Passage
Sun Poems

Brooks, Gwendolyn
Blacks: Collected Works
Report From Part One
To Disembark
Winnie
Primer for Blacks

Browder, Anthony T.
From the Browder File

Brown, Claude
Manchild in the Promised Land

Brown, Sterling
Collected Poems of Sterling Brown

Carruthers, Jacob
The Irritated Genie
Science and Oppression
Essays In Ancient Egyptian Studies

Cesaire, Aime
Discourse on Colonialism
Collected Poems

Chinweizu
Decolonizing The African Mind
The West and the Rest of Us

Cliff, Michelle
The Land of Look Behind

Clifton, Lucille
Good Woman: Poems and a Memoir 1969-1980
Next: New Poems

Cortez, Jayne
Coagulations: New and Selected Poems

Cress-Welsing, Frances
The Isis Papers: The Keys to the Colors

Cruse, Harold
The Crisis of the Negro Intellectual
Plural But Equal

Davis, George and Clegg Watson
Black Life in Corporate America

Diop, Cheikh Anta
The African Origin of Civilization
Pre-Colonial Africa
Black Africa: The Economic and Cultural Basis for a
Federated State
The Cultural Unity of Black Africa

Douglass, Frederick
Narrative of the Life of Frederick Douglass

Drake, St. Clair
Black Folk Here and There: An Essay in History
and Anthropology
The Redemption of Africa and Black Religion

Du Bois, W.E.B.
The World and Africa
The Souls of Black Folk
Black Reconstruction in America
The Autobiography of W.E.B. Du Bois
Dusk of Dawn
(Anything by Du Bois)

Dunbar, Paul Laurence
Collected Poems

Dumas, Henry
Rope of Wind

Ark of Bones
Goodbye, Sweetwater

Ellison, Ralph
Invisible Man

Evans, Mari
Black Women Writers — 1950-1980
I Am a Black Woman: Poetry
Nightstar: Poetry

Fanon, Frantz
The Wretched of the Earth
Black Skin, White Masks
A Dying Colonialism

Fields, Julia
East of Moonlight

Frazier, E. Franklin
Black Bourgeoisie
The Negro Family in the United States

Fuller, Hoyt W.
Journey to Africa

Fuller, Neely
The United Independent Compensatory Code/System/Concept

Gaines, Ernest J.
In My Father's House
A Gathering of Old Men
The Autobiography of Miss Jane Pittman

Gary, Lawrence E. (ed.)
Black Men

Gayle, Jr., Addison
The Black Aesthetic (ed.)
Richard Wright
The Way of the New World
Wayward Child: An Autobiography

Giddings, Paula
When and Where I Enter: The Impact of Black Women on
Race and Sex in America

Gilbert, Herman
The Negotiations

Gordon, Vivian
Black Women, Feminism, and Black Liberation: Which Way?

Greenlee, Sam
The Spook Who Sat by the Door

Hale, Janice E.
Black Children: Their Roots, Culture, and Learning Styles

Harding, Vincent
There is a River

Hare, Nathan & Julia
The Endangered Black Family
Bringing the Black Boy to Manhood
The Black Anglo-Saxons (Nathan Hare)
Crisis in Black Sexual Politics (eds.)

Hayden, Robert
Collected Poems

Head, Bessie
A Question of Power

Himes, Chester
Third Generation
If He Hollers Let Him Go

Hooks, Bell
Ain't I A Woman

Hurston, Zora Neale
Mules and Men
Their Eyes Were Watching God
Tell My Horse
Moses, Man of the Mountain
Dust Tracks on a Road

Jackson, John G.
Man, God and Civilization
Christianity Before Christ
Introduction to African Civilization

Jackson, George L.
Blood in My Eye

James, George G. M.
Stolen Legacy

Johnson, James Weldon
Autobiography of An Ex-Colored Man

Jones, Reginald L. (ed.)
Black Psychology

Jordan, June
Civil Wars

Karenga, Maulana
Introduction to Black Studies
The Husia

Kawaida Theory: An Introductory Outline
Kwanzaa: Origins, Concepts, Practice

Kelly, William Melvin
    A Different Drummer
    A Drop of Patience
    Dancers on the Shore

Kenyatta, Jomo
    Facing Mount Kenya

King, Jr., Woodie (ed.)
    New Plays for the Black Theatre

Ladner, Joyce A.
    Tomorrow's Tomorrow: The Black Woman
    The Death of White Sociology

Landry, Bart
    The New Black Middle Class

Madhubuti, Haki R.
    Don't Cry, Scream
    Book of Life
    From Plan to Planet
    Enemies: the Clash of Races
    Earthquakes and Sunrise Missions
    Killing Memory, Seeking Ancestors
    Black Men: Obsolete, Single and Dangerous?

Mandela, Nelson
    The Struggle is My Life

Mandela, Winnie
    Part of My Soul Went With Him

Marable, Manning
    How Capitalism Underdeveloped Black America

Marshall, Paule
Brown Girl, Brownstones

Martin, Tony
Race First

McAdoo, Harriette Pipes (ed.)
Black Families (2nd edition)
Black Children (with John Lewis McAdoo)

McKay, Claude
Selected Poems
A Long Way From Home
Banana Bottom

Monroe, Sylvester
*Brothers: Black and Poor — A True Story of Courage and
Survival*

Moore, Mafori and others
*Transformations: A Rites of Passage Manual for
African-American Girls*

Morrison, Toni
Song of Solomon
Tar Baby
Beloved

National Urban League
The State of Black America 1989 (annual report)

Neal, Larry
Hoodoo Hollerin Bebop Ghosts
Visions of a Liberated Future

Nettleford, Rex M.
Identity Race and Protest in Jamaica

Ngugi, Wa Thiong'o
Petals of Blood
Devil on the Cross

Nkrumah, Kwame
Ghana: The Autobiography of Kwame Nkrumah
Neo-Colonialism: The Last Stage of Imperialism

Nobles, Wade
Africanity and the Black Family
*Understanding the Black Family: A Guide for Scholarship
and Research* (with Lawford C. Goddard)
African-American Families: Issues, Insights and Directions
(with Goddard, Cavil and George)

Obadele, Imari
Free the Land!
Reparations Yes! (with Lumumba and Taifa)

Padmore, George
Pan-Africanism or Communism

Parks, Carole (ed.)
Nommo: A Literary Legacy of Black Chicago 1967-1987

Perkins, Useni Eugene
Home is a Dirty Street
Harvesting New Generations
The Explosion of Black Chicago Street Gangs

Pinkney, Alphonso
The Myth of Black Progress
The American Way of Violence
Red, Black and Green: Black Nationalism in the United States

Randall, Dudley
The Black Poets
Homage to Hoyt Fuller

Reed, Ishmael
  Reckless Eyeballing
  Flight to Canada
  The Last Days of Louisiana Kid
  Writin' is Fightin': Thirty-Seven Years of Boxing on Paper

Robeson, Paul
  Here I Stand

Rodney, Walter
  How Europe Underdeveloped Africa

Rogers, J. A.
  Sex and Race Vol. 1-3
  Great Men of Color, Vol. 1 & 2

Sanchez, Sonia
  I've Been a Woman
  Love Poems
  Under a Soprano Sky
  Homegirls and Handgrenades

Shakur, Assata
  Assata

Smith, Barbara A.
  Home Girls

Southern, Eileen
  The Music of Black Americans

Soyinka, Wole
  The Man Died
  Ake
  Season of Anomy

Staples, Robert
  *Black Masculinity: The Black Male's Role in American
                Society*
  The Black Family: Essays and Studies
  The World of Black Singles

Steady, Filomina Chioma (ed.)
  The Black Woman Cross-Culturally

Terry, Wallace
  Bloods

Toomer, Jean
  Cane

Travis, Dempsey
  Real Estate is the Gold in Your Future

Van Sertima, Ivan
  They Came Before Columbus
  Journal of African Civilizations (ed.)
      Blacks in Science: Ancient & Modern
      Black Women in Antiquity
      Nile Valley Civilizations
      African Presence in Early Asia
      African Presence in Early Europe
      Great African Thinkers (Cheikh Anta Diop)
      African Presence in Early America
      Great Black Leaders Ancient and Modern
      African Presence in World Cultures

Walker, Alice
  The Color Purple
  In Search of Our Mothers' Gardens
  Living By the Word
  Horses Make A Landscape Look More Beautiful
  The Temple of My Familiar

146

Wallace, Phyllis
Black Women in the Labor Force

Walters, Ronald W.
Black Presidential Politics in America: A Strategic Approach

Walton, Hanes
Invisible Politics: Black Political Behavior

Washington, Booker T.
Up From Slavery

White, Evelyn C.
Chain, Chain, Change: For Black Women Dealing with Physical and Emotional Abuse

Williams, Chancellor
The Destruction of Black Civilization
The Rebirth of African Civilization

Williams, John A.
The Man Who Cried I Am
Sons of Darkness, Sons of Light
Jacob's Ladder

Williams, Richard
They Stole It But You Must Return It

Williams, Terry
The Cocaine Kids

Wilson, Amos
The Developmental Psychology of the Black Child

Wilson, Julius
The Truly Disadvantaged

Woodson, Carter G.
The Mis-education of the Negro
(anything by Woodson)

Wright, Bobby E.
The Psychopathic Racial Personality and other Essays

Wright, Bruce
Black Robes, White Justice: Why Our Justice System
Doesn't Work for Blacks

Wright, Richard
Black Boy
Native Son
Uncle Tom's Children
The Outsider
White Man, Listen!
Black Power

X, Malcolm
The Autobiography of Malcolm X

Salaam, Kalamu ya
Our Women Keep Our Skies From Falling
Revolutionary Poems
What is Life

Yette, Sam
The Choice

Non-Black Writers

Agee, Philip
Inside the Company: CIA Diary on the Run

Amnesty International 1988 Report (a yearly report)

148

Barraclough, Geoffery
Turning Points in World History

Batra, Ravi
The Great Depression of 1990

Beit-Hallahmi, Benjamin
The Israeli Connection: Who Israel Arms and Why

Berry, Wendell
The Hidden Wound

Boyd, Billy Ray
For the Vegetarian in You

Bradley, Michael
The Iceman Inheritance

Brown, Dee
Bury My Heart at Wounded Knee

Brown, Lester R. and others
State of the World 1988 (a yearly report)

Carnoy, Martin
Education or Cultural Imperialism

Chomsky, Noam
The Culture of Terrorism
Pirates and Emperors: International Terrorism in the
Real World
The Chomsky Reader (ed. by James Peck)
On Power and Ideology (The Managua Lectures)
The Fateful Triangle: The United States, Israel & the Palestinians

Chorover, Stephan L.
From Genesis to Genocide: The Meaning of Human Nature
and the Power of Behavior Control

Coates, James
Armed and Dangerous: The Rise of the Survivalist Right

Cockburn, Alexander
Corruptions of Empire

Deloria, Jr., Vine
We Talk, You Listen
Custer Died for Your Sins
Behind the Trail of Broken Treaties

Domhoff, G. William
Who Owns America Now?

Flynn, Kevin and Gerhardt, Gary
The Silent Brotherhood: Inside America's Racist Underground

Frederickson, George
White Supremacy

Gabler, Neal
An Empire of Their Own: How the Jews Invented Hollywood

Galbrath, John Kenneth
The Nature of Mass Poverty

Gilder, George
Men and Marriage
Naked Nomads
Wealth and Poverty

Ginzburg, Ralph
100 Years of Lynchings

Gould, Stephen Jay
The Mismeasure of Man

Hapgood, Fred
Why Males Exist

Harrington, Michael
The Other American
The Vast Majority
The New American Poverty
Taking Sides

Harris, Marvin
Cows, Pigs, Wars and Witches: The Riddles of Culture
America Now: The Anthropology of a Changing Culture
Cannibals and Kings: The Origins of Culture
Our Kind

Herman, Edward S.
The Real Terror Network: Terrorism in Fact and Propaganda

Josephy, Jr., Alvin M.
Now That the Buffalo's Gone

Kennedy, Paul
The Rise and Fall of the Great Powers

Kiernan, V.G.
America: The New Imperialism
From White Settlement to World Hegemony

Kozol, Jonathan
Illiterate America
Death at An Early Age
Rachel and Her Children: Homeless Families in America

Lappe, Frances Moore
Food First
World Hunger Twelve Myths (with Joseph Collins)

Lerner, Gerda
 The Creation of Patriarchy

Lessing, Doris
 Prisons We Choose to Live Inside

Lewis, Norman
 The Missionaries: God Against the Indians

Macdonald, Andrew
 Turner Diaries

Machiavelli, Niccolo
 The Prince

Malefijt, Annamarie de Wal
 *Religion and Culture: An Introduction to Anthropology
  of Religion*

Martinez, Thomas and John Guinther
 Brotherhood of Murder

Matthiessen, Peter
 In the Spirit of Crazy Horse
 Indian Country

Mead, Margaret
 Male and Female
 Keep Your Powder Dry

Mendelism, Kurt
 The Secret of White Domination

Momaday, N. Scott
 House Made of Dawn
 The Names

Montagu, Ashley
The Natural Superiority of Women

Nader, Ralph
Big Boys: Power and Position in American Business

Omang, Joanne and Neier, Aryeh
Psychological Operations in Guerrilla Warfare: The CIA's Nicaragua Manual

O'Reilly, Kennedy
"Racial Matters": The FBI's Secret File on Black America, 1960-1972

Puzo, Mario
The Godfather

Raspail, Jean
The Camp of the Saints

Robbins, John
Diet for a New America

Russell, Bertrand
Unpopular Essays
The Basic Writings of Bertrand Russell

Schaef, Ann Wilson
Women's Reality: An Emerging Female System in a White Male Society

Schur, Edwin M.
Our Criminal Society

Seager, Joni and Ann Olson
Women in the World (An International Atlas)

Skinner, B.F.
Beyond Freedom and Dignity
Science and Human Behavior

Sklar, Holly
Trilateralism (ed.)
Reagan, Trilateralism and the Neoliberals

Spence, Gerry
With Justice for None

Stokes, Bruce
Helping Ourselves: Local Solutions to Global Problems

Tivnan, Edward
The Lobby: Jewish Political Power and American Foreign Policy

Toffler, Alvin
Future Shock
The Third Wave

Tucker, Frank H.
*The White Conscience: An Analysis of the White Man's
Mind and Conduct*

Turnbull, Colin M.
The Human Cycle

Tzu, Lao
The Way of Life

Tzu, Sun
The Art of War

Ward, Churchill and James V. Wall
Agents of Repression

Weyler, Rex
*Blood of the Land: The Government and Corporate War
Against the American Indian Movement*

Wilhelm, Sidney M.
Who Needs the Negro?

Williams, William Appleman
Empire as a Way of Life

Zwitny, Jonathan
*The Crimes of Patriots: A True Tale of Dope, Dirty Money
and the CIA*
Vicious Circles: The Mafia in the Market Place
Endless Enemies: The Making of an Unfriendly World

Twelve Secrets of Life

There are people in this world who live their entire lives without knowing anything about themselves, culturally or biologically. Many of these people run from any identification with their origins, especially if their origins are outside of mainstream America. Most of these people have little accurate knowledge about their bodies and generally depend upon the so-called "experts" for information about their health.

Learning to take hold of one's life is very difficult in a culture that values property over life. This is the same culture that developed the concept of "planned obsolescence" and throw-away underwear. Most Black people in this country are wards of the state. This dependency has rendered many of them neutral in the fight for Black liberation. Therefore, it is mandatory that Afrikan Americans develop "survival and development strategies." We must be able to disconnect from the oppression around us, whether it's political, economic or of a more personal form coming from friends, family members or co-workers. Negative people always will want to involve others in their defeated lives.

Beware of people trying to make their history, culture and traditions yours. Beware of people trying to put their troubles and fears onto you. The road to a life full of *stress* surely is paved with one's inability to say *no* to destructive behavior or activity in the home, on the job, in the streets or in singles bars at happy hour. Knowing one's capacity to deal with the damaged lives of others, as well as one's own "developing" life, can be the difference between *life* and *death*. The road to curing stress, anxiety and frustration is understanding the source of stress, anxiety and frustration. This is not easy because most of us live too close to the surface of life and seldom investigate underlying meanings or reasons for actions. The only messages most of us hear are the ones announcing the arrival of money or pleasure.

We are all prisoners of bad habits. People in the West generally do not "die" natural deaths. We kill ourselves in any number of ways: bad nutritional practices, lack of exercise, unchecked stress, obesity, alcohol and drug addiction, smoking, suicide, poverty, etc. Learning to say goodbye to negative people and situations is extremely difficult if one has grown up with such. Destructive behavior is learned from one's environment, (i.e., culture). Bad habits are acquired, and the habitual mind is very dangerous to the developing self.

This brings me to the bone of change: the ability to look at one's self honestly and design a personalized program for change. This program must include inner exploration, inner investigation, contemplative solitude, professional consultation and inner transformation. In order to effectively deal with a weakness, the weakness needs to be acknowledged. All people have inner selves. However, most do not discover their inner power until it's too late. Most people are transfixed in the past, hypnotized by past defeats or failures, and often they do not understand the sources of denial at a personal or professional level. We don't know where we want to go because we don't know where we've been; nor do we know where we are now. I am not talking about a geopolitical definition but one that connects us to each other regardless of the "systems" endured around the world.

Most people have experienced *rejection* and, therefore, many people build their lives around *not being* accepted. This terrible burden is a frequent reaction to being Black in a white-controlled world where one is rejected even before one is able to see the rejector. Learning what not to do can lead one to *what to do*. However, that is like going through the back door to open the front door. The inner self determines the outer self. Walking away from destruction, saying *no* to foolishness and silliness, refusing handouts and ridding one's self of debilitating habits is the road to wholeness.

Yet, there remains an inner emptiness in most of us. We live in a culture that respects, protects, praises and rewards people with power. And, this power is generally defined as the domination of people, things, ideas, resources and property. Therefore, we find ourselves dominated by the people who are able to play the power game the best.

The fight or quest for power, *as* the norm and ultimate definer, dehumanizes the seeker of truth. A culture built upon the ownership of people and things works against harmonious relationships and pits people against one another for the control of each other. Returning to the "self" becomes even more difficult, especially if one has never been there. And, in a wasteful and property-oriented culture, there ceases to be a "self;" there are just "things" and "others." Therefore, the inner or autonomous self is back-seated to the life of "acquisition" and misdefined "good life."

Chattel enslavement in the United States has been replaced with "material" and "mental" enslavement.

The secrets of a good and productive life are not really secrets. They are mainly common sense activities/actions that have been lost in modern Western life. Most people, due to their struggle for economic survival and misdirection, are too busy trying to keep up with people who have lost their way. *We must return to our source.* Start today by giving *yourself* an hour each day to reach for a *new you.* Start with finding and defining your own *space.* This can be in your home, at a library, under a tree, in a museum or along the path that you walk on each day. Seek a new *solitude* with yourself. Inner reflection requires an understanding of the meditative tradition. Study is in order. Slow down. Quiet your insides, and bring your *outer self* to a slow walk. Start today. If you don't, you may not be able to say no when the order is given to kill your own people. Remember, strengthen the insides and the outer will come.

1. *Self-knowledge*

The Ethiopians have a saying, "A cat may go to a monastery, but she still remains a cat!" Afrikans brought to America are still Afrikans. *Yes,* we have been changed. But, knowing one's self is key to knowing and understanding others. If a person hides from self-understanding or self-knowledge, his or her life will be built upon a bed of quicksand that promises slow but certain confusion, pain, self-doubt and lonely death.

All people need to take charge of their lives. The more a person understands her or his mind and body, the less she or he will destroy it. Ignorance breeds weakness and fear. One's history and culture are as important to good life as food and water. If you don't know who you are, you will be forever fighting other people's wars.

All people, if they are to develop, must ask the simple and correct questions that define life. Why are we here? Where did we come from? What is our purpose in life? Are we here to serve others or ourselves? Self-knowledge leads to self-understanding, which is the path to becoming a whole person. Remember the Afrikan proverb, "Wood may remain ten years in the water, but it will never become a crocodile." First, find the reasons for your own existence and condition. Respect learning. Seek to be *world class* in everything that you do. The best way to do this is through study, work and more study and work.

2. Family

People are shaped by other people and culture. All people have/had mothers and fathers. However, not all mothers and fathers are responsible. Therefore, Black families are undergoing a transition. If one is asked to list the five most important ingredients for the development of a good and productive person, family would be at the top of the list, far ahead of money, cars, clothes and fame.

Working families provide serious love. Members learn self-love and self-worth in functional families. Most importantly, a person's self-esteem is heightened in a family that is goal-oriented with members who are about the business of making life better. Families do fruitful things together, thereby giving their members a sense of oneness and collective doing. Families represent a lifeline among skyscrapers, clear water in sewage.

Families live in houses or apartments that they *make into homes*. A family's home is a refuge from a hostile world. When a person returns home, it is expected that he or she will find peace, welcome, warmth, food for body and mind, protection, love, support and rejuvenation. It is said in Afrika that "living is worthless for one without a home."

Children learn values and morals first in a family context. Integrity, truthfulness, responsibility, honor and shame should be taught first in a family situation. Therefore, one's philosophy of life is taught first at the family level. The one institution that a "developing" or "oppressed" people *cannot* do without is family. Nonfunctioning families will produce nonfunctioning people.

3. Community

There is an Ethiopian proverb that states, "To one who does not know, a small garden is a forest." That's what a family is in relationship to a community. A working community is the closest ecosystem that feeds, stimulates, supports and nurtures families. Communities are impossible without families, and families are strengthened and directly influenced by community-based institutions like houses of worship, schools, universities, businesses, cultural centers, etc. However, the major function of a working community is to make the lives of all its residents livable and enjoyable. This is why ethnic groups form communities. Communities provide not only historical and cultural connections but also *familiarity*. Working communities are like self-contained units that fight the powers that be in order to maintain their existence. The leadership that emerges from a community is one whose allegiance is to that community and the families living in it. When a community fails, its residents are in trouble. When a community's institutions are dying or nonexistent, there is no community. The families are the trees, and the community is the forest. If the forest is alive and well, the family will receive the oxygen needed for life.

4. *Avoiding Stress*

Most people worry too much about things they can't change or control. This is why strong families and strong communities are necessary. They help insulate individuals and define the world in more realistic terms. Families put the world into context, thereby rendering meaning. Part of the stress problem in the United States is related to incomplete definitions, a misunderstanding of the purpose of life, an inability to cope, the necessity to keep up with the neighbors and living with *lies*.

To avoid stress one must examine one's self truthfully and without shortcuts. A Senegalese proverb states, "A healthy ear can stand hearing sick words." Thus, the road to health and a stress-free life is the acceptance of the sickness that revolves around one's own life. This requires a fresh start, a new spirit and the ability to attack each day while searching for happiness that is not defined by the ownership of people or things. Therefore, one must:

1) Seek truth and base one's life on it.
2) Understand one's own culture, history and traditions.
3) Be family-oriented — biological family or social family. Every individual needs loving people in her/his life.
4) *Change*: Remove bad habits from one's activities.
5) Seek life-giving and life-saving ideas.
6) Not fear failure as one works for "success."
7) Redefine success out of one's own needs and realities.
8) Realize that to be wrong is not failure, just a detour in the path to "success."
9) Value the simple things in life.
10) Seek interdependency rather than dependency.

11) Be productive. Avoid too much television. Be creative. Learn a craft. Take up exercising. Keep the body and mind active.
12) Slow down one's life.
13) Be more selective about the food one eats.
14) Be more selective about the people with whom one forms friendships.
15) Seek quality rather than quantity.
16) Cease the use of alcohol, drugs and cigarettes.
17) Learn to say *no* to destruction.
18) Attack one's own fears.
19) Try to see her/himself as others see her/him.
20) Never blame others for one's mistakes.
21) Not let anger cloud one's mind.
22) Avoid harming others unless they seek to harm her/him.
23) Let nothing stop one's search! Always consciously move from unawareness to awareness. Gravitate toward people who are doing good work. Seek inner harmony. Other people cannot provide one with ultimate happiness; they can only make one dependent upon them. Dependency brings on stress. Do not avoid problems. Learn to relax. Cultivate interests that will force a change in actions and attitude. Share love.

Life is, indeed, a path. The knower knows the right one to take. A stressless life is available to those who are willing to study and seek joy in less costly and destructive ways.

5. Critical Thinking

Very seldom are people taught thinking skills. Early in childhood we are told to use our minds, but how to use them is generally left to the individual. Answers to the stresses of modern life, for the average person, have been condensed to thirty-minute sitcoms and one-hour dramas. Solutions to most minor illnesses can be found in thirty-second commercials, and most psychological problems are now handled by radio talk show hosts.

Thinking for one's self is not easy, especially if it's been done by somebody else all of one's life. The mind is often captive by the insignificant. We generally have been taught to listen, do and believe without question.

It has become much *easier to believe than think.* Thinking requires introspection, investigation, silence, definitions, contemplation, challenges, competition, instruction and study. Thinking also demands that a person be curious about the world, its people, its animals, its vegetation, its existence.

Most people who think critically about the world are doers. They are problem-solvers. Thinkers become teachers, doctors, judges, professors, poets, writers, artists, musicians and designers. They are thoughtful people who are always looking for better answers. They go beneath the surface of problems. They do not settle for the easy questions or answers about life.

6. Discipline/Motivation

Very little that is worthwhile is accomplished without discipline. Discipline is a learned process; we are not born knowing it. Parents are children's first teachers of discipline. However, if a child is to move into adulthood with any chance of doing well (i.e., being productive and living a stressless life), he or she will have to learn self-discipline.

Part of the discipline process is the ability to separate desires from needs and prioritize one's life. In a highly material culture, it is easy to lose one's way. The unimportant becomes important, and fruit exists as something to be eaten out of cans. Knowing when to say *no* and knowing one's own limitations is critical to self-discipline. Being able to attack the difficult methodically and not allow the easier temptations of life to interfere with self-development is self-discipline.

Motivation is another important aspect of discipline. There must be something to drive us to move beyond the limiting expectations of losers; that something is *motivation.* Often motivation is the result of wanting something material, like a car. If this is the case, a person arranges his/her life in a way that his/her work, play, creativity, etc. is in line with acquiring that car. However, the type of self-motivation I am thinking of is that which inspires people to be better than they believe they can be. Self-discipline and motivation are the fruits and vegetables of which superior gardens are made.

Most people in urban centers over-eat and, as a consequence, are over-weight and in bad health. People are popping pills for everything: pills to get up with, pills to force bowel movements, pills to lower blood pressure, pills to lose weight, pills to gain weight, pills to put one to sleep and pills (drugs) to cure everything from pot bellies to appetites. The West's answer to illness and disease is to develop another pill.

Over-eating is bad enough, but add to that the consumption of non-food (junk and processed garbage) and you have a crisis. The saying "You are what you eat" is not just a slogan, it's the *truth*. It is only logical that we develop physically and mentally from what we take into our bodies. It defies logic to think that we will have a healthy nation when the great majority of restaurants in the country are "fast food" outlets. Health is greatly curtailed when a person's primary diet consists of double cheeseburgers, sodas, potato chips, french fries, more soda, tomato catsup, milk shakes and desserts made from plastics.

Develop a diet that is in keeping with the natural flow of nature. Try moving toward a diet based on live foods, such as fruits, vegetables, grains, seeds, beans and plenty of *clean* water. In Nigeria, there is a saying that states, "Meat does not eat meat." The eating of meat has been a major contribution to poor health in America. (See "What's Food Got To Do With It?") Study the preventative health aspects of proper nutrition. Move toward 50% raw food and 50% cooked foods. Learn how to combine foods properly for eating. Investigate *fasting* and *colonic irrigation* as components of *preventative health*.

Why do young people look so old in the United States? Why are so many bellies hanging over the belts of young people and senior citizens? Even though "health" is a growth industry, it is mainly touching the affluent few who can afford $400+ a year health club memberships. To maintain a healthy mind, a youthful disposition, an eagerness about life, an active sex life and the strength to do productive work, one *must* exercise. Mind and body are connected; each person must find (design) an exercise program that will keep him or her healthy. Here are a few suggestions:

A) *Walking*. Most people walk, but do they know that by increasing their speed and using a little more arm motion, walking becomes one of the best exercises known? When done properly, walking is an excellent overall workout. Jogging in moderation can be added for those who are in good health and need a little more stimulation.

B) *Cycling.* Bike riding is not just for children; it is one of the best exercises available.

C) *Swimming.* The best way to exercise every muscle in the body is by swimming.

D) *Tennis, volleyball and other low contact sports.*

E) *Yoga.* The best way to stretch is to practice yoga. Yoga is part of a particular philosophy of life that stresses peace and good health. For many people in the world it is a way of life.

F) *Breathing.* Deep breathing three or four times a day is rejuvenating. Breathe in through the nose, pulling oxygen to the stomach; breathe out slowly through the mouth.

Most health consultants recommend that you consult your doctor before starting any new physical development program . I also encourage this because for any program to work, the participants must exercise at least forty minutes four times a week.

8. *Spiritual Search/Reciprocity:*

Always seek answers to the reasons for life. The religion one practices is not as important as the practice itself. Most "world" religions are based upon *doing good* in this world. Beware of cults. Beware of any philosophy of life that makes human beings into deities and places man or woman at the center of the universe. Seek a *way of life* that is non-conflictual but is self-protective. Study all spiritual paths. Study all religions. Pay particular attention to Afrikan spiritual knowledge. Learn to meditate, and try to bring quietness into your life. Study the works of the great spiritual thinkers. Bring more contemplation into your life. Beware also of the misuses of patriarchy in *all* world philosophies.

Reciprocity is a common Afrikan value. The giving is just as important as the receiving. When one smiles at a person, a smile is expected in return. Life's expectations are built around doing good for those you love. If doing good is *the way* in one's life, and if there is any justice in this universe, good should return to one. Only give what you can, and always receive in the spirit of the giving.

9. *Cultural Interaction:*

In most urban areas, visible and active Afrikan American cultural institutions have developed. These institutions generally have low budgets and, therefore, need to be sought out by interested individuals. Of course, the major cultural and spiritual institution in the Black community is the church. However, most Black churches still operate out of a white Christian-Judaic tradition, and that must be understood. Yet, due to the Black liberation struggle of the last thirty years, many ministers have reevaluated their teachings and have begun to preach from a more Afrikan-centered perspective.

We should be aware of the national professional organizations that are working in the best interests of Black people. For example: National Council of Black Studies, African Heritage Association, National Association of Black Social Workers, Association for the Study of Classical African Civilizations, National Black United Front and others.

Involvement in local Black men's and women's groups will give immediate support to persons looking for another way. Become more involved in cultural celebrations: Juneteenth; Black Liberation/History Month (February); Kwanzaa (Dec. 26-Jan. 1); Martin Luther King, Marcus Garvey and Malcolm X birthday observations; etc. The major point is that all people, especially children, need cultural interaction frequently. If one is to be one's self, one must be surrounded by and submersed in one's culture.

10. *Self-Reliance/Ambition:*

America was built on the backs of Afrikan people who were enslaved by whites. The "greatness" of this country was made possible by the "free" or slave labor provided by Afrikan people for over 300 years.

The education that most Black people have received in this country has prepared them to work for others. Most of our people are workers who produce wealth for others. America was also built on small and medium-size businesses. This move toward multinational and world capitalism has been very detrimental to the worker, both Black and white.

We must become more self-reliant in economics, politics and education. We cannot continuously depend on former slave masters and their allies to aid Black people. We must prepare our children to start, operate and succeed in their own businesses. We must move into the business cycle of this country and the world as entrepreneurs and owners.

11. Creative Production:

Enjoy life. Do things that bring you happiness. Life is too short to spend it in front of a television set, lost in the lives of others. If you do not have a hobby or art in which you now partake, think about learning something new. The world is too large and complex for a person to be confined to the southside of Chicago. Explore life. Travel, even if it's to neighboring states. However, if possible, travel abroad; nothing expands the mind like experiencing other cultures.

We often are able to find ourselves through our creativity. Whether one writes, paints, dances, acts or plays music, the more one practices these and other arts, the less stressful he or she will be. Become multi-talented; a person who can do many things well will be in greater demand. Remember, you do have a choice. A Cameroon proverb states, "Knowledge is better than riches." We Afrikan Americans say, "Knowledge leads one to riches."

12. Adapting to Change:

The world is a far different place than it was one hundred, fifty or even thirty years ago. The economy has changed drastically. The politics of the country are less exclusive. The production of food, by and large, has been taken over by large agri-business companies. Most urban water is polluted, and the education that a child receives in an urban school system is sub-par.

A person need not only be adaptable to change, he or she must be able to see change coming and initiate change. I'm not asking the reader to go into the business of forecasting the future, but it is important that one understands where the world is going in the areas of race, economics, politics, environment, food production, education, arts, etc.

Finally, a people (as well as an individual) needs to be able and ready to take its destiny into its own hands. As we liberate our minds, our bodies must follow. We must be prepared to run institutions, organizations, cities, states, nations (i.e., the world) — not as lone gun-slingers among hostile cultures but as participants who understand the necessity of *interdependence* and *sharing*.

We must not come as beggars or buyers but as men and women who understand that the value and worth of most people are tied to their indigenous and creative production. Poverty is slavery, and it *is* criminal that the world's wealth is controlled by a *very* small group of men. We cannot depend on rich people to share their wealth. Everything has an end, and as the Nigerians say, "The bird flies high, but always returns to earth." Those who control the world's wealth and resources are being pulled back to the earth every day.

REFERENCES

Gardner, David C. & Beatty, Grace J. *Stop Stress and Aging Now: The Methuselah Manual.* ATRA, 1985.

Null, Gary. *The Vegetarian Handbook: Eating Right for Total Health.* St. Martin, 1987.

Robbins, John. *Diet for a New America: How Your Food Choices Affect Your Health, Happiness & the Future of Life on Earth.* Stillpoint, 1987.

Samskrti & Veda. *Hatha Yoga Manual I.* Himalayan Publishers.

Samskrti & Franks, Judith. *Hatha Yoga Manual II.* Himalayan Publishers, 1982.

Sher Barbara & Gottlieb, Annie. *Wishcraft: How to Get What You Really Want.* Ballantine, 1987.

Five Most Often Used Excuses
Black Men Give Black Women

It takes more than *love* to make a marriage or relationship work. Love between partners is a glorious start, and for young people it may represent the answer to all questions. However, for more mature and experienced partners, there are other values just as important as love.

Following one's heart *only* may lead a person to a life of unhappiness and confusion. Serious relationships are built and sustained not only on heartfelt feelings but also on the degree to which partners are willing to "give up" a part of their lives to each other. The *sharing* component often is lost in the "new view" of relationships. However, a successful relationship — whether it leads to marriage or not — requires trust; responsibility; communication; productive partners; realistic worldviews; cultural knowledge and compatibility; discipline; clear definitions of fathering, mothering and parenting; and a supportive extended family. Most young people are floating in the upper stratosphere during their "first" love, and listening to their extended family is not one of their criteria for success or happiness. Therefore, two of the values they *must* learn are *patience* and *listening*, especially where elders and family are concerned.

The essence of this short essay is to call Black men on the games that most of us have been taught to play. Pulling the covers off of this "mean-spirited" and often unknown habit of *lying* and *running from relationship to relationship* only shows how Black men and women are shadows of each other. Once the shadow fades, neither of them can develop. We must face each other when we smile.

As I see it, after much consultation with Afrikan American men and women, these are the five excuses Black men use most often to avoid commitment and responsibility:

1) *You don't understand me!* Anytime a Black woman arrives at the crucial point of truly understanding the brother she is with, he says she doesn't understand him. Somebody is wrong; generally, it is the brother. Most Black men fear analysis of their actions from anybody, especially

the sisters with whom they are living or relating. This denial of reality is not uncommon among Black men. Generally, the woman a brother is with knows him better than anyone, with the possible exception of his parents and siblings. The Ashanti proverb states, "It is the wife who knows her husband." Until Black men can honestly face themselves and communicate with themselves, they will not be able to relate meaningfully to Black women. Understanding one's self starts with an admission of not understanding.

2) *Yes, you are right, but...!* Few Black men are willing to admit to errors or mistakes. Even though the sister may have read the brother to the bone, he cannot allow her the last word. This inability to be honest and accept responsibility when one is clearly at fault is a problem among many Black men. The truth and/or evidence may be staring him in the eye, but he can't bring himself to acknowledge it. This reminds me of the Afrikan proverb that states, "He who cannot dance will say: 'The drum is bad.'" Facing reality is difficult enough, but lying to one's self about reality can be tragic. Listening to one's partner, rather than challenging her every utterance, is maturity. However, in a patriarchal culture, seldom are men able to mature to the point where women are regarded as equals. Therefore, the *"but"* will always remain in the conversation.

3) *You are too good for me!* This excuse is probably the closest to the truth. Clearly, there are many women who are not internally ready for relationships, but by and large it is the brothers who plead unworthiness, which is an admission of failure — whether they mean it to be or not. By downplaying and questioning his own qualities, he is attempting to put the woman on the defense and solicit sorrow and understanding. If the sister has "been around the block," she will see through this immediately. She will understand that this man is not willing to make a long-term commitment and is not strong or honest enough to face the woman with the truth. Many Black men avoid the truth like it is a drug that will keep their penises soft. This excuse is given mainly to women who are educationally, professionally and/or financially superior to the men. Due to the nature of the patriarchal society, most men are unable to accept this type of relationship on a long-term basis. The exception is men who are secure and productive in their lives.

4) *I need my space!* Generally, this comes from brothers who couldn't define space if their lives depended on it. Often, they don't have a pot to pee in, but they are ready to call it quits and run. There may be another sister or the current relationship has moved to the point where a "higher" commitment needs to be made, articulated and practiced. These space-based brothers are generally men who have children and who have not developed/matured to the point of being fathers. Somehow in their early mis-education, they were taught that parenting is women's work, that house work is women's work, that diaper changing is women's work and that being involved in such interferes with one's manhood. Too many Black men are destroyed because of this. All space is what one makes of it. However, when space is shared, obviously couples have to talk about its usage. All people, especially in a highly competitive culture, need a place to "cool out," relax and be themselves. That's part of the definition of a home.

5) *I don't have any money and I don't have the time!* The *man* is on my back. This is the brother who is working on a job that demands a lot of time. Generally, his mate knows little about his finances, and he is always crying "broke." When the relationship started, nothing was too good or cost too much. However, as the months and years rolled by, the lack of communications around resources, enlargement of responsibility and probably undisciplined spending have led to financial problems. Rather than sit down like a mature adult and come up with a plan to *save* and pay bills, he just cries "poverty." The *time* question is very important. Most Black men do not have enough money. However, they do have time. If one's time (quality time) is not given to the relationship, where is it going? If relationships are to mature, if couples are to develop, time is more important than money because maturity, wisdom and wealth do not come overnight.

I am sure that many readers will argue against these five excuses. There are many others, but I've tried to condense them to those excuses that cut across class or economic lines. It must be clear that most Afrikan American men in this culture have not been taught to communicate with their mates, children, family, friends or themselves. This inability to face one's self, one's critics and one's actions is the basis for self-deception. A man has to be intimately in touch with himself in order to touch others.

The value of being able to touch and be touched is fundamental to quality relationships. The Tanzanian people have a saying: "Do not mend your neighbor's fence before looking to your own." Men in America have not been taught to be introspective or honest with themselves. Patriarchy not only demands that men be the providers, protectors and law givers, but it also suggests that men are *always right*. One cannot grow within such a definition. To avoid questions, dodge responsibility, accept false reality and hide from the music that Black men need in their lives can only bring regression. Remember, "a healthy ear can stand hearing sick words." We should try to live our lives without excuses, alibis and self-promoting lies. Most of us are disconnected from the security of family permanence. We are the people of concrete, and concrete cracks when it gets too hot. A returning to the earth is in order.

Before Sorry: Listening to and
Feeling the Flow of Black Women

The Vietnamese people could not have won their war against the French or the United States if the Vietnamese women had not particpated as first-line combatants and support troops. Female fighters were also instrumental in Nicaragua, Mozambique, Zimbabwe and many other nations in their wars for liberation. Front-line combat for women is not universal, but as valuable and functional support personnel, women have made a contribution which is beyond question. Many nations are learning from firsthand experience that a nation which restricts the equal participation of its women in all things political, economic and social *will remain second rate.*

In the opening procession at the 1988 Olympics in Seoul, South Korea, the picture that again confirmed the unequal status of women in the world was the sight of delegation after delegation marching past the review stand with few, if any, women among them. The countries that had the fewest female athletes and support staff are located in Afrika, Asia and Central America. The ruling pattern of most cultures, and most certainly Western culture, is the dominance of the patriarchy. In the United States, white males control everything of value and, therefore, wield awesome power over Black women and men in all of the life-saving and life-giving areas of society: law, economics, education, politics, military, religion, entertainment, sports, language, mass media and culture.

The Misdirection of Men

Most men in this country have been socialized to treat women like children. In fact, in many cases, children may have it better; they are not expected to be perfect. To imply that women are equal in America is like saying that deer don't have predators. A friend of mine, a minister who is considered rather progressive, confessed to me in a moment of weakness that he opens and closes his prayers thanking his male God that he's not a woman. Also, there was a recent photograph in *The New York Times* (12-1-88) of fifty Jewish feminists praying at the Wailing Wall in Jerusa-

173

lem. They were carrying the sacred text of Judaism, the *Torah*, and were dressed in prayer shawls and yarmulkes. The orthodox rabbis were furious. According to the *Times*, Rabbi Meir Yehuda Getz, who is in charge of the site, said, "A woman carrying a *Torah* is like a pig at the Wailing Wall." The point of these two stories is that male chauvinism (or sexism) is culturally based, and most, if not all, cultures practice it. Few men or women are exempt from its deadly hold.

The place and status of women in the world is dispicable. Women comprise over one half of the world's population, yet male children are still preferred in most cultures. Women's power most certainly is not commensurate with their numbers. In the case of women, large populations have not translated into clout. Joni Seager and Ann Olson reported in their eye-opening *Women in the World Atlas*, "For women, there are no developed countries. Although some places are clearly better for them to live in than others, it is not always true that the relatively rich countries of the world provide better circumstances for them as women than do poorer countries." Other facts documented by Seager and Olson include:

- In Afghanistan, 4% of eligible girls are enrolled in secondary school; in Australia, 88%.

- In Angola, fewer than 1% of adult women have access to contraceptives; in Belgium, 76%.

- Women in Ghana bear an average of over six children; women in West Germany, fewer than two.

- In Jamaica, the maternal mortality rate stands at 106 mothers' deaths for every 100,000 births; in Norway, there are fewer than eight deaths per 100,000 births.

Most women world over, but especially those in misdeveloped countries, find themselves in a state of powerlessness, dependency and inequality at all levels of society. There are profound differences in the status of Black women and white women in the world. The statistics presented in *Women in the World Atlas* make this clear. It is also evident that all women have been locked out of history-making, science-making and art-making. The only clear area of creativity on which they have a monopoly is baby-making.

One of the few studies that attempts to capture the status of Black women internationally is *The Black Woman Cross-Culturally*, edited by Filomina Chioma Steady. The significance of this book cannot be overstated. Dr. Steady and her contributors focused on the roles of women of Afrikan descent in the United States, Afrika, Caribbean and South America. The picture that emerges from this anthology reveals that: 1) Afrikan women are truly world women; 2) the problems Black women face worldwide are complex, and cross-cultural solutions do not necessarily work; 3) racism (white world supremacy), sexism, inequalities in wealth and lack of opportunities keep Black women dependent; 4) women are not the "weaker sex;" and 5) Afrikan women world over are fighting for enlightened partnerships with their men while actively resisting the domination of Black and white men.

I do not believe that the lives or futures of Afrikan American women should revolve around the thoughts, actions, wishes, demands or strategies of men. Men, mainly white men in our lifetime, have controlled, ordered and reordered the cultures of this planet to our detriment. Hundreds of millions of people, mainly children, go to sleep each night begging for food, shelter, clothing and small happiness. Most of the wealth on this earth is directly or indirectly concentrated in the hands of a few men. Out of a world population of 4.5 billion plus people, less than 5% control the world's wealth, and that percentage is getting smaller each year. If such a state of affairs is not *criminal*, I don't know the meaning of the word. In the United States, power is in the hands of a small white "power elite that is the leadership group of a property-based ruling class," according to William Domhoff's *Who Rules America Now?* This ruling class is 95% white men, and generally the 5% white women who are part of this elite are there by nature of their inheritance.

The White Male System and Its Partners

Ann Wilson Schoff in her book *Women's Reality* clearly understands the white male rulership in this country. She calls it the "white male system" and makes clear distinctions between the white male system and individual white males. The following is her definition of the white male system:

> It is the system in which we live, and in it, the power and influence
> are held by white males. This system did not happen overnight, nor
> was it the result of the machinations of only a few individuals; we
> all not only let it occur but participated in its development...it con-
> trols almost every aspect of our culture. It makes our laws, runs our
> economy, sets our salaries, and decides when and if we will go to
> war or remain at home. It decides what *is* knowledge and how it is
> to be taught.

This definition is important in part because she simultaneously defines the white world supremacist system. It is obvious that white men are the main benefactors, but the system could not survive or prosper without white women. Yes, white men and white women fight; yes, white men control and manipulate white women; yes, white men define white women's place in the white male culture. However, the bottom line is this: *white people could not exist without white men and white women working overtime to reproduce themselves.*

The only way white people are created in this world, other than from gene pools or some other abberation, is by whites mating with whites. If a white person mates with any other person of color, the offsprings will not be white. Period. Therefore, it is clear that what really exists between white men and white women is a family battle that takes on different forms — depending on the country, politics, economics, education and white peoples' proximity to other races, especially Black people.

Vivian Gordon in her book *Black Women, Feminism and Black Liberation: Which Way?* clearly delineates the difference between white women's struggle and Black women's struggle. In her discussion on civil rights and women's studies, she makes a very telling point:

> The perspective of most women's studies programs is that Black
> and White women have suffered a common experience of oppres-
> sion which is gender-specific. There is a pervasive unwillingness
> to acknowledge the distinctinly different nature of oppression for
> White and non-White women. Seldom is attention given to the ex-
> tent to which White women have benefited from the oppression of
> Black women and/or have been active participants in racism.

Dr. Gordon's insight on the triple oppression all Black women face (racism, sexism and economic oppression) makes her book must reading for serious men and women. Her main position, however, is that Black women and white women do *not* share a common history, especially when it comes to oppression; that "white economic exploitation varies drastically for Black and White women;" and that "White women benefited from and participated in the oppression of Black women." Her clear analysis throws water on white women/Black women coalition triangles and shows how historically they have hurt mainly Black women. Dr. Gordon's book is an impassioned yet studied call for renewed cooperation between Black women and men as partners in this most difficult of world struggles.

Back Home

Where does this brief and incomplete discussion leave us? If I've been clear, it is certain that the first line struggle for Black liberation is solidly rooted in the relationship developed between Black men and women. Our buying into other people's systems, struggles, worldviews and values has all but destroyed us. Our rush to become "integrated" Americans has brought us much pain and misery and has had a debilitating effect on Black family life.

The smiles that used to be reserved for each other can be bought on street corners in strange cities. Our love for each other has gone the way of the 45 rpm records. Too many Black lives have been reduced to a killing *purposelessness*. Due to the inability of a significant number of Black people to analyze large social forces, they continuously blame other victims and themselves for our condition. This state of affairs must be rejected and replaced with a value-based culture that stresses enlightened partnerships.

In his very powerful essay, *Beyond Connections: Liberation in Love and Struggle*, Maulana Karenga outlines four basic "alienated arrangements" around which many Blacks build their lives. His analysis is so apropos that it is necessary to share it with you. These arrangements, all based on and reinforced by Western society, are 1) the cash connection; 2) the flesh connection; 3) the force connection; and 4) the dependency connection.

According to Karenga, the cash connection is the most basic and pervasive relation, stems from situations in which the power of money

...becomes, not only a means to control, define and deform, but also a *means of existence.* As a means of existence, money becomes a key social relation, a key social power, the power to satisfy human needs. And such a power is critical and highly sought after possession, *for those who control the means to satisfy human needs at the same time control those humans with those needs.*

Men control the money and other key resources of the world. The flesh connection, as an outgrowth of the cash connection, occurs when

...women and men...become commodities themselves — objects to buy and sell, own and dispose of at will. The natural form and context of sexual desire and practice between women and men, then, are distorted and deformed in a commodity society...And thus, human erotic impulse and need are transformed into a flesh connection, an exchange mediated by money and other economic arrangements. Joined to this process and practice is the obsessive emphasis on sex which pervades this society and blocks our minds through the mass media. This combination in turn gives rise and spreads to the *sexual commodity form* — the systematic commercial appeal to sensuousness through the packaging and selling of the human body — mainly, woman.

Dr. Karenga expands the theory of the flesh connection to the question of pornography and sees its proliferation, "rooted in and reflective of social and sexual pathology."

This society's emphasis on force and violence manifests itself not only in the media but also in White America's historical and current treatment of Blacks and other people of color. The force connection results when society's views and tendencies are internalized and practiced in Black male/female relationships.

Karenga defines the final arrangement, the dependency connection, as

...a logical and inevitable outgrowth of the others. To be seduced to trading sex and self for economic and physical security, to be defined in terms of your organs rather than in terms of your wholeness and to be threatened and beaten into submissive silence and compliant cooperation in your own defamation as a full human, can only imply and impose an unhealthy and anti-human dependence. Women are locked into various forms of reciprocal sexual deference and dependency which always demonstrates male dominance.

Dr. Karenga is quite profound in his message and one can't do it justice with just a few quotes. His compass is a sharp one.

White men have put the burden of the racial and economic problem on the victims. This is like forcing the former enslaved who had been locked down for four hundred years suddenly to run a race against seasoned white marathoners. And, when the Black victims lose the race, they are blamed without examination or explanation for being lazy, unprepared, genetically inferior, uneducated and any number of other debilitating adjectives. As non-thinking victims (i.e., white property), most Blacks have accepted white definitions and worldviews. The damage that has been done to our families is catastrophic.

Mass Media: Loud Noise

Most people do not realize the extent to which outside forces affect their lives. The culture we live in is such a powerful force in shaping and guiding our lives that it seems natural to follow its directives even to our own detriment. One of the major transmitters of ideas, images, attitudes, futures, etc. to the average person, is mass media — mainly television. I've heard women talk about the characters in the soap operas as if they were family. Television is the ever present communicator that reminds us our dream falls short of the American ideal.

Jerry Mander in his *Four Arguments for the Elimination of Television* effectively illustrates how television has aided in completely altering life in America over the last forty years. By the age of seventeen, the average young person will have spent over 15,000 hours in front of the television, compared to 11,000 hours in the classroom. Thus, a technological, commercial and uncontrollable medium that appeals to the lowest common denominator has a monopoly on the socialization of most people. Couple such power with all the other problems facing young people and young couples, and it is truly a wonder that any relationships work.

The world is such a complex place, but television is able to solve most problems in thirty minutes (actually twenty-one minutes in between commercials) or an hour. Its message is simplistic and appeals too often to the easy way out. Popular culture (of which television is a part) more often than not pushes an escapest philosophy, whereas the difficult task of confronting and solving problems is seldom taught. People find themselves locked into easy negative answers like running away, taking drugs, overeating, having excessive sex, drinking alcohol, acquiring material possessions, etc.

This image of Black people was reinforced in the highly acclaimed prime-time two-hour CBS Special Report, *The Vanishing Black Family — Crisis in Black America*. In his authoritative "official" manner, Bill Moyers, the Texan "liberal," gave us the final word on the Black family in America: a smooth, well-scripted victim's viewpoint that was ahistorical, short-sighted, stereotypical, racist and destructive. Much of the destructiveness in Black life is the result of racist, economic and political decisions about Black life of which *most* people are unaware. This is very evident in the socialization of young people, and the *Vanishing Black Family* very smoothly used Black people to blame Black people for the mess we are in.

New Moves: Enlightened Partnerships/Loveships

The key to responsible, respectable and long-lasting relationships/loveships is an understanding of societal forces, unfiltered communication and effective follow-up by couples. The ability to talk about problems before the fighting starts is the sign of mature people who have some understanding of the complexity of life. Black couples must understand that "Black love" in the United States is much more than a commitment between two people; it is also the realization that there are political, economic, historical, racial, familial and emotional forces impacting upon that loveship.

Most Black men in America are afraid of strong, intelligent, independent and self-reliant Afrikan American women. If a Black woman has such attributions and is "beautiful" too, her problems with men will double. So-called "plain" women, or women who dress "down," are more acceptable under certain circumstances because they are viewed as less of a threat than the more "physically endowed" women with whom most men would probably want to sleep. In short, men are frightened by the intelligence of these women but highly tempted by their beauty.

The "fear" of women that exists among many Black men runs deep and often goes unspoken. This fear is cultural. Most men are introduced to members of the opposite sex in a superficial manner, and seldom do we seek a more indepth or informed understanding of them. Man's first view of women is as mother and maybe later as sister, aunt, grandmother and, finally, as lover. In 98% of a young man's life, he sees women as babysitters, cooks, house cleaners, day workers, nurses, waitresses, sales women, pre-school and elementary teachers and any number of other "care-giving" occupations defined as women's work. It is not necessarily the *service* that these occupations offer that restricts women; rather, it is the *value* that *society* attaches to the occupations that is demoralizing and restrictive. Generally, men in comparable occupations, like long-distance truck drivers or garbage collectors, make almost twice the salary of pre-school or elementary teachers. Which jobs are more important? Women have it rough all over the world. Men must become informed listeners. The hope and future of Afrikan American family life rides on the strength of Black loveships.

There are two books that Black men and women need to be aware of as they work to improve their lives: *Strategies for Resolving Conflict in Black Male and Female Relationships* by La Francis Rodgers-Rose and James T. Rodgers and *Focusing: Black Male/Female Relationships* by Delores Aldridge. These are two information-packed but easy-to-read books that discuss the racial myths, game-playing, stereotypes, economic inequalities and cultural dynamics that influence Black life. Just as important, both books give down-to-earth suggestions to aid couples in finding their own answers. Both books are must reading.

Finally, if we know what our problems are and we are intelligent, we must act. Black men must become proponents, perpetuators, actualizers and cheerleaders for solid Black loveships, or enlightened partnerships. Here are a few suggestions:

1) Always listen to your partner. Often this listening needs to be done at the times when you feel least up to it. But, try to put yourself into her *space* and open your ears and mind to the destruction or beauty in her day.

2) Reciprocity: Be on the giving side. Even though it is natural to expect kind actions, don't measure your love-moves solely on hers. Never forget important days: birthdays, anniversary, the

days she gave birth to your children, etc. Develop a sharing mode of life with your loved ones.

3) Always make her feel special. Never take your relationship/ loveship for granted. Never tire of saying "Thank you," "I love you," and "I'm really lucky to be with you." Think of original ways of displaying your love for her.

4) Involve yourself in all aspects of housework. Especially if both partners are working, they need to sit down and split up the cleaning and maintenance of the apartment or house. Housework is not women's work; it's just dirty work that men evaded and "redefined" as women's work.

5) Be involved in the birth of your children. Study the birthing process. Once the child is born, be involved in parenting beyond picking the baby up and kissing him or her.

6) Involve your partner in all important and not-so-important decisions. Even if she doesn't seem to be interested — involve her. To build a life together requires few secrets and input from all. Most women are socialized to leave all important decisions to daddy.

7) Encourage your lovemate to improve herself. Help make time for her to pursue her interests outside of the home. Create an atmosphere in the home that will encourage her to reach for her dreams.

8) Try to keep some excitement in her life. Do special things for her, especially when they are least expected — trips, gifts, letters and poetry written to her, etc.

9) Make sure she has her own space and time. Her life need not be built around yours. The two of you must move as a family that is still aware of individual needs. Encourage her to excel in whatever areas that are important to her. For the family to have meaning, there must be meaning beyond family.

10) Accept the blame for your own imperfections and try to change for the better. This can be done through study and renewed practice.

Remember, the deepest hurt is the hurt inflicted by lovers. To remain lovers is hard work; it is not natural. Everything grows old; the key to beautiful tomorrows is involvement in a loveship that ages gracefully. We are bound to make mistakes in our loveships; the key is to learn from them.

If Black women do not love, there is no love. As the women go, so go the people. Stopping the women stops the future. If Black women do not love, strength disconnects, families sicken, growth is questionable and there are few reasons to conquer ideas or foe. If Black women love, so come flowers from sun, rainbows at dusk. As Black women connect, the earth expands, minds open and our yeses become natural as we seek

quality in the searching
quality in the responses
quality in the giving and loving
quality in the receiving
beginning anew
fresh.

REFERENCES

Aldridge, Delores. *Focusing: Black Male/Female Relationships.* Chicago: Third World Press, 1990.

Domhoff, William G. *Who Rules America Now?* Englewood Cliffs: Prentice-Hall, Inc., 1983.

Gordon, Vivian V. *Black Women, Feminism, and Black Liberation: Which Way?* Chicago: Third World Press, 1987.

Karenga, Maulana. *Beyond Connections: Liberation in Love and Struggle.* New Orleans: Ahidiana, 1978.

Mander, Jerry. *Four Arguments for the Elimination of Television.* New York: Quill, 1978.

Rodgers-Rose, La Francis and Rodgers, James T. *Strategies for Resolving Conflict in Black Male and Female Relationships.* Newark: Traces Institute Publications, 1985.

Schaef, Ann Wilson. *Women's Reality.* San Francisco: Harper & Row, 1985.

Seager, Joni and Olson, Ann. *Women in the World Atlas.* New York: A Touchstone Book, 1986.

Steady, Filomina Chioma. Ed. *The Black Woman Cross-Culturally.* Cambridge: Schenkman, 1981.

A BONDING

For Susan and Khephra, August 20, 1989

we were forest people.
landrooted. vegetable strong.
feet fastened to soil with earth strengthened toes.
determined fruit,
anchored
where music soared,
where dancers circled,
where writers sang,
where griots gave memory,
where smiles were not bought.

you have come to eachother in wilderness,
in this time of cracked concrete, diminished vision, wounded rain.

at the center of flowers your craft is on fire.
only ask for what you can give.

do not forget bright mornings, hands touching under moonlight, filtered
water for your plants, healing laughter, renewing futures. caring.

your search has been rewarded, marriage is not logical, it's necessary.
we have a way of running yellow lights, it is now that we must claim
the
sun in our hearts. your joining is a mending, a quilt.

as determined fruit
you have come late to this music,
only ask for what you can give.
you have asked for eachother.

What's a Daddy? Marriage and Fathering

I

One need not go back over the statistics detailing the decline of Black children born into two-parent households. The figures do not speak well of the Black community. Marriage, whether "legal" (sanctioned by the courts), or common law (people deciding to live together without legal documents), is on the decline. However, the babies do not stop coming, and the *music* and *love* so badly needed in the rearing of children are disappearing quickly in the Afrikan American community.

We know that children will come. The circumstances in which they mature is where much of the problem lies. Leon Dash, in his important book *When Children Want Children*, clarifies for the uninformed and misinformed the reasons why single Black teenage girls have babies. His study notes the lack of self-esteem, self-love and self-confidence in most of these young women. However, the revelations that are the highlights of Mr. Dash's work are 1) culture plays a unique and important role in understanding the differences between Black life and white middle class life; and 2) many, if not most, Black teenage pregnancies are not accidental. The misunderstanding of the Black cultural models among white decision-makers is not new. However, the evidence that most teenage pregnancies represent a *survival strategy* is not openly discussed in the Afrikan American community and is of critical importance.

Stable families and communities are absolutely necessary if we are to have productive and loving individuals. Marriage represents the foundation of family. Without marriage (that is, some bonding tradition that sanctions and forces "partners" into commitments beyond the bedroom), families would soon die; or other types of families would form. Families are the foundation for community. Like a family, a functional community provides security, caring, wealth, resources, cultural institutions, education, employment, a spiritual force, shelter and a challenging atmosphere. Families and community shape the individual into a productive or nonproductive person. Without family, without community, individuals are left to "everything is everything."

Male/female bonding (marriage) is necessary if we are to rebuild viable and serious families and communities. Ideally, children should be born into a family where mother and father have made an emotional as well as a legal commitment to each other. Too often in the Black community, many of its members, mainly men, don't want to go the legal route to marriage. Many brothers disrespect the "white man's laws" and will not acquire marriage licenses. They would rather just jump over a broom. This is a delicate problem; I have little respect for most of such laws. However, *we are in the United States.* When I drive, I carry a driver's licence I got from white people because it is the law; if I drive without it and get caught, I will go to jail — without passing go. For the emotional and economic protection of the children and mothers, I strongly suggest all marriages in the Afrikan American community be legalized according to the "laws" of this land. These are a few reasons:

1) The license provides emotional security for women and children; if a father decides that it's over, the mother will have an easier time obtaining child support.

2) The license represents a government sanction. Therefore, it's the legal community's OK for such an event. The license adds an importance to the act that goes beyond the two people involved.

3) The legalization of marriage forces partners to struggle with each other at a higher level when times are hard. Without a license, brothers and sisters can "walk" at the slightest problem or provocation.

4) In cases where separation is necessary, brothers too will have legal claim on their children.

Marriage is not a vacation or a prolonged holiday. Eighty percent of marriage is work, compromise, adaptation, changes, intimate communication, laughter, confusion, joy, smiles, crying, pain, crises, reeducation, apologies, mistakes, more mistakes, new knowledge and love. If children are involved, include parenting and repeat everything above twice for each year of the marriage. If the marriage lasts for more than fifteen years, the couple probably should add *wisdom.* Of course, one may ask, "What about the other twenty percent?" I presume that even in a successful marriage the couple will sleep.

II

Fathers are the missing links in the lives of many young Afrikan Americans. In an increasingly dangerous and unpredictable world, absent fathers add tremendously to the insecurity of children. It is common knowledge that children function best in an atmosphere where both parents combine and compliment their energies and talents in the rearing of children. Even if pregnancy is an accident, it is clear that once a decision is made to bring a child to term, the rearing of that child cannot be accidental. Most children are born at the top of their game, *genius level*. It is the socialization process that turns most creative, talented and normal children into dependent and helpless adults. There are many aspects to child-rearing, but I would like to stress six:

1) Children need love and need to love. Provide a safe, secure home that is full of warmth, love and challenges. Parents should be complimentary in their parenting and not take anything for granted. Involve extended family in your parenting, especially grandparents and aunts and uncles.

2) Teach by example. Spend quality time with children. Provide options. Give children an open book on growth. Listen to them. When possible, give full answers to their questions, but encourage them to find answers on their own. Be slow to criticize, quick to congratulate.

3) Be conscious of building self-love and self-esteem in your children. Provide a cultural home where self-images are positive and warm, where Afrikan American culture is lived and taught in a natural and non-dogmatic manner.

4) Introduce your children to the unlimited possibilities of life. However, explain to them the necessity of work, discipline, study and patience.

5) Homes should be nonviolent. Parents should be slow to criticize each other in front of children. Arguments should be kept to a minimum. In single-parent homes, criticism of the missing parent in front of the child should be infrequent and/or tempered with understanding.

6) Housework is not women's work and should be shared equally by all, especially if both parents work outside the home.

III

In a patriarchal society, Black men must be able to offer their families a measurement of protection and, at a minimum, basic life-giving needs, such as clothing, shelter, food, education and security. The West and most of the world define manhood as the ability to protect and provide for one's family. If a man doesn't do that, according to most cultures, he is incomplete (i.e., not a man). A good many Black men are not able to deliver in these two areas. Here are some of the reasons:

1) White world supremacy (racism) — Black men are the major threat to white male rule.
2) Failure of integration — Many Black men believe(d) America's big lie of the melting pot theory.
3) Failure of national and local welfare system — the development of a beggar's mentality among many Black people.
4) Failure of public education.
5) Changing economic system — increased dependency on the state.
6) Our replacement in the market place by white women and teenagers.
7) Loss of self-respect, self-esteem and self-love.
8) Ignorance of one's own history and accomplishments.
9) Unawareness of changing world realities.
10) Lack of skills — especially business skills.
11) Fear.

For conscious men, none of this should be new. However, in this *war* situation that we live in, the circumstances demand that Black men rise to the *challenge*. And, a great part of that challenge is to be responsible husbands and fathers. Without both, a bright future is doubtful. Being a good and fruitful husband and father may be the most *difficult task facing Afrikan American men.*

We now live in a time, a first in our history, when there are millions of Afrikan American children with absent fathers. Other than the period of chattel slavery, there has never been a time when the absence of Black fathers has been so grim. This tide of absent, unavailable, nonfunctioning fathers must be reversed. There are *no easy solutions.*

Fathering for most Black men is learned on the job. Generally, by that time, for many fathers it is too late. There are few classes in fathering. However, fathering *is* taught; it's a learned process. Most Black men give very little thought to the lifelong commitment that fathers *must* make to their children.

Children learn to do most things by watching and imitating their parents or care-givers. Formal education starts generally at the age of five for most children, and at two and a half for the blessed few who are able to benefit from Headstart or private schools. Children learn to be mothers or fathers by observing and studying their mothers, fathers, grandparents, aunts, uncles and television.

These days most Black boys learn to be fathers by watching the wind (i.e., spaces reserved for missing fathers). Many of them also receive instruction in fathering from their mothers' discussions about absent "dads" or whatever names these men are given. If there is anything clear about the Afrikan American community, it is that women are having serious difficulty teaching Black boys to be men and, by extension, to be fathers.

However, this not a condemnation of Black women who are trying, against great odds, to raise their sons into responsible and recognizable Black men. The facts suggest that many of them are not succeeding, and the facts also suggest that it is *ignorant, stupid* and *insensitive* to blame Black women for not *raising strong Black men.* The music in these women's lives is little, and to be left *alone* to raise the children may be an impossible task for many of them. However, we do know that millions of Afrikan American women do rise to the challenge and are responsible for millions of Black men who have made "successful" transitions from boyhood to manhood.

Again, it is not easy. There is a difference between raising children and rearing them. Mari Evans, in a very important paper, "The Relationship of Child-Rearing Practices to Chaos and Change in the African American Family," states:

191

...raising (children) is "providing for," while rearing is "responding to." Raising can be satisfied by providing the essentials: food, shelter, clothing and reasonable care. "Rearing" is a carefully thought out process. Rearing begins with a goal and is supported by a clear view of what are facts and what is truth (and the two are not necessarily synonymous). Rearing is complex and requires sacrifice and dedication. It is an ongoing process of "preparation." Joe Kennedy reared presidents; the British royal family rears heirs to the English throne; and when a young African doctor, born in the continent and presently in self-exile in a neighboring country because of her ANC (African National Congress) commitment was interviewed on the news recently and was asked if she was not afraid for her four-year-old son, given her political activism, said, "He has a duty to lay down his life for his people. He is my son, but he is also the son of an oppressed people," she announced the rearing of a "race man."...Obviously something different, some carefully thought out process, some long-range political view is present when one has a clear sense of one's own reality and therefore intends to rear presidents, rulers, or free men and women.

I think that Mari Evans, in her own unique and poetic manner, has set forth the challenge for Afrikan American people, the rearing of "race men and women."

If fathers give some thought to this, it should become clear that fathering (i.e., parenting) is also a political act. As a colonized people fighting for survival and development, Afrikan Americans must see our children as future "warriors" in this struggle for liberation. Mari Evans defined colonization as "suppression and exploitation designed to keep a people powerless, dependent, subordinate, and mystified." Again, we are at war for the minds, bodies, souls, spirits and futures of our children. Ms. Evans states it this way: "Child-rearing should be the primary concern of an oppressed people, and although the rearing of race men and women is obviously a stressful, complex and tedious process, it should be entered into at birth."

I want to make it clear that Black men cannot depend on others to do our job. Fathering must be as important to us as love-making (sex). It is easy to make babies but difficult to rear them. Below is the Afrikan American Father's Pledge that all Black men should consider:

Afrikan American Father's Pledge

1. I will work to be the best father I can be. Fathering is a daily mission, and there are no substitutes for good fathers. Since I have not been taught to be a father, in order to make my "on the job" training easier, I will study, listen, observe and learn from my mistakes.

2. I will openly display love and caring for my wife and children. I will listen to my wife and children. I will hug and kiss my children often. I will be supportive of the mother of my children and spend quality time with my children.

3. I will teach by example. I will try to introduce myself and my family to something new and developmental each week. I will help my children with their homework and encourage them to be involved in extracurricular activities.

4. I will read to or with my children as often as possible. I will provide opportunities for my children to develop creatively in the arts: music, dance, drama, literature and visual arts. I will challenge my children to do their best.

5. I will encourage and organize frequent family activities for the home and away from home. I will try to make life a positive adventure and make my children aware of their extended family.

6. I will never be intoxicated or "high" in the presence of my children, nor will I use language unbecoming for an intelligent and serious father.

7. I will be nonviolent in my relationships with my wife and children. As a father, my role will be to stimulate and encourage my children rather than carry the "big stick."

8. I will maintain a home that is culturally in tune with the best of Afrikan American history, struggle and future. This will be done, in part, by developing a library, record/disc, video and visual art

collections that reflect the developmental aspects of Afrikan people worldwide. There will be *order* and *predictability* in our home.

9. I will teach my children to be responsible, disciplined, fair and honest. I will teach them the value of hard work and fruitful production. I will teach them the importance of family, community, politics and economics. I will teach them the importance of the Nguzo Saba (Black value system) and the role that ownership of property and businesses plays in our struggle.

10. As a father, I will attempt to provide my family with an atmosphere of love and security to aid them in their development into sane, loving, productive, spiritual, hard-working, creative Afrikan Americans who realize they have a responsibility to do well and help the less fortunate of this world. I will teach my children to be *activists* and to *think* for themselves.

Along with the Afrikan American Father's Pledge, I would like to share with you Madhubuti's Home Rules:

Madhubuti's Home Rules (for children)

1. Don't lie, don't steal, don't cheat.
2. Don't embarrass your family; listen to your parents and other responsible adults.
3. Always do your best and improve on yesterday's work; develop a work attitude.
4. Learn as much as you can; always expand your knowledge-base.
5. Seek quality in all things rather than weakening quantity.
6. Always be creative; do not settle for easy answers or conclusions. Think for yourself and learn to be responsible for your decisions.
7. Learn from mistakes and always oppose that which is not good.
8. Do homework and housework each day.
9. Avoid alcohol, drugs and cigarettes.
10. Respect elders.

11. Be a self-starter, self-motivator; do not wait on others to set high goals/standards for you. Always seek the best and avoid the "crowd" mentality.
12. Never forget who you are and always speak up if you feel that you have been wronged.

We have to keep our children active, and it is never too early to prepare them for the outside world. Listed below are required skills for Black children. This list was compiled with the help of the brothers of the National Black Wholistic Retreat Society:

1. *Community and Family Service* — Volunteer once a week at a church or community center, working with young people or senior citizens

2. *Domestic Chores* — Cooking; gardening; ironing clothes; storing food; sewing; cleaning house; washing clothes; shopping for food

3. *Repairs*
   Car: Change oil; change tire; fix flat; check fluid levels
   Home: Plumbing — understand and repair water and sewer lines
          Electrical — replace outlets and light switches; make a lamp
   Bike: change flats

4. *Academic Challenges* — Read at least one new book a month; develop computer skills; learn to play chess/checkers; practice math; learn at least one foreign language

5. *Religion* — Understand Christianity, Judaism, Islam, Maat, Confucious, Hinduism, Taoism, Buddhism, etc.

6. *Physical Fitness* — Swim one mile; run five miles; bike fifty miles; walk ten miles

7. *Interpersonal/Family Relations* — Male-female; male-male; female-female; parenting; problem-solving skills; sex/healthy love-making; reciprocity; family history

8. *Outdoor Skills* — Camping; fire building; compass and map-reading; knowing the city in which one lives

9. *Communications*
   Ham Radio — Novice license

10. *Transportation* — Riding a bike; driving a car; taking public transportation

11. *Defense* — Learn some form of martial arts; become competent with firearms

12. *Finance* — Banking (savings, checking, mortgages); stocks and bonds; insurance; wills and estates; credit unions

13. *Travel* — Local; national; international

14. *Health and Nutrition* — First aid; CPR; stress management; proper diet (vegetarian or low-fat); meditation

Finally, Black life in the United States is full of stress. If a "plan" for child-rearing has not been developed individually, parents should consult the "literature," professionals and grandparents for support and direction. Again, life is not easy, but we do have a choice: live or die. If we are men, we must make the decision to live and develop.

Afrikan American men must have a *greater* commitment to family and community. Families should probably be started later, after one has accomplished other tasks. It is clear that once two people decide to join hands as a family and, most certainly, once children arrive, those parents *must* dig in for the long haul. The parents' lives are not *just theirs anymore*. Their lives also must be shared with their children. More importantly, parents must understand that *often* their own "enjoyment," "adventure," "play time," and, yes, "happiness" may have to be sacrificed for the "joy, adventure and happiness" of their children. This is part of what it means to be a parent.

Our first responsibility with children is to give them opportunities, to provide them with options that most of us *never had*. That's what development and Black struggle are all about. This means, in very plain language, that where one used to party or "go" every weekend, such activity must be reduced to once a month or every six weeks. The point is that our *time* and *resources* must go to rearing strong, creative, intelligent, culture-conscious Afrikan American children who will work for a better world. This also means partners may have to endure some unpleasantness in relationships that they wouldn't if children were not involved. What else is new? That's life — if one makes a bed, one has to sleep in it. Rearing successful children will make us better people, be our insurance in old age and protect us from having to repair broken adults.

What's Food Got to do With It?

Personal Energy, Economics, National Resources and Vegetarianism

As a young man, seldom could I go an entire hour without blowing my nose. It seemed as though I had a perpetual cold. During the spring, summer and fall of each year, my life was complete misery if I didn't take all kinds of antihistamines (i.e., drugs) to temporarily arrest my sneezing, running nose and watery eyes. I visited doctor after doctor with the same results, a prescription for a new and more powerful drug. At the age of twenty-six, I decided to take my health into my own hands.

At that time, the late sixties, health was not the "in" thing. Health food stores and restaurants were not as plentiful as they are today. In fact, the Black community of Chicago had only one of each. Today, Chicago has six stores and two restaurants owned by Afrikan Americans. However, during that period, with the exceptions of Dr. Alvenia Fulton and Dr. Roland Sydney, the proximity of Chicago's Black community to "natural" health was extremely limited. Both Dr. Fulton and Dr. Sydney have been untiring in their advocacy of a natural, drug-free way of life. Their example and commitment have been sources of inspiration to me. And, of course, one must also include the extraordinary efforts of Dick Gregory.

However, I first encountered an alternative way of eating by reading Elijah Muhammad's *How to Eat to Live*. By that time (1967), I had excluded pork from my diet. The Nation of Islam had created two foods that were popular in the Black community — bean soup and bean pies. Mr. Muhammad's basic message to me was 1) people eat too much food in this country, 2) people are eating the wrong "foods," and 3) there is a need for self-discipline. Around the same time, the slogan "You are what you eat" began to appear, especially at outdoor concerts and events where "natural" foods were being served. This saying makes a great deal of sense to me because it reflects the fact that one's actions can make or break her or his physical well-being. Once food enters one's body, the body, in all of its unique complexity, has to deal with it. For example, if a person consumes junk food, even if the body regurgitates the food, the food still will have negative effects on the body.

By 1970, Johari Amini-Hudson (the poet/scholar, now a chiropractor in Atlanta) decided that she would seriously study alternative healing systems. As she collected information, she shared it with me. I had already started to eliminate meat from my diet. This helped my upper respiratory problem, but not until I gave up milk, ice cream, eggs and other dairy products and learned how to combine foods did I really begin to feel the difference a "correct" diet makes in one's life. I was less tired; my energy level doubled almost immediately.

The major thing I learned is that by eliminating certain "foods," or better yet, junk foods, from my diet, I was able to experience better health. However, this move toward a total and balanced vegetarian life-style took a great deal of time and plenty of study, as well as trial and error experimentation with my body. Through the process of use and nonuse, I was able to measure the effects that certain foods have on me. For example, when I stopped eating white bread in the sixties, I switched to whole grain wheat bread, not realizing that I am allergic to wheat. Eventually, I changed to non-wheat bread and seven grain breads with a minimum of wheat. Also, I had very bad reactions to milk and ice cream. It was not until 1971 that I found out the milk producers' ad campaign of "Everybody needs milk" was a lie. Cows' milk is generally best for only cows. The enzyme necessary for digestion of milk is lactose, and over 80% of Black children have no lactose in their intestines.

I realize that each person's body is different. And, my search for my diet took some time to "perfect," but it was worth every minute. Ultimate health slows down the aging process. For me, the six major life necessities that preserve and build the body, reduce stress and keep one sexually alive and creative are 1) a vegetarian diet; 2) exercise, yoga and breathing; 3) productive work; 4) reciprocal love; 5) knowledge of what to avoid and what to add to one's life; and 6) slow time and introspection.

Life is too short to be slowed down with a lot of illness. Illness, in most cases, is a direct result of bad habits. We live in a culture that glorifies bad habits, from smoking and drinking alcohol to doing designer drugs. We are encouraged to run the streets at night rather than sleep. We are encouraged to raise our children on processed and fast foods, and we wonder why they can't concentrate, remain still for over thirty seconds, run a block without dying or find joy in any activity that requires them to use their minds.

Everything is connected. My search for the "correct" diet was also a search for the "correct" way of life. This search took me into other areas of study, such as the environment, conservation, population, food production, energy and health care systems. What I've learned over the past twenty years is that Western technology and science is very destructive to individuals, the society and the environment. This is not to infer that there have not been any "advancements," but it is to suggest that most of the time and money invested in Western research and development have not made people healthier — even though some people may be living longer. However, what *is* certain is that the "health" business is healthier and wealthier.

We can't drink the water in urban or rural areas. To breathe the air in Los Angeles or New York City during most hours is a guarantee of upper respiratory problems. Most processed foods, which make up the majority of American diets, are robbed of their nutritional value. Ninety percent of medical doctors are ignorant of the benefits or hazards of diet. According to John Robbins in *Diet for a New America*, out of the 125 medical schools in the United States, only thirty have required courses in nutrition, and the training in nutrition received during four years of medical school by the average U.S. physician is 2.5 hours. More often than not, the average American diet consists of "fast" foods from "fast" restaurants, which leads to fast deaths.

Any time a nation allocates over 40% of its national budget to defense rather than to the betterment of its people's lives, something's wrong. Any time a nation *gives* over $150 billion to private enterprise — the savings and loan industry — and can't come up with a fair, yet comprehensive national health plan for its citizens, that nation is uncaring, insensitive, incompetent and, yes, capitalist. Welcome to America. Money before people is the creed and policy in the U.S. If a culture or society is to be humane, it must be people-oriented with much of its resources going toward the care and development of its people — especially the young and elderly. This is not an impossible task, and since the U.S. is not going in that direction, individuals, families, groups, communities and organizations must act on their own.

What is a Vegetarian?

There are several types of vegetarians. Most people think that vegetarians eat all raw food, including flowers and hay. The simplest definition of a vegetarian is a person who doesn't eat anything that runs away. Vegetarians avoid flesh or warm-blooded animals. A complete vegetarian diet consists of plant foods only: fruits, grains, legumes, nuts and seeds. *Lacto-vegetarians* include milk and the products of milk, like cheese and ice cream in their diet. *Lacto-ovo-vegetarians* include milk and eggs in their diet. There are other variations, but the only one that may be of importance to most people is the *vegan*. A vegan is not only a total vegetarian but one that does not use any products made out of animal parts, such as leather or wool.

Health

There are over thirteen million vegetarians in the United States, and according to Gary Null in his *The Vegetarian Handbook*, "Throughout most of the world, vegetarianism is the rule, not the exception." Many people changed their diets because of failing health. They recognized that the "traditional" balanced diet recommended by the American Medical Association was not healing them. Many of these people may not be able to articulate the reasons for change, but they realized that change was necessary. They knew that there must be another way because the food they were eating did not help to eliminate asthma, colds, sore throats, depression, arthritis, constipation, ulcers, teeth problems, obesity, fatigue and many other degenerative diseases brought on by improper diet, stress and lack of exercise.

Ethics — New Values

I am against any kind of killing. The killing of animals for food is barbaric and *not necessary* to feed all the people on the planet. Meat, for most people in this world, is a luxury. However, in the West, meat and other flesh is the main course, and vegetables have been reduced to side dishes. According to John Robbins' *Diet for a New America*, the industries of the Great American Food Machine (also known as the meat, dairy and egg industries) "don't want you to know how the animals have lived whose flesh, milk and eggs end up in your body. They also don't want you to know the health consequences of consuming the products of such a system, nor do they want you to know the environmental impact." This book is *must* reading for anyone who is concerned about the life-threatening effects of meat-eating on the mind, body and environment. The inhumane treatment of animals solely for the production of a "tender steak" is horrible. As John Robbins suggests:

> Increasingly in the last few decades, the animals raised for meat, dairy products and eggs in the United States have been subjected to ever more deplorable conditions. Merely to keep the poor creatures alive under these circumstances, even more chemicals have had to be used, and increasingly, hormones, pesticides, antibiotics and countless other chemicals and drugs end up in foods derived from animals. The worst drug pushers don't work city streets — they operate today's "factory farms."
> But that's just the half of it. The suffering these animals undergo has become so extreme that to partake of food from these creatures is to partake unknowingly of the abject misery that has been their lives. Millions upon millions of Americans are merrily eating away, unaware of the pain and disease they are taking into their bodies with every bite. We are ingesting nightmares for breakfast, lunch and dinner.

Economics and Conservation

Common sense tells us that fruits, vegetables and grains are more economic than beef, chicken or fish. If one increased his or her vegetable intake proportionately to his or her decrease in the consumption of flesh, the savings would be substantial. Patronizing the produce stand rather than the butcher shop will open up a whole new world of health and wealth. This change in life-style will also aid the small farmers in their battle against Agribusiness. According to Gary Null in his book, *The Vegetarian Handbook*, "Land is capable of supplying food for nearly fourteen times as many people when it is used to grow food for people rather than crops to feed livestock." The cost of breeding and slaughtering animals, processing and packaging meat requires up to sixteen times the energy, land, water and raw materials needed to produce the same poundage of grain.

Personal Choices

Freedom in America has its down side. Freedom to die is just as tempting as freedom to live. In fact, most Americans unknowingly choose slow death rather than illness-free life. Medical care in the United States is curative rather than preventive. The Great American Food Machine, throughout its billion dollar advertising campaign, has determined the eating plan for most Americans. American doctors' reliance on drugs and the knife to "cure" people should be a national scandal, but it is not. We all have choices. However, one's eating and exercise habits are formed early, and they are difficult to change. If a person is raised on fast food and cooked food (generally over-cooked) only, the chances of attracting that person to non-cooked fresh vegetables and fruits are few. Generally, a person has to face a serious crisis in his or her life before life-giving and life-saving changes are contemplated.

Before that crisis comes, and it will surely come if we are not caring for our bodies, let's review a few facts from *Diet For A New America*. According to John Robbins, the meat, dairy and egg industries (the Great American Food Machine) tell us that animal products constitute two of the "basic four" food groups. What they do not tell us is that there were originally twelve official basic food groups before these industries applied enormous political pressure to cut out the other non-meat/dairy foods. We are told by the meat, dairy and egg industries that we are well fed only with animal products, but what they do not tell us is that the diseases which are commonly prevented, consistently impeded and sometimes cured by a low-fat vegetarian diet include:

Strokes	Heart disease	Osteoporosis
Kidney stones	Breast cancer	Colon cancer
Prostate cancer	Pancreatic cancer	Ovarian cancer
Cervical cancer	Stomach cancer	Endometrial cancer
Diabetes	Hypoglycemia	Kidney disease
Peptic ulcers	Constipation	Hemorrhoids
Hiatal hernias	Diverticulosis	Obesity
Gallstones	Hypertension	Asthma
Irritable colon syndrome	Salmonellosis	Trichinosis

This short essay cannot possibly address all of the reader's concerns. I hope I've raised some questions and evoked an eagerness in the reader to do her/his own research. From experience and study, I learned that it is not time alone that ages the body. When the negatives outnumber the positives in one's life, watch out for illness. Improved health is found in one's saying *yes* to life. In doing so, one must cease consuming coffee (and other caffeine-laden foods), smoking (cigarettes and herbs) and drinking alcohol. Alternatively, one should seek enlightened advice and consider these ten points:

1) Get six to eight hours of sleep a night.
2) Drink at least a half gallon of *clean* water a day. Remember, most tap water is polluted.
3) Bathe everyday — seek cleanliness.
4) Exercise *at least* forty-five minutes, four times a week.
5) Start each day with fifteen minutes of deep breathing; try to bring life-giving oxygen into your stomach.
6) Avoid, if possible, most processed foods. Move toward a 50/50 diet, 50% uncooked and 50% cooked. Start each day with fruit and fresh juices. Always under-eat rather than stuff yourself.
7) Be creative — creativity and longevity go hand in hand. Emotional and spiritual health aid in physical health.
8) Make sure that there is continuous *love* in your life. Make your family a priority.
9) Practice reciprocity — try to give and receive with an open heart and mind.
10) Study — always seek life-giving and life-saving information. *Be disciplined.*

The following is a list of holistic practictioners across the country: Johari Amini-Hudson, D.C.—Decatur/Atlanta, GA; Thabiti H.N. Cartman, D.C. —Chicago, IL; Ndugu Khan, N.D. — Houston, TX; Paul Goss, N.D. — Los Angeles, CA; Roland Sydney, N.D. — Chicago, IL; Alvenia Fulton, N.D., Ph.D. — Chicago, IL; Jifunla C.A. Wright, M.D. — Detroit, MI; Asar Ha-Pi — Chicago, IL

Remember, "You are what you eat" is not just a hip slogan to throw at friends; it's common sense at its highest. What's food got to do with it? Everything.

REFERENCES

Benjamin, Harry. *Commonsense Vegetarianism.* England: Health For All Publishers Co., 1950.

Boyd, Billy Ray. *For the Vegetarian in You.* San Francisco: Taterhill Press SF, 1987.

Giehl, Dudley. *Vegetarianism: A Way of Life.* New York: Barnes & Noble Books, 1979.

Goss, Paul. *Forever Young.* Published by author, 1985.

Gregory, Dick. *Dick Gregory's Natural Diet for Folks Who Eat: Cookin' with Mother Nature.* New York: Harper & Row, 1974.

Kondo, Nia and Zak. *Vegetarianism Made Simple and Easy.* Washington, D.C.: Nubia Press, 1989.

Lappe, Frances Moore. *Diet for a Small Planet.* New York: Ballantine, 1971.

Lappe, Frances Moore and Collins, Joseph. *World Hunger: Twelve Myths.* San Francisco: Grove, 1986.

Null, Gary. *The Vegetarian Handbook.* New York: St. Martin's Press, 1989.

Robbins, John. *Diet for a New America.* Stillpoint, 1987.

Ten Ways to Live Longer by the editors of *Prevention Magazine, 1982.*

Vegetarian Times magazine, one of the best sources of current and accurate information on vegetarians.

The Five Daily Battles that Most Black People Fight in America

Denial of reality is a psychological problem. People who are not in control of their lives are taught to abuse themselves mentally and physically. However, this abuse is often defined as adapting, accommodating, going along with the program, or, as the brothers say, "being real." Being real or not, the pain that all Black people have suffered in this country would fill volumes of horror stories. Briefly, these are five wars that are fought daily by most Afrikan Americans:

1. *Color*

I started writing this piece on October 19, 1987 — the day of the modern stock market crash that was named "Black Monday." The fact that it was called "Black Monday" rather than "white Monday" is a lesson for those who are willing to listen. The stock market worldwide is an economic game that many white people play. There are very, very few Black players. The point is that when anything bad happens in the white world, it is always a *Black* day. Color, unlike class, religion or country of origin, has defined Afrikan American people in the West. Everyday, in and out of the Black community, we are confronted with the reality of race. (See "Nothing Black but a Cadillac.") Color determines reality for Black people in America far more than anything else.

2. *Poverty*

America was built on the backs of enslaved Afrikan people. After Emancipation the Afrikans were promised forty acres and a mule. White people did not deliver on the promise. Not given a "fair" or "equal" chance to catch up, Black people have become almost totally dependent upon the state or national government. White people kept Afrikans in chains for four hundred years, forcing us to help build an empire; then they took the chains off one day and told us to compete with them, the very people who

207

profited from our labor. It is just about impossible to catch a people with a four hundred-year head start without resources, institutions, education, finances and land. The poverty of Afrikan American people in the United States is not of our own making. Traditionally, Black people have been a land-based people that used the land and its gifts wisely. The move from land to concrete has disrupted the lives and institutions of Black people. Black people are truly the real miracles in the West. However, poverty persists and it is now taking its toll on the best and the brightest of our youth.

3. Hair

Anytime the vast majority of a people spend a good part of their days, weeks and months changing the texture, color and style of their hair into the texture, color and style of a people unlike them, this speaks volumes about that people. Black people *battle* with their hair every day. When babies are born into the Black community, the two things that are immediately noticed, after the sex of the baby, are the *color* and *hair texture*. The hair is watched and groomed very carefully, in hopes that it will not turn "bad." Again, if one is told all one's life that his/her hair is "bad," then it shouldn't be uncommon that most Black people, women and men, spend *productive* hours trying to change and accommodate their hair to the prevailing fashion. We should teach our children very early that Europeans have European hair, Asians have Asian hair and Afrikans have Afrikan hair. Many women change their hair not only because they've been taught to, but also because their Black male partners demand it. The men change their hair because they are confused. To take the hair of Afrikan Americans, brutalize it and try to change it into "European" hair cannot be anything but a lifelong losing battle.

4. Fear

Fear in the Afrikan American community is the great equalizer. The use of terror by white people has been a very effective war strategy. Any serious study of European history reveals that the major threat they hold over the people they control is "death." White world supremacy could not maintain its control if it were not for the fear shared by oppressed people worldwide. Such fear manifests itself in a number of ways: death, imprisonment, loss of jobs, loss of material possessions, loss of status or fame, loss of financial resources, etc. White people have the power, will and determination to keep Afrikan American people in their "place." This "place" will always be subservient to whites. Only a few negroes will be able to escape, and they will generally be used as the examples of what is possible. Black people have been the glue holding white people together; we have been the reason there has not been a second civil war in the United States. "A white dog does not bite another white dog when Black dogs are present," goes the Afrikan proverb.

5. *Language*

This is the most subtle battle we fight. Most Afrikan American people are without their indigenous language. Language is crucial to identity and culture. The language used by Blacks in the United States is almost 100% English. However, it is "Black English," a language that has grown up in the Black community and is a legitimate and effective communicative tongue. The in joke in most English departments (college and high school) around the country is that Black people are incapable of speaking, writing or creating in English. Of course, this is not true, but misinformation is not uncommon among ignorant and arrogant people. Most professional Black people are bilingual; they speak "Black English" and the languages of their respective professions. Most of them understand the necessity of both languages and have adapted their speech accordingly. Just like other cultures, the way Black people communicate within their community is legitimate and, more importantly, it is *right*. But, when we move in and out of other communities, we will be more effective if we speak their languages — whether their languages are French, German, Hindi or English. Language has been a major tool that whites have used to deny Blacks entrance into corporate America. The key to language is to understand that even though Europeans and Americans have used it to belittle other cultures, no people has a monopoly on the spoken or written word. The influence of a language, to a large degree, depends upon the *power* of the nation advocating that language.

Black people are often captives of false arguments. The five "battles" are not insurmountable. They require that we face and conquer the individual and collective doubt in us. Self-knowledge cures self-fear. The capacity of a people to succeed in battle depends, in part, upon its own definitions and its ability to actualize such definitions on a broad scale. European-Americans have been quite successful at doing this. Afrikan American people must understand that "he who lives with an ass makes noises like an ass." Such noises are not our destiny.

The S Curve, Double Circle or Infinity:
Serious Solutions for Serious Men

Cracking the Code, Finding the Key. What is the Hook?

There are many ways of looking at the world other than those methods taught in the West. There are, in fact, universal truths such as love, non-love, violence, happiness, poverty, health, sickness, hunger, greed, wealth, struggle, politics, ignorance, etc., which are contemplated daily in all cultures by women and men seeking more beautiful and beneficial ways of life.

The limitations of vision, the inability to rise above the restrictive barriers of a culture and the conforming expectations of peers and family are each partially responsible for the lack of individual and group development among Afrikan American people. Learning to accept and deal with failure does not make one a failure. However, knowing only failure in one's self and in others close by doesn't speak loudly for other possibilities.

In the United States it is much easier to accept success — in all of its various forms — because most people, from birth to adulthood, are taught directly and indirectly to expect and seek success. Success in the West generally is measured by the possession and control of people and things (i.e., ownership). Therefore, if one doesn't have homes, cars, gold credit cards, property, clothes, fame, money (not the kind earned from weekly assembly line pay checks) and lots of "beautiful" and "successful friends," one is not really considered materially substantial in the Western context.

However, this type of "success" without a measured understanding of one's wholeness in relationship to the earth, its people, its animals and vegetation is just about impossible — if "success" is only defined by the acquisition or ownership of people and things. Success in an Afrikan and humane context is not defined by joining the killers of the world. Success, redefined, is the ability of our people to negotiate *difficulty* and deliver answers, resources and bright possibilities for ourselves as well as the majority of the world's people.

211

Often the secrets of life are so clear and simple that we refuse to accept them because such insights didn't cost a minor fortune or levitate from some European brain factory. For example, a great many people in this country abuse themselves on a daily basis by consuming unfiltered, polluted tap water and sugar (in all of its forms) without question. That such consumption of tap water and sugar is harmful is an accepted fact among *knowers*, but such simple knowledge is hard to find in the literature read by "everyday" people. Moving "everyday" people to the status of *knowing* is the challenge and is part of the responsibility of those who know. *We all do what we've been taught to do* — I've written this in most of my books from *From Plan to Planet* (1973) to *Killing Memory, Seeking Ancestors* (1987). Moving from ignorance to knowledge, from unknowing to knowing, is very *complex* at one level and quite *simple* at another. However, it is certain that such travelling will require much more than a good rap from a knowledgeable person — though it may start there. Generally, the knowers among us are everyday people in our communities. Many of them are unappreciated, little known, overworked and often three steps from poverty and despair.

I

If one *thinks* and *feels* in a historical context — that is, weighing both the negative and positive forces that influence certain events — one's analysis and interpretation of experience will more often than not be closer to the truth. In thinking about the truth, one also *feels* the truth — gut reaction is important here. A historical mode of *thought* and *feeling* enables the *thinkers* and *feelers* to go beyond the limiting acts of present day arrogance and self-righteousness.

If one possesses in-depth knowledge of other times, places, cultures, and peoples, chances are that one's perception and analysis of past, present and future events will be more accurate. Historical *reasoning* and *feeling* provide one with a context in which to search for *content*. Two excellent examples of this are Dr. Chancellor Williams' *The Destruction of Black Civilization* and Ayi Kwei Armah's *Two Thousand Seasons*. These two books could not have been written without a passion for historical reasoning and an understanding of *feeling* as an analytical tool, especially since most scholars and serious writers are taught to be empirical and objective without introducing their emotions into a work. The enlightened concept of history speaks to an intimate and non-superficial awareness of *culture* — that is, culture in its most liberating definition, which would include an understanding of the interconnections that, love, health, history, education, literature, food, politics, religion, nationalism, economics, sports, entertainment, language, war, peace and race have to each other locally, nationally and internationally.

If cultural history is presented properly, that is, in a way that doesn't dull the mind, it may produce students who will be less likely to jump to easy conclusions and misguided judgements. A critical selection of data and a serious study of cultural and historical facts can heighten one's interpretation and understanding of local, national and world events. Also, a raw, undisciplined evaluation of data outside of cultural/historical knowledge will probably lead to ill-defined answers, easy solutions and long tomorrows absent of beauty or truth. The study of culture/history in a context of logic (reason) and feeling (emotion) can sharpen one's mental skills and heighten one's appreciation of cultural/historical differences and political and economic realities of all people, whether they be rural, urban or a mixture of other unknown qualities.

However, the real significance of cultural/historical study is that it places cultures, peoples, nations and the world into a frame-of-reference that explains a people's current place in the universe. For example, it is helpful to know that Ethiopia was not always on the doorstep of starvation but once was a world leader in the production of food and knowledge. It also is useful to understand that this beggar's mentality that has crept into the Black community is recent and does not have a historical precedent prior to our coming to the Western Hemisphere. The Chinese have a saying: "Fool me once shame on you, fool me again shame on me." It has been stated also that two types of intelligence exist: intelligent intelligence and stupid intelligence. Where are we? I think that many of us have turned our lives over to "experts" and "specialists," thereby refusing to attack the difficult questions in our lives because of fear, ignorance and the acceptance of the recent history of Afrikan American failure and disappointment in America.

II

Life is definitely rough when ignorant people talk about how ignorant other people are. In measuring the noise in our community, we must be

213

able to distinguish between the false and the real. Too often we will accept men in $2,000 tailored suits with 10¢ tailored minds because our definitions of good and valuable are distorted. Our values often are misplaced and focused on how one dresses, the car one drives, the size and location of one's house or where one vacations, rather than on those things that *really* matter.

We all have our horror stories. Few of our people are exempted from the brutality of America. As the end of the 20th century approaches, one is not assured by the forecast of the future of Afrikan American people. It is easy to overlook the obvious in the United States: three million plus homeless people, sixty million functional illiterates, historically high unemployment, a deadening drug problem, an environment that's losing its ability to withstand pollution, etc. Men and women make their own history, but they do it within the cultural climate of their time (i.e., the historical, political and economic realities that allow or discourage such movement). For example, Afrika is poor and not as productive as it has been or should be because of internal difficulties (nation by nation), but also because of its colonial past and present. And, yes, we are aware of the fact that it is much easier and less embarrassing to place most of the blame on former colonialists or, as in the Afrikan American case, former slave masters, than to *take hold* and transform ourselves. For example, if one were to look at today's Uganda in its utter devastation and desperation, a quick unknowing answer to its problem would be, "It suffers the legacy of colonialism." The answer is partially correct. However, a closer look also would take into account the last thirty-plus years of "independence" under Milton Obote and Idi Amin, two Afrikan men who abused power as if it had been ordained. The continued slaughter of Uganda's people and destruction of the land intensified under Black leadership. This example is not the exception. All over the Black world, from the Sudan to Chicago, Black men (and some women) abuse position and influence at the expense of their people and others.

It is instructive and painful to note that unlike other non-Afrikan former colonial or occupied nations (such as Singapore, India, China, South Korea and Japan), there is not one sub-Saharan Afrikan nation that produces or supplies to the Western world *any* refined Afrikan produced product that is used daily in most homes. For instance, VCR's are 100% Asian, much of the cotton clothing sold in the U.S. comes from India, and the U.S. automobile industry has been crippled by cars coming from Japan.

My point is the decline that Africa and its people have experienced over the last 1,000 years has not stopped, and her children who have been scattered worldwide have not been much help in bringing about such a reversal. Unlike the Jews, Arabs, Japanese, WASPs and others, Afrikans have few, if any, international effective structures working *unselfishly* for Black people. This is partially because the standards which most of us live by have been compromised to the point that in many quarters mediocrity is viewed as advancement. Concepts like integrity, morality, honesty and excellence are given lip-service as many of our teachers and leaders outdo the world in saying one thing while they do the destructive other.

III

The S Curve, Double Circles, or Infinity: Solutions

When a woman or man moves to a level of *knowing*, she or he ceases to be *reactive* and becomes *proactive* (i.e., a positive worker and an example). This is important because our people have enough talkers and rappers. The ability to inspire a crowd or congregation temporarily to do good work is not necessarily a great art; the key is to produce many people and leaders who internalize good work concepts and constantly and consistently do productive and developmental work.

In thinking about this, the letter "S" continues to jump in and out of my mind. In doubling the "S," as in man and woman (or partners) facing each other in a position of love-making, you get double circles or the sign of *infinity*. A man reaches a level of completeness only with a woman of like mind. If a man or woman is with a partner of unlikeness, only confusion can result. Therefore, our journey takes on another path when a partnership of completeness is made. The curve of the "S" is also important from a cultural standpoint because we are a circular people. That is, our lives revolve around the rejoining of the circle (families, communities, the Afrikan world), whereas the unbroken line of the circle represents our people in this land as well as the diaspora.

Therefore, if we concentrate on the S curve of double circles, we see that there exists a value-based system — a system of thought and action that can break the chains that have tied us to Europe and other false concepts of squares, sky scrapers, greed, individualism, sexism, selfishness, silliness and separation.

The S Curve (short definitions)

Source — For all people there are beginnings, in-betweens and endings that are renewing themselves.

Soil — Earth as life-giver, receiver, and renewing energy.

Seeing — Has very little to do with eyesight. Vision, insight.

Soul — The third eye of knowledge, where imagination dwells, where strength dwells.

Self — Faith in one's self is not egocentric pop psychology but is only an extension of one's willingness to accept and seek growth that leads to self-esteem.

Spirit — The willingness to fly into the face of denial. Spirituality, the connecting of the inner-self with the negative and positive temptations of the world.

Strength — Secure in one's history, traditions and present. Responsible. Standing up to evil and corruption.

Structure — All people, especially children, need order and predictability in their lives.

Searching — Trying to find meaning in all questions. Self-knowledge as a starting point.

Security — Knowing, feeling, giving and receiving love from family and extended family.

Study — A way of life that is as important as eating and breathing. Understanding that fruitful study is the foundation of a *knowing* person.

Student — Ongoing, for life. A seeker of knowledge.

Serious — Approaching the world with an attitude of understanding that goes beyond the normal or expected.

Space — One's private place for regeneration.

Stop-time — A time for contemplation and change. A point of reevaluation.

Smile — Laughter, the healing mechanism that is free but seldom understood or used.

Simplicity — An appreciation of the quiet; the search for quality within the unnoticed. Not moved by brand names.

Silence — Quiet time. Slowing running to a walk. Understanding one's internal needs for the absence of noise. Learning to listen.

Stillness — Ability to hear the heartbeat of one's future. A photograph or music that slows one's pulse.

Solitude — Aloneness. Welcomed isolation, a pacing that opens one up to other possibilities.

Sharing — Social network, family, children. The interaction of social institutions that impact on one's quality of life.

Saving — Frugality. The putting aside of resources for the future.

Service — The giving of one's talents to those less fortunate.

Specialness — The feelings one has for one's self and those one loves.

Support — Putting oneself in a position to offer knowledge or resources as needed.

Subtle — A way of functioning that does not underestimate another's intelligence.

Stimulate — Ability to pull the best from others and self. Self-motivated and sure starter.

Struggle — The only way to approach life in the United States. Without struggle, one is only an observer and victim. Conscious organizing.

Shining — Having touch with an internal light.

Saneness — A quality of being that allows one to function intelligently under all circumstances. Always trying to make practical sense.

Speaking — Multilingual. Watching one's words carefully. Avoiding perpetual talking. Having something to say and knowing when to say it.

Skepticism — Always questioning. Not accepting the easy answers or people who perpetually smile with their hands out.

Substance — A quality of being for which we must strive. Quality. Knowledge. Wisdom.

Success — The maximization of one's natural gifts and talents for a fruitful and meaningful life for one's self, family and people.

Steady and ready for Sisters — Having internalized the S curve and more.

Negatives

Siege — People under siege very seldom can create.

Separation — Individuals who are separated from each other, their history and culture will only invite confusion.

Shame — When everything is everything, nothing is nothing — a state of life where values cease to have meaning and anything goes. Honor is replaced with pleasure.

Stress— The psychological beating of the mind and body. A *major* killer of Black people.

Stale — Rotting. Mental retardation. Backwardness beyond saving.

Silliness — Jerri curls on men and women who are supposed to be able to think for themselves. Adults who play rather than think. Superficiality in values and knowledge.

Sameness — The melting pot theory that continues to burn Black people.

Sexism — The idea that men are the center of the universe and that women exist to serve men, children and dogs.

The S Curve (long definitions)

Source:

For all people there are beginnings, in-betweens and endings that continue to renew themselves, and in the absolute spread of time, there are only seconds separating the three. Very few people understand all three. Where one comes from is as important as where one is now or will be tomorrow. Afrika is not an accident of nature. Therefore, Afrikan people — wherever they may sleep — are there for a purpose. The scattering of Afrikan people around the world is not a punishment but an unfocused and improperly defined mission. The meaning of the mission will not and cannot become clear unless we return to the understanding of the *source*. This returning is not necessarily a physical journey because Afrika itself is in a state of questioning. This journey is a movement toward acceptance, acknowledgment and discovery (or finding); also it is one of admitting ignorance and questioning surroundings. The true meaning of Afrikan people in America is much more profound than a quest for food stamps or the Presidency. Our being here is more of an answer than a question. It is clear that the energy of Afrikan American people flows throughout the rivers and sunsets of America and the world.

Soil:

Earth is life. One of the most obvious misunderstandings of earth as life-giver is when an adult or child's answer to the question "Where does fruit come from?" is, "The *supermarket.*" Indeed, the answer — most certainly, in the child's context — may be correct. However, in the overall order of life, it is an uninformed answer. Few people have abused the earth like Europeans. The rush to Western technology and industrialization has reeked serious damage on the earth in the name of progress. Soil (earth) as the provider of life is without question. We need to understand the life cycle of plants, animals and insects if we are to become more responsible in our approach to food. When people are raised on concrete rather than soil, their lives take on other shapes. Often their lives are full of crack(s); not only are their days drowned in drugs, they are defined by breakage. When one loses the connection to the earth, the land becomes like any other commodity — something to be bought, sold and used for making money rather than saving lives. From the damaging effects of acid-rain to the greenhouse effect, it is clear that the current rulers of this earth are sleepwalking toward *dust and dirt* rather than Black, bountiful soil. Remember, the only thing that nobody, anywhere is making any more of is *land.*

Seeing:

Most of us do not see; we are looking. *Seeing* has very little to do with eyesight. In fact, if eyesight is necessary for seeing, why are there so many intelligent blind people? Seeing, in this context, has more to do with *vision*, the type of vision that Stevie Wonder and Ray Charles possess. *Vision.* That's how a people escapes the trap of mediocrity. Not that mediocrity on occasion is dangerous, but the problem arises when mediocrity becomes the accepted norm or goal. Seeing means eclipsing *sameness* and being able to meet the challenges of life at a more meaningful level. *Seeing* is the encouragement of creativity and the actualization of one's personal gifts or talents. Often, such seeing comes in the form of poetry, novels, music, drama, visual arts and dance. The seers that produce visionary works in America often are destroyed because the populace cares more about the sayings and doings of entertainers, sports figures and news anchor people than those of writers, artists and thinkers.

The seers, the prophets in the United States, generally are those persons who have been systematically locked out of the benefits of the nation.

Soul:

The insight of any people can be seen in its creations. Soul, in its most representative form, in fact, is the essence of a people. Soul is, indeed, a special food, but it is not pork chops with white rice and gravy. Often the unexplained energies we receive that get us through the day or week have to do with what is inside. The ultimate soul is the knowing and forgiving soul. Within the soul is the third eye of knowledge. It is where imagination dwells. Imagination is as close as one can get to creating something out of nothing. If one has soul, she/he has balance, heart, hearing, unknown capacities and vision. Soul is the voice in music, the speaker in poetry, the narration in fiction, the feet in dance and the language in drama.

Self:

Belief in one's self should be subordinate only to belief in one's people and in a higher order that regulates all of us. One must develop a reasoned humbleness about one's own powers because it is clear to the knower that something else is working in this universe. Therefore, faith in one's self is not egocentric psychology but is only an extension of one's willingness to accept and seek growth. One's faith in self should be intuitive. It is also the perception and understanding that there is an order in life — a sense of wholeness with a special direction. Intuitive faith or belief allows for change and encourages a certain flexibility in one's actions. Therefore, faith or belief in one's self has a profound and far-reaching psychological effect. Faith or belief in one's self is the basis for all good work. Faith in one's ability allows one to become centered and focused in a direction that will provide fruit for self and others. The major and most rewarding approach to the self is to determine how best to become a creative and productive person as part of a self-reliant community. Self-knowledge means a gut and an intellectual understanding of one's self in connection to other peoples, cultures and races. Self-knowledge, if it is working, means self-love.

Spirit:

This is the brilliant force that has sustained our people all over the world. It's the articulate answer that rides the drumbeat throughout the Black world. Spirit focuses on the will to fly into the face of denial. Spirit provides the stimulus to live and create. Spirit is that quality in all of us that pushes us beyond the expected. It's the fighter's, dancer's, performer's secret weapon. It is spirit that takes the ordinary and makes it look like talent. When we talk about a person with *spirit*, we are talking about that which is extraordinary in a person's actions, heart, giving, beliefs and example.

Strength:

Saying no to weakening pleasures. Discipline. Avoiding the easy, the quick, get-over attitude. The ability to go deep into one's self for energy and fire. The ability to accept responsibility for ideas and actions that advocate that which is good, just and right. Ongoing mental and physical development, from lifting weights to lifting one's mind. Firmness in the mouth of evil opposition. Seeking ways to work for a functioning future. Learning from one's errors. The ability to admit mistakes and apologize for one's negative transgressions against self, family and people. Healthy and ready to support and encourage the good in all people. The ability to smile and show serious compassion and love for children. Processing the *will* to tackle the difficult obstacles in one's life. Not giving in to the quick fixes, unhealthy temptations and smiling lies. Always fighting corruption and deception.

Searching:

Trying to find meaning in all questions. Knowing that looking is far more than having one's eyes open. Seeking a purpose in life that is beyond the meaningless quest for material things and quick fixes. The defining of relationships: people to people, woman to man and children, man to woman and children, humans to animals and vegetation. Seeking answers through continuous study. Knowing that imperfect questions will only lead to incorrect answers and confusion.

Study:

Study is the contemplative search for the betterment of self and others. This involves quiet meditation on things that are valuable and necessary for human development. To be is to know. Knowing is a process. The most important parts of the process are 1) wanting to know; 2) understanding where knowledge and information can be found; 3) having the ability to distinguish between useful and non-useful knowledge; and 4) allowing useful knowledge and information to have a positive impact on one's life. Daily study is the key to knowing. If you have valuable knowledge, the world will come to you.

Student:

One who seeks and is open to life and its many secrets. A receiver of magic, garbage, hope, possibilities and bright tomorrows. Ongoing for life. One who questions most things and will not settle for easy answers or easy solutions. A book to the student is like food to the hungry. Questions to the student are like chalk to a blackboard or a basketball to the NBA.

Serious:

An approach to life that denotes an understanding of the complexity of the world. A person is serious when she or he accepts responsibility for making life better and more rewarding for self, family, extended family, community, one's people and the world. Seriousness is the necessary attitude for action. Knowing when to act is the compliment to a serious attitude. One who possesses this quality approaches the world from the position of a builder and developer.

Space:

A place to regenerate: home, temple, church, mosque or center where one's energy is restored. Nature-parks, libraries, museums, areas where one can meditate and contemplate one's place in the universe. One's private area, an area that is an extension of one's personality, where one

223

seeks strength, knowledge and peace. A place to which one wants to return often. One's space can be personal or collective.

Smile:

Laughter heals. Smiling often and at the right time makes life easier. Life cannot be serious twenty-four hours a day. One must learn to relax and let go. Do things that make one happy, such as spending time with children. Laughter and smiles will surely come if one is around children enough. Be careful about taking one's self too seriously.

Simplicity:

Learn conservation. Walk sometimes rather than ride. Take trains or buses rather than airplanes. Read books rather than watch television. Look for answers in the unexplained. Barter rather than buy all things. Simplicity lies in the enjoyment of art, music, literature, drama, dance, nature, learning and other activities that cost little or no money. It is the quality within the quiet and the unnoticed. Simplicity means back to basics; seeking the natural order of life; moving toward less complication in one's life. One who is simplistic seeks the true and renewable fundamentals of a functional life.

Silence:

Listening to one's own heartbeat. The absence of noise. The ability to communicate without words. A new level of hearing. An appreciation of calmness. A quality of hearing that is regenerative.

Solitude:

Without distraction. Building one's internal self; aloneness. Welcomed isolation. Meditation. Prayer. Clearing the mind. Connecting the mind to the body and spirit. Restoring order in one's life. Thinking time. Invaluable spacing.

Sharing:

Giving when least expected. Reciprocity with community, mate and children. The realization that giving is the best way to receiving. One cannot contribute positively to a functioning community unless one is willing to share beyond the limited expectations of others.

Struggle:

Life is not easy, never has been. To struggle means to reject the victim's role. One who struggles is a rejuvenated fighter — lifelong. She/he is organized, prepared and multi-talented. To struggle is to understand complexity; to pick one's own battles. There cannot be fruitful progress without struggle.

Skepticism:

We were born wanting to know. The art of questioning is lost or developed very early. Most people accept style over substance, junk food over nourishment. We must return to the difficult questions — and expect serious answers. Beware of people who have all the answers to every question without skipping a beat. To have doubts is healthy.

Substance:

A person's actions will ultimately define him/her. Words are fine, but as they say on the block, "You can't beat the drum without hitting it." Be slow to give answers, quick to be the example of the answer. Value knowledge. Realize that wisdom comes from study, work, building, creation and production.

Steady and ready for Sisters, family, community, people and world. Understanding the S curve and other philosophies of life. Mastering the S curve. Seeking and accepting quality and excellence as normal. Looking for that which compliments and encourages beauty in relationships. Able to lead and accept leadership. Loving the sisters, their music and motion. Willing to work for their happiness. Knowing that their happiness will make us happy. Realizing that our women represent source and smile. Knowing that the two selves must connect and grow as one. Maintaining a spirit that stimulates the soul, which gives strength to serious students of love, life and saneness. Avoiding silliness and shamefully sexist acts with a passion. Subtle and simplistic in one's approach to our women and to life. Speaking with wisdom in acknowledging the specialness of Afrikan women.

Finally, I must emphasize several points. We must be skilled doers in this world — walking and working with a humility that is focused on wellness. "Research shows that people who are driven by ambition, goals, and achievements only are more prone to illness than those who place more stock in *harmonious* relationships." Secondly, we must take responsibility for the wellness of ourselves and our people. This means that we must free ourselves from sickening doctor/patient relationships and be careful about looking to other so-called experts to make us well. We must become more adult-like and responsible in *attacking that which is not right* in our lives and communities. Thirdly, we must eat correctly — that is, we must take responsibility for everything that goes into our bodies and our children's bodies, as well as make sure that our families, extended families and friends are aware of life and life-giving alternatives. The most appropriate diet that I've chosen for myself is based on the correct use of fruits, vegetables, whole grains, beans, sea vegetables and clean water. To that I add daily study, yoga and meditation — to connect one to a higher inner self, to exercise the inner and outer body with the mind. Also, a good program of physical exercise is necessary. I suggest walking, cycling and swimming.

It is clear also that one must have an unwavering faith in one's self, our people and the possibilities of the future. This cannot be a blind *faith* but one based upon adherence to study and creative production. This can happen by developing support networks that include but go beyond the extended family. Such networks as sisterhoods, brotherhoods, child-care centers, schools, political organizations, food co-ops, businesses, boys' and girls' clubs must be committed to life. If they are to function in our best interests, each will approach life in a way that fosters optimum benefits for its members. For example, we must be political, but we do not have to become politicians.

It is beauty, security, health, love, enlightenment and happiness we seek. We can only find such music in a functioning social familyhood whose members are aware of its source, soil and soul, and who are able

to see themselves as searchers for spiritual strength — coming as serious students to a space for study and reflection, devoid of stress or staleness, absent of people who find value and energy in sameness that produces silliness without stop-time. Our laughter should be smiles promoting a healing simplicity, rich in silence, stillness, solitude and silver that encourage sharing, saving, service, support and intellectual specialness. All subtly stimulating a shining, sure saneness that makes sense for our struggle, while speaking firmly and skeptically with substance to the promised success we so heartfelt need and
work for
making us steady and ready for
sisters,
family,
extended family, community
world.

MOTHERS

for Mittie Travis (1897-1989), Maxine Graves Lee (1924-1959),
Inez Hall and Gwendolyn Brooks

"Mothers are not to be confused with females
who only birth babies"

mountains have less height
and
elephants less weight than
mothers who plan bright futures for their children
against the sewers of western life.

mothers making magical music miles from monster madness
are not news,
are not subject for doctorates.

how shall we celebrate mothers?
how shall we call them in the winter of their lives?
what melody will cure slow bones?
who will bring them worriless late-years?
who will thank them for hidden pains?

mothers are not broken-homes,
they are irreplaceable fire,
a kiss or smile at a critical juncture,
a hug or reprimand when doubts swim in,
a calm glance when the world seems impossible,
the back that america could not break.

mothers making magical music miles from monster madness
are not news,
are not subject for doctorates.

mothers instill questions and common sense,
urge mighty thoughts and lively expectations,
are impetus for discipline and intelligent work while
making childhood exciting, unforgettable and challenging.

mothers are preventative medicine
they are
women who hold their children all night to break fevers,
women who cleaned other folks' homes in order to give their children
        one,
women who listen when others laugh,
women who believe in their children's dreams,
women who lick the bruises of their children and
give up their food as they suffer hunger pains silently.

if mothers depart their precious spaces too early
values, traditions and bonding interiors are wounded,
morals confused, ethics unknown, needed examples absent and
crippling histories of other people's victories are passed on as
        knowledge.

mothers are not broken-homes,
they are gifts
sharing full hearts, friendships and mysteries.
as the legs of fathers are amputated
mothers double their giving
having seen the deadly future of white flowers.

mothers making magical music miles from monster madness
are not news,
are not subject for doctorates.

who will bring them juice in the sunset of their time?
who will celebrate the wisdom of their lives,
the centrality of their songs,
the quietness of their love,
the greatness of their dance?
it must be us,
able daughters, good sons
their cultural gift,
the fruits and vegetables of their medicine.

We must come like earthrich waterfalls.

III. Worldview

"We still need the essential Black statement of defense and definition. Of course, we are happiest when that statement is not dulled by assimilationist urges, secret or overt. However, there is in "the souls of Black folk" — even when inarticulate and crippled — a yearning toward Black validation."

Gwendolyn Brooks
from "Requiem Before Revival"

Why Foreign Policy Is Foreign
to Most Afrikan Americans

International affairs has to do with relationships, the reasons these relationships exist, and in whose interest they exist. It also has to do with power — raw, unadulterated force and fear, the kind of fear that makes men piss in their pants and blow their brains out. Such power has forced nations to spend 60% of their national budgets on weapons systems, as their people seek nourishment from the garbage of tourists. In the last quarter of the 20th century, on the heels of modern computer technology and satellite communication, the conducting of foreign policy is still the game of running the world.

Simply stated, the relationship that one country has with another country or countries is defined as its foreign policy. A nation's foreign affairs can range anywhere from trade to "constructive engagement," from scientific, cultural and educational exchange to war. Generally speaking, the foreign policy of a nation is set by its ruling body — in the United States, the executive branch. In effect, the President is charged with the formation of a foreign policy that must be, at some point, confirmed by the Congress. To really understand a nation's foreign policy, serious study is required. Most people in the United States, whites as well as Blacks, do not have any idea about what this country is doing around the world, with the possible exception of its "War on Terrorism" that is explained in the thirty-second slots each night on the evening news. This country's foreign policy is calculated in body counts as the sophisticated theft of nations goes unnoticed. The roles the CIA and KGB play in the world's destabilization seldom are explored in the popular press.

The citizen-consumer in the United Stated plays checkers and video games, while the world-runners (politicians, businessmen, military and academia) continuously restructure the world's chessboard. Unlike the game of chess learned during youth, opponents on the world stage do not start with equal chances to checkmate. The game of world-running is fixed according to Holly Sklar's book, *Trilateralism*. The stakes are too enormous to be left to the skill or luck of a single player. These are gigantic gang wars in which the combatants fight without referees or rules. The major gangs are the United States and the North Atlantic Treaty Organization versus the Soviet Union and the Warsaw Pact. Each gang, with some consultation with its membership, has carved up the world into "Spheres of Influence."

What is clear but not talked or written about in great detail is that white people, who are less than 9% percent of the world's population, *run it all*, and that all others fall into one of the two camps or into the ineffective nonaligned nations. White world supremacy, operating in the areas of business, law, education, language, religion, sports, entertainment, military and foreign affairs, is the most serious problem facing Afrikan Americans and other people of color, argues Neely Fuller in the *The United Independent Compensatory Code/System/Concept.*

The function of a gang is to acquire, develop and protect one's turf (its economic market). Thus, the analogy of a nation to a gang is not too far-fetched. The old Anglo-Saxon proverb, "The only successful war is the one that is won," operates daily in the Pentagon and on the streets, which is why the United States can, with a confident arrogance, ignore the World Court's decision condemning its activities in the not-so-"secret" war against Nicaragua. This is also why the USSR and the USA can, with little difficulty, tie up those votes in the United Nations that they feel go against their best interests. The United States and the Soviet Union are modern gangs that, in the final analysis, listen only to each other. And even though each country speaks a different language and operates out of dissimilar cultural imperatives, each one's message is the same, *we run it.*

To fully understand the foreign policy of the United States, one has to have a lot of time and an appreciation for serious money. The major stimulants for the foreign affairs of the United States are its "national security" and profits. Imperialism may be a little understood word on the block, but for most of the world it is a dangerously nonnegotiable reality. The large gap between rich and poor countries; the involvement of politics and international economics; and the effective use of economic and military power to create dependency, exploitation and dominance speak to the type of imperialism (economic control) at which the United States is the reigning master. The foreign policy of the United States is predicated on three principles: 1) expanding markets; 2) national security and anti-communism; and 3) global, economic and political hegemony. At one level, this is deep stuff which will require the average person to give up evenings, weekends, holidays and even dating to grasp its meaning. But, on the other hand, there are some close-to-home and recent observations that may help clarify the crippling influence of U.S. foreign policy.

Ferdinand Marcos, the recently deceased former dictator of the Philippines, ruled that country by using force and crony capitalism for more than twenty years. Marcos, on a salary less than that of the lowest paid state governor in the United States, amassed a fortune that is estimated to be somewhere between $3 and $19 billion. Only his widow, mistress, accountants and lawyers know the exact amount, and they are talking only to each other. Today, 72% of the Philippine population lives in poverty, compared with 27% in 1965. In twenty years of dictatorial rule, Marcos killed, imprisoned and politically crushed his opponents with the aid and blessing of the United States government. What did the United States get out of this deal? The use of land in the Philippines for U.S. military bases. From Lyndon Johnson to George Bush, U.S. foreign policy in the Philippines has been structured around the needs of the U.S., at the cruel expense of the Filipino people.

The poorest country in the Western Hemisphere is Haiti. Jean Claude "Baby Doc" Duvalier and his father before him ruled that small nation like a family business for over a quarter of a century. The poverty is so great in Haiti that fresh water in one's home is viewed as a luxury. The military and economic oppression was so effective that most people involved in progressive political actvity could expect instant imprisonment, torture or death if caught. If a young person cried for food, work and education, she or he was in danger of being branded a communist. The United States provided millions upon millions of dollars in aid to Haiti; little, if any, went directly to the people. Trickle-down economics has not arrived in that part of the world.

The way Baby Doc showed concern for his people was by driving through town with his wife, throwing coins to the populace. However, in February of 1986, the "Baby" and his family fled in the night, with the United States providing the taxi service. Before he left, he had robbed the country white. According to *The New York Times*, he left less than $1 million in the central bank. Corruption in Haiti was a prerequisite for success. The former dictator's wealth is estimated to be between $300 and $900 million, all stolen from the Haitian people. He and his wife are believed to have real estate and monies stashed throughout the West, mainly in the United States, France, and Mexico. Marcos and Duvalier are both looking for a home, and they're doing it in style.

The final example is South Afrika. The history of South Afrika, in broad terms, closely resembles that of the United States. George M. Frederickson, in his book *White Supremacy: A Comparative Study in American and South African History,* draws many cogent parallels. The most obvious is that Europeans settled both lands and on each continent, slowly but effectively instituted a reign of terror designed to reduce and subjugate the indigenous population. In the U.S., the term "genocide" would be a polite description of the "success" Europeans have had in reducing the indigenous population and securing the North American continent. The white South Colonialists of South Afrika, with much help from their Euro-American brothers, still are working at stealing Afrika.

What is obvious, however, is that the annihilation of Afrikan people has not worked and will not work. What has worked is the effective neutralization of many Afrikan people and their reduction to a dependent people in their own land. Also, the whites, through the use of rewards and punishment, have been able to divide the Blacks into battling factions that fight each other rather than the true enemy. This is the classic victim's reaction to oppression. The white colonialists, with their ideology of white supremacy, have developed a system of calculated terror that functions like a well-oiled machine twenty-four hours a day, 365 days a year. Presently, there are over 7,000 Black Afrikans who are being detained in South Afrikan prisons without charges or legal representation.

The white minority (about four million of the population) has structured a completely separate and unequal system that is designed to totally contain the movement and development of the country's majority Black population (25 million plus). The national government has classified and segregated everything from education to housing, politics to food production, employment to sports, entertainment to health care. This system of hatred and social disease flourished in part because of the United States and other Western nations' support and, in particular, through the use of multinational corporations such as IBM, Ford, General Motors and others. The bottom line is that the U.S. chose to fight communism by instituting a boycott against Poland and initiating a private war against the people of Nicaragua, but all it can do for Afrikan Blacks, in the wake of ten Black deaths a day and indescribable oppression, is talk. The major excuse the administration gives is that "constructive engagement" is working, but few actually give the real reasons why this country continues to back such a racist regime.

First, the whites of South Afrika and white Americans are blood brothers. Secondly, the U.S. imports from South Afrika over $1 billion a year in chromium, manganese and platinum for its industrial, economic and military uses. The human rights of people of color are secondary to the national defense and profits of the United States. Bantustans of South Afrika are similar to the Black ghettos of the United States. The racial and economic deprivation our brothers and sisters suffer in South Afrika actually exists in the U.S. but at a much more subtle yet effective level. In fact, many Afrikan Americans do not believe that they are oppressed. To fully explain this will require another essay. However, it is clear that America's Black "permanent underclass," with its high unemployment, frightening illiteracy, enormous prison population, homelessness and huge addiction to drugs and alcohol, is a dependent and enslaved people. To truly comprehend the state of Black America would require a social science course in itself (see Pinkney's *The Myth of Black Progress*). Blacks here are just a boat ride away from the type of enslavement that exists in South Afrika. Think about this: people in the U.S. seldom, if ever, talk about a permanent white underclass. The racist duplicity and contradictions of U.S. foreign policy can be easily illustrated by examining U.S. actions in Grenada, Libya, the Middle East, Chile, Ghana and other nations. The U.S. actions in the Philippines, Haiti, Israel and South Afrika represent state terrorism at its highest stages. The people of the Philippines and Haiti actively are initiating change that has little to do with the corrective actions of the United States. This country jumped on the train of the Haitian and Filipino people when it saw change in the wind. South Afrika remains a serious problem that has Third World War possibilities if substantive changes do not come soon.

There are several observations here for Afrikan Americans: 1) all people do what they've been taught to do, and most of them act in the way that they perceive is in their best interest; the basis for these actions are both cultural and biological; 2) Black people in the United States, most certainly since 1865, have been concerned mainly with surviving and developing in the Western Hemisphere. The majority of Black people have forgotten their holocaust — the middle passage. Many Black people also have forgotten the genocide committed against the indigenous people of this land, those persons renamed Indians or Native Americans. Most

Blacks understand by now that treaties and contracts with the Western world are like sports records — made to be broken.

Generally, the Afrikan American's view of the world is colored by his or her view of himself or herself. That is, acculturation has prepared Blacks to see what they have been taught to see and to believe what they have been taught to believe. The saying "It is easier to believe than think" is quite apropos for the Black situation in the United States. Foreign policy is foreign because most Afrikan Americans have been too busy trying to master, translate and understand domestic policy.

Whereas serious struggle is multifaceted, most Blacks are still one-dimensional and strait-jacketed to a European-centered worldview. Many Blacks are like smokers who believe the warning label on the package is for someone else. Death and taxes are indeed certain; but for the chained mind, slavery is too. It is difficult to win a war when people have to buy weapons from the enemy. Most buyers will never be sold or given weapons from the top of the line. Nations are not taken seriously when they can't do fundamental things like feed themselves. Imperialism has reached its highest stage when the sons and daughters of a given nation, mainly from the First World (Afrika), study abroad and choose to stay and participate in the building of that nation, rather than return home. The brain drain from the First World is unbelievable and crippling to that continent.

The war, whether on the battlefield or in the classroom, is with ideas. Actually, ideas run the world. Foreign policy is fashioned in the popular as well as the national culture. We can see this from the foreign policy of the Catholic Church, where every few months the Pope goes on diplomatic trips around the world. And, most certainly, we can see it in the popular culture with such movies as *Red Dawn*, *Rambo*, *Rocky IV* and the popular *Top Gun*. Ideas are important. Two bad ideas are 1) the view of Black people as a minority people in the world; and 2) the suggestion that Afrikan countries should continue to tie their currency and development to Europe (i.e., the West). My point is that Black people represent over one billion people in the world; if Blacks cannot recognize our own strength worldwide in terms of numbers, land mass and resources and cannot organize such vast wealth, we are lost. Cheikh Anta Diop, in his book *Black Africa*, calls for the formation of a United Black Africa into a single economic and cultural federated state. It is quite clear that white people are organized at a world level for the perpetuation and continuation of their rule. Afrikan people can do no less.

236

Very seldom will an Afrikan trained at Harvard Business School or the London School of Economics create self-reliant ideas out of that academic experience unless he or she is a Kwame Nkrumah, W.E.B. Du Bois, Nelson Mandela or Patrice Lumumba. The only time a great many Black people get involved in U.S. foreign policy is in its implementation as foot soldiers in foreign wars. Black people are the people who fight the wars for this country against other people of color around the world. Recent examples are Vietnam and Grenada.

If Afrikan Americans ever are to have a serious impact on U.S. foreign policy, accurate information is needed. At the end of this essay, there is a list of books, newspapers, magazines and quarterlies with which the interested reader can start. The major rules to follow in gathering data about the world are 1) do not depend on *one* source of information; 2) be flexible by studying materials of both right and left political views; 3) take political science courses at local universities; 4) travel whenever possible to other nations; 5) make friends with foreign students, visitors and citizens; 6) start a personal library; 7) work with progressive Black organizations; 8) attend foreign policy lectures that are open to the public; 9) form foreign policy study groups; 10) don't become overwhelmed with what you will discover; and 11) watch and consult legislators on foreign policy issues.

The attitude one brings to this subject is crucial. Don't be afraid to admit ignorance. The world we live in is very political and extremely complicated. Most things in this world are political, from the food one eats to the clothes one buys. The Western world is Eurocentric, racist, sexist, class-conscious, and youth-oriented. If a person is Black, conscious and living in America, one thing is absolutely certain — he or she is *fighting daily* or has been defeated.

The United States uses over 60% of the world's natural resources but is the home of less than 7% of the world's people. Much of those resources come from Afrika. If one cannot see the inequality in this arrangement, it only confirms the effectiveness of Western acculturation and the dominance of the Eurocentric worldview. The most important foreign policy issue facing Afrikan Americans is our relationship to Afrika. Blacks in the U.S. must pressure the State Department and Congress to pursue a just and balanced policy. We can learn from the Polish and Jewish people in their capable lobbying for Poland and Israel. Afrikan Americans will remain powerless pawns in the international chess game unless Afrika and its future become central in Black thought and action. The 21st century

237

is upon us. Memory is calling, and this generation will truly be judged by its children — if they are alive and productive. Using the knowledge and technology of the present, we must pull from the wisdom and vision of our foreparents to issue on this earth a better world.

REFERENCES

Any bibliography of this inexhaustible subject can only be very selective

Agee, Philip. *Inside The Company: CIA Diary*. New York: Lyle Stuart, 1984.

Aliber, Robert Z. *The International Money Game*. New York: Basic, 1987.

Barraclough, Geoffrey. *The Turning Points in World History*. London: Thames Hudson, 1979.

Biko, Steve. *I Write What I Like*. San Francisco: Harper & Row, 1986.

Brown, Lester R., et al. *State of the World 1986*. New York: Norton, 1986.

Cline, Ray S. *Secrets, Spies & Scholars*. Washington, DC: Acropolis, 1978.

Cohen, Benjamin J. *The Question of Imperialism* . New York: Basic, 1973.

Diop, Cheikh Anta. *Black Africa: the Economic & Cultural Basis for a Federated State*. Chicago: Chicago Review, 1987.

_____ . *The Cultural Unity of Black Africa*. Chicago: Third World Press, 1987.

Dower, John W. *War Without Mercy: Race & Power in the Pacific War.* New York: Pantheon, 1986.

Dunnigan, James F. and Bay, Austin. *A Quick and Dirty Guide to War.* New York: 1986.

Fallows, James. *National Defense.* New York: Random House, 1981.

Franck, Thomas M. and Weisband, Edward. Eds. *Secrecy & Foreign Policy.* London: Oxford University Press, 1974.

Frederickson, George M. *White Supremacy.* New York: 1981.

Fuller, Jr., Neely. *The United Independent Compensatory Code/System/ Concept A Textbook/Workbook for Thought, Speech and/Or Action For Victims of Racism .* Washington, DC: published by author, 1984.

Garwood, Darrell. *Under Cover: Thirty-five Years of CIA Deception.* New York: Grove, 1985.

Hanlon, Joseph and Omond, Roger. *The Sanctions Handbook.* New York: Penguin Books, 1987.

Herman, Edward S. *The Real Terror Network.* Boston: South End Press, 1982.

Kolko, Joyce. *America and the Crises of World Capitalism.* Boston: 1974.

Kwitny, Jonathan. *Endless Enemies.* New York: Congdon & Weed, 1984.

Nalty, Bernard C. *Strength For The Fight: a History of Black Americans in the Military.* New York: Free Press, 1986.

Nkrumah, Kwame. *Neo-Colonialism.* New York: International Publishing Co., 1966.

Pinkney, Alphonso. *The Myth of Black Progress*. Cambridge: Cambridge University Press, 1984.

Sampson, Anthony. *The Money Lenders*. New York: Peter Smith, 1988.

Sklar, Holly. Ed. *Trilateralism*. Boston: South End Press, 1980.

Smith, Anthony. *The Geopolitics of Information: How Western Culture Dominates the World*. New York: Oxford University Press, 1980.

Stockwell, John. *In Search of Enemies*. New York: Norton, 1984.

Williams, Chancellor. *The Destruction of Black Civilization*. Chicago: Third World Press, 1989.

Wright, Bobby E. *Psychopathic Racial Personality and Other Essays*. Chicago: Third World Press, 1989.

Newspapers

New York Times	*Philadelphia Inquirer*	*The Final Call*
Washington Post	*Chicago Tribune*	*In These Times*
Wall Street Journal	*Miami Herald*	*The New York Sun*
Los Angeles Times	*The Buffalo Challenger*	*Christian Science Monitor*

Quarterlies and Magazines

Foreign Affairs	*The Nation*	*Commentary*
Foreign Policy	*The Progressive*	*Black Scholar*
The Return	*The New Republic*	*Mother Jones*
New African	*The National Review*	*New International*
West African	*Black Books Bulletin*	*Covert Action*
African Concord	*African Guardian*	*Zeta*
Essence	*African Commentary*	*Focus*
New York Review of Books	*Crisis*	*North Star*

BLACKS AND JEWS:
THE CONTINUING QUESTION

I was asked by a friend to participate in a forum concerning Black/Jewish relations in Chicago. I refused because I do not believe that such forums are useful without fundamental changes in economic and political relations in this city. My friend then requested that I make a few comments about Black/Jewish relations as I see them, to be broadcast over Chicago public radio. I said yes for four reasons: 1) a friend requested it; 2) there are other views from our community that have not been articulated, 3) this subject is not new to me; and 4) our children deserve more than we are receiving on this question from our leaders and the media. (See the recent *Esquire* article, "The Uncivil War," by Taylor Branch — 5/89.)

To say that Blacks are anti-Semitic is as absurd as saying that Jews are anti-Israel. This issue of Blacks and Jews in Chicago has been blown all out of context and has put some Blacks in an undefensible position of responding to the statements of one man that were, at best, ill-informed and insensitive. The larger issue is not one of Blacks and Jews but of Blacks and white people. The historical, racial, political and economic (i.e., cultural) relationship of Black people to white people, of which Jews are an integral part, has not been approached or analyzed in a reasoned manner in the media or back rooms.

To isolate the gigantic problem that Black people face worldwide, that of white world supremacy, to a fight between Blacks and Jews is to support and legitimize the victim's approach to Black struggle and world realities. Often the victim's approach to a question is ahistorical; it's like saying the holocaust didn't happen, when, in fact, there have been many holocausts throughout history. One such holocaust was the rape of Afrika by Europeans and the scattering of Afrikan people around the world to provide free labor for Europe and her colonies. And according to Chancellor Williams' *The Destruction of Black Civilization,* Walter Rodney's *How Europe Underdeveloped Africa* and George Padmore's *Africa: Britain's Third Empire*, over 65 million Afrikan people perished during the Euro-Asian trade in Afrikan men, women and children. Another example was the European colonization of the Western Hemisphere that destroyed nations of indigenous people (over twenty million); those who are left in the U.S. occupy reservations and a new name, "Native Americans" — sounds like something generic. The German's killing move against its own citizens, mainly Jews, is the holocaust with which most Americans are familiar. The Jewish holocaust remains on the consciences of most literate people because the Jewish people — and rightly so — will not let the world forget. This non-forgetting strategy, along with a Jewish armed force, collective white guilt and aid, helped to create the modern state of Israel, which occupies land that used to be Palestine.

One of the most effective weapons the Jewish people have at their disposal is the labeling of a person or group as anti-Semitic. It is no secret in the Black community that many Blacks will take up Jewish battle before even thinking of their own because, all too often, many Blacks see the Jewish struggle and the Black struggle as one and the same. The quickest way to be designated a surefire, out-in-the-open anti-Semite is by openly confronting the Jewish influence in America, especially in regards to Israel. History, facts and the search for truth often are backseated to long-held positions that allow little room for change, compromise or peace. In an enlightening article, "The Illusion of Jewish Unity," in the June 16, 1988 issue of the *New York Review of Books*, Rabbi Arthur Hertzberg examines the geopolitical nature of the Jewish question. Rabbi Hertzberg states that taxpayers in the United States, of which Black people are a significant part, support Israel to the sum of over three billion dollars a year. This may, indeed, be new information to a great many Black people because prior to Rev. Jackson's raising the right questions in his run for the Presidency, it was assumed that foreign policy of the United States was not the concern of Afrikan Americans. The Jewish influence on the foreign policy of this country is awesome, especially when it comes to Israel. See Paul Findley's *They Dare Speak Out*; the former Illinois congressman dared to criticize Israel, and the Jewish lobby, the American-Israeli Public Affairs Committee (AIPAC), was instrumental in seeing that he did not return to Congress. Another important contribution to this ongoing debate is Edward Tivnan's *The Lobby: Jewish Political Power and American Foreign Policy*. Mr. Tivnan makes it very clear that the job of AIPAC — the only registered lobbyist for Israel on Capitol Hill — is to push and advocate pro-Israel legislation and to soften, intercept and quiet all criticism of Israel.

However, the Jewish need to be involved with the "Black Question" has always been strong. From the Herbert Apthekers to the Theodore Drapers, from the Irving Howes to the Herbert Gutmans, from the Norman Podhoretzs to the Norman Mailers, the Jewish influence over "Afrikan-American" scholarship and ideological development is unbelievable. Their input is unrelenting, and many of the current problems of the Black struggle are a result of our becoming too dependent on Jewish, WASP and other people's interpretations of Black history, life and culture. One of the most recent Jewish contributions to this is Weisbord and Kazarian's *Israel in the Black American Perspective* (Greenwood, 1985).

My argument is not against the Jews bringing forth their own worldview around the Afrikan American question. *My concern is the uncritical acceptance of their worldview and the inability of the work of Black thinkers and activists to find its way into print.* The majority of Afrikan American people are basically left with a Eurocentric, white Judaic-Christian analysis of Black struggle, and any discussions of politics, race, economics, education, religion, politics, culture, law, etc. generally are clouded by this limited perspective.

Such a perspective distorts the Civil Rights and Black Power movements of the sixties. There is no Black/Jewish coalition or alliance in existence among the majority of Black and Jewish people, and there never has been. That *some* Blacks and Jews have worked and struggled together is unquestionable. However, if one understands the concept of coalitions/alliances, one talks about a combining of equals, partners or co-operating decision-makers. This state of affairs never has existed between the majority of Blacks and Jews or between Blacks and any whites. The participation of Jews in the Black struggle of the fifties and sixties was more image, money and decision-influencing than anything else, according to Harold Cruse in his important study, *The Crisis of the Negro Intellectual.* Cruse and others point out that Blacks represented (and still do) a buffer zone for the Jews in regards to their Anglo-Saxon-Irish-Italian-Polish-German (i.e., white) brothers. The Blacks' move toward liberation (which some define as civil rights), after careful inspection, clearly points out that the Black struggle aided Jews and other ethnic whites to a much greater degree than it did Black people. According to Lewis A. Coser and Irving Howe in their book, *The New Conservatives*:

The American negroes have served as a kind of buffer for American Jews. So long as deep-seated native resentments and hatreds were taken out primarily on blacks, they were less likely to be taken out on Jews. If Jews have been the great obsession of Christianity, blacks have been the great obsession of America. And as long as this condition existed, both organized and spontaneous hatred in America concentrated on blacks and only secondarily on Jews.

This should not be odd or earth-shattering if one truly comprehends the type of war that is being waged daily in this country and in much of the world against Black people. Jews have sophisticatedly linked the Black struggle to theirs, and it has worked beautifully for the most part. This linkage began to unravel in the sixties when S.N.C.C. (Student Nonviolent Coordinating Committee) began to question the international nature of Jewish struggle, especially in its relationship to Palestine and South Afrika.

Is there a Jewish conspiracy to rule the world? I don't know. But Jewish-Americans, WASPs, Irish-Americans, Italian-Americans and Polish, Japanese, Greek and French-Americans actively participate in world and domestic capitalism. And the Fortune 1000 companies haven't been dismantling industrial America and shifting much of its manufacturing to European and Third World countries because of altruism. The controlling of world markets and resources is nothing new to global capitalism or socialism. The capitalists just do it better. The major capitalists in the world are white. There are Jews among them.

In an analysis of the annual *Forbes* lists of the 400 richest Americans, Edward S. Shapiro in the winter 1987 issue of *Judaism* makes it very clear that the Jewish presence in monied America is significant but not dominant. Of the *Forbes* 400 richest American families, over 100 are Jews. Therefore, "twenty-five percent of the richest Americans comes from a group which is less than three percent of the general population. By contrast, the *Forbes* list contains only a handful of Italians, no Hispanics, one Black, and a couple of Eastern Europeans, groups which outnumber Jews." Mr. Shapiro also states:

> ...a disproportionate number of America's ordinary millionaires are also Jewish and the per capita income of American Jews is also far higher than in that of the general population...Furthermore, of the fourteen American billionaires, at least four are Jewish: Marvin

Davis, the Denver oil mogul and former owner of Twentieth Century Fox; Leslie Wexner, America's leading merchant and head of the Limited, Inc. women's apparel shops; and the Newhouse brothers, Samuel and Donald, who control America's greatest privately owned newspaper, magazine, and book publishing empire.

Does such wealth control America or the world? No! Mr. Shapiro also points out that Jews are "still rare in corporate America where power is in the hands of the insurance companies, banks and industrial corporations that are controlled by non-Jews." However, such wealth does have immense influence in America and, in particular, Black America. Much of the wealth in Jewish America, according to Gerald Krefetz's *Jews and Money: the Myths and Reality* and Stephen Birmingham's three books, *Our Crowd, The Grundees* and *The Rest of Us*, comes from real estate, retail, publishing and entertainment. *All four areas impact daily on the lives of Black people in terms of where we live, what and where we shop, what we read and who makes it in the entertainment field*, one of the few areas that Black people dominate as performers. (Also see, Neal Gabler's *An Empire of Their Own: How the Jews Invented Hollywood*.)

Blacks can appreciate and understand the Jewish dilemma. (See the May 24, 1988 issue of the *Village Voice*, in which a discussion moderated by Nat Hentoff, "What's a Jew to Do?" explores the issue of Israel, United States, South Afrika and the world.) However, Blacks never have had the luxury of actually making the complete separation of Jews from other whites. The Jews in their day-to-day associations with Blacks, in many cases, have not allowed this. In fact, there are constant reminders of Jews not only being Jews but white also. James Baldwin in his essay, "Negroes are Anti-Semite Because They're Anti-White," states:

> ...the Jew is singled out by Negroes not because he acts differently from other white men, but because he doesn't. His major distinction is given him by that history of Christiandom, which has successfully victimized both Negroes and Jews. And he is playing in Harlem the role assigned him by Christians long ago: he is doing their 'dirty work.'

Many Jews are in an identity crisis; however, this is generally among the young and is not a problem for the Jews that make life and death decisions. Since Jews have used Blacks as buffers for so long, many now feel threatened by those Blacks who question the actual meaning of such a relationship. Those Afrikan Americans that do question such a relationship are in the acute minority. Few, if any Black publications explore the relationship with any type of seriousness. When the question is raised publicly, it is generally a reaction to a Black calling Jews out of their name or questioning their influence in Black affairs.

Several things need to be emphasized:

1) We live in a global world, and just as Jews are concerned about Israel, the Irish about Ireland and the Polish about Poland, Blacks too must be concerned about Afrika, specifically South Afrika where the descendents of Europe rule with gestapo tactics. And South Afrika's continued existence as a white supremacist nation, in part, is dependent on the United States, Western Europe, Israel, Japan and a few Afrikan nations.

2) For Blacks to advocate Black or Afrikan American nationalism is not odd or racist or unusual in a world context. In fact, most people — Jews included — who are in control of their own cultural imperatives act in a self-protecting and self-reliant manner that is a form of nationalism and may have either religious or secular roots. In fact, that which is odd, racist and unusual is that there are not more Black people advocating Black nationalistic ideas. This, of course, has to do with the effectiveness of the acculturation/seasoning process and the Black commitment to the American promise of integration and fairness, even as such misconceptions destroy many Black people daily.

3) Jews and most white people who negotiate with the Black community at a policy level are informed and have done their homework. Often the criticism of whites and Jews that comes from the Black community is personal and highly emotional — which in itself doesn't make it less valid, but in the political arena such responses are less effective if they can't be immediately documented or collaborated, thereby leaving them open to counter-criticism and dismissal. The study of other cultures and people cannot be left to academia, who are often too removed from the Black community or have been co-opted and thus are not effective. If we are to confront our critics and/or adversaries, we must know them well.

246

4) This issue of knowing and not forgetting one's history is of paramount importance. The self-protecting manner in which Jews define, project and carry out their own worldview is another lesson we can learn from them. The power of Black people is diluted and often not actualized because of forced amnesia. Whether Blacks reside in Brazil, the United States, the Caribbean, Asia or Afrika, the two grains that divide us are non-communication (i.e., language and contact) and other people's definitions.

One of the many strengths of the Jewish people — and they must be admired for this — is that they build institutions. Therefore, when a response is needed to a particular problem, question, or attack, they are able to act quickly and decisively at an individual and institutional level. And this response comes from many quarters, such as the pages of *Commentary*, *Midstream* and *The New York Times*; as well as organizations like the Anti-Defamation league of B'nai B'rith and the American Jewish Congress. That former President Reagan and Jesse Jackson took the human rights issue, which was first raised in reference to the Black situation in the United States in the sixties by Malcolm X, to the U.S.S.R. is another sign of Jewish determination. Mr. Reagan and President Bush have yet to be as forceful about the human rights and majority rule of Blacks in South Afrika.

It's time for Blacks to stop being the pawns in the word-games of others. Our youth are wasting away in imitation schools, overloading the few drug programs available, filling up the prisons, being forgotten in mental institutions and dying faster than the statistics can record their forgotten bodies. The Black testing time has passed. Does this mean that some Black people and some Jewish people cannot work together, grow together and struggle against evil together? Absolutely not, this has happened in the past and will undoubtedly continue. However, *Chicago Sun-Times* columnist Vernon Jarrett is correct in pointing out the Black/Jew double standard in the Jewish criticism of Blacks without restraint. Therefore, it is very difficult for many informed Blacks to forget the Jewish anti-Black feelings expressed by Jewish leaders such as Norman Podhoretz. His now infamous position, "My Negro Problem — and Ours," appeared in the February 1963 issue of *Commentary*.

> The hatred I still feel for Negroes is the hardest of all the old feelings to face or admit, and it is the most hidden...by the conscious at-

247

titudes into which I have succeeded in willing myself. It no longer has, as for me it once did, any cause or justification (except, perhaps, that I am constantly being denied my right to honest expression of the things I earned the right as a child to feel)...Color is indeed a political rather than a human or a personal reality and if politics (which is to say power) has made it into a human and a personal reality, then only politics (which is to say power) can unmake it once again. But the way of politics is slow and bitter, and as impatience on the one side is matched by a setting of the jaw on the other, we move closer and closer to an explosion and blood may yet run in the streets.

The difference between Blacks and Jews is that we do not see Norman Podhoretz as the only spokesperson on Jewish thought and, therefore, do not go off half-crazy because of his racism and ignorance.

It is clear to most Blacks in the United States that the majority of Jews are not rich, not politically influential and not in control of U.S. media, science, education, economics or legal system. They have influence, yes, *but not control.* (See G. William Domhoff's *Who Rules America Now?*) This is important because Israel could not *exist* without the aid (some call it welfare) from the United States. Israel received over $3 billion in aid in 1988 from the U.S. This comes to about $10 million each working day. This money doesn't include the millions of dollars that are raised by the various Jewish organizations. My point is that Afrikan Americans contribute through taxes and as individuals to the upkeep, survival and development of Israel. I've yet to hear a *thank you* from Jewish leadership. If Afrikan Americans received $3 billion a year from any source, we would not have too many problems that couldn't be solved.

There is a lesson in all of this: 1) Jews take care of their own, using monies and resources from wherever they are available; 2) they are a highly literate and political people that keeps their struggle in the minds-eye of most people worldwide; 3) regardless of the criticism, they are always on the offense; 4) they have stopped apologizing for being Jewish and have developed visible Black spokespersons like Julius Lester and Sammy Davis, Jr. to advocate their cause.

A final point that often is overlooked is that violence against Jews by Afrikan Americans is just about nonexistent. I am not aware of any Black people in the U.S. organizing to do harm to Jewish people or Jewish institutions. Nor am I aware of any organized or individual acts of violence by Black people against Jews or their institutions. It seems to me that the rift between Blacks and Jews is mainly verbal.

In the Black community of the eighties and nineties, Jews have been replaced on the front line (commercial) by Arabs and Koreans; if we criticize them, are we anti-Arab or anti-Korean? Like the Jews, Poles, Italians and Irish, we must elevate our struggle to a world level and seek life-giving and life-saving answers that will positively resurrect our communities. As long as we are reacting to other people's definitions and programs, pro-action among the knowers in the Afrikan-American community will be futile. Today Afrikan American people in the United States are *a majority people with a minority complex,* and this comes from the uncritical acceptance of other people's ideas, dreams, visions and definitions. However, there is a significant number of Afrikan American people that will never go back to acting out the definitions of others. Change is in the wind and a whole lot of people are upset, not only Jews.

Malcolm X: Diamond in the Coal

There is not a day in my life that I do not think about Malcolm X. His picture, along with those of Garvey, King, Lumumba and Hoyt Fuller, rests on the wall above my desk. It often reminds me of the influence he had on me and millions of other Black people of my generation. To have become conscious in the early sixties is to have been touched by the truth of Malcolm X. That is beyond question. He was the man that gave my generation a *voice*. His presence, his example, his stand against the greatest human evil to confront our people — *white world supremacy and its creation, negroes* — is stamped upon my mind forever.

The short life Malcolm X, formerly Malcolm Little, was ended as El-Hajj Malik El-Shabazz. His travel from a self-hating victim to a politically conscious and learned spokesman-organizer for Black people via the Nation of Islam (under the guidance of the Honorable Elijah Muhammad) is what legends are made of. His journey from the streets to prison to proactive statesman in Afrikan American struggle is well chronicled in his *Autobiography of Malcolm X*, written with the assistance of Alex Haley. His autobiography should be read by all Black people, especially the young. It was Malcolm X who understood that what one could change does not need to be eliminated. Most certainly, he saw in himself and in Black people eminent possibilities for positive and lasting change (i.e., development).

There are many images that define Malcolm X. His unique articulation of Afrikan American struggle without bowing, scratching his head or tap dancing is the clearest. He lived with facts, and in all of his confrontations (and that's what they were) with reporters, media hosts, public officials and others he gave more than he got. The clarity and conviction of his arguments helped to unglue many negro-minds from the myth and hypocrisy of white people and Eurocentrism. He handled himself and the language like a young, undefeated fighter. He was *always* reading; seldom did we see Malcolm X without a book, magazine or newspaper. He was, what is called today a "quick study."

He received the respect of younger and elder brothers, not because they feared him but because he had proven himself time and time again; he had tested fire. How could one not remember the photograph of Malcolm X at the window of his home, with weapon in hand, guarding his family? Betty Shabazz and their girls — Attalah, Qubilah, Ilyasah, Gamilah Lamubah, Malikah Saban and Malaak Saban — all quiet and sincere, engaged (in their own public and private ways) in a battle that was still being defined, a war that was/is often beyond explanation or comprehension, yet very dangerous. Malcolm X as student, teacher, spokesman, organizer, leader and family man represented the type of man that did not put style before content, image before thought or reaction before analysis. His suits were not tailor-made; nor were his ideas or actions. His message was clear water and music for a thirsty people searching for a new dance.

Malcolm X was not perfect; he made mistakes and on many occasions, to friend and foe, admitted error. But, who among us during the difficult sixties did not error? The Malcolm X difference was that he did not allow his mistakes to destroy him; he learned from them and took succeeding steps with careful deliberation. No, he was not perfect, but he was moving toward a kind of working perfection. Whether or not he would have arrived we do not know. However, the odds are it would have been a well-fought battle. El-Hajj Malik El-Shabazz was cut down—brutally murdered in the prime of his life by negroes blinded by a self-righteous ideology that created in them (and others) a killing-field mentality. For them, the easiest and quickest answer to serious and embarrassing questions was to kill the questioner; bury the message and messenger.

The short life of El-Hajj Malik El-Shabazz is without parallel in Afrikan American struggle. His impact is immeasurable, his message undying, his integrity legendary, his commitment unquestioned and his significance and contribution are still growing. In fact, it was Malcolm X and the Nation of Islam that first popularized the using of Black as the correct designation for people of Afrikan descent in America. It was also Malcolm's Organization of African American Unity that made the ultimate connection between Black people here and Black people in Afrika, Asia, the Americas and elsewhere. Somehow I don't feel that the current debate over what we should call ourselves would have taken up too much of his time. Black and Afrikan American had entered his lexicon already married, and a divorce seemed unnecessary. Ossie Davis, a man who is usually careful with his adjectives, called him our "Black Shining Prince." He did shine, as in illuminate, and the light that glowed behind his ever present glasses should always burn in us, our children and their children until the evil that killed him and *continues to kill* millions of our people yearly is plowed into the earth never to rise again.

Malcolm X, the name most people remember him by, was the complex, serious, multifaceted, quick-smiling man who doubted and questioned, doubted and questioned until inaction would have been viewed as endorsement of the hypocrisy with which he could no longer live. He tried in his own unique way to give answers to those difficult and murderous times. To forget and not honor his contribution is to give quarter to the enemies of Black people and, in effect, bury memory and history in an unmarked grave.

Our commitment to Black world struggle, and Afrikan American struggle in particular, ideally should be no less than his. To not try and reach his level of seriousness is to acknowledge our own failure and, just as important, would be a confirmation of Black impotence. Such inaction will confine us to the garbage bins of history, and people worldwide will continue to use Black people as the catch-line in their jokes. If anything can be said about Malcolm X, it's that he was not a comedian and he didn't sell wolf tickets.

A common saying in the Black community is "If you don't know where you are going, any road will take you there." Remember that the ideal may not be the "mountain top," but may be the path to the top; life is, indeed, a process. Certainly, El-Hajj Malik El-Shabazz never stopped learning and he, unlike most of our leadership, truly respected and believed in the ground-rooted and untouched power of Black people. It is good that we can now talk of Martin Luther King and Malcolm X in a way that is not conflicting. They both loved Black people and gave the ultimate gift that one could give to our people, their lives. Jeff Stetson in his very powerful play "The Meeting" examined the possible connection between the two of them. It is clear that the work of Dr. King will be remembered and advanced. To remember and celebrate the life of Malcolm X is fine. However, I believe it is time that a nationwide effort is launched to build a living memorial or institution for the life-work of this monumental man. The form that such a structure would take is not for me to say. All I can do is join the call for it and be willing to be a part of a national effort to make it a reality.

Malcolm X, El-Hajj Malik El-Shabazz, our Black Shining Prince, the diamond in the coal, did not "know his place" in America or the world.

As a consequence, he was dedicated to making "other places" for all people, especially those of Afrikan descent. His short, yet beloved journey into our lives marked his presence as true prophet and insightful seer. His heartfelt fight should still be our fight; his preparation and seriousness must be duplicated in Black communities across this land. In doing so, we not only rejoice in what he left us, but we also appreciate the genius of his vision because when the *word* is finalized, we know — without doubt or hesitation — that Malcolm X, El-Hajj Malik El-Shabazz, gave us *a way*; and he often smiled while doing it.

New Steel Screaming in the Wind:
Hoyt W. Fuller

Clearly there are losses that are irreplaceable, examples that are indispensable. Hoyt W. Fuller has joined our ancestors. Hoyt W. Fuller died in March of 1981. His journey is an early and unexpected one, is a hurting exodus, but in any language *gone means gone* and as to the thousands of people and students he touched, as important as some of them are, none will occupy the chair of the teacher. So it is. What remains are memories of a unique *Afrikan Freedom Fighter*, his magnificent body of written work, scores of his ideas that need acting on, and an army of people that his spirit of urgency connected with and transformed.

I have not met many "true" Black men in my time, and therefore without concrete images of what Black manhood is, I have had to study and reconstruct a definition that is consistent with 20th century realities. In my estimation, some of the qualities that best exemplify new Black manhood are cultural and moral integrity, competence, psychological security and stability as a Black man, sensitivity to the needs of one's people, a strong work ethic, a culturally-based mindset, an unquenchable thirst for knowledge (truth), a winner's attitude toward life, an insatiable love for Black people (especially the children), revolutionary unpredictability, and an unstoppable willingness to struggle against any odds for the liberation of Black people. This was Hoyt Fuller, Black man extraordinaire. His credo was a simple one: *Liberation for Black people is possible.*

Yet, too, he knew that liberation was indeed unlikely without strong Black men and women whose first obligation was securing their own vision and historical direction. He understood the complexity of the human heart and realized the extent to which many Black men and women had made the "easy compromise," resulting in their effective neutralization. He was not one to hide behind excuses:

> But what clogs in the heart is that Black men know what they do. They know. The flight to Kappa-Omega is not blind. If red blood deserts the veins, then substitute tomato juice. When white men

255

deride the manhood of those they degrade, what they mean is this: men do not beg for freedom, men take their freedom. Only fearful fools confuse real manhood with slapping backs and guzzling booze...These are games children also play...Far too many Black men lack seriousness. They are content being slaves. "Making it" is the religion, and "success" is the god we worship. It is no cliche. What do we "make it" to?...they know. The only source of power in the race is in the people, the plain ones. Marcus Garvey knew that. Elijah Muhammad knows..."Power lies in the People." *(The Turning of the Wheel*, I.P.E., 1972, Chicago)

Hoyt Fuller knew the power of the Black collective, yet he was also the example of the fired-up, conscious individual. He felt that a people's Liberation was indelibly tied to individuals and their institutions. Acceptance of the status quo was never in his game plan. For him, a people's liberation was not only a material reality but was mostly reflected in their day to day spiritual and political (i.e., cultural) development. He represented the epitome of the paradoxical man. He was tormented and imprisoned, yet he was free. He would often comment, "I am not home in America," as he fought daily against the piles of excrement that America forced on his people. Actually, the world was his prison, even though there were places in this world where he was less hurried, more relaxed and constantly productive. However, the larger questions remain: How was this man different? Did his passage among us impact our lives positively?

Hoyt was analytical but not aloof, an idea man but not actionless. He constantly involved himself with the daily construction of a means toward an end and seldom was confused in his ideas or acts as to the ultimate end: liberation. He profoundly understood that the lack of action infecting the great majority of Black people, especially the men, is not genetic or biological. Rather, it is the result of hundreds of years of special, intensified conditioning, which also destroyed other cultures, such as the indigenous people of the Americas. He knew deep inside that constant and consistent motion toward the affirmative is absolutely necessary. Not to act, not to function consciously in the best interest of one's people was, to Hoyt, unthinkable and merely a way of accepting the world on the terms of others.

In essence, Black inaction was acting against Black action. Do nothingness, translated into negative acts, has left us terminally confused and frightened. However, in this precarious existence, Hoyt dared to see potential in us, and based upon much study, enormous travel, and his own varied life experiences, he seldom fell prey to false expectations. His truths were continuous and earthshaking:

> The American educational system, as it is, is not designed for the benefit of Black people, who are oppressed by that system; it is not designed to facilitate the regeneration of a people it has calculatedly debased; it is not designed to liberate the spirit of the sons and daughters of Africa nor to enhance that spirit nor to thrill at its soaring; the American educational system is not designed to encourage the destruction of the American political and economic system, no matter how cruel and debilitating embattled minorities may find that system.

> The American educational system, as it is, is designed to benefit and to maintain the status and well-being of the white middle-class majority; it is designed to train the personnel and to maintain the ideology which will ensure the perpetuation and endurance of the American political and economic system, which is now, and always has been, hostile to the ultimate aims of the Black minority which serves it. (*Black World*, May 1974).

His motion was to change and upset, to dethrone current Euro-American interpretations and correct them with a perspective (his word) that spoke to the realities of his people and other people of color. For certain, he was not seeking to replace a white falsehood with a Black one. Intellectual honesty and an accurate reading of history would not allow for such nonsense. He knew that the process of freedom was always open to debate and interpretation.

Nor was he a fighter for some vague notion of universality or world humanism. He was too culturally grounded to be sidetracked into never-never land. Plainly stated, he was a Black (Afrikan) man first, and then a citizen of the world. He, as far as I know, never apologized for this honor, but functioned for the seventeen years of our friendship in a way that forced Afrikan Americans either to accept themselves and work toward our collective self-interest or crawl back into the closets of scientific slavery. He was not one to avoid confrontation and fought very well with words and fists. If anything was truly important to him, it was not to make truth out of lies. His commitment to authenticity and to facts was unquestionable, and is exemplified in his editorship of *Black World* and *First World* magazines, and in his only published book, *Journey to Africa*, (Third World Press).

Unlike most of us, Hoyt Fuller seldom chose the easy route. He was a warrior of the first rank and did not pick false battles. He sought the eye of the needle. He knew that one cannot reason with the majority of white people (and their negro lackeys); therefore, they are to be feared and organized against. He felt that Black murder in the United States had become legitimate, yet our best responses to it were ribbon wearing and promises not to make such murder a political issue. Hoyt was not an excuse maker and often stated:

> ...power makes concessions only when challenged by counter-power...But we know what we do and what we fail to do. After nearly 400 years of racist subjugation, Black people have no justification for repeating the cycle of hope and disillusionment. If we do not seize the instruments of power and use them, we must admit that it is our terribly conscious choice. (*Black World*, December, 1972).

He was the classic race man, not superficially wearing his culture on his back, but carrying it within him to the point where if you were in his presence, and an enemy of our people, the racial and cultural intensity of his personality would force reactions from you, in the positive or the negative.

There is an uneasiness among our people. Contrary to misinformed belief, Ronald Reagan is not a dumb actor; he is in fact a superb screen writer, director and an integral part of the Western production team that is bent on the absoluteness of their emerging order. Hoyt prepared some of us. These new interpreters voicing opinions disguised as facts will be resisted with the forces of volcanoes and the strength of the elephants.

The fight against this white conservative and neo-conservative united front was Hoyt's special project. He warned us. Well, it's for real, and above ground. Cowboys, American pie, and Real Stuff are back in force with another crop of "new negroes," led by the likes of Thomas Sowell, Samuel Pierce, Mel Bradley, Arthur Fletcher, William O. Walker, Thad Garrett, Martin Kilson, Glenn C. Loury and Wilson J. Williams. These preachers and posing princes, clowns in scholar's roles, will not have an easy time of it. Hoyt had often stated that the "task is monumental, and it is not easier by the diversionary tactics of the game-player. It is imperative that the Black Community know the difference between the committed and the comedians." His truths could devastate. Hoyt is not to be mourned but emulated, his actions duplicated a thousand times:

He will be missed, not lost among papers
remembered in midnight study cells
and early morning runs.
remembered as an originator of
wisdom
from a vision that was sound and sane
steadfast and tempered
Tempo between songs and dance   between
. fist and articulation   call him
fresh music
screamingly dangerous

Sang beauty first
notice the eyes of children
locate their living and eating space
try and smile now.
run with and against the common wind
do damage for damage   be
unpredictable with map and compass
and weapons pressed against the cheek
Catch fire and fire
notice
there is an uneasiness among us
window shades are drawn,
people talk in nods and whispers
babies are again born in homes,
people are picking up books and nails
and anxiously listening to grandparents.
there is sunrise on the horizon
Pass this word quickly and quietly
there are rats in the streets.

Poison is needed.   Now.

Bobby Wright:
Genius in Honest Search

How does one measure greatness?

There are few Black men or women today in the "right" place, or position, asking the penetrating questions and demanding answers and corrective actions to the racial situation in the United States and the world. Generally, Black people are viewed as pitiful pawns in an international game of control and manipulation, and our worldwide misuse is an accepted by-product of business as usual.

The loss of Dr. Bobby E. Wright is magnified a hundredfold because he was the constant swimmer, the energized professional, the concerned and loving family man, the Garveyite race man; always a step or two ahead of the accepted theories masquerading as insight and knowledge. Dr. Wright was a man who had fought to get to the "right" place in order to ask the "right" questions and demand and force the "right" actions.

It is true that we do not recognize greatness among us. Our measurements of importance are generally faulty and speak mainly to the superficialities of life e.g., from where one lives, the type of clothing one wears, the car one drives, to the number of bodyguards that one employs to carry bags and open and close doors. Dr. Wright cut through dishonesty with a passion. He, as a clinical psychologist, understood the mind of an enslaved people. He knew the mental state of a people caught in a world stolen and remade for Europeans. His view was that the high Afrikan standards that gave the world civilization were now confusing or nonexistent. Dr. Wright was a visionary with standards, values, integrity and convictions. In essence, he was a man who valued Afrikan traditions and culture.

He died in the prime of his thinking. He was involved in honest search. His presence was a stabilizing force for all people who had recently become anchored to video machines and sightlessness. He understood the power of ideas, and was constantly cutting through nonsense and mediocrity. His concern was for the widening distance between the haves and have-nots, the job-givers and job-seekers.

Bobby's love was conditional and selective. He had been burned often by the call of "Blackness" and "Brotherhood." His work, more than most in his profession, is a telling indictment of white world supremacy, and within his multidimensional approach he recognized and gave us a way of dealing with this evil. However, Bobby could not talk as fast as he was thinking, even though he often tried. It seemed that his mind was always rushing, going jet-like from idea to idea, leaving most people on the bus of a wasted Western culture. He was fire and energy, thoroughly original, possessor of a monumental mind in a sea of lobotomized small thinkers.

He focused and unsettled us. In his short life, he seldom spoke of his own future. He knew of a death worse than personal physical passing, that of a people unaware of their own promise. Dr. Wright was a thorn in the brains of Black men and women posing as leaders. In many of them he diagnosed a deep dishonor that disqualified them for their trusted positions. His last words were a warning to his friends and associates, "Watch the leadership, especially those proclaiming *their* God-given answer to the problems of Black people."

He was a fighter within the eye of the volcano,
a listener in the midst of the hurricane,
a lover unafraid of giving tears of laughter,
a scientist seeking bright and moving moments,
a deliverer of truth within the truth,
a tree displaying roots and beauty,
a good and honest man,
carrying wisdom,
carrying future.

It is an honor to publish him.

My introduction to Dr. Wright's collection of essays, *Psychopathic Racial Personality and other Essays*.

262

Nothing Black but a Cadillac:

Color, Power and Identity in America

Color, economics and other cultural manifestations are what separate people in the United States. Most people of color, regardless of consciousness, see the pigmentation of their skin as the major reason for exclusion, denial, stereotyping, caricature, bigotry and racism. People of Afrikan descent are designated by people in the dominating culture in the United States as negroes, niggers, coloreds, Black so-and-sos or slaves. Generally, the "place" of a Black person is decided before his or her educational, economic or political status is known. White America and *all* of the Western world think and act in *color.*

Culture, biology and class differences are crucial definers of people. However, in the United States, a person's color impacts on his or her present and future in such a way that money, no matter how much a person has, is at best a tonic that cannot cure the disease of white world supremacy (racism); but like most "drugs," money can temporarily arrest the deadly bite. Racism has done serious damage to the psyches of all people. Whether one observes the Untouchables of Asia, the dark-skinned people of Europe and America or the Blacks and "coloreds" of South Afrika, the common battle fought by all of them on a daily basis is one of survival and development in a world that judges and categorizes them, first and foremost, by the pigmentation of their skin. This is a worldwide phenomenon, but it is most pronounced in white-dominated societies like the United States, Canada, Europe, Australia, U.S.S.R. and South Afrika.

In this century, it was Marcus Garvey, W.E.B. Du Bois, Carter G. Woodson, E. Franklin Frazier, Frantz Fanon, Malcolm X and others who articulated the duality and finality that color plays on the Western conscience. The inability of most people of Afrikan descent, (i.e., Black people) to accurately define themselves within, as well as apart from, the dominating white (Euro-American) culture speaks loudly to how victims accommodate themselves to the oppressor's worldview. Such accommodation is beyond acculturation; it's mental slavery without chains. The internalization and acceptance of white people's values, life-style, desires, worldview, (i.e., culture) with little selectivity, has been defined as *seasoning*. The clearest example of this mindset is working at a worldwide level each day as Black people battle with themselves and their biology to look like, act like and talk like white people. This is most evident in Black people's efforts to straighten their hair and lighten their skin. And, this sickness is not confined to the Western Hemisphere. Recently, the *Los Angeles Times* (12-6-88) in an article by Mawusi Afele, a Ghana-based writer, reported that "skin-bleaching continues to be popular among women in the West African country despite warnings from doctors that it is a dangerous practice." However, this bleaching of one's face is not indigenous to West Afrika; it started here in the "good old USA" by 20th century negroes.

Taylor Branch in his *Parting the Waters*, a massive study of Martin Luther King and the Civil Rights struggle, states, "...almost as color defines vision itself, race shapes the culture eye — what we do and do not notice, the reach of empathy and the alignment of response. This subliminal force recommends care in choosing a point of view for a history grounded in race." The white response to the majority of the world's people, who are not white, is indeed grounded in race. More than any other factor in the Eurocentric context, *race* defines, categorizes, tracks, destroys and redefines cultures. The color question in America has a way of driving most people into silliness and/or madness.

The word *Black* as defined by non-Black people (as well as millions of Black people) is still: devious, dark, soiled, dirty, forbidding, disastrous, amoral, evil, wicked, sinful, fiendish, inhuman, treacherous and diabolic. Many Afrikan Americans still instruct their daughters not to marry men darker than they are. Those whom many Blacks call "Black-Black" or "jet Black" men, as well as dark-skinned women, are still back-seated and made to stand in the "shadow" of light-skinned people. When some of our children are upset with each other, the invectives they call each other are often preceded by the word *Black* as in, "You Black bitch," or "Black son-of-a-bitch," or "You Black mother fucker," etc. Who has not heard and repeated the popular folk put-down of Black people:

> if you're white you're alright
> yellow you're mellow,
> brown stick around, but if
> you're Black step back.

The point of all this is that we must be very careful not to go back to the pre-sixties and let the word *Black*, the description we selected for ourselves, revert without question or opposition to its most common negative uses. "Black" for us is a *political designation*. We've always said that "Black" is synonymous with Afrika and, therefore, represents a particular history and culture.

The argument that no one is really white or Black is irrelevant when culturally the color symbols have reached the height of political myths, and these myths have been accepted as truths. To exclusively define Black people in the United States as Afrikan American only denies history, culture and reality. If one truly understands the multi-ethnic, multilingual, multi-religious (i.e., multi-cultural) continent that Afrika is, one realizes that what is really called for are accurate definitions. If we are really Afrikans — as I believe we are — what does that mean?

In terms of cultural diversity, Afrika is at the apex of complexity. Afrika is not homogeneous. From the Arab-dominated north to the European-controlled south to the Afrikan-populated middle, Afrikans have yet to reach a consensus on something as vital as a continent-wide workable definition of Pan-Afrikanism. However, the question for Black people in America is, "What part of Afrika do our foreparents come from?" Are we Nigerians, Ghanaians, Tanzanians, Kenyans or Ethiopians? Are we the daughters and sons of Algeria, Libya, Chad, Zambia, Angola, Zimbabwe or Liberia? What language(s) have we lost? Is our natural tongue Fanti, Ga, Hausa, Ibo, Swahili, Shona, Tswana, Zulu or Kamba? According to Kofi Awoonor in his *The Breast of the Earth*, there are about 800 major languages in Afrika. Yes, Blacks in America are Afrikan people, but is there, or should there be, more to that definition? I think the answer is that we don't know. Therefore, do we accept and identify with all of Afrika? I think the answer to that is yes, but it still is an incomplete answer.

When white people in the United States recognize their respective ethnic backgrounds, they are Polish Americans, Irish Americans, Italian Americans, Jewish Americans, etc. Most of the time they simply refer to themselves as white, but they do not see a conflict in using both terms. Seldom do white Americans define themselves as European Americans. Most whites in America do have some memory or connection to their former homelands and wouldn't dare define themselves as something as ambiguous as the entire continent — European Americans. In fact, if it weren't for Black people, whites in the United States — if we can believe their history — would be at each other's throats. The glue that keeps white people "together" is Black people. Toni Morrison, in a recent *Time* interview (5-22-89), states it this way:

...black people have always been used as a buffer in this country between powers to prevent class war, to prevent other kinds of real conflagrations. If there were no black people here in this country, it would have been Balkonized. The immigrants would have torn each other's throats out, as they have done everywhere else. But in becoming American, from Europe, what one has in common with that other immigrant is contempt for *me* — it's nothing but color.

The point I'm trying to make is that "Black" as a designation of a people, of course, is not accurate if we naively conceive of the Afrikan American presence here without a specific history and racial context. However, the historical, political and cultural reality of the United States is that color has always been *the* overriding issue here and in much of the world. Therefore, if Black is, indeed, a political reality rather than a "human" one, should not Black people control such a reality? And politics, in the final analysis, is the acquisition, use and distribution of power. It seems to me that our focus should be on taking any political reality that affects us and making it work for us, on our own terms. This is partially what the struggle of the sixties was about — *redefinition.*

People who have dark skin, which is a genetic and biological condition, have been defined as negative by white people worldwide. Would it not be in Black people's interest (especially that of their children), and in keeping with today's geopolitical construction, to take such a reality and make it *positive*? Most certainly white people, who are European, are not giving up or running from "white." Why? They've defined "white" as *the best of everything*, and most of the world has bought into their political definition. Poet and thinker Gwendolyn Brooks put this perspective in a manner that we all can understand in her essay "Requiem Before Revival:"

I give whites big credit. They have never tried to be anything but what they are. They have been and will be everlastingly proud proud proud to be white. It has never occurred to them that there has been or ever will be ANYthing better than, nor one zillionth as good as, being white. They have an overwhelming belief in their validity.

266

Not in their "virtue," for they are shrewdly capable of a very cold view of *that*. But their validity they salute with an amazing innocence — yes, a genuine innocence, the brass of which befuddles most of the rest of us in the world because we have allowed ourselves to be hypnotized by its shine.

The key, of course, is that all political realities in part depend upon how a people, any people, defines itself and struggles to actualize a worldview it considers *necessary for its development or beauty*.

Dark-skinned people, Black people, if you will, should be moving toward greater accuracy and extension. We are an Afrikan people that has been scattered and brought to this land. We must not ever forget that the horror perpetuated on us was not only an economic move by white people, but our people also represented the exact opposite of the white (European) worldview. In their destruction and denigration of us, white people found themselves, for we, in color and life-style, did not and could not fit the European (white) model. The two things that people of Afrikan descent share are *color* and *negative experiences with white people*. Whether we wish to accept it or not, our Blackness is now a political, historical (i.e., cultural) reality in this land. Not using "Black" doesn't mean that it will go away.

We cannot give up "Black" as long as it is not redemptive and as natural and/or lifegiving as water. We must use "Afrikan American" because it does connect us to land, history, culture that do represent our source, spirit and soul. We are an Afrikan people, but we are also part of a larger Afrikan community worldwide that has suffered mainly because we are Black. It was Gwendolyn Brooks who stated, "I share *Family*hood with Blacks wherever they may be. I am a *Black*, and I capitalize my name." If Afrikan people controlled the images of this world, this perspective wouldn't be necessary. Until that day, the choice is not either/or but an intelligent use of both, "Afrikan American" and "Black" with a capital "B."

Final Words/World

Question: Do I think all white people are racist, evil, bad and corrupt? No, but those who are are clearly in the majority and are the ones who hold power and determine the future of my children and my neighbors' children. The oppressed in the United States have the unusual quality of looking evil in the eye and denying its existence. This quality is not genetic, it is learned. To be a part of an oppressed culture is to be hidden from knowledge, from knowing.

Wendell Berry's *The Hidden Wound* confirmed for me that there are some white men of good will who are quietly and loudly talking to their own people about the "wound" of racism. However, talk is fine and books attacking racism are great, but the key to enlightenment is to interest the majority of white people, especially those who have power, in looking at their own history as honestly and as brutally as possible and initiating life-giving and life-saving corrections. I know that the great majority of whites cannot and will not do this, and herein lies the problem; enlightened words are like tear drops in a desert if they are not heard.

Four recent books (*Racial Matters: The FBI's File on Black America, 1960-1972; The Silent Brotherhood: Inside American's Racist Underground; With Justice For None;* and *Brotherhood of Murder*) confirm the validity of my position: white America would rather destroy itself from the inside than share power, wealth or influence with "former slaves." The FBI's annual "Uniform Crime Reports" clearly points out that the main criminals in the United States are white people. From drugs to white collar crimes, from homocide to organized crime, white men are the reigning kings. Yet, Black men are portrayed day after day on television, in newspapers, and in magazines as the chief thieves and boogiemen in the country. That's like saying the main predator of the elephant is the mosquito.

I hope that this book has been helpful to the reader in his/her consideration of another point of view concerning the status of Black people. I would like to think that my views are realrooted. I didn't have a grant or research monies to write this book. Eleven years (off and on) of work went between these covers. After completing *Enemies: The Clash of*

Races in 1978, I was "whitelisted." Speaking engagements and poetry readings across the country were cancelled, and I found myself without employment for about a year. Whether or not I'll be whitelisted as a result of this book doesn't really matter. Sometimes change only comes after a shaking up. I'm reminded of the words of Doris Lessing from her book, *Prisons We Choose to Live Inside*:

> It is particularly hard for young people, faced with what seem like impervious walls of obstacles, to have belief in their ability to change things, to keep their personal and individual viewpoints intact. I remember very clearly how it seemed to me in my late teens and early twenties, seeing only what seemed to be impregnable systems of thought, of belief - governments that seemed unshakeable. But what has happened to those governments like the white government in Southern Rhodesia, for instance? To those powerful systems of faith, like the Nazis, or the Italian Fascists, or to Stalinism? To the British Empire ... to all the European empires, in fact, so recently powerful? They have all gone, and in such a short time ... It is individuals who change societies, give birth to ideas, who, standing out against tides of opinion, change them. This is as true in open societies as it is in oppressive societies...

As a revolutionary poet/activist/intellectual, it is my responsiblity to challenge the state, to point out contradiction and hypocrisy, to offer solutions and to, if possible, be an example of one who lives an honorable life. I've grown tired of men who only demonstrate respect for Black women when they are trying to get something out of them. It is important that we be able to admit error (especially to Black women), learn from our errors, apologize if necessary, and keep on growing.

I'm not optimistic about the reception of *Black Men: Obsolete, Single, Dangerous?* because I do not think that America, in relationship to race, has matured very much since the sixties. Many people, Black and white, will deny the deadly role white world supremacy (racism) plays in the world and in the destruction of Black people. Hopefully, I have not excused the transgressions and limitations of my own people in this regard. We still have mountains to climb. The power of conscious and committed individuals is our major hope. Don't give up; remain activists. People are naturally innovative and creative. The beauty of jogging uphill is being able to run down the other side. I'm going to try to write some new poetry

now, continue to publish new and innovative Black writers, try to inspire
new students
and each day
meet the
sun with a
smile
as I attack
this ever present
mountain.

one love,

H.R.M.

Yes

for those that want:
every woman a man
every man a woman,
every person an education and willing work,
for all people
family, food, clothing, shelter, love,
frequent smiles and children swimming in glorious happiness.

for every elder a home, blooming health, few worries,
good teeth and fun-filled thank you's.
for all people,
liberating culture,
the full love of laughing children who
have been bathed in the caring eyes of
family, friends, nation.

for all people,
the inner glow that radiates peace and wisdom,
the confirming smiles of knowledge known,
the confident walk of music heard,
the quiet presence of having accepted and created beauty.

for Afrikan people
an unspoken understanding that
this is the center we gave the world

this is civilization.

About the Author

Haki R. Madhubuti is the Director of the Institute of Positive Education and Editor of Third World Press. The author of sixteen books of poetry, literary criticism, and essays, he has been poet - in- residence at Cornell University, Howard University, Central State University, and the University of Illinois - Circle Campus. He is the recipient of awards from the Illinois Arts Council and the National Endowment for the Arts. Recently his work has been highlighted on *CBS News Nightwatch,* National Public Radio's *All Things Considered, The Washington Post, The New York Times, Essence* magazine, *The Chicago Tribune, The MacNeil/Lehrer News Hour,* and Black Entertainment Television.

His published books are *Think Black* (1967), *Black Pride* (1968), *Don't Cry, Scream* (1969), *We Walk the Way of the New World* (1970), *Directionscore : Selected and New Poems* (1971), *To Gwen, With Love* edited with Francis Ward and Patricia L. Brown (1971), *Dynamite Voices: Black Poets of the 1960's* (1971), *Kwanzaa: A Progressive and Uplifting African-American Holiday* (1972), *From Plan To Planet* (1973), *Book of Life* (1973), *A Capsule Course in Black Poetry Writing* co-authored with Gwendolyn Brooks, Keorapetse Kgositsile and Dudley Randall (1975), *Enemies:The Clash of Races* (1978), *Earthquakes and Sunrise Missions* (1984), *Killing Memory, Seeking Ancestors* (1987), *Say That the River Turns: The Impact of Gwendolyn Brooks* (1987) and *Black Men: Obsolete, Single Dangerous? The Afrikan American Family in Transition* (1990).

Mr. Madhubuti earned his MFA from the University of Iowa and is a professor of English at Chicago State University. He lives in Chicago with his wife and children.

ALSO AVAILABLE FROM THIRD WORLD PRESS

Nonfiction

*The Destruction Of Black
Civilization: Great Issues
Of A Race From 4500 B.C.
To 2000 A.D.*
by Dr. Chancellor Williams $16.95

*The Cultural Unity Of
Black Africa*
by Cheikh Anta Diop $14.95

Home Is A Dirty Street
by Useni Eugene Perkins $9.95

*Black Men: Obsolete, Single,
Dangerous?*
by Haki R. Madhubuti $14.95

*From Plan To Planet
Life Studies: The Need
For Afrikan Minds And
Institutions*
by Haki R. Madhubuti $7.95

Enemies: The Clash Of Races
by Haki R. Madhubuti $12.95

*Kwanzaa: A Progressive And
Uplifting African-American
Holiday*
by Institute of Positive Education
Intro. by Haki R. Madhubuti $2.50

*Harvesting New Generations:
The Positive Development Of
Black Youth*
by Useni Eugene Perkins $12.95

*Explosion Of Chicago
Black Street Gangs*
by Useni Eugene Perkins $6.95

*The Psychopathic Racial
Personality And Other Essays*
by Dr. Bobby E. Wright $5.95

*Black Women, Feminism And Black
Liberation: Which Way?*
by Vivian V. Gordon $5.95

Black Rituals
by Sterling Plumpp $8.95

*The Redemption Of Africa
And Black Religion*
by St. Clair Drake $6.95

How I Wrote Jubilee
by Margaret Walker $1.50

A Lonely Place Against The Sky
by Dorothy Palmer Smith $7.95

Fiction

*Mostly Womenfolk And A Man
Or Two: A Collection*
by Mignon Holland Anderson $5.95

Sortilege (Black Mystery)
by Abdias do Nascimento $2.95

Poetry and Drama

To Disembark
by Gwendolyn Brooks $6.95

I've Been A Woman
by Sonia Sanchez $7.95

My One Good Nerve
by Ruby Dee $8.95

Geechies
by Gregory Millard $5.95

Earthquakes And Sunrise Missions
by Haki R. Madhubuti $8.95

Killing Memory: Seeking Ancestors
by Haki R. Madhubuti $8.00

Say That The River Turns:
The Impact Of Gwendolyn Brooks
(Anthology)
Ed.by Haki R. Madhubuti $8.95

Octavia And Other Poems
by Naomi Long Madgett $8.00

A Move Further South
by Ruth Garnett $7.95

Manish
by Alfred Woods $8.00

New Plays for the Black Theatre
(Anthology)
edited by Woodie King, Jr. $14.95

Children's Books

The Day They Stole
The Letter J
by Jabari Mahiri $3.95

The Tiger Who Wore
White Gloves
by Gwendolyn Brooks $5.00

A Sound Investment
by Sonia Sanchez $2.95

I Look At Me
by Mari Evans $2.50

Black Books Bulletin

A limited number of back issues
of this unique journal are available
at $3.00 each:

Vol. 1, Fall '71   Interview with
                   Hoyt W. Fuller

Vol. 1, No. 3   Interview with
                   Lerone Bennett, Jr.

Vol. 5, No. 3   Science & Struggle

Vol. 5, No. 4   Blacks & Jews

Vol. 7, No. 3   The South

Order from **Third World Press**
7524 S. Cottage Grove Ave.
Chicago, IL 60619

Shipping: Add $1.50 for first book
and .25 for each additional book.
Mastercard /Visa orders may be placed
by calling 1-312/651-0700

WORDSWORTH AND THE POETRY OF ENCOUNTER

Wordsworth

AND THE

Poetry of Encounter

FREDERICK GARBER

UNIVERSITY OF ILLINOIS PRESS

Urbana, Chicago, London

© 1971 by The Board of Trustees of the University of Illinois
Manufactured in the United States of America
Library of Congress Catalog Card No. 71-157888
ISBN 0-252-00184-2

To Marjorie, with thanks

Contents

Preface

IN HIS ESSAY "On Wordsworth and the Locke Tradition" in *The Seventeenth Century Background*, Basil Willey speaks of what Wordsworth had, perforce, to do when he set out to work in a world without myth: as the individual poet alone in an order he needed to rebuild for himself, Wordsworth had to make "a record of successes; of successful imaginative dealings with the world of eye and ear." [1] The purpose of this book is to say something about those successes, their limitations, and the meaning of the affirmations within them, and about how difficult it was for Wordsworth to earn any successes at all. Few were complete, and some were not nearly so. Indeed, there is a mode of Wordsworthian poetry which is about the chanciness of success, and one of the arguments of this book is that aspects of that mode find their way into most of the poems of Wordsworth's great decade, the years from 1798 to 1807. The difficulties involved in Wordsworth's experience have come more and more to be a concern of modern criticism of his work, and that movement is a healthy one. This criticism has nothing to do with neo-humanist attacks, which are now mainly history, though it also rejects much of the sense of Wordsworth's meaning put forth by a major predecessor of the neo-humanists who was one of Wordsworth's supporters, Matthew Arnold. By and large, most commentary on Wordsworth, and not only the most

[1] Basil Willey, *The Seventeenth Century Background* (1934; reprinted, New York: Doubleday Anchor, 1953), p. 301.

ix

routine material, has dealt with what David Ferry calls "the 'Arnoldian' tendency to take Wordsworth's vocabulary of feeling at face value, saying that he gave us back the simplicity and force of our emotions."[2] I feel, as do Ferry and others, that there are ways of understanding Wordsworth which can take into account the uneasiness apparent even in many of his greatest moments. It is probably with Raymond Dexter Havens's *The Mind of a Poet* (Baltimore: The Johns Hopkins Press, 1941) that this quality in Wordsworth's experience received the first elaborate charting of some of its contours, though Havens generally confined his remarks on that subject to the ministry of fear, which is primarily a childhood educative experience. There is, I think, a good deal more to the uneasiness than that, and what there is can be found even more sharply in Wordsworth's adult years as his capacity for knowing grew. Certainly we have come to see that there are more uncertainties in Wordsworth than those in childhood, more even than in the mature versions associated with the "Immortality" ode's nostalgia for lost forms of vision or in the sense of sad changes that comes out of the stanzas on Peele Castle. Key documents in this regard are John Jones's *The Egotistical Sublime* (London: Chatto and Windus, 1954) and Geoffrey Hartman's *Wordsworth's Poetry, 1787–1814* (New Haven: Yale University Press, 1964), though in the background are A. C. Bradley's essay in *Oxford Lectures on Poetry* (1909; reprinted, London: Macmillan, 1934) and G. Wilson Knight's great study "The Wordsworthian Profundity," in *The Starlit Dome* (1941; reprinted, London: Methuen, 1964). Clearly we should bring into question the idea of a warm, welcoming nature as a *pervasive* element in Wordsworth. This means, essentially, that the record of successes was not easy to come by.

The problems I deal with begin from Wordsworth's awareness of what shares the world with him. That awareness holds within itself several ways of knowing, most of which I touch upon to one degree or another. The argument, then, is about epistemology, though I have not felt it necessary to go into the

2 David Ferry, *The Limits of Mortality: An Essay on Wordsworth's Major Poems* (Middletown: Wesleyan University Press, 1959), p. ix.

material on Wordsworth's background dealt with in books such as Newton P. Stallknecht's *Strange Seas of Thought* (Bloomington: Indiana University Press, 1958), Melvin Rader's *Wordsworth. A Philosophical Approach* (Oxford: The Clarendon Press, 1967), and Arthur Beatty's *William Wordsworth. His Doctrine and Art in Their Historical Relations* (1927; 3rd ed., Madison: University of Wisconsin Press, 1960). These books suffice in themselves, and all readers of Wordsworth are in the debt of their authors.

The knowing I am most concerned with has to do with object-consciousness. Not all of the romantics have Wordsworth's sense of this, though Keats does very often, and Coleridge and Shelley have it in certain modes. Byron and Blake do not, for reasons that have much to do with their awareness of theme and archetype as structuring principles, ideas that are as romantic as any that Wordsworth and Keats hold. The obverse of object-consciousness, and it is a question I am particularly concerned with, is the activity of the speaker as witness of himself; this too is knowledge, and it is often in form startlingly like that which dwells with the presence of objects. I have not done more than touch lightly on the kinds and areas of knowledge that begin from a transcendence of sense experience, mainly because this is a very different mode from the subjects of my interest in this book.

One term perhaps needs some explanation. The poetry of object-consciousness is the poetry of a meeting. I use the term *encounter* somewhat technically, to mean not just a meeting but what is, in more than one sense, a confrontation. Encounter need not imply antipathy though it always points to a tension, an antagonism, simply because those elements which meet in an encounter are necessarily somewhat different. The closely associated idea of hierarchy has to do, to begin with, with the great chain of being, though the full meaning of hierarchy is by no means confined to that traditional structure. The relationship of these terms to the body of my argument will come clear as the study progresses. It begins with a long exploratory analysis of one poem to set up a limited paradigm which may not contain all of the variations but which is complete and suggestive in its outline. Wordsworth's fascination with what can be learned from a meeting with palpable immediacy is evidently somewhat contagious.

I quote throughout from *The Poetical Works of William Wordsworth*, ed. Ernest de Selincourt and Helen Darbishire, 5 vols. (Oxford: The Clarendon Press, 1940–49, Vol. II, 2nd ed. 1952), cited as *Poetical Works*. I use the 1850 text in *The Prelude*, ed. Ernest de Selincourt, 2nd ed. rev. by Helen Darbishire (Oxford: The Clarendon Press, 1959), but cite the 1805 text when it is relevant to my argument.

Permission has been granted for the use of previously published materials as follows: *Bucknell Review*, "Wordsworth and the Romantic Synecdoche," 1966; *English Studies*, "Point of View and the Egotistical Sublime," 1968; *Studies in Romanticism*, "Wordsworth at the Universal Dance," 1969. A section from Chapter Three was read at the 1969 meeting of the Modern Language Association. Several pages took their earliest form in a doctoral thesis under the direction of René Wellek, to whom I am grateful for his profound intellectual presence. The Research Foundation of the State University of New York helped to forward the preparation of the book with a summer research grant.

And Jacob was left alone; and there wrestled a man with him until the breaking of the day. And when he saw that he prevailed not against him, he touched the hollow of his thigh; and the hollow of Jacob's thigh was out of joint, as he wrestled with him. And he said, Let me go, for the day breaketh. And he said, I will not let thee go, except thou bless me. And he said unto him, What is thy name? And he said, Jacob. And he said, Thy name shall be called no more Jacob, but Israel: for as a prince hast thou power with God and with men, and hast prevailed. And Jacob asked him, and said, Tell me, I pray thee, thy name. And he said, Wherefore is it that thou dost ask after my name? And he blessed him there. And Jacob called the name of the place Peniel: for I have seen God face to face, and my life is preserved.

Genesis 32:24–30

C'est pourquoi je ne puis pas me perdre dans l'exaltation ou la simple définition d'une notion qui m'échappe et perd son sens à partir du moment où elle déborde le cadre de mon expérience individuelle. Je ne puis comprendre ce que peut être une liberté qui me serait donnée par un être supérieur. J'ai perdu le sens de la hiérarchie.

Camus, Le mythe de Sisyphe

> Could you have said the bluejay suddenly
> Would swoop to earth? It is a wheel, the rays
> Around the sun. The wheel survives the myths.
> The fire eye in the clouds survives the gods.
> To think of a dove with an eye of grenadine
> And pines that are cornets, so it occurs,
> And a little island full of geese and stars:
> It may be that the ignorant man, alone,
> Has any chance to mate his life with life
> That is the sensual, pearly spouse, the life
> That is fluent in even the wintriest bronze.
> Stevens, "The Sense of the Sleight-of-Hand Man"

CHAPTER ONE

Knowledge of Encounter

"The Solitary Reaper"

Behold her, single in the field,
Yon solitary Highland Lass!
Reaping and singing by herself;
Stop here, or gently pass!
Alone she cuts and binds the grain,
And sings a melancholy strain;
O Listen! for the Vale profound
Is overflowing with the sound.

No Nightingale did ever chaunt
More welcome notes to weary bands
Of travellers in some shady haunt,
Among Arabian sands:
A voice so thrilling ne'er was heard
In spring-time from the Cuckoo-bird,
Breaking the silence of the seas
Among the farthest Hebrides.

Will no one tell me what she sings?—
Perhaps the plaintive numbers flow
For old, unhappy, far-off things,
And battles long ago:
Or is it some more humble lay,
Familiar matter of to-day?
Some natural sorrow, loss, or pain,
That has been, and may be again?

Whate'er the theme, the Maiden sang
As if her song could have no ending;
I saw her singing at her work,
And o'er the sickle bending:—
I listened, motionless and still;
And, as I mounted up the hill,
The music in my heart I bore,
Long after it was heard no more.

Wordsworth's encounters with other people or with natural objects have a variety of dimensions about them to which this poem bears particular witness. The statement of the reaper's solitude in the title, while sufficient to point out that she is alone, cannot by itself carry the import her isolation holds for the entire situation. A partly alliterative series of words whose meanings intersect at a number of points—single, solitary, by herself, alone—emphasizes unobtrusively but with incessant reiteration that this object, the girl, is separated from all other similar objects, the presence of which would impinge upon her uniqueness in the situation. It is not so much that she becomes progressively more alone (although in a sense this does happen) as that each word forces her, with increasing intensity, toward the center of the observer's vision. Concurrent with this movement is another, set going by a different group of words joined alliteratively not only with each other but also with the first group—singing, sings, strain, and sound. As the observer becomes more aware of the intensity of the girl's isolation, he begins to perceive her not only as alone but as alone and singing, each of these aspects so much part of the other that they make a wholeness in themselves which leads into the greater wholeness of the girl in her context. Further, by pointing out that she reaps, cuts, and binds the grain, he places her in action; he does not, apparently, want the solitary singer to be removed from movement or to be disembodied.

Some of her characteristics, clearly, have been heightened and intensified, but very many more have no place whatsoever in the activity which is the encounter of the observer and the girl. Although the singer is placed solidly in her surroundings, she is in no way described as a *particular* individual (which is not to say that she loses her unqualified uniqueness). No ex-

4

ternal, personal features come through. Such a condensation of the qualities of the object in its context leaves only those characteristics which have a function in the encounter. The object becomes not so much more purely itself (it may, but this is not a Keatsian event of negative capability) as a pure distillation of what has meaning for the observer. The idiosyncrasies of the observer's perception, then, are not only determinative of what he sees but also self-reflecting and impossible to hide. In other words, the experience reflects less of the object than it could, while the observer becomes more aware of what is most personal about himself. The object never loses its integrity though, at least when the observer respects it, which in his great days Wordsworth usually did. For human figures the experience is less a departure from humanity (in fact, it may be a move closer to it) than from irrelevancy, while the observer, in a converse action of expansion, opens up a great deal of himself that may have been only latent had this odd meeting never occurred.

The high point of the encounter in "The Solitary Reaper" takes place on a level which is not below intellect but beyond it or cutting across it. Such a para-intellectual communion becomes possible here because the observer does not understand the language the girl is singing, Erse, and therefore has consciousness of the words not as fully elements of language but only as sound patterns supporting and reinforcing the other sound patterns within the melodic line of her song. Thus, even the song itself is stripped down to those radical elements which contribute their part to his total apprehension of the meaning of the whole encounter. Their contact (or rather, his contact with her) goes beyond the ordinary intellectual dimension of communion toward another level, which depends in part on the kind of imagery through which he places her in the context. The girl's singing is compared not to that of other people but to the sounds of birds; she is linked to the animal world, though not in quite the way that the leech-gatherer, through the images of rock and sea-beast, becomes for a while something other than human. In "The Solitary Reaper" the creatures are mentioned partly to show that she is not at all like them but is something else altogether, even if human song and bird song

5

are at some points analogous. (The effect in "Resolution and Independence" is similar but is achieved differently.) This girl never ceases to be human, not only because of what he can see of her but primarily because what she sings is of basic human concern. Or at least he guesses it is, since he cannot really know; but this affirms only a gently ironic undertone, a running, good-humored qualification that should never be entirely ignored.

At every point in such situations there is the difficulty of maintaining the necessary discreteness of the object during the process of encounter, at the same time as the object undergoes the transformation the whole encounter forces upon it. One of the ways this is done is to keep discovering alien elements within the object which put it either in another realm of being or, more simply, in a different section of humanity, such as a child or a foreign girl. The thoroughly familiar too easily becomes wholly a part of us, while the intensified awareness of difference tends to objectify and make distinct. Indeed, the swamping of the object by the self is an unusual occurrence in the poetry of Wordsworth's great decade because the encounter as he experiences it depends as much upon what happens to the things outside as upon what happens to him. Both poles have to be affected to forestall the dangers of solipsism, which creates another kind of situation with another kind of meaning that cannot be the meaning of an encounter. Wordsworth takes seriously the need to protect the integrity of the object, partly because his own integrity (i.e., his true place in the situation) has very much to do with the integrity of the objects he sees outside of himself. Along with this impulse to protect the object goes his fascination with the dialectic within the meetings which are truly encounters between himself and what he is not. Observing, as Wordsworth shows it happening, is no static confrontation. The encounter begins with one way of seeing which leads to others, varied in scope, meaning, and quality but all offering an increase in special kinds of knowledge which open up more of his surroundings as well as more of himself.

In this and similar poems, because the experiences they describe cannot be static, Wordsworth has to make the "I" a protagonist, a participant in an action (which may or may not be a narrative) and not merely an observer. In the first stanza of

6

"The Solitary Reaper," the speaker looks on at things outside of himself, saying nothing about the fact that he cannot understand the girl's song and pointing out only as much of what is immediately present to him as is necessary to show that she and he are in a particular kind of place together. He is standing at one spot, probably on the hill referred to later, watching her in the field which is part of a vale that hints at depths ("profound") beyond where they are now. The second stanza moves rapidly into something exotic and strange (his choice of illustration emphasizing his remoteness from the object and thus its discreteness), but the shift in location indicates mainly that he has gone from looking outward to looking within. Her physical actions, of which a fuller description would have tied him more closely to the scene, took a subsidiary role in the previous stanza, and thus it was easier for him to shift inward without any noticeably harsh juncture. The reader focuses mainly on what the observer is musing about rather than on where he is musing from. Then, in the third stanza, some aspects of the immediate moment and circumstances return sharply with the line "Will no one tell me what she sings?" and they bring with them the high point in the intensity of his desire to understand her song. Yet the stanza is only minimally concrete. He is still in the grip of the communion induced by the encounter, still to a great degree within himself, although now more of what is immediately external to him enters in than it did in the second stanza. Though far enough out of the mood so that he can be eager to know the meaning of her song, he is by no means out of it completely. With the appearance of a balanced and actively concrete interplay of inner and outer, and thus a drifting away of the contemplation and a loosening of the tension of the encounter, the poem comes full circle. The action that had been frozen starts again as the girl goes on reaping and he leaves.

Wordsworth uses the comparative absence or presence of the immediately felt physicality of the scene to denote the degree to which perception is directed inward, toward the observer's consciousness and the images that flash within him, or outward, toward the girl and her surroundings. In other words, we watch not only the girl but the whole complex of activities involved in the poet's watching of the girl, the effect the encounter has upon him. His activity of seeing dances around the object, clearing it of the irrelevant, seeing himself and it together with the focus moving from the object to his sense of other kinds and places and then back to the object again. Thus, the movement in and out of the self of the protagonist is only one of a number of movements in other dimensions that dance in a delicate counterpoint in Wordsworth's poem. For example, in the second stanza the girl is seen as a focal point in space (between the Arabian sands and the Hebrides) and, in the third stanza, in time. A variety of ways of seeing and organizing the results of sight come to a center at this girl. The pressure of each of these ways coming, with its own intensity, to meet the others at this one point brings the communion to a terrifying pitch and exalts the girl more than any mere statement could. It is as if the presence that rolls through all things had arrived at a point of ultimate intensity in her. The stranger, the outsider, watches her and sees the complex harmony of the dimensions which surround and lead toward the figure of the girl. Ultimately he reaches a highly pitched moment, the fleetingness of which is partly overcome by what the moment does to him. He never ceases to be a stranger, but the possibility of a kind of communion—imperfect and transient but possible nevertheless—has been verified through the occurrence. No absolute union can take place, no full identification with the object, no giving up of his self in order to understand hers fully. Her discreteness is never in question; nor for that matter—and this will bring pain later—is his.

Out through the center of his experience—that is, as he stares at the girl and his vision takes motion—there moves an expanding awareness which enlarges areas of knowledge within him and without. From the girl as center he comes to see an immense wholeness, with the bleak, damp, cold Hebrides on one side and their opposite in the Arabian sands, with a spectrum including man and animals (united in the act of singing), and with a movement from past time to present through a song which seemingly has no ending. The whole pattern is classically Wordsworthian. Even some of the briefer lyrics, such as the one on daffodils or "A Night-Piece," hold centers within themselves which open into a variously denoted but thoroughly consistent series of dimensions. Still, the variety of modes of expansion seems limited only by the number and complexity of the kinds of experience possible to him. The mode familiar from "Tintern Abbey," for example, appears several times in *The Prelude*, but on the whole there seem to be few experiences recorded in his work which share the general characteristics of that mode. It is surely erroneous to call the process in "Tintern Abbey" a mystic experience, since there is in it no ultimate union (there neither is nor can be at any stage in Wordsworth's development), but it does offer an analogy to numerous forms of religious ecstasy. His awareness of physicality, first that of outside objects and then his own, diminishes to the point where only the most essential functions still hold:

> Until, the breath of this corporeal frame
> And even the motion of our human blood
> Almost suspended, we are laid asleep
> In body

and he becomes *almost* a pure consciousness, holding lightly but firmly onto livingness through his not quite extinguished functions, the comparative purification of which does much to guarantee the coalescence of his own life with the life within things. Such passages turn out to be about himself rather than about what he sees, primarily because what he sees can only be recorded, not demonstrated. There is another, equally familiar instance in Book Four of *The Prelude*, where, though he says nothing about an insight into universal life, his soul moves effortlessly into what seems to be a state of purity:

> Gently did my soul
> Put off her veil, and, self-transmuted, stood
> Naked, as in the presence of her God.
> While on I walked, a comfort seemed to touch
> A heart that had not been disconsolate:
> Strength came where weakness was not known to be,
> At least not felt; and restoration came
> Like an intruder knocking at the door
> Of unacknowledged weariness.
>
> (150–158)

Here are all the negations in the rhetoric of the mystic way, but the language is that of analogy only: his soul does what it does *as* in her God's presence. The focus is necessarily on process, not on whatever it is he came to know. Further, there is here, as in "Tintern Abbey," a hold onto functions which are still, though just barely, working; there is no unequivocal removal from palpability:

> —Of that external scene which round me lay,
> Little, in this abstraction, did I see.
>
> (160–161)

The further he gets from palpability, the less he has to say about what he sees; but however far he gets in this special mode among the possibilities in his experience, he still, in some way, usually leaves a fingertip touching at substance. Those childhood experiences in which the senses absolutely blanked out are not, then, the same as this kind. But even in those experiences a barely concealed fear drives him to grope at walls and trees, to touch physicality with love and fright. He seems always to have been aware of all the meanings of being out of one's senses.

Neither of these modes of experience is like the spots of time, prominent in part from Wordsworth's theorizing about them, where there is an extraordinarily intense sensitivity to the immediacy of the presence of things outside of him—things animate or inanimate but always occupying palpability, like the girl with a pitcher on her head or "the single sheep, and the one blasted tree." Of yet another kind (and quite unlike the spots, with their tendency to apocalyptic vision) are those moments of which Wordsworth spoke to De Quincey, when the sudden cessation of any kind of intense observation or expectation leads to an instantaneous, unexpected, and penetrating awareness of some other thing or things that fall into his view. His comment to De Quincey hints at special claims for what he could perceive under these circumstances, "a pathos and a sense of the Infinite, that would not have arrested me under other circumstances." [1] The claims, however, are only now and then borne out in poems based on such a pattern of action, where a strained attentiveness, either physical or perhaps only a rapt attention to oneself, stops very abruptly and is followed by a moment of un-

---

[1] Thomas De Quincey, "William Wordsworth," in *Literary Reminiscences* (Boston: Ticknor and Fields, 1861), I, 314–315.

usual apprehension. Events as various as the skating scene in Book One of *The Prelude*, the lover's journey to his lady in "Strange Fits of Passion," or the walk in "A Night-Piece" show a pattern like this, a sequence of events, the plot of which is the same in each case whatever the difference in specifics. But a sense of the infinite can be found in the first two of these, the skating scene and "Strange Fits of Passion," only with the most unusual insight and probably with very little accuracy. More relevant to the hungry expansion of consciousness of which Wordsworth spoke to De Quincey is the relationship of "A Night-Piece" to the ascent up Mt. Snowdon. In these cases, and especially in the ascent, all that Wordsworth claims is borne out.[2]

Still, whatever the differences among these modes and whether or not they involved the removal of physicality, each was clearly and primarily an affair of significant epistemological excitement. They could include a vision of apocalypse, a steady gaze into the life of things, or merely the recognition of the sudden beauty of a star; but every one shaped out an increase in what he could know and therefore what he could be and do. Of the making of self there is no end, though it complicates in tone as he moves out from the making at the beginning:

> Many are our joys
> In youth, but oh! what happiness to live
> When every hour brings palpable access
> Of knowledge, when all knowledge is delight,
> And sorrow is not there!
>
> *(Prelude, II, 284–288)*

Every circumstance of excited self added something to him. Wordsworth tends to use images of assimilation, especially of food, to describe those occurrences when he is aware of what is happening.[3] His greedy soul demanded a continual accretion

---

[2] The similarity of "A Night-Piece" and the passage on the ascent has been noted by James Kissane in "'A Night Piece': Wordsworth's Emblem of the Mind," *MLN*, 71 (1956), 183–186.

[3] For example, *The Excursion*, I, 205–210:

> Sound needed none,
> Nor any voice of joy; his spirit drank
> The spectacle: sensation, soul, and form,

of experience at a number of levels, preferably at the highest available, though ultimately of any kind so long as he had some form of intense experience and therefore more knowledge of what was outside of him. All this was due, in part at least, to his primary and incessant interest in what was inside of him, which he knew more about as he discovered more of the meaning of external things. In Book Five of *The Prelude* he called such knowing "knowledge not purchased by the loss of power," certainly in contrast to the kind bought by the Moralist characters in "A Poet's Epitaph":

> to whose smooth-rubbed soul can cling
> Nor form, nor feeling, great or small;
> A reasoning, self-sufficing thing,
> An intellectual All-in-all!

One of the meanings of power for Wordsworth was the capacity (quite literally) for imaginative experience.[4] It was power in this sense that the characters in "A Poet's Epitaph" slowly gave up as their souls lost the roughness that implies receptivity.

In a curious shift of metaphor from smoothness to restriction, Wordsworth points out very frequently that the only reprehensible kind of knowledge is that which leads to shrinking of self. Both metaphors are present in "A Poet's Epitaph," which speaks of an "ever-dwindling soul." He had established the metaphor of expansion early, in relation to the hunt for sublime images during his walking tour in Europe with Robert Jones. He writes to Dorothy in September 1790: "It is the end of travelling by communicating ideas to enlarge the mind; God forbid that I should stamp upon mine the strongest proof of a

---

> All melted into him; they swallowed up
> His animal being; in them did he live,
> And by them did he live; they were his life.

Herbert Lindenberger argues that Wordsworth draws the image of nourishment from Boehme and the Christian mystics through Coleridge; see *On Wordsworth's Prelude* (Princeton: Princeton University Press, 1963), pp. 308–309.

[4] See Raymond Dexter Havens, *The Mind of a Poet* (1941; 2nd printing, Baltimore: The Johns Hopkins Press, 1951), II, 472–473.

contracted spirit." [5] He carried the idea into a discussion of *The Excursion* in 1815: "The soul, dear Mrs. C. may be re-given when it had been taken away, my own Solitary is an instance of this; but a soul that has been dwarfed by a course of bad culture cannot after a certain age, be expanded into on[e] of even ordinary proportion." [6] And the old comments (and punishment) from "A Poet's Epitaph" echo deep into *The Excursion* itself:

> Enquire of ancient Wisdom; go, demand
> Of mighty Nature, if 'twas ever meant
> That we should pry far off yet be unraised;
> That we should pore, and dwindle as we pore,
> Viewing all objects unremittingly
> In disconnection dead and spiritless.
>
> (IV, 957–962)

It appears, then, that the palpable access which leads to a knowledge of self leads also to an increase in self, the images dwelling on expansion as though he were growing fat on experience. The imagery of capaciousness in the quotations just above is repeated in a variety of moods in *The Prelude*, which shows how the self can increase, with finesse and subtlety, its capacities for response: "Thus daily were my sympathies enlarged" (1805 version, II, 181). Indeed, such knowledge could do nothing but increase itself merely by being itself, since it led to power and thus to a further capacity for more of the same kinds of knowledge and power again. Its possibilities seemed to be without end. Certainly nothing seems to have convinced Wordsworth that his sense of their endlessness was the last deception of all, though he may have guessed at it: "as the mind grows serious from the weight of life, the range of its passions is contracted accordingly." That, without irony (and

---

[5] *The Letters of William and Dorothy Wordsworth. I. The Early Years. 1787–1805*, ed. Ernest de Selincourt, 2nd ed. rev. by Chester L. Shaver (Oxford: The Clarendon Press, 1967), p. 32. Hereafter cited as *Early Years*.

[6] *The Letters of William and Dorothy Wordsworth. III. The Middle Years. Part 2, 1812–1820*, ed. Ernest de Selincourt, 2nd ed. rev. by Mary Moorman and Alan G. Hill (Oxford: The Clarendon Press, 1970), p. 188. Hereafter cited as *Middle Years*, Part 2.

sadly without the recognition of the need for it), is from the "Essay, Supplementary to the Preface" of 1815.

How the knowing takes place varies in detail from one situation to another, depending in part on the internal state of the observer, in part on what happens to him and what causes it to happen. In "Resolution and Independence" the fluctuating stability in his moods combines with the strangeness of the old man and with the specifics of landscape to make possible the quality of vision in the meeting of his own uncertainties with the thorough certainties of the old man. "The Solitary Reaper" particularizes still a different set of circumstances: the stranger in a strange land gropes for certainties at a level of discourse lower than the one on which certainty (which is partly a knowledge of their shared humanity) is actually given to him. He has to break through, by accepting it, the impossibility of knowing the details of her song, and what he learns he could not have learned without that effort. The power that comes from such knowledge is ordinarily defined first in the food the situation offers and later, perhaps, in the shape of a poem. One of the central activities in "The Solitary Reaper" is the manifestation of the learning he goes through as he shifts in attentiveness to the things outside of himself. Each event in the increase of self is as unique as what he learns from it.

The process of the intensification and extension of awareness is therefore a process of encounter. In it the self comes to meet something outside (some aspect of a person or an object—something); it is an event in which the self may break through to a fleeting, incomplete, but definite understanding of something about the world of the other, an understanding which can result in a permanent increase of self and its knowledge. Both late and early he saw limitations, of different kinds depending on the source. But in every case such heightening as there was came out of the activities in the process, and the consciousness of consciousness was his awareness that he was going through it. In the activity of encounter, and coming out of it, is the energy which, controlled and channeled, could lead the experience into the wholeness of shape of a poem.

The lineaments of the encounter seem clear enough. The observer comes upon an object which, because he and the object carry their idiosyncrasies into a (therefore) idiosyncratic meeting, affects him in a way for which no previous meeting could prepare him. It often affects him with an impulse, sometimes painful in its urgency, sometimes hardly noticeable at all, to establish some conditions through which he could get into the object's world. From a number of Wordsworth's poems in which the impulse is not only conscious but also eager, it would seem that overtness of intention leads, if not to a failure of understanding, at least to its surprising establishment on a level other than the one on which the observer is consciously working. If the mute stones speak for Wordsworth, it is not always because he kicks them. His struggle to understand the reaper's song is fruitless; his awareness of their shared humanity reaches him at a far more profound level. The passionate, agonized attempt to establish some kind of relationship with emblems of spring in the "Immortality" ode leads to a failure, and eventually to a series of affirmations which may have only a verbal reality. On the other hand, the lyric on daffodils shows him to be quite aware of the process as it is happening to him; he recognizes only one aspect of it, that he is a bit happier now than before he saw the flowers. Only later, in that case and others, does full recognition come. We do know that the observer has to be in a state of readiness for the experience (though he is never aware that he is), a state which surely cannot be willed into being since the element of surprise is so often essential for encounter to start happening. If there is expectation, as in the process described to De Quincey, it is nearly always an expectation of something very different from what he is actually going to meet. He cannot know that he is about to encounter something quite other than himself, something that will surprise him into an impulse no less compelling because he may be unaware of being compelled. And when he does meet the object—the field of daffodils, the soldier, the voice of a woman calling a greeting in a strange land, the moon shining over Mt. Snowdon—the result does not take long to come about, although the fullest effect may not be recognizable for some time. Cassirer speaks of a somewhat related experience as being like a spark jumping a gap in a flash of intense emotion.[7] A transient and inimitable encounter occurs, and it brings together into a momentary situation of wholeness (never of a blending of identities) the disparate and discrete worlds of the observer and the observed, creating a continuity between them which may leave pain or joy for a memory, but creating it nonetheless. Understanding takes place at some level, for only a moment but certainly for at least that moment. A number of tensions had been building up until then, based perhaps on his loneliness or other uncertainties, on what he should be feeling at that moment and cannot, or, quite differently, on simply an excess of exuberant delight. The causes are various, but the tension is always there and always finds an equal and opposite tension coming at it from outside, possibly not seeking him (that important point is always at question) but finding him all the same. Curiously, but consistent with the whole pattern, those rare situations in which Wordsworth does put off physicality, because they do not depend on an encounter with anything, lack the impression of a tension coming from the opposite direction, although there may well be an influx of knowledge and power all the same. The following is worth requoting for this context:

> Gently did my soul
> Put off her veil, and, self-transmuted, stood
> Naked, as in the presence of her God.
> While on I walked, a comfort seemed to touch
> A heart that had not been disconsolate:
> Strength came where weakness was not known to be,
> At least not felt; and restoration came
> Like an intruder knocking at the door
> Of unacknowledged weariness.
>
> (*Prelude*, IV, 150–158)

In response to an external object, then, Wordsworth rises to what can only be called a moment of exaltation. His reactions are as variable as what he sees and what he is. They range from the several kinds of fear involved in *The Prelude* and elsewhere (the fear in the boat-stealing scene is actually quite different

[7] Ernst Cassirer, *Language and Myth*, trans. Susanne K. Langer (New York: Harper, 1946), p. 33.

from that in "Nutting") to his complex delight in the daffodils and in the imaginative junction of the existent and the historical in "Yew-Trees." The tonality is always unique. Unrepeatable but not necessarily inexpressible, the variations depend on the supple, shifting nature of the thing out there and on the equally flexible and mobile mood of the observer. Clearly, such an experience could not be redone, not only because it could not have been predicted or expected or chosen but also because the combination of circumstances is simply too farfetched to achieve again. All such experiences are primary in the sense that they offer the necessary conditions for an act that could lead to the making of a poem. But they are primary also in being a kind of experience so unique and oddly naïve that no parallels (or, in some cases, antecedents) can be thought of. Each event has that sort of naïveté which can come about only through an extension of sophisticated awareness. The observer, in fact, can be so moved by the unpredictability that he may pretend to transfer all of its uniqueness to himself—in part, it would seem, because he can feel more comfortable and accurate in asserting his own uniqueness than he can in asserting the uniqueness of anything else. In his delight he rarely forgets his ignorance. It then appears, or at least he claims that it does, that no other receptive self had ever existed. He can thus parody Genesis and the Rousseau of the *Rêveries* both at once:

> You look round on your Mother Earth,
> As if she for no purpose bore you;
> As if you were her first-born birth,
> And none had lived before you!

The self is not everything that it experiences, but it is just as unique as the experiences it runs through. The result for Wordsworth is a poetry which is concrete and self-concerned, the paradoxical incarnation of the plot of a moment of experience beyond expectation or repetition.

The exaltation of the moment of encounter drives the observer to an extreme pitch of consciousness of all that he sees and of himself in that context. The experience expands the normal bounds of awareness, and as the intensity subsides, it leads into a withdrawal that is partly a retreat but not fully one, because the normal bounds had probably spread out to include the new areas of awareness. In "The Solitary Reaper" a movement parallel to and in some ways identical with the learning process referred to earlier flows inward from concreteness and then back again to the song and history and finally to the observer's departure from the scene. Keats offers a version of this radical pattern in "Ode to a Nightingale" but complicates the pattern by having the speaker transported, in fancy, to the center from which the song radiates, in an effort to force the encounter onto another level which would make possible a knowledge beyond what seems to be offered to him. Because of a sudden withdrawal—"Forlorn! the very word is like a bell / To toll me back from thee to my sole self!"—he has to return to the garden in Hampstead, while the bird goes off in another direction:

> Adieu! adieu! thy plaintive anthem fades
> Past the near meadows, over the still stream,
> Up the hill-side; and now 'tis buried deep
> In the next valley-glades.

The drama of the encounter, its inevitable frustrations and probably inevitable areas of misunderstanding, and all the pain of necessary withdrawal are nowhere more clearly urged than here: "Was it a vision, or a waking dream? / Fled is that music: —Do I wake or sleep?"

In Keats's poem the tension is not resolved but takes another form, appropriate to the nature of the special experience that had unfolded. With Wordsworth, however, the encounter ordinarily comes full circle, and the observer, as the pressure gradually eases, becomes temporarily composed. Each of the participants in the experience settles back into a more or less normal pattern, the sentiment of being still spread, as usual, over all.

However obvious the value of such experiences may be (for what is known and for the exuberance in knowing), we have to take several steps back to see why an act of knowing of the sort in question has such special force for this observer and is so desirable to him and others like him. He is often, though not always obviously, an uncomfortable observer. Fear had been educative in his youth, and all through his creative phases he felt a generally subliminal discomfort over mortality and its hindrances which he somehow learned to live with. But the observer is consistently a stranger, an outsider alone and with difficulty becoming aware that he is separate and has to learn to live with that too. In some cases the stranger takes the role of an intruder, breaking in where he has no business, into a life that shares no part of his life but may be forced to notice him. "Nutting" is an instance of this, as is also the scene in Book One of *The Prelude* when, as he goes about setting snares,

> moon and stars
> Were shining o'er my head. I was alone,
> And seemed to be a trouble to the peace
> That dwelt among them.
>
> (314–317)

The imagery of rape in "Nutting" underscores the forceful intrusion of his distinct otherness.[8]

But the role of the stranger, even when recognized as such, has other possibilities of fulfillment. What the stranger knows has its own value. Apartness can be overcome, though never completely, and the outsider, though he may remain a stranger still, can recognize elements in the experience that may make a relationship possible. The stranger is rejected, it seems, only when he forcibly intrudes himself or when he tries to will a relationship into being. The observer in "Ode to a Nightingale," one of Keats's most Wordsworthian poems, does both of these, which may be part of the number of reasons for his questioning whether the experience ever really occurred. Curiosity, perhaps, or merely a gentle surprise could lead to other kinds of contact. A poem like "Stepping Westward," which has as a ground the observer's recognition and acceptance of his strangeness in a strange land, indicates the possibility of a brief but completed experience in which the outsider is recognized and accepted through a gratuitous act that emerges, ultimately, out of shared humanity. That sharing is part of the theme of

---

[8] See Ferry, *The Limits of Mortality*, p. 25, for an interesting extension of this point, and cf., for a more positive view of the tone of the poem, Alan Grob, "Wordsworth's *Nutting*," *JEGP*, 61 (1962), 826–832.

his three related Scottish poems, "Stepping Westward," "The Solitary Reaper," and "To a Highland Girl," where the sense of foreignness takes the convenient form of a passage through strange lands where he is both alike and different. In other romantic hands, and in later ones, this could be the imagery of nightmare. That it is not usually so in Wordsworth (though there are times and some poems when it is nothing else) has to do with what he came to see that even the stranger can know.

The outsider, temporarily perhaps but definitely, can be welcomed into a community. If a number of Wordsworth's lyrics base their inner movement on the outsider's urgent wish to enter, *The Prelude* as a whole shows the impulse on a larger scale and shows how it came about that communion was necessary at all. Like Milton, Blake, and Byron, Wordsworth writes of the resolute ambiguities of innocence and experience. *The Prelude* is ultimately about Wordsworth "unparadis'd" and the specifics of a return to a higher innocence which is, among other things, a good deal less frantic than the earlier one. At the center of the experience, he descends into a hell of rootlessness and separation from all value, that is, of a thorough divorce from anything which could establish him as part of a larger context of being. A curious fragment entitled "Incipient Madness," dated probably in early 1797, shows the observer grasping in his desperate isolation at a false semblance of life, something with which he can establish even an illusory contact. And from what he saw (in an early occurrence of the metaphor) he drew food to nourish his helplessness:

> I crossed the dreary moor
> In the clear moonlight: when I reached the hut
> I entered in, but all was still and dark,
> Only within the ruin I beheld
> At a small distance, on the dusky ground
> A broken pane which glittered in the moon
> And seemed akin to life. There is a mood
> A settled temper of the heart, when grief,
> Become an instinct, fastening on all things
> That promise food, doth like a sucking babe
> Create where it is not. From this time

That speck of glass was dearer to my soul
Than was the moon in heaven.[9]

This is the closest that Wordsworth ever got to explaining the
day-to-day sense of what happened to him in his bleakest period.
All of his subsequent poetry shows that he never forgot what
it was and what it meant to have experienced this. Here and elsewhere Wordsworth can speak of an incapacity for meaningful
encounter so thorough that the self is split in two, the impulse to
communion coming from that part of self of which he is most
aware, the part that searches for the other. It could be a bitter
parody of the story Aristophanes tells in *The Symposium*. That
his isolation was nearly but not quite total and that the change
was not radical but only temporary indicate the continued
though subterranean presence of his capacity to save himself
from the blankness of the ego that stares at its aloneness. If encounter brings a kind of harmony and wholeness, then here
where the divided self stands fragmented is where the whole
process has to begin. The fragments were somehow kept joined,
so that when he had to work out a version of wholeness again,
he found that an absolute communion with his true self, and
thus a wholeness of being, was not as far away as it had seemed:

Then it was—
Thanks to the bounteous Giver of all good!—
That the beloved Sister in whose sight
Those days were passed, now speaking in a voice
Of sudden admonition—like a brook
That did but *cross* a lonely road, and now
Is seen, heard, felt, and caught at every turn,
Companion never lost through many a league—

[9] *Poetical Works*, I, 314–315. I shall deal at some length with this fragment
later. It is mentioned by Mary Moorman in *William Wordsworth, A Bi-
ography. The Early Years. 1770–1803* (Oxford: The Clarendon Press, 1957),
p. 286, where Mrs. Moorman notes the relationship to "The Ruined Cottage."
For further remarks on the relationship and suggestions on the dating, see
Mark L. Reed, *Wordsworth. The Chronology of the Early Years, 1770–1799*
(Cambridge, Mass.: Harvard University Press, 1967), pp. 193, 337–338. See also
Jonathan Wordsworth, *The Music of Humanity* (London: Thomas Nelson,
1969), pp. 7–8. There are important quotations from manuscripts in *Poetical
Works*, V, 377.

Maintained for me a saving intercourse
With my true self; for, though bedimmed and changed
Much, as it seemed, I was no further changed
Than as a clouded and a waning moon.

(Prelude, XI, 333–344)

Though *The Prelude* envisions the possibility of a complete separateness in which no living encounter can be thought of, much less accomplished, in "Ode: Intimations of Immortality" the possibility becomes in part an actuality and brings out a frantic, useless effort to force a relationship. One of the triumphs of the ode is its blend of lyric and elegiac into a mode quite unlike anything Wordsworth, and probably anyone else, had ever produced. Giving form to this mode, and indeed making it possible, is Wordsworth's most complicated and accomplished use of the image of the intrusive stranger, trying to break in but this time with the awareness of his separateness very much in the center of his concerns. The versions of intrusiveness in "Nutting" and Book One of *The Prelude* show no such awareness, unquestionably because they are dramatically earlier than his epic descent. Both "Stepping Westward" and "The Solitary Reaper," though, which are related in a number of ways, show the acceptance of the stranger (who is, it should be noted, not intrusive in these poems) and show also his clear recognition that he is an outsider and very grateful for any understanding he can reach. But in the "Immortality" ode there is awareness and no acceptance, and what makes it even bleaker than the apparently worse situation in *The Prelude* is the indication that nothing can keep those fragmented parts of his being together. Separation of the kind shown in the ode is permanent, total (though restricted to one part of his being), and conscious, worse than he had ever experienced in his post-Godwinian hell. What the ode shows is what Wordsworth feared most from the time of his early disillusion. His need for meaningful encounter and therefore his manner of writing poetry stemmed to a great extent from such fears.

The metaphor of travel that gives bone and substance to *The Prelude* is implied in the ode, though it only rarely rises to the surface as it does frequently throughout the longer work. On the metaphor, Wordsworth builds, in the ode, an image of distance that develops naturally from the idea of travel but, not unexpectedly, begins more and more to stress the spatial aspects involved in moving from one place to another, especially the space between where he is now and where he has come from. *The Prelude*, again, makes this point in a manner that clarifies the position of the observer in the ode:

> A tranquillising spirit presses now
> On my corporeal frame, so wide appears
> The vacancy between me and those days
> Which yet have such self-presence in my mind,
> That, musing on them, often do I seem
> Two consciousnesses, conscious of myself
> And of some other Being.
>
> (II, 27–33)

The days of childhood have so much "self-presence" in his mind because he feels their distance from his present, remembering self. Contained and sufficient, they are so far away that they have an existence of their own, quite independent of the existence of the observer, as the "self" in "self-presence" implies: "self" is a qualifier, putting all the emphasis on the individuality and independence of what he remembers, on its discreteness apart from him. In the first four stanzas of the ode, Wordsworth had had to verify that discreteness all over again in a series of images which are as much of his own childhood as of any specific children he may observe. Thus, when the poem arrives at the emergence of its own version of the travel-distance metaphor, the emergence carries with it all the melancholy of a separateness beyond reconciliation which had been defined by the first four stanzas with chilling clarity:

> Hence in a season of calm weather
> Though inland far we be,
> Our Souls have sight of that immortal sea
> Which brought us hither,
> Can in a moment travel thither,
> And see the Children sport upon the shore,
> And hear the mighty waters rolling evermore.

For what so frightened Wordsworth, what the ode is essentially about, is the real presence, not merely the possibility, of an absolute strangeness brought clearly into sight through the failure of encounter. He, after all, is the only one to whom "there came a thought of grief." And his feeling that he has wronged the season has, like most of his statements here, something desperately self-convincing about it, since it is a feeling he can share only with himself: the imagery and the scene described make clear that everyone else was too busy and happy to notice. The "timely utterance," therefore, was only for himself—no one else needed it—and could have brought only a consolation, for there is no genuine wholeness possible with what he wanted (and wants) to join. Everything outside is spring, but the poem shows the observer well into that stage when custom lies upon him "heavy as frost." The type of joy he sees outside, the joy of spring analogous to "the innocent brightness of a new-born Day," has only poignancy for one who is now in the autumn (the fall) beyond innocence.[10] The elaborately patterned fourth stanza renders in considerable detail the increasing frenzy and desperateness of his desire to force into being a kind of community that can never again open up for him. He sees and feels and hears (though he should have known that would not be enough) and tries by a series of insistent repetitions of word and syntax to hammer out a community of understanding, but the emotion is all on his side, no one else notices, and nothing arrives from without. The peak of the crescendo—"I hear, I hear, with joy I hear!"—has to be false, then, since only he can know and feel it. The emotion subsides and becomes an underlying anxiety he cannot quite allay. The inevitable confrontation with the truth now faces him.

But if he cannot establish a form of community here, he can certainly do so elsewhere, and the rest of the poem tries to show how. At the least, the ode is clearly not the farewell to

[10] Cf. *The Prelude*, XII, 31–37:

> The morning shines,
> Nor heedeth Man's perverseness; Spring returns,—
> I saw the Spring return, and could rejoice,
> In common with the children of her love,
> Piping on boughs, or sporting on fresh fields,
> Or boldly seeking pleasure nearer heaven
> On wings that navigate cerulean skies.

power that it used to be called; if anything, it shows how power can increase and expand by the encompassing of new depths through new knowledge. Lionel Trilling argued that the ode is no farewell, pointing out the insufficient structure of the child's solipsistic world, insufficient, that is, for the adult as poet.[11] But solipsism is only the most striking form that a failure of encounter can take. Ironically, then, there is both a harmony and a symmetry of opposites, fearful indeed, between the child in his innocent solipsism, cut off from contact, and the observer looking out from his prison in the world of experience. The solipsistic child can meet only himself. The same is true of the observer, but only he, of the two, can know that and can know what genuine encounter entails. The child who sees the world as "fallings from us" cannot reach out to anything and probably does not want to. For the observer, who does want to, it is too far away. There are other ironies: for example, the child is also an outsider when he first arrives, but the lost prince is welcomed into a kind of community; yet the community is one in which he can participate most meaningfully only after he has lost his childhood. But after that he can write his poetry because he can then place out there situations other than the impossible ones (a return to the world of his own childhood being the most impossible), and out of these he can make up a universe in which communion on every level becomes a limited, occasional, sporadic, but genuine reality. The ode is remarkable for the purity with which it affirms, probably in spite of him, the difficult, radical ambivalence of Wordsworth's feelings. He does, after all, speak with a praise that approaches reverence of the moments that dazzled him in childhood. And nowhere in the ode does he indicate that what came to him afterward was the necessary distancing without which there can be no poetry. (Perhaps it is only our humanist prejudice that puts the child's insufficiencies into the poem as we interpret it: not only can we not understand him, but also we sense that the boundedness of his world must be close, in some ways, to that of an intelligent animal.) If the observer all through Wordsworth's poems

[11] Lionel Trilling, "The Immortality Ode," in *English Romantic Poets: Modern Essays in Criticism*, ed. M. H. Abrams (New York: Oxford University Press, 1960), pp. 123–143.

has to learn and keep learning all that he is not, he can never forget exactly what he is, though that too has to be learned again at each moment of encounter or of the failure of encounter, and that too is an area of knowledge that continues to increase. In the ode the loss and gain involved can never be measured on any available scale. Given that situation, the ambivalence built into the experience requires that the poem be open-ended: as Wordsworth defines the lineaments of this process of knowing, no resolution of allegiances is possible, and any attempt at it is a falsification.

Thus, the ode is neither a hymn to declining powers nor quite a welcome of new ones, but an explanation of how powers come to exist at all and of what they cost. And their cost is as much in anxiety over what is imaged forth for the future as in the loss of certain childhood experiences that probably have great value. He can know what is outside of him now, and that is very good and leads to the making of poems. But the beginning of the ode (and the whole poem has to be read with the beginning in mind) shows at least one instance in which these powers failed, and that ominous note sounds as a sour undertone throughout the whole poem. What happened to the observer in those early stanzas is very close in kind to what happened after Godwin had gone and there seemed to be nothing there except himself. In the ode he insists that his isolation is only partial, though permanent, and that as a stranger he is irreconcilable only to his early self as imaged in the other children. But to combine in the same thought both this experience and the one after Godwin and the French Revolution is at the least to foresee the genuine possibility of a total failure of the capacity for encounter, which would lead to an intolerably thorough isolation. If the ode shows the emergence of new powers from old, it also indicates that a time when there are no powers at all is never beyond possibility. In *The Egotistical Sublime* (London: Chatto and Windus, 1954), John Jones argues brilliantly and convincingly that Wordsworth needed solitude in order to create, that in solitude he accepted and rejoiced in the uniqueness of personality, and that his solitaries discover and explore relationship with the unified series of disparate things and qualities that make up the universe. But it seems to me that

26

we have to go further than this and point out how Wordsworth's occasional uneasiness betrays, by its sporadic emergence, that he came by his understanding of solitude and relationship only with a great deal of exertion and anguish. For even his greatest moments had enough uncertainties within them to show how difficult they were to come by and to control and, finally, to understand. Solitude is fine when relationship is possible, but the possibility of relationship—indeed its very nature—had first of all to be established. Solitude without relationship is isolation and radical loneliness. That is what Wordsworth feared and fled.

Yet the power to mitigate, if not entirely to offset, the fullest consequences of the possibility of the failure of encounter lay in the organization of the moments of encounter themselves. Encounter was difficult enough to achieve and obviously impossible to hold. The partial overcoming of strangeness was a moment of such magnitude, and for so many reasons, that its preservation became necessary, surely for the fullness of its imaginative richness, the awe, wonder, and insight of moments like those in "Stepping Westward." But there is surely also more than a hint that the preservation of the moment of encounter could forestall the blankness of the thorough isolation that is never, before his smug days, entirely beyond what he can envision. The romantic emphasis on the redemptive value of poems took various forms, but the emphasis was pervasive, forceful, and insistent. What poetry redeemed from and for was also variable, but the possibility of loneliness of the bleakest sort, coupled with the pressures of mortality, was usually there and had to be faced. Wordsworth was luckier than many, partly because he could draw on areas in which he was both stable and interested. He drew particularly on the fact that those areas encompassed things and people, solitary trees and herdsmen both, objects nearly always at the center of what he saw.

CHAPTER TWO

The Presence of Singularity

THE WORLD that Wordsworth describes is a world of plurality, of discrete and not completely knowable objects. All of the complication of his reaction to the physical world has its ground not only in his own exceptionally complex reacting self, of which he has given the best account, but also in the more mysterious, oddly precise, but never perfectly defined network of things outside of him. His own rather firm ideas about the qualities of what he looked at (by 1815 Wordsworth was firm about most matters), though we would like more information, have the virtue of making several points clear:

> Having had the good fortune to be born and reared in a mountainous country, from my very childhood I have felt the falsehood that pervades the volumes imposed upon the world under the name of Ossian. From what I saw with my own eyes, I knew that the imagery was spurious. In nature everything is distinct, yet nothing defined into absolute independent singleness. In Macpherson's work, it is exactly the reverse; everything (that is not stolen) is in this manner defined, insulated, dislocated, deadened,—yet nothing distinct. It will always be so when words are substituted for things.[1]

Wordsworth wants clarity of outline as intensely as Blake does, and for some of the same reasons: the object has to be essentially itself and no other, and it has to reveal that it is through the qualities of its distinct presence there in front of him. Whatever

---

[1] "Essay, Supplementary to the Preface," in *Poetical Works*, II, 423–424.

its place on the great chain, the object is as idiosyncratic as the observer who stares at it. And if he does not always project into the object his glory in his own discrete individuality (of course he does so at times), Wordsworth would at least assume that whatever is out there shares in the quality of inimitable self-hood; and the sharing, or the realization that there is something to share, is one more way by which he can link himself with what he sees outside. His protection of the discreteness of the objects he experiences, his refusal—in the great decade and occasionally later—to overwhelm them with his own urgent, impelling being, is in part a protection of his own individuality, which he does not want to lose by blending it with another or by being swamped. The later Wordsworth of *The Excursion* and the egotistical sublime offers an unwitting parody of this urge to protect his separateness, a parody which almost, para-doxically, defeats the urge. For in overwhelming everything with his swelling self (and thus compromising his separateness by putting himself in everything), he removes most of what is inexplicable from outside; but in doing so he begins a curve back toward the solipsism of early childhood. For various good reasons he never gets there. Ironically, in the Wordsworth of 1815, whatever his professions, so many of the poems show him swamping the object he wanted to protect that we can assume what is proven elsewhere and frequently, that he was no longer perfectly aware of what he was able to do. Yet his very in-sistence, in the supplementary essay of 1815, indicates that the problems were still very much in his mind and surely never ceased to occupy him.

The distinctness of the object is, then, primary and without qualification. But the object is distinct in a context, distinct as one of other discrete things, not absolute (pure and unattached) or independent (unattached and alone) or single (without con-text). What Wordsworth calls "absolute independent single-ness" affirms a state of isolation, complete aloneness. An insu-lated object, locked within the walls of its own being, *has* to be dislocated, without that place in a context which has exceptional importance for Wordsworth in defining what the object means. Such an object is therefore deadened, Wordsworth insists, since to be without any share in the life that moves everywhere outside is to have no life in oneself. Again, and without any re-markable frankness, the observer wants for the object what he also wants for himself, for to have no life in this way is to be spiritually dead, to go without the possibility of a genuine en-counter (however limited and imperfect), and thus to be radi-cally separate until life returns in a miraculous reincarnation, if it ever does. The ironies in the analogy are heavy. Wordsworth had developed them early, in the last of the group of poems on death he devoted to Lucy: in death the only context offered —and the offer is firm—is to be one of a world of unconscious things, rocks and stones and trees. If our life makes a meeting possible, our death gives us an ultimately stable, uniform con-text, beyond consciousness and therefore beyond the anguish of separation. Death has many meanings in this group of poems, but in the last poem it is also, though not exclusively, the figure of a kind of life.

Yet, though degrees and kinds of relationship seem infinitely variable, this is, after all, a world of things, of whatever degree of consciousness. Macpherson's work, then, is a fraud, and not for the most obvious reasons. Wordsworth, characteristically, denies the authenticity of Ossian because of the way that things are seen, or actually not seen, in the poems. Substituting words for things means, for Wordsworth, ignoring the difficult rela-tionship out of which come those words which can tell of things seen and touched. The substitution of words for things falsifies the facts of the process by which language emerges from a meeting of the world and the self. Language has to be not only the reporter of an encounter but also the testimony and proof that it took place. Wordsworth's attack on Macpherson is there-fore one more instance—from a different direction and in terms somewhat less familiar—of his continual rejection of any kind of obstruction, personification or whatever, that comes between the observer and what he sees (which also includes what he feels about the things seen). What is worse about Macpherson, though, is not so much the veiling of the object because words take the place of things as an ultimate fraudulence because there really is no object out there for one to experience. This guaran-tees that Macpherson cannot speak truly. Wordsworth himself was of varying opinion about the success with which words can get through to an embodiment of things, but he never doubted that they should try to do so.[2] He said in 1829 that "words are not a mere *vehicle*, but they are *powers* either to kill or to animate."[3] The point here is not only the power *in* words (not merely *of* them) but further, that something has to be there to be killed or animated. Words define a thing as it is seen and carve new meanings out of it. One motion of the self experiences the thing, and another works to create something more than an equivalent of the experience. Macpherson short-circuits this process (and is therefore essentially uncreative) by experiencing apparent *verbal* equivalents and then trying to shape these. But he is shaping only words into words, not things into words. What he does can be only a lie about the process and about what objects are like.

And Wordsworth was compulsive about the truth of what he saw (within and without himself) and of what it was like for him to see what he did. The obsession with accurate analysis comes out quite explicitly in the same supplementary essay of 1815: "The appropriate business of poetry, (which, nevertheless, if genuine, is as permanent as pure science,) her appropriate employment, her privilege and her *duty*, is to treat of things not as they *are*, but as they *appear;* not as they exist in themselves, but as they *seem* to exist to the *senses*, and to the *passions*."[4] The object gets into the poem, then, insofar as it has an effect on the observer, and what we really watch, apparently, is the effect and not the object itself, the consciousness at work on the thing and not the thing as it stands there in itself. This, clearly, is one version of the variety of answers Wordsworth came up with to a question he worked on continually. The question is whether poetry is this way because its job is to deal with consciousness—that is Wordsworth's answer in this passage—or whether it has to be this way because it is only consciousness which poetry can safely assert to know. The quotation does make clear that the qualities of the object as they

[2] See David Perkins, *Wordsworth and the Poetry of Sincerity* (Cambridge, Mass.: The Belknap Press, 1964), pp. 86–90.

[3] *The Letters of William and Dorothy Wordsworth. The Later Years. I, 1821–30*, ed. Ernest de Selincourt (Oxford: The Clarendon Press, 1939), p. 437. Hereafter cited as *Later Years*.

[4] *Poetical Works*, II, 410.

appear in the poem are the result (not the sum) of an encounter of seer and seen, and therefore of the activity disclosed in the meeting manifested in the poem. The qualities exist as part of the activity and take their substance and meaning from it. A description of the object, then, has to be approached through a devotion to the reality of the encounter and that high point at which something comes to be known to the observer. What he knows about the object that appears in the poem are the facts of the object in encounter. The object, therefore, because it is what it is, has a large share in defining the shape of the activity in which it is one of the acting participants. Everything that the activity meant to the observer and everything that took place in it should in some way be present and discoverable in the qualities of the object as it appears in the poem. The solitary reaper has about her only those qualities which can define what the encounter meant to the stranger observing her. If the qualities in some cases are probably (or disputably) not part of the object but *only* within an observer's consciousness of it, Wordsworth will often dramatize that distinction, as is indicated by the number of situations he records that have to do with superstition or hallucination. But whatever the distinction (and it is never without ambiguities at every point), the poem of encounter is the narrative of a meeting.[5]

It follows, then, that the qualities in a poem by Macpherson must be untrue since they cannot be the record of an encounter that has actually, somewhere, taken place. Macpherson offers false knowledge: it has the appearance of being grounded in the substantiality of a meeting, but an examination of its nature reveals that there is no more truth about it than about any other mere verbalism. A closely related idea, involving another kind of knowledge but with echoes of similar language, appears in a passage on Coleridge in Book Six of *The Prelude:*

> I have thought
> Of thee, thy learning, gorgeous eloquence,
> And all the strength and plumage of thy youth,
> Thy subtle speculations, toils abstruse

[5] Various degrees of the ambiguities in Wordsworth's perception are discussed in C. C. Clarke's *Romantic Paradox. An Essay on the Poetry of Wordsworth* (London: Routledge and Kegan Paul, 1962).

Among the schoolmen, and Platonic forms
Of wild ideal pageantry, shaped out
From things well-matched or ill, and words for things,
The self-created sustenance of a mind
Debarred from Nature's living images,
Compelled to be a life unto herself,
And unrelentingly possessed by thirst
Of greatness, love, and beauty.

(294–305)

This is much less direct and therefore less easily conclusive than is the passage on Macpherson in the essay. Wordsworth does not say that Coleridge's knowledge of things is false, although he makes the same accusation of verbalism. He argues only that what Coleridge knows is solipsistic because it is parthenogenetic, born of a virgin mind untouched by the grossness of palpable things outside, the things and the qualities about them that make the words that define the meaning of a meeting. Yet, considering the terms of his attack on Macpherson, Wordsworth would have had to call this knowledge dead because it is insulated, isolated. That he does not do so indicates a curious but comprehensible hesitancy and ambivalence, based partly on his self-assurance in dealing with Macpherson: he feels on sounder ground attacking thingless poetry than thingless ideas. The passage on Coleridge is more serious but also darker and more tentative than "Expostulation and Reply," which it resembles in juxtaposing these kinds of knowledge. If we prefer the serio-comic exposition of the lyric, that is not only because of its more accomplished and assured stance but also because Wordsworth has located in the tone of "Expostulation and Reply" a more satisfying attitude toward the complexities in question.

The significant awkwardness of the passage on Coleridge finds further explanation through the necessary pairing of that passage with another, some lines earlier in the same book but close enough so that they have to be examined together. The passages seem to move toward a serious, jarring contradiction, but in fact they do not since Wordsworth is speaking of different ways of knowing. In the earlier one he tells of a man, shipwrecked with others on an uninhabited coast, who wanders occasionally from his fellow sufferers to console himself with a

33

book on geometry. He would take the book "to spots remote
and draw his diagrams / With a long staff upon the sand" (151–
152). Wordsworth's comment, when he turns the passage
toward his own interests, dwells on the attractions of the for-
getfulness that this intellectual world can offer:

> Mighty is the charm
> Of those abstractions to a mind beset
> With images and haunted by herself,
> And specially delightful unto me
> Was that clear synthesis built up aloft
> So gracefully; even then when it appeared
> Not more than a mere plaything, or a toy
> To sense embodied: not the thing it is
> In verity, an independent world,
> Created out of pure intelligence.
>
> (158–167)

But why is this independent world a supreme fiction and the
other, the one in which Coleridge spends his intellectual life,
vague, rather botched, and unanchored? The difference, for
Wordsworth of the highest importance, lies in the nature of
the world of geometry, which deals with figures—observable
things—that his shipwrecked wanderer can, if he wants to,
sketch in the sand. Coleridge, according to Wordsworth's comment, could not possibly level his intellectual world into the
forms of observable reality. (There is a warm, sad, self-directed
irony in Chapter XIII of the *Biographia Literaria,* framed by a
partly self-mocking discussion of the use of mathematical structures in metaphysics and ending with an abrupt and still dazzling definition of the Imagination.) Plato, we remember from
The Republic, found mathematical forms, though part of the
higher, intelligible world, to be a kind of bridge between that
world and the physical world of appearances. If its models remain imperfect, they can at least be models, things palpable and
immediate. This points to where Wordsworth stood, with the
greatest of shakiness, in regard to the presentness of things.

One of the central issues in modern criticism of Wordsworth
has to do with the ambivalence of his relation to the physical
world and in particular with what C. C. Clarke calls "the equiv-

ocal solidity of Wordsworth's real, solid world of images." [6] Geoffrey Hartman has shown how Wordsworth's urge toward apocalyptic vision, to which nature leads him, is bound up with an uncertainty about it that drives Wordsworth back toward nature.[7] Wordsworth's equivocation and uneasiness are significant indications of an ambivalence about physicality which he seems to have had up to the days of certainty enshrined in *The Excursion*, when he solved the problem of whether to embrace or reject by placing the world of objects into an interesting but subsidiary role. There is no poem by Wordsworth in which physicality is not, in some way, an issue: presentness and substantiality are either there, or he claims they are there, or he wants them to be there, or they had been there. He cannot, it seems, stop talking about things even when he wants to leave them for a while. We have seen that even at a moment of vision he can, apparently, hold onto some physicality if he wants to, and he frequently wants to. Even when he does not do so, he is generally quite specific in pointing out how much physicality had been involved: the question is always there even when the kind of knowledge toward which he reaches is far beyond things. However matter-of-fact the poems may be, they are always and in some way a matter of things.

An important passage in Book Eight of *The Prelude* goes part of the way toward clarifying some of the causes of Wordsworth's ambivalence:

> Yet, 'mid the fervent swarm
> Of these vagaries, with an eye so rich
> As mine was through the bounty of a grand
> And lovely region, I had forms distinct
> To steady me: each airy thought revolved
> Round a substantial centre, which at once
> Incited it to motion, and controlled.
>
> (426–432)

The very presence of the object stimulates intellectual activity while simultaneously guaranteeing, through its stability, that the

[6] Clarke, *Romantic Paradox*, p. 73.

[7] Geoffrey Hartman, *Wordsworth's Poetry, 1787–1814* (New Haven: Yale University Press, 1964).

activity is in some sense coherent and therefore has an element of truth within it. Its presence creates excitement, order, and truth all at once and all equally powerfully. For Wordsworth there is a kind of shape and meaning in the experience that seems to come about only with the object there at that specific place. In short, the object shares at least this with a mathematical form: it is both a subject of knowledge and a control on the validity of a way of knowing. In the above quotation, Wordsworth locks into "substantial" a number of related meanings which the word frequently has for him: it means full, palpable (having substance), and important; "weighty" would be a good synonym, and "essential" has a related multitude of possible directions of meaning. "Substantial" has the same meaning in Book Thirteen, where it is specifically coupled with truth:

> of these,
> If future years mature me for the task,
> Will I record the praises, making verse
> Deal boldly with substantial things; in truth
> And sanctity of passion, speak of these,
> That justice may be done, obeisance paid
> Where it is due.

(232–238)

Obviously this has close affinities with Wordsworth's desire, outlined in the 1800 Preface, to "keep the Reader in the company of flesh and blood," where the question of substantiality ties in with his realism and with the rejection of personifications as not only impediments but also radical falsehoods.

There is, finally, no essential contradiction between Wordsworth's positive support of geometrical life and his qualified, somewhat ambiguous and tentative judgment on the unrootedness of Coleridge's intellectual sphere. Mathematics appeals to Wordsworth because of its special position straddling two quite different areas of reality and also because of the qualified substantiality, through its figured objects, of its mode of knowing. At most levels of apprehension, Wordsworth closely relates, and at times even identifies, palpability and certain varieties of truth. His ambivalence toward the physical makes startlingly clear that substantiality was only partly satisfactory; but a substantial object *does* give a center which defines and orders and

36

clarifies, and it is therefore the revealer of several kinds of truth, kinds that are limited but there to be had all the same. There is the truth of present being and also the truth that the substantial presence of the object lends to the situation by making the situation cohere around it. But the truths *of* things are not the same as the truths outside of them. The truth of being is not the equivalent of the order that presentness gives, and both of these together lead to further kinds of truth which are outside of the situation of encounter and so big that they hold the situation within themselves. The most immediate truth about things lies in their existence as present things, and it is this special truth that things give *absolutely* to the situations in which they are perceived. Their substantiality guarantees that there is something about the situation that can be held onto (literally and all degrees of figuratively). This kind of truth, which is caught up in the qualities of the object as they appear in the poem, is not even all of the truth of the object in encounter, but it has to be known. However ambiguous presentness may occasionally have been for Wordsworth, he knew that it had within its existence as presentness that which he could not comfortably do without for very long, though he sometimes went in directions where he had to do without it. That, as much as anything else, underlies the ambivalence.[8]

Yet the truth about the object in encounter includes the object as it appears in a context. We have seen that a dislocated object is one to which Wordsworth could ascribe no life. Whatever the observer may do with the object in the act of perceiving it and, perhaps, in following through by making it the center of a poem, a perception of the object *in vacuo* is sterile and without meaning; indeed, finally false. If the object gives stability and order to the experience, the experience in turn puts life into the object by affording it the context in which it becomes most completely itself. At the periphery of the observer's awareness of the object are the related facts (and

---

[8] R. D. Havens talks of Wordsworth's use of "presence" in relation to animism; see *The Mind of a Poet*, I, 74–75. But Ellen Douglass Leyburn correctly points out Wordsworth's sense of immediate being in his use of the word; see "Recurrent Words in *The Prelude*," *ELH*, 16 (1949), 295–296. Her remarks on "substantial" (288) are also useful.

only those) of its surroundings. While the object may well be the catalyst that gives order and focus to the surroundings, without them it could never be exactly what it is or do what it does:

> While he was talking thus, the lonely place,
> The old Man's shape, and speech—all troubled me:
> In my mind's eye I seemed to see him pace
> About the weary moors continually,
> Wandering about alone and silently.

The peculiar kind of inner vitality observable in so many romantic poems like "Resolution and Independence" comes from the multiple, interrelated levels of activity created at various points: by the relationship between the object and its surroundings, and by the give-and-take between the observer and the object as it stands at the center of its surroundings. So much activity going on at so many levels could make for incoherence when there is no control given by a central object or by a very clear awareness of all the ramifications of action. At his best, Wordsworth shows an admirable finesse in his control of all of the activities in which the object takes part. For example, in the episode in Book Four of *The Prelude* (1805) where he meets the returned soldier, Wordsworth takes pains to point out that the object is not moving:

> I wish'd to see him move; but he remain'd
> Fix'd to his place, and still from time to time
> Sent forth a murmuring voice of dead complaint,
> Groans scarcely audible.
>
> (429–432)

And yet this quality of stillness becomes so significant a part of the multitude of activities involved in the entire situation that the incident draws much of its effect from the soldier's immobility, as well as from where and what he is. A number of other qualities are involved: the darkness in which the ridge is marked off by the glittering of the moon, the observer's relaxation of awareness, the suddenness with which he comes upon the soldier, the soldier's position just around a bend in the road, and the milestone (in this atmosphere reminiscent of a gravestone) against which he is leaning his gaunt and bony frame. Yet of all these qualities only the second and in part the third involve the observer; all of the others define either the object or those components of the object which are its context. But of course that context could have no meaning for the observer (or at least the special meaning it does have for him) unless the object retained the idiosyncratic qualities it has in that place at that time. Perfectly organic in their wholeness and variety, such moments image, completely and in miniature, the romantic conception of the active interrelationship which takes place among all aspects of the elements in an encounter.

The multiplicity of activities within the interrelationship demands of the observer a careful attention to a variegated group of simultaneously shifting phenomena; but within them some one, single, central thing seems often to stand out and be noticed. The frequency with which a single thing—one unique object standing alone—becomes and remains the center of attention in the poems is remarkable. Wordsworth's use of solitary human figures like the old soldier is too familiar to need demonstration. But there is more than that one kind of solitary involved, for throughout the whole canon of his poems the idea and fact of singularity run up and down the chain of being and enclose all varieties, not only human figures (in fact, not usually people) but the entire range of the elements that make up Wordsworth's broad and variegated world:

> But there's a Tree, of many, one,
> A single Field which I have looked upon.

A skylark or a cuckoo, a yew tree, "the single sheep, and the one blasted tree," a violet by a mossy stone, a sea-beast sunning itself on a rock, as well as Lucy Gray, Michael alone in his valley, and a prattling child conspicuous in a theater—the variety of the kinds of single objects is as impressive as their quantity. And to extend the list is to indicate the overwhelming substantiality, however equivocal and qualified and uncertain, of the world Wordsworth shapes out.[9]

[9] Commentary on Wordsworthian solitude is, with only a few exceptions, confined almost exclusively to the meaning of solitary human figures. For two of the exceptions, see Havens, *The Mind of a Poet*, I, 56, and A. C. Bradley, "Wordsworth," in *Oxford Lectures on Poetry* (1909; reprinted, London: Macmillan, 1934), pp. 141–142.

The variety of forms in which he spots singularity (I use the word to mean both uniqueness and unusualness) should make clear that there is more involved than the solitude of a man alone in a world which may know better than he does what it is going about and doing. The point is not that solitary man is not really alone (he unquestionably is alone) but that he is not the only object which is alone in its kind. Singularity for Wordsworth is, not surprisingly, a problem of the process of knowing that ties in with a special mode of presentness and the facts and pressure of context. One of the more curious passages dealing with these matters occurs in Book Three of *The Prelude*. He had been speaking of the heroic argument of his epic, the development of prowess in individual souls:

> This genuine prowess, which I wished to touch
> With hand however weak, but in the main
> It lies far hidden from the reach of words.
> Points have we all of us within our souls
> Where all stand single; this I feel, and make
> Breathings for incommunicable powers;
> But is not each a memory to himself.
>
> (185–191)

Singularity here has many facets: privateness and separateness, uniqueness and unusualness; all are folded into this word and give to the state Wordsworth describes a quality of being that is precious in its special character. Singularity apparently shows all of these facets at any point within the self (and Wordsworth implies that there are many) where one stands single; and these points are, for the most part, beyond the reach of a search for knowledge that comes from outside. Conventional syntax ordinarily offers a grouping of words that reveals in its structure the presence of some kind of contact, a sharing in an action between subject and object, in this case knower and known. But no such contact seems possible where the object of desire is as private and mainly unknowable as what Wordsworth depicts here. The word he lacks and has to find is a verb. In other contexts, indeed in many others, encounter or some closely similar activity can complete the syntax of the experience. In the unfinished pattern of events described in the above quotation, every element is there except the activity that puts all the others into order. This he tries to supply through his breathings, with admitted insufficiency. Singularity remains an essentially mysterious phenomenon, connected with power and, because of the very difficult problems of communication and "breathings," with a hoped-for contact that will permit the power to push out the limits of awareness. The complex gains in clarity and definition (though the dark corners are not so much brightened as disregarded) when an efficient verb can be offered and the elements on each side of it come into some measure of parity:

> Imagination having been our theme,
> So also hath that intellectual Love,
> For they are each in each, and cannot stand
> Dividually.—Here must thou be, O Man!
> Power to thyself; no Helper hast thou here;
> Here keepest thou in singleness thy state:
> No other can divide with thee this work:
> No secondary hand can intervene
> To fashion this ability; 'tis thine,
> The prime and vital principle is thine
> In the recesses of thy nature, far
> From any reach of outward fellowship,
> Else is not thine at all.
>
> (XIV, 206–218)

Clearly the point of the other passage has been flattened; it is not so much a loss of mystery, though that surely happens, as that the unexplored areas are ignored and therefore remain unexplored. (What the gothic novelists objectified in caverns and dungeons, with tentative exploration and obvious loss, generally remained for Wordsworth somewhere just beyond what he could say.) In this passage, which is surely a conscious echo of the earlier one, the same elements of power and singleness emerge; now, however, with the addition of Imagination (a kind of knowing and perhaps one of the hidden powers), the complex realigns itself very closely with creation and the nature of poetry, as well as with a special kind of love. Wordsworth goes on to talk of the effects of imagining and intellectual loving. Those hidden powers which can come into the light in these circumstances do come out and themselves become the verbs that complete the syntax, creating an order in the elements of the complex he had been describing. So radically important a shift in the pattern means for singularity a change in quality that opens up rich possibilities of development. To be single in these conditions means to be able to tap, as one wishes and with full awareness, elemental resources that have the power to give the deepest of insights into the nature of things. Even more, to be single means to have those resources at reach within oneself. If singularity is now not quite a synonym for power and insight, it comes to be identified with them so closely that those qualities seem indissolubly a part of anything that is alone. Being alone, unique, and single, then, comes to signify having about oneself an association with hidden powers which are difficult to know and never completely knowable. The powers seem tied in with the state of singularity itself, so that something that is alone can, at least potentially, have an immensely potent capacity to reveal the might of hidden forces connected with the insights afforded by imaginative vision. Wordsworth's association of the idea of singularity with that which is absolutely private and permanently partly mysterious, as well as the tie-in of those qualities with insight and power, leads not only to his familiar concerns with his own solitude but to much more, to his sense of what objects are and what they can mean for himself as experiencing man and as creative figure. When he sees a single thing, whatever its status on the hierarchy of being, the facts of its aloneness and presentness come close to completing the conditions under which an explosion of insight is imminent. The form and nature of the explosion depend on the qualities and circumstances of all the participants in the encounter. A yew tree or even a gibbet with its human associations cannot mean the same to him as a girl singing in a strange tongue or an old man appearing out of nowhere (or everywhere).

Whatever a single object may be, it is not diffuse but, quite the opposite, packed and concentrated in intensity. It is not merely alone (that is only the beginning of its definition) but also single, the unique example and representative of its kind. It shares nothing of its most important characteristics with any other like object in the situation, and therefore all that is significant about that kind of object is, for Wordsworth, concentrated in the pure example the observer has in front of him:

We had another fine sight one evening, walking along a rising ground about two miles distant from the shore. It was about the hour of sunset, and the sea was perfectly calm, and in a quarter where its surface was indistinguishable from the western sky, hazy, and luminous with the setting Sun, appeared a tall sloop-rigged vessel, magnified by the atmosphere through which it was viewed, and seeming rather to hang in the air than to float upon the waters. Milton compares the appearance of Satan to a *Fleet* descried far off at sea; the visionary grandeur and beautiful form of this *single* vessel, could words have conveyed to the mind the picture which Nature presented to the eye, would have suited his purpose as well as the largest company of Vessels that ever associated together with the help of a trade wind, in the wide Ocean. Yet not exactly so, and for this reason, that his image is a permanent one, not dependent upon accident.[10]

The point is that one more reaper not only would change the title of the poem but also would spread out and dilute all of the packed intensity that the solitary reaper has, an intensity resulting, as we have seen, from her position at the meeting points of continua in time and space. The situation would become so different that little of its meaning could remain intact. Diffusion means dispersal, concentration the condensation of power which, in any number of analogies, could lead to an explosion of insight.

It is worth digressing briefly to pursue an analogy that may illuminate the kind of power and meaning that singularity has for Wordsworth. One of the most exciting of the intricate webs of imagery that emerge from the Old Testament is a pervasive obsession with purity, an obsession which no other Near Eastern people showed to such a degree. Purity for the Hebrews meant concentrating on one thing, while being one of a kind seemed to go far toward guaranteeing purity for them. Elijah's

[10] *The Letters of William and Dorothy Wordsworth. II. The Middle Years. Part 1, 1806–1811*, ed. Ernest de Selincourt, 2nd ed. rev. by Mary Moorman (Oxford: The Clarendon Press, 1969), p. 508. Hereafter cited as *Middle Years*, Part 1.

hatred of syncretism is paralleled clearly by the Hebraic sense of exclusiveness. Further, the urge toward the centralization of worship at one place is reinforced for the Hebraic consciousness by the image of the Virgin of Zion which underlies Isaiah's great song in II Kings and sounds throughout the prophets. This was a religion that not only could tolerate no other gods (officially at least) but also could never have worshiped saints; it abhorred pantheons because diffusion, as a multitude of images show, meant impurity and adulteration. At some deep stratum of the Hebraic consciousness, duplication was repellent and bred contamination. Jerusalem had to be a maiden for them, and her adversary had to be imaged as the Whore of Babylon. It was a sure instinct that led Jeroboam (in I Kings 12) to move toward breaking up the kingdom by installing a second place of worship. The biblical historians, always ironists, stressed that event. No wonder, indeed, that the image of the holy marriage is monogamous and that apostasy was always imaged as adultery.

There is something of the same intense meaning in the relationship of singleness and purity and power in Wordsworth. In the two incidents in Book Twelve of *The Prelude* which Wordsworth picks out to show what spots of time are like, he emphasizes, sometimes by repetition, that the objects involved are unique, one of whatever the kind is. Along with the "naked pool," mentioned several times in the first situation (it appears again in "Resolution and Independence" as the "pool, bare to the eyes of heaven"), come the single beacon "crowning the lone eminence," the one girl, and of course the mouldered gibbet-mast, emphatic in its presence and aloneness. The girl, the only moving thing, is obviously differentiated in the quality of her being from the other elements in the situation, especially by her activities, but she is like all the others in that she is alone in her kind. In the second example, Wordsworth makes enough of "the single sheep, and the one blasted tree" to indicate that their singularity is, for him, what is most significant about them in that special context: two sheep would be diffusive and therefore be one too many, for the occasion concentrates at one point a series of objects that ascends on the great chain from the tree up through the sheep to the man. The man sits regally between these two individuals in their kind and sits high on a throne, a crag that ascends "from the meeting point of two highways." The scene verges on the allegorical, though as an allegorical image it has no pronounced content. More overtly allegorical, and possessing that content precisely because of its singularity, is the figure of the blind beggar in Book Seven of *The Prelude* (635 ff.). Wordsworth, in fact, had stressed the element of the singular just before that, as prelude to his description, mainly to point out emphatically the concentrated power that comes out of a thing alone in its kind:

> As the black storm upon the mountain top
> Sets off the sunbeam in the valley, so
> That huge fermenting mass of human-kind
> Serves as a solemn back-ground, or relief,
> To single forms and objects, whence they draw,
> For feeling and contemplative regard,
> More than inherent liveliness and power.
>
> (619–625)

The statement is pristine and immensely significant. But Wordsworth is usually less direct, more subtle and compelling in indicating how the singularity of any kind of object in the hierarchy of being is tied in with pressure and therefore power. In the second spot of time, for example, the crag is at the center where two roads meet, two lines of continuum that move in toward it, and it becomes the target of the movement of anything coming down the roads. This is an exact equivalent of the situation of the solitary reaper, on whom is concentrated the force of temporal and spatial continua embodied in the images and questions in the second and third stanzas. Another instance of the centered object as a focus of force is in a letter of 7 October 1804 from Dorothy to Lady Beaumont:

> You must have crossed Whinlatter and will recollect what a lovely and wild road it is among high mountains. One scene impressed me very much—there was neither stone fence nor hedge, nor any work of men but the Road for a considerable way before us between the hills, a mile-stone and a wall upon the sloping ground at the foot of the mountain built by the shepherds in the form of a cross as a shelter for their sheep—it is strange that so simple a thing should be of so much impor-

45

tance, but the mountains and the very sky above them, the solitary mountain-vale all seemed to have a reference to that rude shelter—it was the very soul of the place.[11]

In all of these cases the movement of perception, visual or imaginative, goes from a concern with the continua to end up at those objects which are the centers where the lines of force converge. This pattern in which objects are targets occurs a number of times in Wordsworth's poems and seems to represent one of the modes in which he perceived concentrations of energy. A few of his poems show, at almost a rudimentary level, the bare conditions of the experience. In "Strange Fits of Passion" it is nearly diagrammatic. A triad of elements—the rider on his horse, the moon, and the cottage—are set apart in space with the cottage at the center and the other two focusing on it. The observer, as in so many of these experiences, is in a state of relaxed awareness, half in and half out of himself. His attention, as the situation seems to require, is elsewhere than on the object that is about to become significant. This defines the particular qualities of consciousness necessary for what is to come after:

> In one of those sweet dreams I slept,
> Kind Nature's gentlest boon!
> And all the while my eyes I kept
> On the descending moon.

He moves toward the cottage, the single object at the center, as the moon does from another angle. As each progresses toward the cottage, the tension in the poem develops until the climax:

> My horse moved on; hoof after hoof
> He raised, and never stopped:
> When down behind the cottage roof,
> At once, the bright moon dropped.

And at this point, when the tension reaches its limit, the spark jumps the gap in a flash of intense feeling:

> What fond and wayward thoughts will slide
> Into a Lover's head!
> "O mercy!" to myself I cried,
> "If Lucy should be dead!"

[11] *Early Years*, p. 507.

The form which the poem finally took indicates cogently how aware Wordsworth was of the dangers of dissipating intensity. As it stands, the poem ends just at the moment of the abrupt and irrational shift caused by the sudden, explosive release of tension. The observer had had no full consciousness that such a tension was building (a degree of surprise is probably always necessary), but the poem makes evident that some more subliminal action of consciousness had been following the development of the lines of force all along. Those lines—his own movement and the movement of the moon—in their simultaneous approach to the target cottage, built up a pressure by their continual focusing and forward movement right up to the moment when the moon dropped. And when it did drop, it brought the observer not out of his semirelaxed state but further in toward an irrational leap of thought. (There is a neat reversal of this pattern in "Resolution and Independence," where the observer is brought *out* of an irrational turn of thought by a sudden awareness of the person of the old man.) Wordsworth's usual pattern is to resolve the moment of tension by rounding out the poem with a comment or a return to the original scene, sometimes both. At one point in his writing of the poem, he had rounded it out in his conventional fashion with an additional stanza, but it had been all wrong and later he dropped it:

> I told her this: her laughter light
> Is ringing in my ears:
> And when I think upon that night
> My eyes are dim with tears.

This is not the usual coming to rest, where the object remains at the center of the situation while the observer comes back into control, somewhat sadly perhaps. ("The Solitary Reaper" offers a clear example of that kind of activity.) This is only a dissipation of intensity, the thinning out of a fascinating madness into the light of ordered day. Without this extraneous stanza we are left standing near the cottage, the moment of explosive irrationality only just over, the single object still there and bright. More clearly than in most of Wordsworth's poems, we are aware of just how these experiences happen and what goes into

47

them. If "Strange Fits of Passion" shows the moment at a rudimentary, perspicuous level, the experience in the poem is by no means inchoate but complete and fully developed. Everything necessary is there, particularly that movement in which an object alone in its kind—in this case a cottage of the sort Wordsworth saw a dozen of every day—flashes into a sudden life of its own in which power, singularity, and a strange insight all inhabit the world of this moment.

CHAPTER THREE

The Farthest Reach of Sense

In "Strange Fits of Passion" Wordsworth's experience with the object is relatively pure and direct. The poem has an imposingly present focal object at the center, while the narrative unfolds an action which, though many elements are involved and acting, has as its point and result a presentation of his experience of the elements that were meeting. The poem is so organized that nothing comes between him and what this experience shows that he can know of the central object: everything serves to focus with absolute clarity the bare but complete outlines of the encounter, i.e., his experience of himself experiencing the object in its context. There is nothing for him to go around and get through, and in the language of the poem there is nothing which calls glaring attention to itself and thus away from the directness of his experience of the contextual object. What Wordsworth wants here, obviously, is a straight road through to the action, as thorough an immediacy of understanding of the whole encounter as language and pure action would permit. A version of this insistence upon a special kind of immediacy lies behind his rejection of Macpherson's poems, for their language is not a road to the understanding of encounter but a block to it. The words which shape our understanding of our experience of things should offer the least possible hindrance to such understanding. Words are mediating instruments and thus, to begin and end with, are not able to hold all of what they point to. But the success of the poem of encounter, whatever the limitations of the medium, ought to be thought of in terms of how close the poem permits us to get to all the available facets of the meeting presented within it. Macpherson's work is a multi-dimensional lie, then, because it gets at none of these aspects of truth. When Wordsworth attacked the language of Gray, he did so because of its fuzziness, its inability to offer precise, accurate information about all that Wordsworth wanted to know. Language cannot be taken out of a self-contained, incestuous verbal world and used to chat about how one goes and experiences things. Gray, like Macpherson, had the direction of words and the process of using them all wrong.

The close involvement of Wordsworth's insistence upon immediacy of understanding with his sense of truth in action and in presence worked to create patterns of imaginative comprehension, patterns which are as much definitions of modes of perception as they are ways of thinking out what poems could be like. For example, I have indicated how singularity means for Wordsworth a concentration of intensity. But surely he dwells on single objects alone in their kind, things more often than people but people too, because he could get closer to understanding when there were no distractions of duplication. Dispersal of intensity (the intensity which comes necessarily with immediacy) is a danger that increases with the distance from the object. That distance, he knew, can come not only from actual removal but also from the diffusiveness resulting when concentration has to be divided. There are various kinds of Wordsworthian seeing, but the kind associated with the objects in encounter requires all that can be drawn up of concentrated, intensified force, even if the force is concentrated without his complete awareness (we remember the element of surprise that seems almost requisite at some level of the meeting). Aloneness in kind, then, comes to be the condition for a special kind of knowing because of what it can offer toward an immediacy of understanding.

So important to Wordsworth were this complex of conditions and the related questions of truth and presence that he deals with them at all stages of his development, particularly in his ideas on the language and modes of poetry and, for a time at least, even in his social concerns. But the need for immediacy also had a frequently determining effect on the landscapes in which his figures and the few things which surround them find a place to be. Obviously, part of the reason that his landscapes were so often bleak and stark has to do with the physical world out of which he drew the forms of his vision. But Wordsworth had learned early how the materials at his hand could be molded to become not only bright instances of various objects but also the forms through which a mode of vision could achieve its most precise expression for him. A single object in a bare landscape offered a means of capturing and, for a meaningful duration, holding onto an awareness of the meaning of the presentness of the object that few other kinds of situation could approach in intensity, directness, and purity. If the single object creates through its own starkness a condition in which attentiveness finds no diversion, then the right kind of landscape in which to place the object makes for a greater intensification of the same activities. The difficulty of imagining Wordsworth in the tropics comes less from any particular idea about what is or is not in the natural world than from what would have to be considered a breakdown in the consistency with which his landscape communicates.[1] In a lush landscape the quality of the world is determined largely by the overwhelming weight of the quantity of things in it. It is a world of which the tone and therefore much of the meaning work out of mass and diversity, especially out of the mass of diversity. It sends its meaning out through a quantitative sense of presences moving from everywhere toward the observer, whose attentiveness has to be extraordinarily multiple in kind and direction. The meaning of a thing in a world like this draws much of its content from the thing's being one of a constantly active myriad. But the world of the bleaker Wordsworthian landscapes has to deal with other modes of seeing, modes possible only because they come out of a situation where diversity is rare and often undesirable. A landscape uncluttered except for the most integral properties, and with very few even of those, is one in which bleakness may come to be seen primarily, and positively, as a way of being without interference. Thus,

---

[1] Aldous Huxley's "Wordsworth in the Tropics," in *Do What You Will* (London: Chatto and Windus, 1929), pp. 113-129, is typical of the cranky anti-Wordsworthianism of the years between the wars.

all of the conditions would be there for a very full and direct experience which would be truer in a certain kind of truth, the kind that comes from knowing more of the facts about what he does and what the presence of external things does to him. The starkness of a Wordsworthian landscape, therefore, usually goes without the overtones of fear and malevolence that emerge from the similarly stark landscapes of Thomas Hardy. It is not a matter of what Hardy does or does not put into them, for very often his landscapes and those of Wordsworth seem nearly identical, indeed physically almost interchangeable. With Wordsworth the starkness can set up the basis for a gorgeous illumination, and that could never happen with Hardy. Wordsworth could not hope for the same knowledge of the presence of the object under other, lusher circumstances which reveled in quantification. One meaning of purification has to do with distillation, the removal of the disturbingly diverting and the distractingly irrelevant. The purest knowledge comes from the most thorough cleansing of the doors of perception.

Wordsworth experimented with a number of approaches through which he attempted to get closer to knowing the truth of his experience and the truth (as far as words can give it) bestowed by substantial presence. It is worth reiterating that the knowledge given through language may well, for Wordsworth, be imperfect because incomplete; but the relevant quotations make very clear indeed that he never made up his mind about this matter and that, though he was often certain that language could do miracles, he was often uncertain about the extent of its reproductive (not necessarily transforming) powers. Here is a form of "substantial" again, in a less confident usage than most we have seen:

> The days gone by
> Return upon me almost from the dawn
> Of life: the hiding-places of man's power
> Open; I would approach them, but they close.
> I see by glimpses now; when age comes on,
> May scarcely see at all; and I would give,
> While yet we may, as far as words can give,
> Substance and life to what I feel, enshrining,

Such is my hope, the spirit of the Past
For future restoration.
(Prelude, XII, 277–286)

All through Wordsworth's poetry, from some very early passages through *The Excursion* and later poems, an image runs which was clearly and strikingly an attempt to solve some of the problems indicated in this passage. He appears to have felt that if he could experience the presence of the object while the presence was only just there (but very definitely there), he could reduce the difficulties language has in dealing with substantial things, at the same time as he could still work with the kind of truth that presence bestows upon an experience of encounter. One of the most curious and fascinating of his experiments in this vein is his use of a disembodied voice, a voice which is all that a poem gives about a central object in it. No body is ever seen in the poem, though it may be mentioned; there is only the sound of the voice. The voice need not be singing, although in most instances in Wordsworth and the other romantics in whom it occurs, the voice is a voice of song—often, for obvious reasons, that of a bird. Most important is that a voice be there, pure and at the center of the experience. Many of the conditions are set up in one instance early in *The Prelude.* The young Wordsworth had been out riding with friends, had visited a ruined abbey with them, and later recalled:

> that single wren
> Which one day sang so sweetly in the nave
> Of the old church, that—though from recent showers
> The earth was comfortless, and touched by faint
> Internal breezes, sobbings of the place
> And respirations, from the roofless walls
> The shuddering ivy dripped large drops—yet still
> So sweetly 'mid the gloom the invisible bird
> Sang to herself, that there I could have made
> My dwelling-place, and lived for ever there
> To hear such music.
>
> (II, 118–128)

The abbey, as he indicates a few lines earlier, was for them not the seat of pleasurable melancholy it could have been but a moldering structure that was "a holy scene." Within this holy place at a moment of darkness after a storm, when the physical qualities of the place took on the touches of minor eighteenth-century fiction that Wordsworth could apply now and then, a single voice emerged. The wren, alone and invisible, changes through its voice what could have been rather ordinary gloom into a condition where the observer feels that the voice makes possible for him a kind of home. Through the voice the stranger is welcomed into a place that was not his own. The bird is almost not there, yet it is definitely there, still available to the fleshly ear and therefore still in the world of the senses and capable of warming it.

This passage shares with a poem like "Strange Fits of Passion" the status of being a pristine, fully developed version of an experience of encounter. The single object at the center of each experience shares with a stark landscape and uncluttered diction the relative purity that brings closer the possibility of a more immediate understanding. Yet the difference between the cottage in "Strange Fits of Passion" and the voice of the bird coming out of the ruined abbey is more than one between inanimate and animate objects, however important that difference can be for Wordsworth. There is also, and crucially, the difference between visual and aural experiences, between the more and the less complete presence, between one to which several senses can at least potentially respond and another where there is nothing to see and feel but only to hear.

The disembodied voice is for Wordsworth the final point to which an object can be purified and still retain a tie to the sensuous reality of things. In the Preface of 1815, when he speaks of his use of the cuckoo's voice in "To the Cuckoo," he mentions almost casually and in passing what is surely one of the primary facts in the experience. He quotes from the poem—"Shall I call thee Bird, / Or but a wandering Voice?"—and then goes on to comment: "This concise interrogation characterises the seeming ubiquity of the voice of the cuckoo, and dispossesses the creature almost of a corporeal existence; the Imagination being tempted to this exertion of her power by a consciousness in the memory that the cuckoo is almost perpetually heard throughout the season of spring, but seldom becomes an object of sight." [2] Here the first occurrence of "almost" carries a great deal of freight: the voice of the cuckoo, like all disembodied voices, remains within the elements of the physical world, however much it strains to the edge of another. The senses still give us access to it, although the quality of the access is more pure, direct, and immediate than it could be in any other case involving the senses. Wordsworth never presents a disembodied voice without grounding it carefully, if only by a brief gesture, in the physical scene out of which it emerges, so that it has a place and context that are solidly palpable and immediate. The voice itself, though, is at the outer limits of sense experience, the most perfect version of the immediacy Wordsworth sought. In a passage some lines after the one on the wren and obviously to be thought of with it, Wordsworth speaks of the "power in sound"

> To breathe an elevated mood, by form
> Or image unprofaned; and I would stand,
> If the night blackened with a coming storm,
> Beneath some rock, listening to notes that are
> The ghostly language of the ancient earth,
> Or make their dim abode in distant winds.
>
> (II, 305-310)

Sound sets his awareness going toward experiences high and mysterious: these are the outermost reaches to which he can go at this moment; but the reach is the reach of the senses, and the sense involved is the one which to Wordsworth is the most spiritualized of all, as the lines following this passage make eminently clear.

For Wordsworth as for Keats there was a crucial distinction between the "sensual ear" and whatever it is (Keats called it "the Spirit") that gets to know "ditties of no tone." It may be that for Wordsworth as well as Keats the unheard melodies were sweeter. At any rate, his experimentation with the idea of a disembodied voice allowed him to play with the limits of sensuousness and the meaning of those limits to see how far he could take them before the senses lost their epistemological capabilities. Through the voice, he could explore the forms

[2] *Poetical Works,* II, 437.

of knowing involved when sensuousness reaches so pure a point that it quite nearly refines itself out of existence. The disembodied voice is just this side of the line where he has to change to a new set of epistemological tools to cope with new modes of meaning.

The problem and this experiment toward a solution were by no means Wordsworth's alone. The romantics' concerns about the meaning of immediate physical experience—and they were fascinated by the mazes of physicality—were never separable from their ideas about what is beyond this immediate moment of sense. For a romantic no moment was to be thought of as completely isolated. It always made up a segment of a continuum, perhaps of a sequence in time or space, frequently of another kind of progression that began with rock and flesh and led to another mode elsewhere. The moment stands as a center, a walled point of focus which can be breached, though with difficulty, and can lead the poet out into a climate of knowing very different from the one the moment immediately holds. This leap beyond immediacy enclosed a wide spectrum of possible attitudes and results, ranging from the most earthbound (usually involved with a transition to another moment in time) to an urgent reach toward dissolution in other variously named but always transphysical elements. The activity of leaping was in itself an insistence that moments were never completely circumscribed. It was, then, an assertion that the manifold dimensions of romantic experience had within them a coherence, the existence of which is proven because the moment can be breached and seen to relate to other moments at other places that are not here and now. Of course this was generally more a hope than a firm statement of fact: the romantics were not unusual in asserting the existence of a truth at the same time as they were setting about to find out if it were true. Here, at the center of one of the most difficult romantic problems, the poets worked their way toward affirmations which turned out to be as variable as they and their special concerns.

On one level romanticism moved toward a new shape of coherence, new understanding that would emerge, inevitably it was hoped, from contemporary perceptions of order. The poets went on a hunt for images that could serve as instruments for the discovery of the order that was presumably there. The idea of the moment as a walled center meant that bridges had to be built out of it, conduits that would lead the poets back and forth among all the major modes available to them. One of these bridges was the image of the disembodied voice. All of the major English romantics made various use of it, but what Wordsworth did with the image is peculiarly his own. It is, therefore, worth exploring a few experiments by some of the other poets in order to define more exactly how the image ties in with Wordsworth's sense of the presence of things just barely out there.

A notebook entry by Coleridge about the voice of a shepherd boy in Scotland sits at one end of the spectrum, pointing to the simple presence of the sensuous fact: "Never, never let me forget that small Herd boy, in his Tartan Plaid, dim-seen on the hilly field, & long heard ere seen, a melancholy *Voice*, calling to his Cattle!" [3] As simple as it is, this brief observation shows that in even the least complicated use of the image a richly awesome quality (something more than the merely mysterious) comes through as primary. At the other end of the spectrum is Byron's Manfred:

> Oh, that I were
> The viewless spirit of a lovely sound,
> A living voice, a breathing harmony,
> A bodiless enjoyment—born and dying
> With the blest tone which made me!
>
> (Act I, Scene ii, 52–56)

Manfred wants only dissolution, a leap out of the physical toward pure, fleshless sound. Most examples, though (and all of Wordsworth's), fall somewhere between these extremes, building on the awesomeness of the voice to make of it a bridge toward other areas of experience, earlier or later ones or those absolutely different. Typical of many is the effect of "the viewless skylark's note" on the speaker in Coleridge's "Reflections on Having Left a Place of Retirement": he hears an "unearthly minstrelsy," what the heart can know of an exalted mode when a song comes through purely. But in this poem Coleridge does nothing with what the image can show of the poet in love and dread, that

---

[3] *The Notebooks of Samuel Taylor Coleridge*, ed. Kathleen Coburn (New York: Pantheon Books, 1957), I, no. 1471. The italics are Coleridge's.

ambivalent fascination with physicality that illustrates and defines the romantic sense of things. Wordsworth shows it and so
do Keats and Shelley, from whom there are significant illustra-
tions of what romantics could do with this image that focused
so many of their concerns. But the voices that sound in Keats
and Shelley have only an apparent similarity to the kind of
material with which Wordsworth usually worked. Shelley's
skylark and Keats's nightingale are, like Wordsworth's wren or
his cuckoo, images of joy. The difference between Wordsworth
and these others grows out of vastly divergent perceptions of the
weight of physicality and, through no surprising extension, of
the pain of human mortality.

A comparison of several poems should make the differences
clear. In Keats's "Ode to a Nightingale" the movement toward
a change in the nature of the sensing self (and Keats's whole empathic mode is, finally, nothing less than a death of the self)
begins with a numbing of sense but ends up by proving only
that the weight of physicality has to be borne. Still, nothing
about Keats is ever simple. The road out of the senses, which
tell about and feel mortality, leads toward a bird just barely
within the sensible world, a bird he cannot feel or see but only
hear. Yet the road itself is lush and exotic (stanza two), and
when the urge finally drives him into the heart of darkness, he
finds there an extraordinary intensity of sense experience (stanza
five). To leave completely, therefore, means to go beyond the
lovely richness of all this. If he rejects the pallid thinness of de-
caying men, he knows too that the temporal world surrounding
them can be thick with a luxuriance that is its own sweet and
immediate delight. (The romp on the Grecian urn, where the
same ambivalence shows in another form, discloses far more
uncertainty about relative values than does the song of Yeats's
Byzantine artifact that, beyond the flesh, still looks and sounds
like a bird.) The voice, then, is bridge and more: it entices him
toward easeful dissolution to the tune of ecstasy, but it never
gets him there. The whole poem is a complex monument to
conflicting impulses and calls all of the values within it into
question. So does Keats: as much as any other factor, his ambivalence (which is major and invulnerable to human consolation)

prompts the ambiguous ending, the questioning of the experience as it was.

In Shelley's equally complicated case, there is implied throughout a clear recognition of the various realms and their distinctness, with barriers of varying density (veils and glassy domes) as persistent impediments everywhere. Yet the voice of a woman singing in "To Jane: 'The Keen Stars Were Twinkling,' " the best of a number of similar poems, shows that there are indeed bridges and that passage across them can be easy, ecstatically so. Still, the world from which he moves is so richly sensuous and multidimensional in quality, indeed so infused with sensuality, that there is no question here of distilling physicality to a fine and pure point. The voice, the bridge, is not, for very good reasons, disembodied. He is more straightforward and more certain than Keats is about wanting to keep everything, to have it all at once. When he does move across in this poem, he moves to a world equally opulent in sense but of a pure unity, "where music and moonlight and feeling are one." In "To Constantia Singing," of which similar remarks can be made, a further element is added, that kind of death to an ecstatic song which looks to be so rich a possibility in Keats's "Ode to a Nightingale." Shelley takes over fully the image of a disembodied voice with the "unbodied joy" in "To a Skylark," where he moves even closer to Keats though he shares a special awareness with Wordsworth. He knows what Keats may well have learned, the inaccessibility of the bird which he can only hear; but Shelley adds more, the clear confession (not just the tentative questioning as in Keats) of a thorough ignorance that he has and would reject. The otherness of the bird, its radical separateness from himself, is firm and without qualification. The bird sings to him out of another world he cannot share and sees what the poet is aware of but sees it so differently that the bird is proven to have a different being, the kind only pure joy can have. The poet cannot cross this bridge, but he can guess where it goes. Most important, he knows very clearly that it is a bridge to another mode of being. (A passage from *A Defence of Poetry* which draws on imagery similar to that in the poem speaks of poetry bringing light and fire from the "eternal regions.") Yet despite his lucid awareness of disparity, the urge he has to share in the bird's knowledge, to be like it in joy and pure intensity, is at bottom an impulse to change the nature of self. The kind of knowledge he wants, seriously though without expectations, means a change in all that he is: the shout, more subdued than that in "Ode to the West Wind," still has the same lineaments and still means the same: "Be thou me, impetuous one!"

Some general differences between these variations on the image and those in Wordsworth can be stated at once. The voice of Wordsworth's wren sings joyfully to him out of a context which he wants to partake of fully but without ever ceasing to be himself. If the voice of the wren comes to him out of no visible body, there is still no indication that he would like to change places with the bird or that he envies its disembodiment. Wordsworth's delight in an image of sensuousness stretched to its limit (in every case that delight is basic and obvious) is to a great extent grounded in his awareness of his own qualities as a special kind of sensing being. If the voice makes his imagination do its own work better, he can then be all the more himself at his best. There is, for him, no activity without a simultaneous consciousness of himself as acting in it. Experiences such as those involving disembodied voices made it possible for him to do more with the powers whose flexibility, range, and subtlety could only increase under such a stimulus. It was, in other words, an enrichment of himself as an experiencing being, and thus he became all the more Wordsworth, and neither different nor less. The voices he tries out on the order of his being usually impel him to an increase in self, not to a shift in its nature. (This will change by the time of The Excursion.) For Keats and Shelley, though, the voices in no way lead toward an increase in the totality of being, despite the intensity of those poets' sense experience in other poems. Rather, the voices lead toward a hoped-for but probably unachievable purification of self. The poems by Keats and Shelley are, more directly than Wordsworth's, about poetry and the artist, and they are unlike most of Wordsworth's poems on the voice in that they draw out images of the pains and ambiguities of human experience to show the superiority of what is suggested by the disembodied voice of the bird. In their poems, the voice is at the farthest reach of sense not for the sake of immediacy or through a fascination with the limits of sense, but to get rid of as much of the burden of physicality as could be dispensed with and still leave communication possible. If they retain the voice, it is in order to make the bird, as an image of the poet or his art, into a being that is all song, all art. This, of course, keeps it meaningful and intelligible to human experience, within the range of what men can know within the confines of this world. At the same time, all human intensity has been refined into a pure image of song. Neither Keats nor Shelley, therefore, grounded as they were in a world where whole areas of delight were still bound up with the senses, could have conceived of communication from beyond the borders of living warmth in the image of a golden, mechanical bird. But, unlike Wordsworth, they held onto the limits of sensuousness only in order to make the voice significant to the sensuous. The sound of the voice, then, while it is joyful for all, has other, surely more ominous implications for them than it does for Wordsworth. They feel all the ambivalence that he does, and some kinds of ambivalence that were probably foreign to him. His is the last step before a new field of experience, theirs the last hold onto the old one.

In "To the Cuckoo," though, Wordsworth does appear to have come near to discovering the kind of meaning Keats and Shelley were to find in their own experiences with disembodied voices. Yet even here the similarity is only apparent, in part because Wordsworth's bird has nothing to do with the song of art, but also, and primarily, because of the process through which the bird comes to have meaning for him. The question in the first stanza—"shall I call thee Bird, / Or but a wandering Voice?"—announces the beginning and the shape of the process. He proclaims that he has chosen deliberately to think of the bird in this apparently limited fashion, not in all the glorious fullness of its total being but only as a voice. The second step in the process comes in the third stanza:

> Though babbling only to the Vale,
> Of sunshine and of flowers,
> Thou bringest unto me a tale
> Of visionary hours.

Here, in this encounter between himself and the bird, there is not the slightest question of his fancy cheating him into thinking he can know very much about the world of the bird. He knows the limits, knows what the bird can and cannot do for him. When he chooses to find a meaning in that song in that context (a meaning that depends, in part, on who he is now and what he has been), he is thoroughly aware that he has no part in the scene that the bird experiences. He knows that he must will into being whatever meaning is in the scene. This is far more drastic than are most poems of encounter. Yet, curiously, there is within it neither melancholy nor a bitter concern for loss. It is still another version, joyful this time, of the stranger who is outside and alone and seems to be looking for a kind of welcome—though it is apparent that he is not seriously looking for one since he knows that he cannot find it here, and furthermore he has other concerns at this point. The separateness of man and his distinctness from the natural are as firmly asserted in this poem as in any by Keats and Shelley. Still, though he is never admitted into the world he faces, he creates a satisfactory situation. He has emphasized the willed process of his relationship with the voice in order to show how aware the stranger is of what he is and what he can never be. Thus, when he addresses the bird as "No bird, but an invisible thing, / A voice, a mystery," it is clear that he has willingly and confidently chosen a mode, with good reasons for doing so.

And in those reasons lies the essential difference between his "no bird" and Shelley's "bird thou never wert." Behind Wordsworth's choice in "To the Cuckoo" stands the impulse to recapture a childhood way of looking at things. It is a mode very like the one in which he saw the world as "an unsubstantial, faery place" where the hard concrete reality of rocks and stones and trees gives way to the "abyss of idealism" that he mentioned to Isabella Fenwick in speaking of his "Immortality" ode. In short, this poem is much closer to Wordsworth's own ode on the loss of childhood's mode of vision than it is to anything Keats or Shelley shaped from what they saw in this world or out of it. But "To the Cuckoo," though it shares concerns with the ode, has within it some similar activities that have different results. In "To the Cuckoo" Wordsworth offers not a transformation of

the physical into the transcendental (if that is what the childhood experience in the ode did offer) but, instead, its transformation into "an unsubstantial, faery place," the locale of "visionary hours." That change has meaning in terms of the way he sees
it happen and of what it shows of himself. There is no question
even considered here of the vision of a world beyond the natural: the change is in the one where he lives and moves now.
His youthful perception could accomplish such changes with
ease, though in his youth he would surely not have pondered
over whether he should distill the fullness of the bird into its
voice, the limit of its sensuous reach toward him. At one point
in his youth he could easily slip out of the senses. Now his world
is perhaps all too sensuous, and the change in his relationship
to it controls a deep change in its meaning for him. Yet Wordsworth tells us that he does manage to bring back for a moment
some aspects of his youthful mode of vision. By concentrating
the presence of the bird into the single element of its voice,
Wordsworth gets as close as he can to making it unsubstantial,
yet he gives it just enough place within the substantial to keep
him (and the bird) safely there. As immediate as that experience
of the bird's song can be, he claims at least that much immediacy
in his reexperience of himself as he was. In what he now does he
affirms that he can bring the mode back, that there is no unbridgeable gap between himself and what he was, and that there
is indeed a unity of being to be discovered in his experience.
He becomes, in other words, more fully himself for recapturing
the mode, and under those circumstances he could hardly want
to distill the fullness of his own self into a voice by identifying
with the bird. He wants, if anything, to intensify his newly re-
discovered awareness of the ties between childhood and now
and to glory in the knowledge that he can so work with things
outside as to make some of the earlier ways come back. The
metaphor of distance in the "Immortality" ode has no obvious
place in this poem, though the situations are much the same;
here he asserts that he can see again in a way which the ode
claims is forever beyond him. This is a poem that is partly about
fullness of self: thus, in purifying the qualities of the bird to the
fine point of its song, he does to it what, in this situation, he did
not want to do to himself. The limits of that unconsciously

ironic gesture are about as far from the modes of Keats and Shelley as one can move.

Wordsworth's own modes of knowing are so varied and extensive, and at the same time so closely involved with each other, that to separate out any one special kind, such as that associated with the disembodied voice, is to risk giving a partial and rather limited picture of a complicated set of activities. On the other hand, his series of experiments with the disembodied voice had its value for him in indicating how his need for a sense of the presence of the object could be compatible with the necessity for protecting its discreteness. Furthermore, some versions of the experiment also show how it was possible for all these demands to be met while pointing toward other kinds of knowledge to which physicality could give access but which were very definitely beyond the physical. At some times such knowledge is apocalyptic, a revelation of universal transformation; at others it is transcendental in the sense of being a more private and circumscribed glimpse into other forms of phenomena which can be led to only by a dissolution of the physical. Obviously these possibilities are not mutually exclusive; indeed, they fade into each other at some areas. The action through which Wordsworth pushes an object to the limits of its sensuousness should perhaps be seen as a gradual but persistent drawing out of physicality to a very fine and pure point. From that point one can choose to rest and move back, or one can move to the obverse of that fine point in another point which begins the expanding road to new dimensions of knowing. One of the most rewarding of all his experiments with the distillation of an object into a voice, the poem "Stepping Westward," permits a glimpse into this process of disembodiment and shows how the voice, heard in a certain way, makes possible the knowledge of other dimensions of experience at the same time as it retains its identity as pure voice. What we are offered is a wide spectrum in which there is room for many varieties of knowing.

The proper place to begin with this poem is with Dorothy's journal entry of 11 September 1803:

> We have never had a more delightful walk than this evening. Ben Lomond and the three pointed-topped mountains of Loch Lomond, which we had seen from the Garrison, were very

majestic under the clear sky, the lake perfectly calm, the air sweet and mild. I felt that it was much more interesting to visit a place where we have been before than it can possibly be the first time, except under peculiar circumstances. The sun had been set for some time, when, being within a quarter of a mile of the ferryman's hut, our path having led us close to the shore of the calm lake, we met two neatly dressed women, without hats, who had probably been taking their Sunday evening's walk. One of them said to us in a friendly, soft tone of voice, "What! you are stepping westward?" I cannot describe how affecting this simple expression was in that remote place, with the western sky in front, *yet* glowing with the departed sun.[4]

The undercurrent of nervous exuberance that runs all through her journals here finds its outlet in the generalized description of the larger physical aspects of the scene. Just before this passage there are some circumstantial sentences which describe the different forms the road took, sentences whose brief, pointed shifts in detailed observation had given a more elaborate texture to the scene than it has in this passage. Thus there has been a move toward starkness. The scene has its own idiosyncratic character, and the travelers and the women they meet have their own particularity, which is defined essentially in terms of where they are and what they are doing there. It is Sunday, and the women are hatless and, we are told, probably strolling for exercise and relaxation. All of these are important facts, as are Dorothy's observations on revisiting a familiar place. The scope is broad, and the details are placed carefully. In the scene as a whole, the sense of expansiveness moves out quite noticeably through all the physical space around the participants.

The material in this passage is calculated to give a wide and detailed breadth of experience that is grounded firmly in the physical world, with the two women part of a context that has a variety of contours and a number of specific points at which the eye can rest. This passage is the first literary stage of the experience, its first embodiment in language. In the next stage, of special interest because so clearly transitional, the elements in the scene have begun to take on different characteristics. That

---

[4] *Journals of Dorothy Wordsworth*, ed. Ernest de Selincourt (1941; reprinted, London: Macmillan, 1959), I, 367. Hereafter cited as *Journals*.

next stage is the headnote to "Stepping Westward": "While my Fellow-traveller and I were walking by the side of Loch Ketterine, one fine evening after sunset, in our road to a Hut where, in the course of our tour, we had been hospitably entertained some weeks before, we met, in one of the loneliest parts of that solitary region, two well-dressed Women, one of whom said to us, by way of greeting, 'What, you are stepping westward?' " The landscape has not really disappeared, though most of the contours and specifics have gone. There has been a further move toward starkness. Still, the note gives quite enough to place the travelers and the women who greet them in a locale that is not merely somewhere but also of a special character: the broad expanse of the lake is beside them, and just ahead is a known destination associated with warmth, but the landscape is still empty and isolated, without any regular or repeated suggestions of human associations. It is in this context that the women appear. The fact that they are well dressed (their lack of hats is no longer mentioned), which in itself was hardly noticeable in Dorothy's description, takes on a particular prominence because of the brevity of the passage and the few facts that receive any mention at all. Obviously the quality of their clothing is on a par in importance with the emptiness of the landscape and the welcoming hut just ahead. The meeting has begun to take on significant shape.

In the poem itself the process of condensation reaches its limit, while certain factors within the experience are developed and intensified to the point where new proportions of emphasis begin to emerge. At the center, like a sound whose echo has unlimited reach, is a disembodied voice. Curiously, the process has turned the poem into a quasi allegory, an effect not unusual in Wordsworth and not at all surprising considering the material he had at hand. The poem shows a moment of transition in the physical world, with the full darkness about to begin but with the sky ahead, "such a sky," still glowing with the fading of the light. Behind the speaker lies darkness, and the ground under him is cold. A stranger in a strange land, he journeys toward the west from where a light still comes by which he can see his way. A question that is really a greeting comes to him from a native of the place through which he is moving.

Looked at in these terms, the situation clearly demands an allegorical reading. The speaker himself finds the impetus to such a reading irresistible and falls effortlessly into that mode of interpretation. His journey toward the west "seemed to be / A kind of *heavenly* destiny," that is, to have a heavenly destination, and he wraps this package up with a tidy climax, testifying to his awareness that he is living a moment of allegory. In the situation he is going through at that moment, he sees an image of man's journey through this world:

> and while my eye
> Was fixed upon the glowing Sky,
> The echo of the voice enwrought
> A human sweetness with the thought
> Of travelling through the world that lay
> Before me in my endless way.

There is surely nothing inherently false about the speaker's interpretation of his own situation. Indeed, it intrigues and clarifies. But at the same time it goes off in a direction that leads away from many of the more interesting facts about the poem. There is, for example, the odd chiaroscuro of the landscape, which makes it look as though the travelers were creating darkness behind them as they went, though here darkness is nothing ominous. Rather, the travelers seem to be closing off all things behind them. The landscape of blacks and grays serves, in its severity, to bring out with concentrated intensity the one item of color, the glow on which the speaker's eye is acutely fixed. We remember the importance of that process in Wordsworth in which his intense concentration on some one aspect of sense effectively promotes the impact of another aspect that comes, somewhat surprisingly, from a different direction. That, of course, is what happens here with this observer, who is greeted by the voice, now apparently no longer attached to any body. It would seem that nearly all of the significant elements in the scene have been purified to their most intense point. The stark chiaroscuro with the glow at its center, the line (a kind of continuum) on which the travelers are moving, and the voice coming at them from somewhere never specified in the poem itself create an acute pressure derived primarily from the condensation to an intense purity of all that he sees. Nothing comes through but color tones, the line of movement, his own eye, and a woman's voice. The two women whom they met have been distilled into the voice of one, a pure sound of greeting. To keep the voice within the woman and to surround her with the particularities of the situation would be to turn the whole action onto another plane, where a multiplicity of sensuous stimuli would create another kind of experience, one which was embedded in the particular. But in the poem as it is, the point is in purity, that limit of the senses beyond which there is something else to know and another way of knowing necessary. The condensation absorbs the allegorical dimension into a purified vision leading inexorably out of this landscape, though the scene moves to the edge of apocalyptic transformation without ever quite getting there. Distilled into a sound, the welcome enlarges in scope and transcends the immediacy of its source to become a heavenly greeting, one that appears to come out of a realm that can confer the spiritual right of travel. But it is a *human* sweetness that the echo of the voice fuses with the thought of traveling, and thus he is still kept here. The greeting, then, is located in both this world and another, for with all its human sweetness it still comes in the form of "a sound / Of something without place or bound," certainly not the form of anything in this realm of things. The voice, because it partakes of each world, is a bridge toward other modes of being, which cannot be confined or defined even in the purified world he has created around him. The outsider, who has not really been unhappy or seriously uncomfortable, finds acceptance from both worlds and is given security as he passes through this one. Events just like these, but without the tones of allegory or apocalypse, happened to the stranger who came upon the voice of the wren in the ruined abbey. An ironic reversal of the central plot occurs in *The Ancient Mariner*: there the outsider's rejection of gratuitous welcome leads to isolation from any order which can welcome, thus making him the complete stranger. Then, through spontaneous love that leads eventually to a welcoming (line 459), there emerges for him the possibility of a new kind of knowing which the stranger has to earn by encountering other strangers. *Peter Bell* offers a parodic version of the basic plot at a level where the outsider learns about welcome through a grotesque lower being.[5]

The difference between "Stepping Westward" and "The Solitary Reaper," poems related in a number of ways, gives an emphatic indication of the difference in kind and therefore meaning between Wordsworth's experiments in two contrasting modes. The reaper is also singing, but the voice is not disembodied, although what we see of the girl is beyond particularity. Her presence is minimal but firm and unequivocal, and what he sees is enough to place her clearly in the field, with the voice coming out of the body of that girl who can be seen alone "at her work, / And o'er the sickle bending." The difference in the relative presence of the women in these poems goes partway toward creating (and is in turn supported by) a difference in the meaning the women have in their particular situations. For the point of embodying the voice of the reaper in a physical presence, however minimal, is to affirm her role and situation in earthly continua, a context including the physical as well as the temporal, both dimensions very much of this world. To make the reaper's voice a disembodied one would be to create a cacophony in which the image of the girl could not support or clarify the context in which he places it. For it is her earthiness, her representative earthiness, that matters. The mode of "Stepping Westward," however similar the locale, is so different that it makes another kind of poem with a form and significance that place it in another continuum where different realms of being come together.

The image of the disembodied voice was so flexible that it could be serviceable to Wordsworth even when his interest in the physical diminished. The kind of knowing involved in object-consciousness, the sense of the presence of things out there, was always of some usefulness (partly through nostalgia, perhaps). In *The Excursion*, where bodiless voices sound through at a number of places, he could so arrange the image that its meaning for him turned quite around from what it had been, becoming the last hold onto the physical in much the same way as it

[5] See my "Wordsworth's Comedy of Redemption," *Anglia*, 84 (1966), 388–397.

had been for Keats and Shelley. He is, in other words, less interested in the knowing available on this side of the voice than in the kind on its other side, what the voice leads him to. Even the old ambivalence has gone. His eagerness to get beyond the voice is evident in Book Nine of *The Excursion*, where he had begun to build an idea "of Age, / As of a final EMINENCE," and where he shapes the outline of a mountain similar to those in the observer's surroundings (the romantic likes to pick up images from his surroundings so that the images can get as close to their meaning as possible [6]). The conventional detachment that the situation on the mountain affords leads him, a bit surprisingly, into the disappearance of the visible world:

> But, while the gross and visible frame of things
> Relinquishes its hold upon the sense,
> Yea almost on the Mind herself, and seems
> All unsubstantialized,—how loud the voice
> Of waters, with invigorated peal
> From the full river in the vale below,
> Ascending! For on that superior height
> Who sits, is disencumbered from the press
> Of near obstructions, and is privileged
> To breathe in solitude, above the host
> Of ever-humming insects, 'mid thin air
> That suits not them. The murmur of the leaves
> Many and idle, visits not his ear:
> This he is freed from, and from thousand notes
> (Not less unceasing, not less vain than these,)
> By which the finer passages of sense
> Are occupied; and the Soul, that would incline
> To listen, is prevented and deterred.
>
> (63–80)

Memories of the vision on Mt. Snowdon are here, but this is different seeing, for all the senses close off except the one receiving the loud voice of the waters, invisible down below. The point of the image is to show what Age is like, its insulated detachment from the myriad voices of insects, leaves, and most

[6] See William K. Wimsatt's classic essay on the subject, "The Structure of Romantic Nature Imagery," in *English Romantic Poets: Modern Essays in Criticism*, pp. 25–36.

things "By which the finer passages of sense / Are occupied." The air he now breathes is too thin for them. Free from their voices and their distractions, he can concentrate on what is beyond the bodily eye. At the farthest reach of sense there is only one sound; but that sound coming through to Age is all that remains of physicality, so that "the finer passages of sense" are now almost unoccupied, and therefore he can go through them to other modes of knowing. Here the voice is a remnant of what no longer interests him; he has no real delight in it. Through the sound of the waters, he has the last contact with sense (which has been unceasing and vain), and when the contact slips all idle sounds will be gone. Yet this is the same image, with the same form, as he made use of with the wren, the cuckoo, the woman in "Stepping Westward," and all the other instances. The process and pattern are the same, but the slant and frame of reference are quite the opposite. The voice is not a welcome but a farewell.

Even here, in a conventional, skillful use of a potentially stunning image, Wordsworth still thinks in terms of object-consciousness; he always had to get a sense of the presence of the object in order to work out the sense of the voice. When he left that mode of consciousness, he worked very differently. Thorough disembodiment of self does not mean for Wordsworth that he ascends a ladder and carries along with him everything he has learned below. A radically different kind of understanding goes to work, with the split coming just beyond the edge to which his experiments with the disembodied voice carried him. We have seen that he could go to the edge and turn back. When he went beyond, he did so because only there could the unheard melodies come through with absolute purity:

> Wonder not
> If high the transport, great the joy I felt,
> Communing in this sort through earth and heaven
> With every form of creature, as it looked
> Towards the Uncreated with a countenance
> Of adoration, with an eye of love.
> One song they sang, and it was audible,
> Most audible, then, when the fleshly ear,

O'ercome by humblest prelude of that strain,
Forgot her functions, and slept undisturbed.

(*Prelude*, II, 409–418)

But that is to talk of other music, not the kind associated
with an encounter in which he might not know more about the
truth of an object than that it was there, had met him, and was
strange.

CHAPTER FOUR

A Synecdoche for Wholeness

DESPITE Wordsworth's public complacency, his world and that of the other romantics usually comes through as a particularly difficult one. Its moments of glory stand out at least partly because they are so rare, sporadic, and unpredictable, and, when they do occur, so brief and evanescent. The necessary loneliness of the self (the "sole self" of Keats's "Ode to a Nightingale") is overcome for a moment in a communion that may or may not be joyful, but it is overcome only for that surprising moment and for no longer. Paradoxes, sometimes painful and sometimes glorious, abound. Chief among them is the quality of the moment itself, subject to the very evanescence, flux, and instability which it alone (or some representative of it) can conquer. But when it does conquer, however briefly, the rewards are exciting and manifold.

What the romantics wanted to assert about the nature of the romantic self has much to do with the qualities and difficulties of the moments in which it glories and, finally, of the world in which the glorying takes place. If there is a sense in which the romantic poet had to remake the wholeness of the world for himself, the prevalence of the organic metaphor indicates that wholeness as such was always an issue. Of the coherence of the self, its contained and idiosyncratic development, Wordsworth spoke at every turn and, in one way or another, in most of his major poems. The truth of encounter was, in part, a truth about the wholeness of this action in which there were no absolutely passive participants. And the sentiment of being was, of course, the awareness of the wholeness of a continuum where all things had at least the fact of existence in common. Some of the difficulty about Wordsworth's world comes because he was unsentimental enough to talk about wholeness while avoiding identification and unification. We know that he was concerned with a sense of totality in the scenes where things happened to him.[1] This too was organicism, a complex whole of elements held tensely together for perhaps only a moment. But organicism is wholeness, not a blending of identities. It is a meeting of necessarily independent elements within a context where they all can function together but cannot cease being their idiosyncratic selves. There was, quite simply, too much around Wordsworth that was so strange that he could see no possibility of more than a partial understanding of most of it, with an occasional glimpse deeper within at a high moment of encounter. In such a world there was no chance for walls to disappear so completely that everything was everywhere in all. Wordsworth never expected what Shelley frequently wanted: he could not become one with anything except himself, and even that had its problems. On the other hand, it was possible to work out the sense of a world shot through with different instances of wholeness in various dimensions, so that organicism became the criterion for stability within and without, for health, and even for a version of piety that picked up many overtones from outworn assertions of order. In this sense of a world, there are dangerous glories that Wordsworth shared with other romantics. For if it is both a duty and a delight to instance wholeness, that function fails when there is division and the self ceases to stand coherently. This is surely the essential cause of the undertone of sin perceptible in most instances of separation and isolation undergone by disjunct romantic selves. The long history of the romantic hero reveals again and again what has to be defined as an awareness that somehow there has been a failure of responsibil-

---

[1] See Hazlitt's essay on Wordsworth in *The Spirit of the Age* (London: J. M. Dent, Everyman's Library, 1955), p. 259: "he would not give a rush for any landscape that did not express the time of day, the climate, the period of the world it was meant to illustrate, or had not this character of *wholeness* in it."

ity: "dann sehne ich mich oft und denke: Ach könntest du das
wieder ausdrücken, könntest du dem Papiere das einhauchen,
was so voll, so warm in dir lebt, dass es würde der Spiegel deiner
Seele, wie deine Seele ist der Spiegel des unendlichen Gottes!—
Mein Freund—Aber ich gehe darüber zugrunde, ich erliege
unter der Gewalt der Herrlichkeit dieser Erscheinungen." [2]
In *The Prelude*, when Wordsworth crawls around in the abyss
whose full depths can only be guessed at (his reticence here is as
remarkable as his candor elsewhere), he makes clear that he
felt something essentially wrong with himself, since a way up
from the abyss was out there waiting for him to make use of
it. What was outside was whole, and if he was not, the fault was
his own and not in the stars. Several familiar phrases sound out
of a fragment of early 1798 from the Alfoxden notebook:

> Of unknown modes of being which on earth,
> Or in the heavens, or in the heavens and earth
> Exist by mighty combinations, bound
> Together by a link, and with a soul
> Which makes all one.[3]

This puts it quite starkly, defining a continuum of apparently
independent entities and therefore a kind of order whose radical
characteristics are wholeness and an element that ties. It is an
order outside of his own order but one that is nonetheless tied
up with his own, since he makes one more step in the continuum
as another independent entity. If there is a sense in which he is
always by himself, always therefore the stranger, it is equally
true that, though alone, he is not untied. At this level of Wordsworth's thinking, all these orders are panentheistic, and his own
comes to be imbued with a persistent awareness of the hierarchy
on the great chain of being. The moment of glory in which
the stranger ruptures the tough wall of self offers, therefore,
not only the conquering of isolation and transience but also a
luminous contact of the self with that which is partly its counterpart in external reality. The moment of encounter is all the
more glorious because of what can come to be known from it: it

---

[2] *Die Leiden des jungen Werther*, letter of 10 May, in *Goethes Werke*,
VI, ed. Benno von Wiese and Erich Strunz (1951; 5th ed., Hamburg:
Christian Wegner, 1963), 9.
[3] *Poetical Works*, V, 340–341.

is worldly and beyond things, orderly and ordering, and at the same time absolutely idiosyncratic and therefore expressive of the uniqueness of his seeing.

For Wordsworth and every other romantic who dealt with similar experiences, the priceless quality of these moments had much to do with what they could offer as solutions to a number of romantic quandaries. But the evanescence of the moment was nonetheless (or therefore all the more) shocking. Concerned as all of the romantics were, the generation of Keats as well as that of Wordsworth, with the flux of time and the self, they had to find some way to get over the difficulties of transience, to retain in all its livingness and incomparableness that rare moment in which the self, in an instant of pure encounter, breaches the boundaries within which it is ordinarily confined. The moment in which the self comes to a further knowledge of its own nature and overcomes its radical loneliness has somehow to be retained without falsification and with all its intricacy of related dimensions. The romantic agony, whatever its single or unmixed bias, took a series of forms which, though perhaps not quite homogeneous, usually had to do with the problems of self in a fleeting world where miraculous breaches of separateness could occasionally happen. What with the difficulties involved in a union achieved through love of another self (as so often in Shelley), an experience connected with the natural world and its people or objects, or perhaps one transcending both concreteness and the ordinary limits of awareness—what with all these and other experiences possible to the romantics, the poets had cause enough for anguish. In a world where the loss of most standards of value had driven them within to the order of the self ("the last place of refuge—my own soul": *Prelude*, X, 415), they hoped that that order, at least, could remain whole. One of the various glories of the moment of encounter was that it verified the wholeness of the self. But added to all these difficulties came others, probably provoked by the pervasive fact of evanescence. Once the moment was completed, there could well be questions about its actuality and about illusoriness in general (as at the end of "Ode to a Nightingale"), or, if there had been no moments for long, about the loss of ability ever to achieve them again, one of the network of themes in Coleridge's

"Dejection." Experiences so unsettling find their most suggestive analogies in the more intense forms of baroque religious poetry.

Yet certain premises were exempt from doubt, most of all the cogency, efficacy, and truthfulness of artistic statement. This is not to say that art has no limitations: we have seen Wordsworth's uncertainty (or fluctuating certainty) about all that words can do. Still, whatever the value of Wordsworth's repeated insistence that he wanted to be considered a teacher or nothing, he shared with every romantic (not excepting Byron with his cozy disclaimers) a substantial belief in the importance of poetry as a way of defining what human experience is like and what it probably means. This importance was not, however, confined to what the poetry said but grew out of fundamental principles in the romantic aesthetics of form. The declaration that the art object is an organic unity reiterates in another field of discourse the idea of a coherent and felicitous wholeness. Here is a primary, specific, and eminently observable version of what the romantic poets all over England and Europe kept trying to define as basic to what they could experience and the way they experienced it. All of the particulars in this closely textured argument move toward supporting the implication, inevitable in a romantic context, that there is a close relationship between the order of the artist's self and the shape of what that self produces. Of the many forms that the relationship took, one of the more suggestive and significant came with the implied homology between the creative self and the created object. We know from figures as diverse as the Coleridge of "Dejection" and Goethe's Werther that only with a wholeness of self can there be a successfully emergent coherence in the object one creates. Thus, if the created object and the creative self are not to be identified (though several arguments come close to that), at the least they can be seen as homologous. Since it is assumed that a coherent organic structure can be produced only by another that is at least equally coherent, it follows that if the object is coherent then the producing self must be so too. (Such arguments tend now and then toward a glaring circularity, but that hardly matters when so many varieties of wholeness are at stake.) The homology of self and product took, for some poets, a further complication of direction with the argument that an

Ultimate Creative Spirit—defined in no matter what framework—has created the microcosmic human self. This, in turn, created another microcosm in which is mirrored the sustained, integrated completeness of its creator and its creator's Creator. (The passage from *Werther* quoted above is very clear about this kind of relationship.) It would be easy to argue, then, that the making of poems is an act of devotion. Further, it would be possible to assert that the possession of a coherent, organic self is another act of devotion and, conversely, that a disjunct self is somehow vile and impious. Variations on this argument about the continuum of microcosms ran all through romanticism, but it would be quite wrong to say that all of the romantics felt exactly what the argument describes. Keats certainly did not. Byron probably did, though, and Coleridge could certainly hold with no other. Wordsworth never went as far as Coleridge, but during and after the spiritual illness detailed in *The Prelude* he came to know with unmistakable clarity that only with an organic, efficacious self could the kind of relationship which for him was devout come into being. The successfully working wholeness of action which was the encounter meant that there came through to the observer an awareness of individual coherences of various kinds and on various levels, all abutting on each other, all part of the same totality of experience though not entirely contained within it. But to know this he had to have made out his own workable completeness.

When the poem is thought of in a context like this, it has to be considered an affirmation of order. Its character as an organism implies an ordered relationship of everything that the romantics wanted to see working harmoniously together. There exists within the organism a thoroughly satisfying organization of the inner and outer worlds of the poet, insofar as those are at all separable for examination. Both worlds appear together in a coherent system in which everything works for everything else as well as for itself, and all planes and dimensions balance each other in such a way as to make wholeness possible without jeopardizing the integrity of any one member. A poem like "Dejection," which has disharmony as one of its themes, asserts by its existence as a successful poem that harmony is possible after all and on a number of levels. That means, further, that at some level the disjunct self must be working successfully. (There is a profound richness in the fact that "Dejection" is a self-contradicting product; there is no such paradox in the "Immortality" ode.) Disharmony, therefore, can be asserted harmoniously. Whatever else they may be, these implications of romantic poetics are hardly wish fulfillment masquerading as aesthetics. More accurately, and considering the dilemmas of the romantic position, such implications go far toward defining the romantic sense of a poem and the reasons which made romantic aesthetics an important way of discussing the difficulties of living in that age.

Other ways of examining the wholeness of self were available to the romantics, of course, and Wordsworth seems to have looked for as many as he could find within the range of his own knowledge and sensibility. Poems, merely in being themselves, could do such examining as well as any other mode of discourse could. Poems which were about encounters had a built-in harmony of reflecting wholenesses, for the special qualities of the moment affirmed much the same values, indeed had much the same organization, as did the order of the poem. Encounter was another kind of tensely ordered, imaginatively compelling whole which was successful in being fully itself, though it may have done no more than point to the difficulties of knowing very much about anything else which was also successfully and fully itself. The poem of encounter would therefore be an affirmation not only of order but also of a multitude of varied versions of it. Here there became possible the loveliest fusion of form and content. But in the case of Wordsworth, typical in many ways, the sense and experience of organicism and wholeness seem to have been arrived at (or, more properly, returned to) only after a sometimes brutal experience of fragmentation and disjunction.

In a way, the shape of encounter has so natural a form that the poem embodying it takes on a wholeness simply by dramatizing the experience. This means that there can be poems that look like fragments but are not, poems in which Wordsworth not only draws the complete lineaments of the experience—sometimes with elaborate thoroughness, occasionally very briefly and sharply—but also most often indicates the conditions of the encounter, how it became what it was as well as the fact that it became so at all:

> ———The sky is overcast
> With a continuous cloud of texture close,
> Heavy and wan, all whitened by the Moon,
> Which through that veil is indistinctly seen,
> A dull, contracted circle, yielding light
> So feebly spread that not a shadow falls,
> Chequering the ground—from rock, plant, tree, or tower.
> At length a pleasant instantaneous gleam
> Startles the pensive traveller while he treads
> His lonesome path, with unobserving eye
> Bent earthwards; he looks up—the clouds are split
> Asunder,—and above his head he sees
> The clear Moon, and the glory of the heavens.
> There, in a black-blue vault she sails along,
> Followed by multitudes of stars, that, small
> And sharp, and bright, along the dark abyss
> Drive as she drives: how fast they wheel away,
> Yet vanish not!—the wind is in the tree,
> But they are silent;—still they roll along
> Immeasurably distant; and the vault,
> Built round by those white clouds, enormous clouds,
> Still deepens its unfathomable depth.
> At length the Vision closes; and the mind,
> Not undisturbed by the delight it feels,
> Which slowly settles into peaceful calm,
> Is left to muse upon the solemn scene.

Wordsworth told Henry Crabb Robinson in 1815 that "A Night-Piece" (which he called "a description of Night") was among the best of his Poems of Imagination "for the imaginative power displayed in [it]." [4] The poem has its counterpart in a journal entry recorded by Dorothy for 25 January 1798: "The sky spread over with one continuous cloud, whitened by the light of the moon, which, though her dim shape was seen, did not throw forth so strong a light as to checquer the earth with shadows. At once the clouds seemed to cleave asunder, and left her in the centre of a black-blue vault. She sailed along, followed

[4] *Henry Crabb Robinson on Books and Their Writers*, ed. Edith J. Morley (London: J. M. Dent, 1938), I, 166.

by multitudes of stars, small, and bright, and sharp. Their brightness seemed concentrated." [5] Certain details are similar to those in the poem, the verbal parallels are clear, and it is also clear that the overall cosmic activities in the poem and the journal entry are much the same. Dorothy's visual acuity usually establishes a total image or event with a few details to ground it in concreteness and give it inner dimensions. But the differences between the poem and the journal entry are so remarkable that the poem becomes quite another experience. Dorothy's description is detached and objective, in a way completely external. There is shown no awareness of an observer watching this or of his watching as part of the activity of the experience. There is, therefore, no change shown within the observer that could parallel the change that occurs outside of him. In those two kinds of change, in the parallels between them and especially the tensions evident there, lie the radical elements of organization in the poem, its fullness and variety of dimensions, and the harmonizing interchange between inner and outer and man and cosmos recorded in the dialectic of the various states.

The state of the observer at each point of the experience in the poem is rendered with care, and the states are such that the external changes in the physical qualities of the heavens (each point of change marked sharply by the transitional "at length") form an exact parallel to what is going on inside of him. In the first stage, the poet sees what the observer apparently does not, although it can be argued that the pensive traveler must have been subliminally aware of the parallel of his own state to the state of the sky since the states follow each other so exactly. As in the lyric on daffodils, "Strange Fits of Passion," and many other of Wordsworth's poems, the observer, mostly within himself but with a hidden sense in touch with the external scene, wakes abruptly and with surprise into another kind of landscape than the one he has been in. His own change follows immediately upon the change in the qualities outside. In all of these poems, he comes upon an activity that contrasts to the general passivity he had been experiencing, a passivity echoed in the world outside. In "A Night-Piece" a smothering dullness is at

---

[5] *Journals*, I, 4.

first the dominant tone of that world and therefore of his state. But it is not merely the heavy colorlessness or the dullness of the contracted circle or the weakness of the light that makes this tone. There is also, and more significantly, the continuous cloud and the absence of chiaroscuro. Thus there is none of that breaking up into acutely delineated patterns of light and dark which for Wordsworth usually indicates the observer's sensitized awareness of the varied qualities of the external scene (e.g., "Stepping Westward"). When the observer is startled into awareness in the second stage, the qualities of the pattern he observes in the sky are seen to have shifted abruptly into an elaborate arrangement including one large spot of light and multitudinous small ones, all etched sharply and brightly against the black-blue background. This signals the change in the range and qualities of the observer's perception. His attention fixes on the moon, a single central object riding majestically in a situation of which it is the master and initial point of focus, though the myriad of stars and what they lead his vision to come subsequently into the midpoint of the picture.

When the veil of clouds is split, the observer sees what is not a new world but another part of the totality that he had always been in without realizing it. The cosmos opens up, and he sees not only that he is part of the context of earth (he is no longer "with unobserving eye / Bent earthwards") but also that he and the earth are part of the fullest of totalities that includes both earth and cosmos. In a characteristic gesture, Wordsworth had prepared for this new knowledge by talking, in the first six lines, of earth and sky together and of the light of the moon that affects the clouds but not the earth. Curiously, the chiaroscuro effect that the breakthrough of the light will create, the "chequering" of the ground, indicates that sky and earth are brought together through the light. (It is worth repeating here that such a breakthrough is usually a sign in Wordsworth of a sudden new intensity in the observer's perception.) The new vision is therefore created by a movement that reveals wholeness, and what the movement creates (here it also reveals the chiaroscuro in the sky) shows that the observer has intensified his seeing and now knows the fullness and the whole.

The act of splitting that had opened the cosmos builds a

strange excitement within the observer that parallels the excitement without, the wind in the tree and the silent but swift movement of the moon and the stars. The order in which the objects and actions in the sky are described shows that he first fixed on the moon, saw it in its place in the whole of the heavens ("glory" here may well be a pun as it probably is in the "Immortality" ode), and then saw the stars, which because of their multitude and diversity receive more detailed description than does anything else, and finally saw the vault encircled by the clouds that had opened up. From his first fixation on a single striking object, the observer has increased the scope of his vision until he sees the framed vault, which looks like an entrance into the deep center of things. The vault, along with his soul, expands and deepens in compass into the unfathomable depths, and here, of course, he can say no more than that what he sees is all there is to see. Now he can only return: "At length the Vision closes." He has had the experience, and he can come back to the original scene with an excited awareness of an increase in himself.

A poem like this not only tells that some event occurred but also shows how it occurred and defines the qualities that had been necessary to make it come about at all. The conditions of the experience and the shape of its development emerge in the details of language and form. The poem and the experience are therefore inseparable, not only because the poem contains the experience and nothing else but, further, because the order of the poem and the order of the encounter are each organic and self-sustaining, i.e., are organized in much the same way. This characteristic kind of romantic poem is a hymn of triumph, whatever its subject. The triumph was there because a certain kind of experience had occurred and the experience could be organized into a special kind of poem. Under these conditions, poetic discourse becomes a type of experience that is about experiencing, action in process, and very often about the high point of encounter, the object that stimulated it, and the total situation that surrounded the meeting and gave it a context. "A Night-Piece" asserts a complicated wholeness by telling of what it does, and at the same time it is itself an instance of another version of wholeness, harmony, and radiance—or rather, of a variety of wholenesses in one. Part of the variety involved is the organic structure of the encounter in which at least two poles establish themselves (one, the object, is the most apparent center of energy). Between both there happens a meeting so complicated that the movements to and fro are difficult to disentangle, partly because they are usually simultaneous. Those movements occur along a dimension containing the observer and the object and bordered by them; but that dimension is obviously only one of the many in the poem. All of the dimensions, though (and this is true of any poem of encounter), are held together by a very active plot which is necessarily dramatic, since the process of encounter leads to an intense point of meeting and then a (usually) gradual withdrawal. Movements, dimensions, and plot all point to the tensions of the encounter, which seem very often to imply a struggle or a series of them. Most obvious are the sort of conflicts in "Resolution and Independence," with its deep inner uneasiness, or the attempt of the hearer to understand the song of the solitary reaper, a conflict that resolves itself, somewhat to the observer's surprise, on another level of awareness. But since much of the action in these poems seems to be taking place without the overt awareness of the observer, there are most likely other kinds of struggle at work. This can occur so subtly that one is aware only of what the current situation, somehow vaguely unsatisfactory, could be but is not. Such is the beginning of "A Night-Piece," where the unpleasing though not offensive dullness in the sky is contrasted to what could happen at those obviously more desirable moments when the light breaks through. Further, in this poem and all others like it, the conflict results in a moment of awe, the mature development of the fear in some of the experiences of childhood. This awe frequently implies a gap in hierarchical status between the observer and what he sees, a gap which makes the moment of communion (the desire for which can be part of the struggle) all the more impressive when it does occur because it involves the meeting of forces which cannot be equal in power. The protagonist in "A Night-Piece" feels what he does partly because he sees how immense the wholeness is.

Still, whatever the lineaments of the struggle and the quality of its content, the beginning of the poem of encounter usually verifies the grounding of the experience in physicality. Sometimes, as in "Resolution and Independence," the texture of the physical comes through in elaborate detail, while at other times the physicality at the beginning seems just on the verge of disappearing or being transformed into something else, a movement seen occasionally in Keats and also in Wordsworth, who could never have written "Ode to a Nightingale" but would certainly understand what was going on in it. The physicality may not become other than it is but develop into an even greater fullness, dwelling on the sense of the presence of the object with all of the richness that the extraordinarily heightened perception of the observer can discover in it. In "A Night-Piece," what he sees never disappears or fades into something else. It becomes, rather, all it can probably ever be for him, which is very much indeed, while it leads him to the edge of an awesome glimpse into the bottomless center of things. In "The Solitary Reaper," though, the girl fades in a sense that is characteristically romantic and particularly Wordsworthian: his vision of her moves from an outward gaze, out to where she is, to an inner gaze, where her substantiality is almost entirely subsumed into the metaphors and the large context in which her song leads him to place her. Yet, and perhaps not paradoxically after all, what he glimpses in "A Night-Piece" is clearly more encompassing in scope than even the grand vision of universal humanity he has through the song of the reaper. Obviously, then, the relative annihilation or fullness of presence of the object has no *necessary* relation to the significance or depth of what he sees.

Dramatic, concrete, organic, itself a symbol of a comprehension of wholeness through the creative spirit, itself an indication of an assertion of will in the face of the potential chaos always there in things—this kind of romantic poem made possible for Wordsworth and those like him one of the finest modes of overcoming the transience of the moments of glory seen or foreseen by most of the English romantic poets. The analogy and affinity of the poem and the experience it recorded gave the poets the opportunity to preserve those moments in which the observer comes to know something more about the world in which he and the thing outside share the same, nearly overwhelming context. Obviously the moments were not always successful and probably (we have no poems to judge by) registered when unsuccessful only as a state of nervousness, perhaps a set of free-floating tensions that turned into unexplained anxieties coming strangely out of some odd situation. Certainly the preservation of the successful moments was a primary concern for Wordsworth, though it seems likely that he was not always thoroughly and immediately aware of why they were successful. But he was profoundly aware of why such moments were important to him. The 1797 fragment called "Incipient Madness" leads with startling clarity into an understanding of one of the reasons behind Wordsworth's passion for encounter.[6]

Even so early a fragment as this one reveals the process involved, although here he shows it primarily through an awareness that what he is doing is a lie. All the more, then, does the process come clear. The broken pane on which he fixed his gaze "seemed akin to life," gave a false semblance of it. But he needed that semblance so badly, needed, in other words, something to which he could establish some kind of a relation, that he would lie to himself in order to fashion what would seem like an encounter. Encounter is a way of asserting that something has meaning; but it is also a way of asserting that there is something out there that has meaning. Further, the self in encounter is the whole self. A fragmented self deludes itself by giving life to pieces of flashing glass in moments of incipient madness. His hunger for communion drove him to that point:

> There is a mood
> A settled temper of the heart, when grief,
> Become an instinct, fastening on all things
> That promise food, doth like a sucking babe
> Create where it is not.

Indeed, as another version of the passage (quoted as a variant in *Poetical Works*, I, 315) brings out, his greedy relation to the flashing piece of glass was desperate, and the greed drove him to the object again and again for reassurance:

[6] *Poetical Works*, I, 314–316. See above, pp. 20–21.

A Synecdoche for Wholeness

I found my sickly heart had tied itself
Even to this tiny speck of glass—it could produce
A feeling of absence [
            ] on the moment when my sight
Should feed on it again. Many long months
Confirmed this strange incontinence; my eye
Did every evening measure the moon's height
And forth I went before her yellow beams
Could overtop the elmtrees oer the heath,
I went, I reach'd the cottage, and I found
Still undisturb'd and glittering in its place
That speck of glass more precious to my soul.

In the text proper, immediately following the episode with the glass is another episode, linked without commentary:

Another time
The winds of Autumn drove me o'er the heath
One gloomy evening: by the storm compell'd
The poor man's horse that feeds along the lanes
Had hither come among these fractur'd walls
To weather out the night; and as I pass'd
While restlessly he turn'd from the fierce wind
And from the open sky, I heard, within,
The iron links with which his feet were clogg'd
Mix their dull clanking with the heavy noise
Of falling rain—I started from the spot
And heard the sound still following in the wind.

But there is no arbitrary juxtaposition here in these classic instances of visionary dreariness, for there is commentary within the forms of the experiences themselves. In one he fastened on a sight which attracts, in the other a sound which repels. One offers a pained, lying security in which there is no warmth, the other a fear much like that he had felt in childhood but which, strangely, ties him in an odd but definite way to something outside because the thing outside can have an effect upon him. In each case a sensuous experience stands at the center, and that which stimulates the sense, though it is not all of what the experience is about, becomes the focus upon which he acts. Moreover, the broken pane and the fractured walls are too closely analogous, not only to each other but also to his state, to be anything other than further elements attracting him and linking together the aspects of each situation into a larger coherence. The move is obviously toward organization and wholeness. He can sense what is needed, though the fragment never gets there. In "Frost at Midnight" Coleridge fastens his attention on an unliving thing and plays with its qualities of being as well as its physical properties, giving it, as Wordsworth gave the broken pane of flashing glass, a semblance of life:

> Only that film, which fluttered on the grate,
> Still flutters there, the sole unquiet thing.
> Methinks, its motion in this hush of nature
> Gives it dim sympathies with me who live,
> Making it a companionable form,
> Whose puny flaps and freaks the idling Spirit
> By its own moods interprets, every where
> Echo or mirror seeking of itself,
> And makes a toy of Thought.

But Coleridge works with assurance where the observer in "Incipient Madness," who can only counterfeit equilibrium, offers a grim parody of the kind of activity in "Frost at Midnight." Coleridge's poem works richly through an elaborate analysis of the unity of being and a form of the continuation of personal identity through father and son. It juxtaposes wholenesses at all levels through an intricate play of scenes in the past and present, and, to justify and contain all of these, it moves through them all back to the physical scene from which the poem had begun. This return to the beginning, enriched through new knowledge, occurs also in *The Ancient Mariner* and is part of the cyclical pattern of spiritual travel that underlies most romantic journeys, whether in the self or outside in the world, in memory or in sequential time. In "Frost at Midnight" the journey begins with an apparently absentminded gaze at a flapping cone of flame which seems almost alive. If "the idling Spirit" sees the shifting flame as a restless image of itself, this central object leads him out in a most Proustian manner to where and what he had been. The willed delusion is efficacious. The observer in "Incipient Madness," though, can see as an image of his spirit only broken glass and fractured walls. His willed delusion has to go further back than does the one in "Frost at Midnight," for the whole point in what he wills is to put something out there from which he can then begin his own move outward. He has, in other words, to make a wholeness of meeting before he can do anything else. His instinct had been accurate in sensing that there, with some one thing outside as a center of energy, he could begin to make out an organic totality. He had the idea of the necessary process. That was as far as he could go.

It is, then, not only the object in his experience that matters to Wordsworth but also how and what the object performs when it gets into the world of a poem. In the lyric on daffodils Wordsworth did not lie to himself. Quite the contrary, he is not even aware of the fullest import of what happened until some time after the event, when he focuses within on the daffodils (a group that functions as one total object) as they have been transformed by the energy of his spiritual life. This is not a false consolation but a delayed one, not a forced and therefore false relationship but one recognized, with surprise, only much later. In "The Solitary Reaper" he has his recognition right at the moment of experience. In each of these cases, the false and the true, the immediate and the postponed, the initial movement comes from the focus upon the object, and that object remains at the imaginative core of the whole experience, no matter how small a part it has in the entire context. The object, in other words, is central though not total, but since it is a way in to the experience for him, it could be used so as to bring the whole context along with it when he focuses on it.

Several issues have to be recalled here. First, we have seen that for Wordsworth there is a close relation between his sense of the presence of a thing (whatever the equivocal qualities of its location or actuality) and the truth of the experience in which it partakes. Not every true experience has this kind of center, but experiences centered on objects do tend, for him, to have various kinds of irrevocable truth about them. The object steadies him, as he said. The second important issue is the familiar one of the function of memory. Somewhat vaguely and without the necessary differentiations, Wordsworth mentions several stages in the involved activities of memory when he refers, in the 1800 Preface, to the actual moment at which the recollection occurs and the original event works its way back to the high point of tension. In a moment of contemplation the entire spiritual event has come along and been renewed. But the usual mode of Wordsworth's process of remembering makes clear that the reexperience probably occurred in roughly the same temporal sequence as the original series of events. That is, the sensuousness (the vision of the object, now experienced with the blissful inner eye) has to come first. Then, as before, follows the emotion he speaks of in the Preface, the emotion which had become locked to the object during the sudden coherence of disparate things, which is the formative activity in an encounter. And, unquestionably, the experience has surfaced with new dimensions and contours, older, richer, and riper than before.[7]

But this is mostly process and very little content. That greed in Wordsworth which led him continually to expand his self in search of new modes of awareness and knowledge drove him also, as he mentions frequently, to store up impressions and images of the physical world. It seems probable that at *some* level Wordsworth was impelled to hoard a stockpile of relics of sensuousness because of a deep fear of loss, an urge to hug to himself all that verified his spiritual wholeness. Isolated impressions were probably mostly pleasurable, though the impressions coming out of the wholeness of encounter were by no means exclusively of any particular tone. And the latter take a good deal of their meaning from their place in a plot whose details are unrepeatable, while the former, because isolated, are very likely of recurrent quality. Both kinds, though, indicate that somewhere he had walked into something that happened to him; they do not indicate a situation where he did the walking in order to make something happen, i.e., a wild attempt to pack together the scattered bits and pieces of what could have been, but was not, a genuine meeting. Memories stored and restored are about the touch of self and also about the touchable which

---

[7] Cf. the letter by Keats to Benjamin Bailey, 22 November 1817, in *The Letters of John Keats, 1814–1821,* ed. Hyder Edward Rollins (Cambridge, Mass.: Harvard University Press, 1958), I, 183–187. See below, Chapter Six, n. 3.

settled, not always to unmixed delight, quite naturally into order with him. When he came upon an object which could affect him unforcedly (the situation in "Incipient Madness" is very like a rape), the memory of that object could stand as reminder and guarantee of what had been a wholeness of relationship. We remember that one kind of truth which he got out of the sense of an object's presence had to do with the way the object gave to the situation a center of stability onto which he could hold. The sense of presence seems also to have contained and communicated to Wordsworth a verification of the genuineness of the meeting.

What comes back up to the surface, then, is both concrete and acted upon by the intangible processes of storage. At the original event and during the workings within himself, neither the density of the object nor what he gave to it could suffice alone. This came to mean that it is not just the object or the experience but the object as it is part of and has the power to re-create the whole experience that matters ultimately to the manner in which he creates.

It may happen, though, that the process of storage will be dispensed with when the impulse to hold onto the object (because of what it has done with and for him) becomes compelling. He is then willing to forgo the process by which it becomes part of himself, by itself, and emerges later transformed, heightened, and intensified. The poem "The Thorn," he told Isabella Fenwick, "arose out of my observing, on the ridge of Quantock Hill, on a stormy day, a thorn which I had often passed in calm and bright weather without noticing it. I said to myself, 'Cannot I by some invention do as much to make this Thorn permanently an impressive object as the storm has made it to my eyes at this moment?' I began the poem accordingly, and composed it with great rapidity." [8] The result is impressive, not because it is about a thorn or even another of Wordsworth's suffering human figures, but through its true focus of interest, which lies in how the old sea captain sees the whole affair.[9] The

[8] *Poetical Works*, II, 511.

[9] Most useful on these matters is Stephen Maxfield Parrish, " 'The Thorn': Wordsworth's Dramatic Monologue," *ELH*, 24 (1957), 153–163. For other

poem sifts out various possibilities, including the one that the action may never have occurred at all but rose, instead, out of the way the rather dim-minded but excitable observer brought into the field of his experience a strange single object with which he met. Whatever the case, whether or not the narrator has actually seen all that he speaks of, he places the thorn at the hub of the situation. Though by no means all of what happened, the thorn stands at an axial point, a center from which the energy of the experience appears to radiate. The first two stanzas and the last one work closely with the object, the description reverberating in a somewhat clumsy manner into various levels of the poem's significance. The object itself is never really transformed or translucent, though it is patently symbolic; the sentimental morality which dominates the poem may have held back whatever could have become of the thorn. Or it may be that the point of view was not such as to make it possible or desirable to do more with the thorn by itself. At any rate, the thorn that names the poem becomes a kind of trigger which releases the total value of the occasion and, because of what it can do, holds within itself the seed of the richness which the experience comes to have for the poet. Were this one of those occasions when the process of storage had been involved, the object would emerge enriched with all that had happened to it, both initially and through the simultaneous accretion and purification that take place when the object becomes part of his inner life. The final step, the poem, need not be taken and involves very much more; but this primary activity has to have happened for the poem of encounter to come about at all.

This is a form of synecdoche, for the object as Wordsworth works with it in the poem is only part of the experience, though perhaps its most tangible part. But in his understanding of it, the object comes to be the seed of what can be said about what happened in the experience. Thus, the reawakening of the object out of its curiously embryonic state comes with the first renewal of the original sensuous impulse, and this can very well

---

views and a brief summary of criticism of the poem, see Albert S. Gérard, "Emblems of Misery," in *English Romantic Poetry* (Berkeley: University of California Press, 1968), pp. 64–88.

serve to bring back restored the totality of the entire spiritual event. As Wordsworth uses the process, there is a continual, reiterated employment of these basic movements. In the movements, objects become not only subject matter but also compelling particulars in the process of creating form. But the object should not ordinarily be considered a catalyst, introduced into a situation in order to change the pattern of relationships within it. Nothing is a more integral part of the whole than this object and the acting consciousness that meets and works with it. The role of the object is to stand alone until around it are reshaped the full dimensions, however far they may extend, of the situation in which it had originally held a crucial position. Such a role and status are exactly the opposite of those fulfilled by personifications, for personifications are abstractions brought into a concrete situation from without, ingested to flesh out body and fullness, while the synecdoche gives substance to them from the center.

If the object can become a synecdoche for the whole experience, it would seem to follow that the way to overcome the flux, to conquer finally and irrevocably the transience of what Wallace Stevens called the "weddings of the soul," is to build a place for the object as the central symbol in a poem which has to be dramatic because its assumptions rest on the re-creation of an experience. The object, then, seen from its position as trigger and as creator of significant form, ought to be considered in the rhetorical structure of the poem as a synecdoche. But in its function as an indicator of the dimensions into which the experience moves and of the wholeness encompassing the varied elements, the object becomes a symbol as well. The synecdoche moves to the center and, though never without its quality as a part, becomes the symbol of the commanding presence of the whole. This happens often for Wordsworth and for others as well. Coleridge's definition of the symbol involves the thing both as synecdoche and as a central signifying particular: "On the other hand a symbol . . . is characterized by a translucence of the special in the individual, or of the general in the special, or of the universal in the general; above all by the translucence of the eternal in and through the temporal. It always partakes of the reality which it renders intelligible;

and while it enunciates the whole, abides itself as a living part in that unity of which it is the representative." [10] It follows also that the poet need not utilize the exact object originally encountered in the biographical experience, if there ever had been such an experience at all. If the object in the poem is not the identical one he had met with and stood over against (we can know if it is only from material outside the poem), it may be an amalgam of several disparate but somehow related objects, a coalescing that could well pack into the poem a complexity no single experience had been able to grant. It would be possible, then, to borrow an alien situation, as Wordsworth did for "The Solitary Reaper," so long as the object in that situation could be both synecdoche and symbol for anything the poet might have felt in his own similar moments, the conditions of which did not offer the right combination of elements from which he could make a poem. "Passed a female who was reaping alone: she sung in Erse as she bended over her sickle; the sweetest human voice I ever heard: her strains were tenderly melancholy, and felt delicious, long after they were heard no more": whatever this passage from Thomas Wilkinson's *Tours to the British Mountains* meant for its author, it brought a number of things together for Wordsworth. Only in cases like this, when the poet borrowed from a foreign experience, can the object be considered a catalyst. The result, though, in the form that finally matters, is essentially the same: the object, part of the whole, serves also as the image that focuses and magnifies the organic world of the whole. The romantic poet's skill in conquering the flux of time, the transience of the "weddings of the soul," comes down to this form for knowing, a form which holds the image of the wholeness of an encounter.

[10] From *The Statesman's Manual*, in *The Complete Works of Samuel Taylor Coleridge*, ed. W. G. T. Shedd (New York: Harper and Brothers, 1871), I, 437–438.

CHAPTER FIVE

The Appropriate Center

THE ORDER within the world of the *Lyrical Ballads* is frequently askew, and always because man has knocked it out of balance. A poem about natural joy like "Lines Written in Early Spring" has more ambivalence about it than a recognition of its animism would be prepared to admit. Indeed it is not a joyful poem, exactly. The observer, like the Hebrew prophets, finds himself caught peculiarly between two dimensions: while he is in the special position of being able to talk about one world which he has experienced deeply, the nature of his being places him in another, and he can never quite forget that. The prophets talked to men about God and to God about man, though never quite sure of a hearing from either direction. Blake and Hölderlin compounded the problem by a mode of organizing the difficulties of this dark time which made illumination very difficult —and very exciting—to achieve. Wordsworth, no obvious my- thographer, still stood in the middle: one of the points of a poem like "Lines Written in Early Spring" is that man is not listening. Like so many of Wordsworth's poems, it speaks of a harmony and a kind of wholeness—

> To her fair works did Nature link
> The human soul that through me ran

—which men in general stand outside of. Here, as frequently elsewhere, the harmony is imaged in natural song. The observer, in a privileged position tuned in to the current of joy, is rather curiously not in a joyful state, however much he may be linked to all joyful things. To him alone "there came a thought of grief," with as yet no "timely utterance" to relieve him. He grieves over a disorder that is ultimately moral but that has come out of what he sees as man's impulse to reject a place in the universal harmony. Yet the observer is clear enough about where he stands in the whole, and he restricts with qualifications his assertions about natural joy: " 'tis my faith . . . it seemed . . . and I must think, do all I can." He cannot measure ornithological thoughts: this is no Keats watching, and momentarily becoming, the sparrow pecking around in the gravel outside his window.

Here it becomes clear that even in those situations in which the observer can take part in the movements of the natural world, he remains in some way alone, and to that degree a stranger. If he is in a privileged position, it is not one which can satisfy him completely: obviously he is different from most other men as well as from the birds whose thrill he cannot measure. Other men cannot feel all that he does and therefore cannot recognize their moral inadequacies. On the other hand, he is still a man, representative of the kind. He is doing what they should do, but because they do not do it, he argues that his own pleasure is somehow tinged or limited. Thus, even though he cannot measure the thoughts of other things, his own thoughts are sufficient to cut into his joy. Man stands over against his own kind as well as all other kinds.

However that may be, in none of the poems of this great nature poet is the human image far from the center, though he was as aware as anyone of his time that the universe was not anthropocentric. In some sense, and always in one or two in particular, the poems concern themselves with some aspect of man in the world, what he is or (for this poet, much the same thing) what he does. Often the preoccupations are such as those in "Lines Written in Early Spring," the kind which for Arnold became much of what Wordsworth was about. But even when he is not concerned about what others are doing or failing to do, he is usually staring at himself, aware, if of nothing else, at least of the fact that he—this man—is going through the process of perceiving. Even when absolutely alone, he fingers his consciousness of himself seeing, partly because his own activity is an eminently observable aspect of the whole context (what he sees always includes himself going through the seeing), partly because the activity is above all and unfailingly fascinating. Hazlitt and Keats were ambivalent about this side of Wordsworth, finding it repellently attractive; they were as fascinated in watching it as he was in going through it. But the consciousness of consciousness is not merely an enraptured display of self to self. At some ultimate point it is a frequently uncomfortable exploration of what it means to be human in a world that is mostly not human, a world that, despite Wordsworth's public and almost professional complacency, never ceases to be difficult. The essential concern is with organized wholeness—existent or nonexistent, psychological, moral, or universal, but a wholeness never without some reference to the place of the human within it, even if that human is himself alone. Order, humanity, and the natural never drop into separate compartments for Wordsworth: man in the world gives to the order of the world a meaning and potency beyond the capacity of any other kind of object it is possible to contemplate:

> When from our better selves we have too long
> Been parted by the hurrying world, and droop,
> Sick of its business, of its pleasures tired,
> How gracious, how benign, is Solitude;
> How potent a mere image of her sway;
> Most potent when impressed upon the mind
> With an appropriate human centre—hermit,
> Deep in the bosom of the wilderness;
> Votary (in vast cathedral, where no foot
> Is treading, where no other face is seen)
> Kneeling at prayers; or watchman on the top
> Of lighthouse, beaten by Atlantic waves;
> Or as the soul of that great Power is met
> Sometimes embodied on a public road,
> When, for the night deserted, it assumes
> A character of quiet more profound
> Than pathless wastes.

> (*Prelude*, IV, 354–370)

This late passage introduces the very early one detailing Words-worth's awesome meeting on the road with the returned soldier.[1] It seems most inappropriate to describe Solitude, as it appears in the person of the soldier, as "gracious" and "benign," for the figure has "a strange half-absence," his height is "a span above man's common measure," and his whole appearance is desolate and simple. The observer, rather uncomfortable, feels guilty for being afraid. The years separating the passage on solitude from the one it introduces brought changes and a very different kind of seeing, one so different that it found graciousness and benignity where there is actually a moving encounter with strangeness. "Gracious" and "benign" belong in the cathedral with the votary, not on a nighttime road that is nearly empty and soundless, where "an uncouth shape" which he can see while he is unseen stands suddenly there near him.

Clearly, whatever the change and the reasons for it, "an appro-priate human centre" had as much potency for Wordsworth in 1798 as it did in the 1830's. The human object as appropriate center took a wide spectrum of forms for Wordsworth, a spec-trum to be enclosed not between the bathetic and the sublime (though that enclosure has its own special interest) but, more pertinently, between sentimental morality and the quality of the greater poems like "Resolution and Independence." In some ways the early poems of sentimental morality are transitional because of their profound involvement in the restrained but anguished exploration of self that Wordsworth was going through in the 1790's. He must have been attracted to senti-mental morality because of the possibilities that could grow from its basic principle, "that man could be stimulated to mo-rality through awakening his compassion for undeserved suffer-ing,— his pity for virtue in distress." [2] Like all didactic theories, this puts the whole weight on pathos as a stimulant to something else, since no didactic poem experiments with arousing emotions for their own sake but for what they can lead to. Wordsworth never gave up the elementary principle of sentimental morality,

---

[1] See *The Prelude*, pp. 536–538.
[2] Oscar James Campbell, "Sentimental Morality in Wordsworth's Narrative Poetry," *University of Wisconsin Studies in Language and Literature*, no. 11 (1920), 24.

though it was absorbed into more complicated conceptions of what a poem can do. But at this early stage, part of its meaning for him was quite probably formed by its ability to create a situation that would stimulate the self into an active emotion, an emotion that by its existence would prove that he had been able to respond to something outside of himself. Involved here, as it was all through the history of sentimentalism, was the implication that one is a good person insofar as he can have such feelings of pity; but behind the implication there surely rested for Wordsworth a gratification that one could feel anything at all. Sentimental morality was one step back from the edge he had seen and skirted in "Incipient Madness."

The process and effect of sentimental morality found echoes and analogues everywhere in Wordsworth. The stress of this mode is on human response to the human, universal man responding through sympathy and identification to the pained world of other men. In its way it is an eighteenth-century sentimentalist parody of Aristotelian catharsis. Its closest analogue is that mode in which Wordsworth is stimulated by non-human objects into feelings very similar to those stimulated by sentimental morality. Here, objects which are not of his kind move him toward compassion and love which are far more likely to be for other human beings than for things which are not men. The "beauteous forms" he mentions in "Tintern Abbey" might ("perhaps"—the qualifications are everywhere) have had

> no slight or trivial influence
> On that best portion of a good man's life,
> His little, nameless, unremembered, acts
> Of kindness and of love.

An ironic misunderstanding of the speech metaphor that runs all through Wordsworth's poetry led to the generally erroneous impression that he chatted amicably with seedlings. However, Wordsworth does come close here to an emblematic use of the natural which makes it less a series of discrete objects than a series of object lessons designed to illustrate the role of man in a universe apparently ordained to serve him. The whole mode, which appears to have grown out of his experience with sentimental morality, had one of its more useful results in the enlargement of scope it gave to the field of his experience. Both sentimental morality and a morally feelingful response to the stimulation afforded by nonhuman objects succeeded in affecting "that best portion of a good man's life," and the fact that both could do so revealed for Wordsworth new patterns of relationship within the outside world and between himself and the various objects outside in that world. A new step toward greater coherence was taken because man and the natural existed not only in a relationship of subject and object but also together as specific kinds of stimulating objects that could bring out the same highly specialized responses in the observer.

Supporting and solidifying this structural similarity (but not to be identified with it) is the concept of the One Life. The concept offers one more reason why Wordsworth should respond to a variety of objects which are other than his kind, since every object which can have a meaningful effect on him shares in the vast complex of Being; indeed, it would seem possible that everything in the complex, just because it is in there, can have such an effect. The sentiment of Being he felt in his seventeenth year (*Prelude*, II, 376 ff.) became the panentheism of "Tintern Abbey" and guaranteed for him the validity of much of his experience: whatever the distinctions in kind, there was a link because of the One Life, and there would therefore seem to be always at least this one point at which a profound and moving understanding of another kind of being was possible. The universe was one vast democracy in which all objects partook of the same Being, and the experience that could make his own private version of the whole comprehend *something* about that of another (no matter that the comprehension was imperfect and limited) was an experience to be hoped for and preserved. In fact, the multiplicity which is Wordsworth shows at any one point a complicated set of motivations for any one activity or poem. What is called his humanitarianism, an early form of which emerges in his idea of sentimental morality, is in part, and not only by analogy, an impulse toward democratization that was strengthened for him by the concept of the One Life. Even the style of the *Lyrical Ballads* takes some of its drive from this same complex of motivations. The leveling influence of the One Life should be thought of as a movement or as a direction of energy, para-dimensional because it is not only horizontal (within the things of this world) but also universal and a property of all things everywhere. Nothing escapes it, all things exist because of it. It would appear to be there, always available for a positive response, in every thing of any kind which was there for him to know.

But there is another movement, another direction of energy. Even in "Lines Written in Early Spring" the sense comes through of a continuum of separate objects whose differentiation is as significant as whatever links them:

> To her fair works did Nature link
> The human soul that through me ran;
> And much it grieved my heart to think
> What man has made of man.

"Human" is there specifically to differentiate his kind of soul from the other kinds in the continuum. This conception has nothing to do with vernal impulses, whose educative effect is very strictly confined to an awareness which has a clearly de-fined effect upon him and his relations with other men. This is, rather, a kind of knowing which, if not quite neutral, has noth-ing to do with valuation drawn from clearer moral categories. It insists upon the apparently redundant "human" because it grows out of a deep and not particularly comforting recogni-tion of another direction of energy. In this other direction, usually defined by Wordsworth through the image of the great chain of being, there is neither democracy nor leveling but a rigid (though living) hierarchy in which there are variegated levels and stages. For if all manner of objects can have analo-gous effects upon him, the difference among those objects sets up an extraordinarily tense interplay with any similarities they might have. The difference is not only that between the ani-mism of a poem like "Nutting" and the spirit that rolls through all things in "Tintern Abbey" and *The Prelude*, although that difference is a related one. The voice of the single wren in Book Two of *The Prelude* or the wandering voice of the cuckoo ordinarily can bring him to various dimensions of experience, but they cannot do for him what the sound of the woman's voice in "Stepping Westward" can do. Nor is the field of daffodils, however grand and encompassing the scope of vision it can bring him to, able to afford the quality or special kind of amplitude involved in his experience with the reaper singing alone in the field. Modes of experience were available to him through the person of a blind beggar or of Lucy Gray that a single sheep or one blasted tree could never offer. And if "A Night-Piece" shows patterns that illustrate a prevalent formal (and therefore epistemological) mode for Wordsworth, what it has no opening to show, no means of impelling into being, was available to him through the "appropriate human centre" of a poem like "Resolution and Independence."

One passage will suffice to show both Wordsworth's dependence on a traditional view of the great chain and his awareness of the simultaneous presence of both directions of energy:

> Enough of humble arguments; recal,
> My Song! those high emotions which thy voice
> Has heretofore made known; that bursting forth
> Of sympathy, inspiring and inspired,
> When everywhere a vital pulse was felt,
> And all the several frames of things, like stars,
> Through every magnitude distinguishable,
> Shone mutually indebted, or half lost
> Each in the other's blaze, a galaxy
> Of life and glory. In the midst stood Man,
> Outwardly, inwardly contemplated,
> As, of all visible natures, crown, though born
> Of dust, and kindred to the worm; a Being,
> Both in perception and discernment, first
> In every capability of rapture,
> Through the divine effect of power and love;
> As, more than anything we know, instinct
> With godhead, and, by reason and by will,
> Acknowledging dependency sublime.
>
> (*Prelude*, VIII, 476–494)

The exceptional value Wordsworth places on an experience of this sort is apparent from the similarity of certain lines in this passage to others in a letter to Walter Savage Landor of 21 January 1824: "even in poetry it is the imaginative only, viz., that

which is conversant [with], or turns upon infinity, that powerfully affects me,—perhaps I ought to explain: I mean to say
that, unless in those passages where things are lost in each other,
and limits vanish, and aspirations are raised, I read with something too much like indifference. . . ." [3] The passage is from
the 1850 *Prelude* and the letter is from the later Wordsworth,
from both of which we could expect a traditional ecclesiastical
coloring (other parts of the letter framing the quotation imply
an identification of the imaginative with religious experience);
but the comparable passage in the 1805 *Prelude* says much the
same about the two directions of energy, though without the
ecclesiastical coloring and with a few interesting differences;
for example:

> Then rose
> Man, inwardly contemplated, and present
> In my own being.
>
> (631–633)

Wordsworth's sense of the grandeur of man grows from a number of sources. In Book Eight of *The Prelude*, he singles out as
especially significant what he came to see of the dalesmen, particularly the shepherds, in the context that enfolded and ordered
their lives. But along with this went the obsessive concern with
the shape and sense of his private self, which he attempted to
understand not only through staring at himself but also by comparing his own nature to what he could know of all the other
kinds of being outside. Wordsworth never learned only one
thing at a time. If his self was often painfully idiosyncratic, it
was still a human self, his private version of universal man:
"Man, inwardly contemplated, and present / In my own being." The activity of comparison was one more attempt to
discover versions of wholeness which abut on each other. It was
thus one more action in the series that shaped his world. Part of
that shape comes clear in the imagery of the 1850 passage
quoted above, which fuses the complementary but opposing
movements of the One Life and the great chain of being: the
"vital pulse" is everywhere, but there are "several frames of
things, like stars, / Through every magnitude distinguishable."

3 *Later Years*, pp. 134–135.

The order is various and multiple, but the order is whole, held in place and in tension by a sense of hierarchy and a sense of shared being. These directions of energy *have* to war with each other because they agree on only one point, that every form of being has a place somewhere in each of them. That means, of course, that the movements meet in every being. The meaning of such a meeting for romantic symbol-making is very great indeed.

The *Lyrical Ballads* of 1798, with one or two exceptions like "Tintern Abbey" and "Lines Written in Early Spring," seem not to have sorted the implications of the two movements into definable categories. These poems dwell, rather, on a combination of sentimental humanitarianism, studies in both normal and abnormal psychology, and the effects of a particular kind of experience of the natural world which ties in very closely with sentimental morality. Although the idea of the One Life appears here and there in the volume, there is no indication in most of these poems that Wordsworth had done any serious worrying about the implications of the great chain as it confronted the universal order of being. In "Simon Lee," for example, the focus of interest is on human qualities and relationships in decay. The poem complicates itself quite beautifully in the last four lines:

> —I've heard of hearts unkind, kind deeds
> With coldness still returning;
> Alas! the gratitude of men
> Hath oftener left me mourning.

A good deal happens in these lines, including the importation into the whole context not only of the observer's reaction to the old man but also, in a not very distant implication, of the potential which the narrator himself has to face. Yet there is no question of any serious elevation of the main figure, who is not seen in the eye of nature or of some vast order perceptible in human experience. There are gestures at placing him in the hands of time, to Wordsworth a dimension of experience always of deep significance, but nothing serious is done with its possibilities. The mode is severely limited in scope and opportunities for development, though what he does with it here is acceptable enough. The mode is even more limited in "Goody Blake and Harry Gill." But in a poem like "The Thorn" there do seem to be possibilities inherent in the kind and quality of material he is using, particularly the object, the woman associated with it, and the context as a whole. Wordsworth, we remember, wanted to make of the thorn an object permanently as impressive as it had been to him at an especially striking moment. Yet the thorn turns out to be an emblem rather than a symbol, and Martha Ray turns out to be nothing much more than a figure less interesting in herself than in her ability to stir compassion in the reader, which might have happened in some cases. There is, in other words, compassion but no transformation, no sense of being tuned in to anything much larger than the context of the mountaintop. This lack of any sense of a larger context may well be qualitatively neutral, but it certainly is limiting and places more of a burden on delicacy of tone than Wordsworth could always bear easily. Most successful in the poem is the manipulation of point of view that reveals the curious, intriguing personality of the narrator. It is, then, a poem that works most comfortably on the plane of psychological exploration that runs all through the *Lyrical Ballads*.

"The Idiot Boy" is another poem in which the narrator's role has some effect on the overall tone, but the effect is minimal, certainly offering none of the general support which this poem so badly needs and which is offered in "The Thorn." More interesting and pertinent than "The Idiot Boy" itself are some of the comments Wordsworth made about it in a letter to John Wilson—not, indeed, the familiar attack on false refinements of language and feeling but, rather, this observation:

> I have often applied to Idiots, in my own mind, that sublime expression of scripture that *"their life is hidden with God."* They are worshipped, probably from a feeling of this sort, in several parts of the East. Among the Alps where they are numerous, they are considered, I believe, as a blessing to the family to which they belong I have indeed often looked upon the conduct of fathers and mothers of the lower classes of society towards Idiots as the great triumph of the human heart. It is there that we see the strength, disinterestedness, and grandeur of love, nor have I ever been able to contemplate an object that

calls out so many excellent virtuous sentiments without finding it hallowed thereby and having something in me which bears down before it, like a deluge, every feeble sensation of disgust and aversion.[4]

However much this attitude may lean toward sentimental religiosity, the hallowing of the object offers possibilities of imaginative exploration to which the hints at the idea of the divine idiot give substantial support. Wordsworth does nothing with those possibilities in the poem, obviously. But his recognition that a human figure can hold within itself various strata of experience simultaneously is a big step in the widening of his perception and lifts him far out of the limitations of the mode of the *Lyrical Ballads.*

Wordsworth took that step somewhat haltingly and wrote a number of poems that led him toward the complete success of others like "Michael" or "Resolution and Independence." One of those transitional poems, "The Old Cumberland Beggar," has particular importance because of what it shows of the difficulties Wordsworth went through in working out the lineaments of his richest imaginative mode. The strange incongruities of this poem emerge from several conflicting impulses which Wordsworth was not able to jell into satisfactory coherence. One of its most serious problems has to do with point of view, which in this poem is so disorganized that it skirts the borders of absurdity. In the first sixty-six lines, the old man comes alive through finely carved details that incarnate a numb misery, something approaching a spiritual numbness. A series of particulars leaves an unmistakable impression of the observer's deep compassion:

> In the sun,
> Upon the second step of that small pile,
> Surrounded by those wild unpeopled hills,
> He sat, and ate his food in solitude:
> And ever, scattered from his palsied hand,
> That, still attempting to prevent the waste,
> Was baffled still, the crumbs in little showers
> Fell on the ground; and the small mountain birds,

[4] *Early Years*, p. 357.

Not venturing yet to peck their destined meal,
Approached within the length of half his staff.

But this beginning section is not entirely impersonal: two judicious references to the observer's own participation, however peripheral, emphasize his personal knowledge of these details:

I saw an aged Beggar in my walk;
. . . .
Him from my childhood have I known.

These tactful gestures serve not only to set off in perspective the description of the old man (this is what *I* saw) but also to furnish the factual basis, the delicate assertion of the truth of the situation (*this* is what I saw). The mood of the passage called for only that much self-reference; more would have put the observer intrusively into a situation where he really did not belong.

Probably because of his preoccupation with the ways in which the self comes to know things outside, Wordsworth had so many difficulties with narrative form (especially as it centers on human figures) that his success with it was often tenuous. Keats and Hazlitt recognized that with Wordsworth emotional distance and personal involvement were in part problems of point of view. In Wordsworth's case it was at times a problem because he would shift his vantage point (usually to some version of a first person) so awkwardly as to disrupt coherence. Aspects of the first-person attitude could carry over into a poem in which the radical experience is alien to them. The intimacy characteristic of that attitude is, at the least, irrelevant if the situation requires, for full effect, something else. "The Old Cumberland Beggar" shows, too bluntly, what can happen: after he creates the brilliant effects of the beginning and sets the conditions for a promising exploration of the situation, Wordsworth bursts into the poem and forces upon the reader a jangling and incongruous rhetoric:

But deem not this Man useless.—Statesmen! ye
Who are so restless in your wisdom, ye
Who have a broom still ready in your hands
To rid the world of nuisances; ye proud,
Heart-swoln, while in your pride ye contemplate

Your talents, power, or wisdom, deem him not
A burthen of the earth!

The cadences tighten, becoming knotted and muscle-bound, paralleling in their stridency the scolding, melodramatic attack upon the statesmen. From this point on, the poem never quite manages to return to coherence. Wordsworth does scatter throughout it a series of instances showing the effect of the beggar on what we might call his constituents. But this hint at a more coherent understanding remains only a gesture, suggesting what the poem could have been. Unsure of his focus, of where he should be in the poem, Wordsworth intrudes clumsily, and as a result the beggar becomes merely a sociological case, an object of charity rather than a man receiving it.

The incoherence of the poem seems ultimately to rest in Wordsworth's curious attitude toward the old man, an attitude which is neither ambiguous nor ambivalent (for these have an inner coherence of their own) but, simply, inconsistent and unsettled. The beggar is so withered and wasted, so light, weak, and old, that

> His staff trails with him; scarcely do his feet
> Disturb the summer dust; he is so still
> In look and motion, that the cottage curs,
> Ere he has passed the door, will turn away,
> Weary of barking at him.

Wordsworth (significantly enough, considering his own visual preoccupations) refers several times to the dullness of the old man's sight and once, along with that, to the mechanical, sub-human monotony of his daily progress:

> Thus, from day to day,
> Bow-bent, his eyes for ever on the ground,
> He plies his weary journey; seeing still,
> And seldom knowing that he sees, some straw,
> Some scattered leaf, or marks which, in one track,
> The nails of cart or chariot-wheel have left
> Impressed on the white road,—in the same line,
> At distance still the same.

It seems impossible to reconcile this very clear portrayal of senility, of an old man so deadened in sensibility that he is hardly aware of his surroundings, with Wordsworth's portrayal at the end of the same old man as a dignified image of freedom, a figure close, for a few lines at least, to others like Michael or the shepherds in the great vision in Book Eight of *The Prelude:*

> —Then let him pass, a blessing on his head!
> And, long as he can wander, let him breathe
> The freshness of the valleys; let his blood
> Struggle with frosty air and winter snows;
> And let the chartered wind that sweeps the heath
> Beat his grey locks against his withered face.

There is in this poem no reconciliation of disparate aspects of a complicated whole but only a conglomeration of discordant qualities. The fragment called "Animal Tranquillity and Decay," which Wordsworth spoke of as an "overflowing" from this poem, presents the old man resigned and composed, hardly senile now, moving along with his full measure of humanity. He is one "who does not move with pain, but moves / With thought." We are told that his composure even excites a certain degree of envy, a feeling scarcely to be expected from what we see of the same beggar in the early sections of the full poem. In those sections his peace comes from spiritual paralysis, but at the end of that poem and in the fragment it comes from "settled quiet," something very different indeed.[5] After the first sixty-six lines of "The Old Cumberland Beggar," which are certainly among the best Wordsworth did of a kind of lucid, detached, compassionate observation, the old man hardly appears again until the end, with so startling a change that little comes through except Wordsworth's still unsettled ideas about him. The attempt to make of the old beggar an image of man in the eyes of nature fails: only at the end does Wordsworth gain sight of him as a man whose qualities could support such an image. For most of the poem it was only the beggar's function that was important, Wordsworth insisting that the beggar should not go into a workhouse because he is too important as an object of charity, giving the people with whom he comes

[5] In a continuation of the fragment, the old man tells the observer that he is on his way to a hospital in Falmouth to see his dying son. Apparently the nucleus of a narrative was forming, and Wordsworth seems not to have wanted to develop it any further. He dropped the continuation in 1815.

into contact the opportunity to do good and feel better. Wordsworth is in the middle, straddling decrepitude and grandeur,
sentimental morality and an impressive vision of man in the
world. However these can be reconciled, he did not manage to
do so here. Coleridge's observations on Wordsworth and
Goethe, with all the qualification and adjustment those observations need, have enough truth in them to light up certain aspects
of "The Old Cumberland Beggar": both poets, he said, "have
this peculiarity of utter non-sympathy with the subjects of their
poetry. They are always, both of them spectators *ab extra*,—
feeling *for*, but never *with*, their characters." [6]

Two years later, in "The Two April Mornings" and "The
Fountain," Wordsworth worked out a more coherent and ultimately more productive apprehension of a character, an apprehension which he felt as deeply as he did that of the old beggar but with more distance and a clearer understanding. The
Matthew poems place man in a context, as Wordsworth had
tried to do at the end of "The Old Cumberland Beggar," man
some*where* in time, subject to the universal movement of decay
and mortality but seen at a particular place in his own development and in the development of others. The speaker, Matthew,
his dead daughter, and the "blooming Girl" whom he does not
wish to be his, all take part in the movement and pattern and

[6] From the 16 February 1833 notations in *Specimens of the Table Talk
of Samuel Taylor Coleridge* (London: John Murray, 1874), p. 211. Coleridge
had mentioned the same point earlier in *Biographia Literaria;* see the edition
by J. Shawcross (London: Oxford University Press, 1907), II, 122–123. In *The
Visionary Company* (Garden City: Doubleday, 1961), pp. 173–178, Harold
Bloom sees in "The Old Cumberland Beggar" an affirmation of the old man's
absorption into nature, "as absorbed as he can be and still retain human
identity" (p. 174). But it seems impossible to distinguish between the near
stasis that Bloom describes and a state of full-blown senility. Bloom's reading
is perhaps the most interesting of the few significant comments on the poem.
H. V. D. Dyson reads the poem helpfully but quite uncritically in " 'The Old
Cumberland Beggar' and the Wordsworthian Unities," in *Essays on the
Eighteenth Century Presented to David Nichol Smith* (Oxford: The Clarendon
Press, 1945), pp. 238–251. See also Cleanth Brooks, "Wordsworth and Human
Suffering: Notes on Two Early Poems," in *From Sensibility to Romanticism:
Essays Presented to Frederick A. Pottle*, ed. Frederick W. Hilles and Harold
Bloom (New York: Oxford University Press, 1965), pp. 373–387. Of first
importance are the comments of Charles Lamb in a letter to Wordsworth of
30 January 1801; see *The Letters of Charles and Mary Lamb*, ed. E. V. Lucas
(New Haven: Yale University Press, 1935), I, 239–240.

unity of the context of time which enfolds them. And it is that context which, in these poems, gives to the figures much of their specific meaning both as individuals and as instances of universal man. Wordsworth has no need to force the elevation of his main character in these poems: the context, firmly and coherently sketched (as it was not in "Simon Lee," which seems a step in the direction of the Matthew poems), elevates the character for him. But giving further significant shape to these poems, and supporting the context of time, are the implications of the One Life and the great chain. The two movements of energy are evident particularly in the quality of the songs in "The Fountain," where Wordsworth juxtaposes human and natural songs to the enlargement of the significance of both. In "The Fountain" Matthew sees that man understands what birds cannot, but he sees also that man is granted such understanding at his own great cost. Memory makes possible for Matthew the pain and joy of being human, the recollection of past love—never felt so much as now—and the knowledge that all of its objects are gone. He is more complicated than the birds and the fountain, but as "The Fountain" especially shows, he still shares with them in a song that is each one's rendition of the harmony of the One Life. Here, as everywhere, the movements intersect in everything that has being, joining and distinguishing, leveling and separating. Any object that confronts him can be the synecdoche of what may well be the most dramatic kind of meeing. Each object, because it is the location and the instance of the meeting of hierarchy and equality, is a potential symbol of the whole in which it takes part and of which it speaks.

What Wordsworth struggled with in "The Old Cumberland Beggar" came much more easily in the Matthew poems, in part because the earlier poem trips over its own clumsy didacticism, in part also because the context fits around the character very firmly in the Matthew poems, while the attempt to locate the old beggar in a universal context fails because the nature of the character is itself so uncertain. The interplay set up in the Matthew poems has within it the outline of an order which became clearer to Wordsworth as he began to recognize what was unavailable to his understanding as well as what he could assimilate into himself. Eventually, though, the order had somehow to be worked into a kind of poetry. And that kind had to be able to move others as deeply, and in much the same way, as his vision of the world had moved him. To do so, to reflect the movements of soul he had experienced in an encounter, such poetry would have to do justice to every form of object and would thus have to give a sense of the immense multiplicity of objects as well as of the context in which they move. At the same time, this poetry had to establish a very clear awareness of what it is to be a man moving in that context. In the *Lyrical Ballads* Wordsworth leaned heavily on tone to get across his sense of the value of the human. If the prop sometimes failed him, surely the essential skimpiness of the content of sentimental humanitarianism contributed heavily to the limitations of dimension which made the tone so difficult to sustain. Wordsworth made a brilliant extension of a style which others had worked out before him: most of the sympathetic characters are types, almost stereotypes, of prevalent kinds of characters in contemporary lyrical ballads.[7] Yet despite the impressive quality of his movement beyond convention, the limitations of the style meant that it was only after a number of public false starts that he could bring together coherently the stresses and demands of humanitarianism with his sense of elemental human grandeur. Transition pieces like "The Old Cumberland Beggar" show what he had to learn in order to enter into and embody coherently his fullest understanding of the human. Indeed, only in the process of developing his modes of embodying it did Wordsworth learn what the image of man in the universal context could mean for him. It took time for his men to grow into a universe large enough and whole enough to hold them.

Some of the transition pieces are as exciting for what they cannot see as for what comes through from them. In 1800 Wordsworth wrote to Biggs with instructions about one of the Poems on the Naming of Places which were to go into the new edition of the *Lyrical Ballads*. He seemed especially concerned about an insert needed toward the end of the fourth poem of

[7] Robert Mayo, "The Contemporaneity of the *Lyrical Ballads*," *PMLA*, 69 (1954), 486–522.

the series, three lines which were "absolutely necessary to render the po[em] intelligible": [8]

Nor did we fail to see within ourselves
What need there is to be reserv'd in speech,
And temper all our thoughts with charity.

The poem, "A Narrow Girdle of Rough Stones and Crags," written that year, stands in mode and content somewhere between the flawed order of "The Old Cumberland Beggar" and the complex unities of "Resolution and Independence"; but "A Narrow Girdle" is itself a very good, strangely neglected poem.

The insert is obviously in the mode of sentimental morality: the sight of human suffering, especially when the sufferer has done nothing to deserve retribution, raises in the observer a compassion that clarifies and defines the moral benefits he receives from the scene. Part of this comes out of Wordsworth's compulsive didacticism. But there is more: something obscure in Wordsworth frequently compels him to put into his comments on a scene what appears to be an insufficient moral tacked onto a poem but what is actually a statement about some form of human relationship. Behind the moral tag, justifying its place in the poem, is an assertion that what he sees has value on the plane of man's relations in this world with other men, no matter what other planes of meaning or existence may be evident in the poem. The assertion points to one kind of meaning that can be drawn out of the situation he observes, a meaning associated with the sympathetic feelings men can have for each other's misfortunes. The impression comes through very strongly here, in "Resolution and Independence," and even in Coleridge's *Ancient Mariner* and "This Lime-Tree Bower My Prison" that many of these statements about the morality of compassion are, on one level at least, an attempt to find familiar meanings in a very strange situation. Perhaps because the plane of compassionate human relationships is a common one, comfortably and easily absorbed into the observer's experience, the tacked-on moral seems at times to be an effort on his part to bring the whole odd and perplexing affair into an area that is more com-

[8] *Early Years*, p. 311.

prehensible, less awesome, and perhaps even less frightening than are the other dimensions to which his seeing has led him. If the moral is insufficient, it is also easier to work with. Sentimental morality never opens up unsettling matters that cannot be eased by compassion.

And there are difficult questions in "A Narrow Girdle of Rough Stones and Crags." The trio of observers, at leisure and dallying with their time, come into a world where there is no leisure for other men, where natural things are either dead or at play or standing in their stately beauty, where nature, ultimately and horribly, appears to be thoroughly without concern for man. Wordsworth, with his usual impressive skill in these matters, first brings into focus a series of scattered, shattered objects, unrelated bits of wreck tossed onto the shore of the lake, things piled incongruously together because useless and dead:

> and, as we strolled along,
> It was our occupation to observe
> Such objects as the waves had tossed ashore—
> Feather, or leaf, or weed, or withered bough,
> Each on the other heaped, along the line
> Of the dry wreck.

From these dead things the observers' attention moves up the scale to objects that play at life and death, objects which the speaker ultimately envisions as driven by a form of the life within all things, imaged in the most familiar symbol for that life, the breeze:

> And, in our vacant mood,
> Not seldom did we stop to watch some tuft
> Of dandelion seed or thistle's beard,
> That skimmed the surface of the dead calm lake,
> Suddenly halting now—a lifeless stand!
> And starting off again with freak as sudden;
> In all its sportive wanderings, all the while,
> Making report of an invisible breeze
> That was its wings, its chariot, and its horse,
> Its playmate, rather say, its moving soul.[9]

[9] There are interesting variations recorded in *Poetical Works*, II, 116.

Yet though these are still dead things, offering only a semblance of life, this is not a neurotic attempt to see life where there is none, to force it into being. The situation here is very like that in "Frost at Midnight" and not like the one in "Incipient Madness." For the wings, the chariot, and the horse are the perceptions of wit or fancy; the observers, too, are playing at things, toying with what they see as they play with their time.

Their next move has to be further up the scale toward life and the kind of natural beauty which can be achieved only after life is granted. But the ironies, already prefigured with the wings and the chariot, are heavy indeed, though not fully apparent until after what follows: nature's gorgeousness takes the form, in the observers' perception of it, of the decadent imagery of Naiads, "the Queen Osmunda," and the "Lady of the Mere," imagery shockingly inappropriate in the light of what follows but chillingly revelatory of the kind of thinking they bring to the scene. What happens next jolts them so much that it temporarily separates the observers.

Now that it has moved up into the circle of genuinely living things, the poem turns toward the highest in life, men. The sound from the fields comes through to the observers as "the busy mirth / Of reapers," the tone of the pretty pastoral which their perception tells them is there. Their choice of imagery does even more than do blunt words like "trifling" or phrases like "feeding thus our fancies" to define with precise accuracy what they are able to know about their surroundings. Earlier the speaker had indicated that there was a mist which had not yet "altogether yielded to the sun," though the mist had not, apparently, gotten in the way of the other objects they looked at. Only now, when they come up close to a man, does the mist block their clear perception. The irony mocks subtly, for it becomes apparent very quickly that there had, in fact, been another kind of mist distorting their vision all this time. The sight of the real man reeks of brutality in what it tells of him and of all men and in what it does to the observers. Suddenly each of them stands alone, forced into himself—"my single self"—by what he sees. (The analogy to the "sole self" in Keats's encounter with the nightingale is perfectly apt.) The man at the shore of the lake, though not yet dead, is close to being as wrecked as the other pieces of flotsam they had come across previously on the shore. Nature's prettiness, still there perhaps, is shown to have occurred in another realm of things, a realm which, though it may have a meaning for them, has no feeling. Now all the ironies come in for their pay: the lake they had earlier called "the dead calm lake" (only now is the phrase seen as ominous) becomes "the dead unfeeling lake"; the symmetry reveals the progress in the process of knowing that outlines the poem. And the movement up the scale of life, drawn with Wordsworth's best casual skill, turns awry because man, the highest of things, can be as wrecked as the lowest, and the lowest do not, or cannot, care. Here the dramatic appropriateness of the insufficient moral strikes hard. It is, essentially, a protective reaction, a recovery from the shock of what they have seen into a mode more familiar and therefore, with all this strangeness around them, more satisfying. Clearly the tag is no answer to what has happened. The reaction, instinctive and stock, fills only a corner or two of this complex, grotesque event, satisfying them primarily by offering a means of coming to terms with what has happened. Yet it does manage to supply what nature cannot, a compassionate awareness (limited and partly selfish though it may be) of the man's plight. Just below the surface is the assertion that man can feel if nature cannot, that human understanding fills some of the gaps in this imperfect scheme. But the assertion never comes into full clarity, and the tag has to suffice as all that the observers can say.

Oddly but forcefully, "A Narrow Girdle of Rough Stones and Crags" affirms a coherent order in experience, an unpleasant one that paradoxically puts man at the pinnacle of living things but shows his eminence as a lonely one and the order as foreign to his interests. Something profound had opened up for these strollers playing with their time, and even if they refused to enclose the full meaning of what they saw in a reaction complex enough to contain it, the profundity remains along with the hints of their fear. Man in nature stands quite alone, with frailty always potential and his own wreckage certain. A confrontation with the actuality of their own mortality does not rise plainly out of the observers' reaction; sentimental morality does not, as a rule, include such thoughts, although "Simon Lee" hints at them. But, like the assertion about man's ability to feel where nature cannot, the confrontation seems ready to occur, though in fact the reaction goes another way. The order revealed in this poem has a subtle but limited coherence. That places the poem several steps ahead of "The Old Cumberland Beggar" with its ungainly attempts, too late in the poem, to assert a boldly expansive scheme where man is part of his natural context and an especially courageous figure within it. In "A Narrow Girdle" distinctions are patterned carefully: differences among natural things and among social classes, distinctions between living and dead and things that play (or are played) at life and death. The order is elaborate and acutely defined, but it is not very pleasant for man. The scale of life goes up to man but no further, makes of man in this poem a high creature but still only a creature. Complex as the order is, it has a painfully limited scope: the two movements are there, but the sense of hierarchy in the poem has severe limits, though it emerges distinctly. Man shares death with the natural world but not, unfortunately, its obliviousness. If he can be grossly inadequate and self-serving in his perceptions, the shock of recognition, when it does come, comes with a vision of horror and not of glory. There, finally, is what jars the observers into reaction: human grandeur never emerges in this poem though man may be at the apex of life.

Wordsworth saw this situation often and never found it very satisfactory. The last two Lucy poems, "Three Years She Grew in Sun and Shower" and "A Slumber Did My Spirit Seal," though written perhaps two years apart, have to be taken as text and commentary or thesis and antithesis, with the poem on the beneficent fostering of Nature being loaded with phrases that turn savagely ironic when read in the light of its companion piece. Nature is nurse in "Three Years" (as it is in the "Immortality" ode) and therefore nurturer. Lucy will feel the continuum within things that echoes from "Tintern Abbey":

> The Girl, in rock and plain,
> In earth and heaven, in glade and bower,
> Shall feel an overseeing power
> To kindle or restrain.

She will feel together with them and will even feel some of what they do. Continuities of all kinds will be established: "beauty born of murmuring sound / Shall pass into her face." Even with these continuities, however, Wordsworth is quite ambiguous, carefully so: she becomes one of the beings Nature rears, but she is a special one who, whatever the blending into context, never ceases to be herself. Yet though her specialness is in her beauty, we are probably not encouraged to read here that human beauty is of a special kind. The poem is full of doors that can be opened to lead away from its general track: Nature will be to her "both law and impulse"; Lucy's will *be* (this means more than that she will share in) "the silence and the calm / Of mute insensate things"; the "feelings of delight" that will shape her body are "vital," a bitter pun indeed.

None of these remarks is quite innocent (Wordsworth never has innocent lines). "A Slumber Did My Spirit Seal," written about the same time as "A Narrow Girdle of Rough Stones and Crags," picks up the overtones of "Three Years" so surely that it must have been meant as the one step away taken by a cold objectivity that reaches for antithesis. Nature is still an impulse and a law, but the impulse is now the energetic push of the earth-ball that whirls her around with all of the other things, the "mute insensate things" to which she is more akin now than ever. Here is true identity: if there had been a continuum of being with a hint at human differences, there is now a continuity with a final and absolute equality.

In the Matthew poems, written after "Three Years" but before "A Slumber," there had been hints at another order, less chilling though not apparent enough to warm Matthew into learning to live with loss. There seems even less of that order in "Three Years" and "A Slumber," though the hints are somewhat stronger in "A Narrow Girdle of Rough Stones and Crags." Wordsworth's fluctuations and uncertainties rose from his acuteness and honesty, but most of all from his concern with the kind and quality of those objects which were not like himself. He was shaping a vision of man surrounded by a variety of orders, some of which meet in him, all of which affect him profoundly. The activity of shaping took Wordsworth uncertainly from the clumsy assertiveness of "The Old Cumberland

Beggar" to the cold coherence of "A Narrow Girdle of Rough
Stones and Crags," where the human ends as insensate wreckage.
To be flotsam among dead things is to share in an order. But
all those things with which he shared carrion qualities had lives
of their own—when they had lives—with which he could share
very little at all. Such points of continuity as there were tended,
frequently, to be overshadowed by that fact.

CHAPTER SIX

Nearness and Distance

IF THE ORDER occasionally chills, that is not so much because of the multiplicity within it (which can delight as well as overwhelm) or the chanciness of the sporadic moments of glory (which do, after all, occur) or even the uninhibited and irrevocable flux (for things come down to him before they go by) as it is primarily because of the strangeness of all the participants in that order. Pater's definition of the romantic in art as strangeness added to beauty has in it much with which Wordsworth could have agreed, especially where Pater stresses the new—that which has not yet been experienced but is not so grotesque as to unbalance beauty or, perhaps most important, that which it is unusual to experience. But if the strange is the unusual for Wordsworth, it is also—what it is not for Pater—the unassailable other, i.e., the strange as the sheerly foreign, that which is so immutably different that the knowing at the center of encounter always has within it an area of questionableness and uncertainty.

To recall several previous issues: Wordsworth, we remember, had argued that "Points have we all of us within our souls / Where all stand single" (*Prelude*, III, 188–189). The wide reverberations of the meanings of singleness here include the sense of the idiosyncratic which is so private and personal that no aspect of the deep center of self can move out and be shared. We have seen that Wordsworth's awareness of this uniqueness within himself impelled him to preserve the integrity of individuality by asserting the distinctness of each individual thing of whatever kind. He wanted to ensure that "the great social principle of life" (*Prelude*, II, 389) did not draw each thing down into itself so that all looked and did alike. The smothering of individuality not only created a lie about the way the world is but also attacked the radical privacy which had to be protected whatever else happened. Arguing against the falsities of Macpherson's style had been relatively simple, but the ease came only because all of the meanings and implications of individuality forever haunted Wordsworth. If the comments on Macpherson's style took the form of calling it a misrepresentation of the way objects are seen in context, the whole idea of what happens to the individual object in context emerges from Wordsworth's knowledge that there is that within the object which is true for no other. All of this led him into a tricky and delicate balance, and the weight of the egotistical sublime guaranteed that he would not always be successful.

But if there are those points within the human which are unassailably other, what there is in something which is not of his kind, something already distant and problematical, compounds the areas and varieties of strangeness to make the nonhuman largely unknowable. The selves linked by the One Life are simultaneously sundered by their positions on the great chain of being. The nonhuman, then, is partly other, something which he can approach and meet and be near to, with which he can even share in a kind of life; but it remains in some part always distant and—because it is strange and permanently so—always potentially frightening. Here, then, are the sources of the chill that the urgently desired order seems occasionally to bring, as it did in "A Narrow Girdle of Rough Stones and Crags." If a man fits into the world, there is that in the world which also fits into it, which shares the context with him but shares very little else.

Wordsworth knew this well, and Shelley and Keats (in certain moods) knew it too; so, for that matter, did most other romantics at one point or another in their experience. Wordsworth's awareness of strangeness is obsessive. It disconcerts at times, at others it forms one element in a complicated harmony, and it never, whatever the effect, appears without surprising

him. It is always part of what the stranger knows, and sometimes it is nearly all of the knowledge that he carries away with
him. He is aware that strangeness is on all sides of the encounter
and that it basically affects the ennobling interchange, limiting
its possibilities, making it, for the most part, a very difficult and
rarely successful process though not quite an impossible one.
In some situations, he points out the strangeness with elaborate
care (e.g., "Lines Written in Early Spring"), probably in part
to protect the truth of the situation, and when he does point
it out, he usually does so with a kind of nervous frankness. We
have already seen several instances of the qualifications he is
driven to make about some of his own assertions. If the qualifications are designed to allay criticisms of statements he knows
some will find unacceptable, they show another fact he knows
but rarely discusses openly: the other which stands over against
him often has little to do even with him, the man who has placed
himself between most men and that which is out there. (This
reaches deep into the meaning of the prophet's role and is one of
the several ties he has with the position of the biblical prophets.)
The Prelude, indeed, is riddled with qualifications: Wordsworth can do more with "to seem" in the appropriate place
than he can do elsewhere with entire lyrics:

> Ere I had told
> Ten birth-days, when among the mountain slopes
> Frost, and the breath of frosty wind, had snapped
> The last autumnal crocus, 'twas my joy
> With store of springes o'er my shoulder hung
> To range the open heights where woodcocks run
> Along the smooth green turf. Through half the night,
> Scudding away from snare to snare, I plied
> That anxious visitation;—moon and stars
> Were shining o'er my head. I was alone,
> And seemed to be a trouble to the peace
> That dwelt among them.
>
> (*Prelude*, I, 306–317)

Perhaps he did trouble the peace, but there was no way to find
out for certain. This event was reported in order to show that
what is possibly a delusion can still have moral effects; even
untruth can have its value for man. But the educative dimen-

sions of the passage cannot block out a more troubling possibility, never spelled out but always there, that what he did made no difference to that peace which was the peace of other forms that being took.

Immediately following this passage is another reported event. Here he clings to a high slippery ridge, and his relation to the world outside of him, the wind and the sky, is balanced precariously on past participles: the blast "seemed" almost to suspend him, and "the sky seemed not a sky / Of earth." The precariousness of his physical position underscores and reinforces the odd uncertainty of his relation to things outside, delicate and chancy in its own way. Nowhere can his grip absolutely relax.

As if to reinforce this tension on a variety of levels, Wordsworth brings in the boat-stealing scene only a few lines later. At one level, of course, there is the argument about the ministry of fear, its efficacy, and its educative value. But here, more clearly than in most other similar events, the dread arises as much from the *difference* of what seems to come after him as from the fact that it seems to come at all:

> from behind that craggy steep till then
> The horizon's bound, a huge peak, black and huge,
> As if with voluntary power instinct
> Upreared its head. I struck and struck again,
> And growing still in stature the grim shape
> Towered up between me and the stars, and still,
> For so it seemed, with purpose of its own
> And measured motion like a living thing,
> Strode after me.
>
> (377–385)

The existence of otherness, its presence and nearness, is sufficient to terrify, no matter what it happens to do. Added to these aspects and as important as any is the uncertainty, the question of whether what looked as if it was out there was really out there at all. Further, since the uncertainty may not have been in the boy but is surely in the man writing about his boyhood (it was the man, after all, who sowed this and the preceding scenes with qualifiers such as "seemed" and "as if"), the fear has lost some shapes only to assume others, more subtle and sophisticated, less obviously shattering, but as discomforting as mature perplexities about otherness can be. All varieties of the meaning of strangeness are in this passage.

But perhaps even other modes of being, though they may come to him out of another realm, have something to share with him. At the least, these other modes, if they did come into his life, came because they represented the relation of some other realm of law to his own world and what he did in it. This is not quite Kafka, because no matter how distant the other realm or how strange its workings in his life, Wordsworth knows well why the other modes come after him. The mystery is in what they are, not in why they are there at that moment in his world.

The situations, then, range on a spectrum in which the mystery is of varying degrees, from partial to near total. The solitary reaper is much like him but with ineffable areas in the context of her world and her self which are forever beyond him. The cuckoo, which lives in the world with him (though the world is different for both), stands on the spectrum between the reaper and the modes of being which seem to approach from a realm of thorough strangeness. No wonder, then, that when his inner vacuity drove him into isolation from other men, he felt entirely alone, fixed into a world where most things were quite different from him and where he was separated, temporarily and sickeningly, from those who were most like him. Much of the thrust of Wordsworth's poetry through the *Lyrical Ballads* and into the middle of the great decade was an effort to reach a point of absolute balance among all the oppositions he knew were out there and within himself. He came to see many possibilities and, eventually, how to work them out. The stranger learned how to face strangeness as he learned more about its opposites and saw that wholes of unimaginable complexity and beauty could be reached for and occasionally seen. In "To the Cuckoo" he grants an entire realm he cannot know, a realm so huge that his part in it is tiny and much of the part has to be fabricated. Yet the intricacy and potential glories in his encounter with the cuckoo come, quite precisely, out of the tension he recognized between the bird's profound otherness and the coincidence of being in which both he and the bird share.

For Wordsworth, to whom learning was an activity so extensive that eventually he could not recognize all of its workings, the existence of the unknowable was bitter, whatever the mask he put over his awareness of it. It was a challenge and a frustration that could reach all the way to terror, with numerous stops along the way. It added every imaginable difficulty to his relationships with a world in which all kinds of objects are out there and have, somehow, to be experienced and ordered. How can he do that experiencing, what is entailed in the process, how much can he actually experience, and what are the quality and nature of what he finally does (perhaps) experience —all of these questions and a myriad of related ones stand around him at every point when he contacts something outside in the kind of encounter which has at its center an experience of knowing. Wordsworth was never indifferent about the process of experiencing or naïve about its complications, however much he asserted qualities about the process ("Thanks to the means which Nature deigned to employ") that grated on many of his readers. Because of the multiplicity of his interests, he could come at the complications from various directions. But because the multiplicity was ultimately subsumed under the central problem of his own order and its station within the world order, the complications remained under a unified heading though they were extraordinarily complex. How, though, to reach to the question of his own and the world's order when there was that within the world which he could never hope fully to understand? Order, after all, is made up of continuities, and although there are, within the world, continuities of all kinds (it was the business of his life to discover them), Wordsworth saw that there were also discontinuities that were impossible to bridge.

Discontinuity, then, is a point at which various questions meet, questions of order and of knowledge and of the possibilities of some kind of relationship with that which is outside and very different. If the fact of discontinuity frustrates his impulse to know because he can never really know otherness (whatever else he can come to know about the object), the frustration has then to be ordered, the pressures turned into a direction which appeases the impulse. It seems quite possible that Wordsworth's self-consciousness about his own processes of knowing is in part the result of his need to turn the frustrated desire to know otherness into a more immediate and satisfying channel. At any rate, he settled eventually not for knowing otherness but for knowing that it is there; and coming to terms with even that fragment of knowledge was in itself an achievement available only after exceptional spiritual labor. For if there was no difficulty in coming upon discontinuity, there was a great deal in learning what to do with it. The drama was ultimately one of consciousness of self, for his self recognized strangeness and tested it in terms of its difference from what he was. And involved with this process of recognition and test was his consciousness of himself going through those very activities, the consciousness of consciousness that made him, like Emma Bovary, both actor and spectator in the world his knowledge gave him.

Discontinuity had its versions, of course, different ones at different times for Wordsworth and also for the other romantics. Shelley could try to drive into being an identification with the West Wind (or rather, of the West Wind with himself), but even in that poem he knew that no such move could ever be more than illusory. In one of his most skillful crescendos, he tries to force a movement upward and out of his own sphere, first to a freedom only just less than that of the wind, then to a plea for a place as the wind's poet, and finally with the full leap into a total identification:

> Be thou, Spirit fierce,
> My spirit! Be thou me, impetuous one!

Here "impetuous" is probably more a transference from his objective opinion of himself than a valid description of the wind's nature, for the poem shows that nothing is more steadily purposeful than the wind. The objectivity hidden in the word moves him down quickly and abruptly to that which is most possible for him in his mortality. He is not what the wind is, though it drives through his world: it is a part of the world but a part unlike him. Between him and the wind there is none of the coincidence of being that for Wordsworth established at least one level of likeness. To be in the same place is not the same as to be continuous: contiguity is no cure for absolute strangeness. Wordsworth knew that too. The being Shelley shares is with the other scatterable things. He and they will be resolved into the elements of earth, air, and water set out in the first three stanzas, while he, in the fourth, will contribute the fire out of his ashes and sparks. These elements suffer no change although their shapes do. And there, precisely, is the continuity on an absolute plane that overcomes the shattering discontinuity of personal death. Shelley reached for another continuum of being to overcome the abyss broken open by death, but the poem offers instead only the loss of self into the selfless but enduring framework of nature's ingredients.

Wordsworth, at times, worked to conclusions much like this, though he says nothing about regenerative transformation within natural movements. In "A Slumber Did My Spirit Seal," the body which goes into the earth as a hunk of stuff takes on an absolute passivity which signals its reduction to the level of mute insensate things. This is no overcoming of otherness, no wild reach into the sphere of the unknowable, but a defeat into a world where, horribly, no distinctions can or need be made. Wordsworth's world was surrounded by shadowy beginnings and sharp endings. In his occasional awareness of natural cycles, there is nothing that reaches the profundity of Shelley's ideas about eternal continuity within recurrent natural processes. Wordsworth was not really interested in recurrence, and cyclical imagery is therefore rare in his work and, when it appears, conventional (e.g., *The Excursion*, V, 390–410). Such images had no place in the overall shape of his thinking. Consciousness and self-consciousness, personality, the unity of being, the difficulties and chanciness of the ennobling interchange, the meaning and being of what faced him out there—all these have little if anything to do with the eternality of the seasons, but everything to do with the quality of the stages which brought him to wherever he is at the moment. Wordsworth's sense of time is severely linear. It is cyclical only in the way that biblical time is both linear and cyclical at once: for time moves without detour or diversion from an old to a new Eden, the earthly to the heavenly Jerusalem, one kind of life among the lakes to another, more knowing kind resulting from a journey through the world of experience. This mode of time is cyclical only because stages seem to reoccur, such as a saving remnant or a sense of firm placement within the context of the natural world. But each reoccurence is on a higher plane, so that what appears to be a cyclical return is actually a segment of an upward spiral, a staircase rather than a ring. Though there are no qualifications in the biblical pattern, where the final state was never reached, or in *The Prelude*, where it was, the "Immortality" ode shows that even in the final state Wordsworth has difficult ambiguities to face. On the other hand, this is clearly no eternal return. If the end is in the beginning, then surely there will be an end, and what happens after that will never disappear to reoccur but will reach its absolute quality. The travel image in *The Prelude* and the "Immortality" ode promises no swing back to the start; nor is anything but an ending implied. Primarily there is only the strong assertion that he has reached that interesting point after coming from all those curious places.

The Christian otherworld, pure spirit's final, fleshless home, offered Wordsworth no solution to the struggle with strangeness but only a long step away from the struggle with much still left to be done. For otherness and a sense of the presence of palpable singularity went together and implied each other. They worked jointly to create the symmetry of the world he walked around in and incessantly felt at to see what he and it could do with each other. The end of his personal part of the physical world would be an end to all this, whatever waited for him afterwards. Wordsworth's late mood of Christian resignation, combined of course with love of the lakes, emerges in imagery so conventional and therefore so out of touch with objects as themselves that the whole complex of relationships thins into predictable interchanges with little tension and few difficulties. But the Wordsworth of the great decade, whatever the ambiguities of perception, had too strong an orientation to the presence of palpable singularity not to regret a *permanent* loss of the body. The world of physicality had an end to it beyond any recourse and had things within it with all the palpability of himself. Those things which he could hear (sometimes only that) and see (with all the tyranny of the eye), which he could climb on and break off and shout to, were things with which he could share the most basic of qualities, palpable presence in this world. Only in those terms, and with an awareness of the entire situation as it has to be constituted to exist at all, does Wordsworth's great struggle with strangeness achieve its fullest meaning.

When he abandoned the struggle, which neither he nor the world of things ever quite won, he left behind many of the conditions out of which he could build that fullness of meaning (the fullness which—it seems impossible to argue otherwise—makes for most of the superb drive and structure that his world of imagination held). The new order could only lower the pitch of these complexities, for it was an order less pressed by temporal urgencies, because one could ignore time, and less distressed by the presence of strangeness, because man had, after all, a better place to go to after the end of things. But the earlier work knew none of this, which is perhaps why, there, an odd sort of desperateness rises to the surface, probably impelled by the urge that we must do now what we ought to do because we shall never again be able to do it. If *The Excursion* offers a release from time's finalities and the uncertainties of temporal order, it never really solves the dilemmas posed by "The World Is Too Much with Us" and all those other poems which imply that our opportunities to do with otherness what we probably can will never be offered again. That is why the sad waste of human powers so frustrated Wordsworth. What he saw men doing or not doing pushed him into mockery and melancholy, sometimes both together: witness not only "The World Is Too Much with Us" but also *The Prelude* and its related lyrics, "A Poet's Epitaph," and the like. He always was aware, at every stage, how knowing and myth could work together if man wanted them to, how man could make of the things out there a world to which some kind of relationship at some points was at least possible. This single basic concern with the ordering of knowledge involved in myth stretches, *mutatis mutandis*, between his earliest good work and the organization of experience that went eventually into *The Excursion*. It occasionally underlies his perplexities about the qualities of the objects over against him:

The world is too much with us; late and soon,
Getting and spending, we lay waste our powers:
Little we see in Nature that is ours;
We have given our hearts away, a sordid boon!
This Sea that bares her bosom to the moon;
The winds that will be howling at all hours,
And are up-gathered now like sleeping flowers;
For this, for everything, we are out of tune;
It moves us not.—Great God! I'd rather be
A Pagan suckled in a creed outworn;
So might I, standing on this pleasant lea,
Have glimpses that would make me less forlorn;
Have sight of Proteus rising from the sea;
Or hear old Triton blow his wreathèd horn.

Discontinuity with the natural falls, apparently, into at least two patterns, obviously very closely related and ultimately shading off into each other. One, seen in this poem, is temporary and can perhaps be overcome by a radical change of heart which will cleanse the doors of perception. The other pattern, unquestionably irrevocable, has to do with the unconquerable foreignness of that which is thickly out there. To see what is involved in the first pattern means to begin to negate it, to work new coherence and potential harmonies into one's way of knowing. But as Wordsworth's own daily workings made very clear indeed, whatever one does with the first, the second remains as it is, a wall to be reached and run into, late for some, soon for others.

In "The World Is Too Much with Us" there are glimpses of a stratum bleaker than that which can be overcome temporarily, by a will to believe. Discontinuity (here imaged as disharmony) was bridged for the pagan by the imagination, which shaped an image of successful encounter by playing on the forms of things until the world was peopled with figures which are anthropomorphic and yet fully divine. But nothing in this poem speaks of truth or points out where the truth lies. There is nothing in it of the coincidence of being or any other factor which could, at least potentially, establish possibilities of genuine encounter. "Outworn" simply means that creeds are at some time fresh and serviceable, and therefore useful in making the world livable, but that creeds—and presumably all other things—come and go. If the poem shows discontinuity at a moment in time, it also argues that time's own disjunctiveness has brought him and everyone else to this pass. The frequently cited analogy to the passage on myth in Book Four of *The Excursion* (631 ff.) has limitations which ought to be carefully noted. In that passage Wordsworth runs through the history of early religions from Old Testament Hebraism to the Persians, Babylonians, Chaldeans, and Greeks. He points out with elaborate care that after the period of the early Hebrews, God withdrew from man but that God then, in his beneficence, left behind the imagination as a gift so that man would not be

> left, to feel the weight
> Of his own reason, without sense or thought
> Of higher reason and a purer will,
> To benefit and bless, through mightier power.
> (667–670)

Clearly these stopgaps are the result of an act of grace, an act done so that man will not be alone in an alien world and therefore see his own kind of being as the height and end of things. He will have help from the imagination until the truth comes, that which will never need replacement because it can never be outworn. And it has come.

The similarities between the sonnet and this passage find echoes in various other comments by Wordsworth on superstition and related matters. These similarities emerge when we see that, for example, the characters in "A Poet's Epitaph" differ from Peter Bell in one important respect, that is, in apathy, an attitude for which Wordsworth could have very little affection. Peter is indifferent to primroses but not to the smile of an ass, rumblings from underground, or the skittering of a leaf behind him. If he cannot respond to the kind of stimulus which is preferred in the Wordsworthian norm, he can respond to another, one of a secondary nature but still to some degree admirable. For Peter has a kind of sensibility, and that is a certain good, while its content is, for the moment, unimportant. It is better to feel something than not to feel at all, and superstition is somewhere on the side of the imagination, as Wordsworth insisted when he said that "he would much prefer being a super-stitious old woman" than a fact-ridden rationalist.[1] Far in back of these remarks are those versions of sensibility and senti-mental morality in which even the most depraved can indicate virtue through a display of deep feelings. In Peter's case the superstitiousness made possible by this sensibility serves as a means of punishment, a comic motif, and an indication of his capability of change and salvation. But behind even the ver-sions of sentimental morality, we remember, was a time when to feel anything at all was very gratifying. *Peter Bell* and "The World Is Too Much with Us" share that deep background too. *The Excursion* has none of it.

Thus, while the sonnet and the passage from *The Excursion* agree that the exercise of imagination is in itself a good, their differences lead to a grim echo of the mode of "Incipient Mad-ness." For if creeds come and go, *The Excursion* asserts the existence of a final and inevitable truth that the sonnet does not acknowledge or at least mention. In *The Excursion* there is an end to speculation, and because of the particular content of that ending, there is the assertion of an end to things when there will be no more need for fluctuations. The sonnet, though, speaks not of a *true* way to order the world but only of a temporary one, and it is one which at the same time he knows to be false. The imagination is seen in the sonnet as an activity which creates a momentary belief; it is in itself not a creed but that which helps to make one. What the imagination does here can make him feel less abandoned ("forlorn"), but it is sufficient only for the moment nonetheless. This was exactly the kind of activity dramatized in "Incipient Madness," though the world in the fragment is much less controlled and stable than the one in the sonnet. In both, however, he is can-did and objective about what he is doing. The raw outline of the same unsettling experience turns up more than a decade after Wordsworth had come out of his most bitter period, and it appears during a time of immense creative success which he was never again able to match. Clearly, the framework of Wordsworth's experience never settled dependably into place

[1] Havens, *The Mind of a Poet*, I, 147.

until he gave up staring at strangeness and embraced the infallible order that holds together the world of *The Excursion.* On the other hand, however much he met that blocked the fervent impulse to knowing, he never took what from a later perspective would appear to have been a convenient second best, the acceptance of imaginative activity as in itself the sufficient and final good. Perhaps such an acceptance would imply the existence of a thoroughly unknowable otherness that stands everywhere outside and fills in all the spaces, so that process-watching makes the only comfortable sense. Wordsworth could never have agreed with what the acceptance implied. He did a good deal of watching of the process of experiencing, but it was not all that he did. He never got so far as to make the process all (it seems doubtful whether any romantic did), though he must have seen that position as a possibility. He should not, then, be read as if he were Wallace Stevens, who derives as inevitably from Wordsworth as he differs in ultimate arguments about the imagination and the knowing of order:

> The poem of the mind in the act of finding
> What will suffice. It has not always had
> To find: the scene was set; it repeated what
> Was in the script.
> > Then the theatre was changed
> To something else. Its past was a souvenir.
> > > . . . The actor is
> A metaphysician in the dark, twanging
> An instrument, twanging a wiry string that gives
> Sounds passing through sudden rightnesses, wholly
> Containing the mind, below which it cannot descend,
> Beyond which it has no will to rise.
> > > ("Of Modern Poetry")

Here sufficiency is accepted with a glorious elegance as final in itself. It could never have been accepted as such by Wordsworth, for whom words alone were never certain good.[2]

---

[2] Hoxie N. Fairchild argues that Wordsworth's sonnet holds "the idea that beliefs which are repugnant to reason are justifiable if they foster the sense of imaginative power"; but this puts Wordsworth closer to a poet like Stevens, if not to the decadents, than he actually is. See Fairchild's "Words-

A poet like Keats, who found other ways that were more than sufficient, could be dazzled by Wordsworth, could imitate him deep into the bones and sinew of his own new kind of poems, and at the same time could find in the older poet a dangerous mass of ego that had to be rejected in principle. The peculiar selflessness that was part of the mode of negative capability seemed to Keats to match nothing in Wordsworth, the old bird who would brood and peacock rather than thin the bright colors of self toward some impossible but conceivable translucence. In some of his moods, particularly in the major odes, Keats saw radical discontinuities as intensely as Wordsworth ever did. But Keats argued that in the kind of empathy involved in the complex of negative capability, objects can be experienced in a fullness so total that no room is left for the experiencer to be himself. Everything that remains of himself hides something of the other; only total loss gives total knowledge. Keats saw and therefore was a sparrow; Wordsworth looked at birds and knew that he could never be anything less than himself. The question is not of desire but of capability, what one actually can do. To become, for the moment, a sparrow pecking around outside in the gravel is to go into a temporary death of the self; one dies into the center of another's being: "or if a Sparrow come before my Window I take part in its existince [*sic*] and pick about the Gravel." [3] This is not sympathy. Wordsworth could feel that, despite what Coleridge said in comparing him to Goethe. Keats is an early exemplar of that aspect of the romantic imagination which is empathic, rejecting feeling-for or feeling-with for feeling-within. The romantic push for knowledge (different for Keats, Wordsworth, and the Goethe of both *Fausts*) led Keats toward the realization that identification adds up to the fullest possible knowledge of another, and he seems not to have felt any qualms about what happened to his self in the process.

---

worth's Doctrine of Creative Delusion," *South Atlantic Quarterly*, 46 (1947), 545.

[3] From the letter to Benjamin Bailey, 22 November 1817, in *The Letters of John Keats, 1814–1821*, I, 186. The best comments on the empathic element in negative capability are in Walter Jackson Bate's chapter on the subject in his *John Keats* (Cambridge, Mass.: The Belknap Press, 1963), pp. 233–263.

Contemporary discussions about empathy, under whatever name, usually connected it with Shakespeare. For most romantics, not only Hazlitt, it was the way of the actor and the playwright (but not of all kinds of either, obviously) and of a certain method of writing poetry which Keats himself never really exemplified. It seems only rarely to have come into clash with contemporary conceptions of what the lyric was and how it operated. And apparently only literal Crabb Robinson wanted to question, however timidly, the propriety of applying dramatic criteria to the romantic expressionist lyric: "We spoke of Wordsworth and Coleridge. Lamb, to my surprise, asserted Coleridge to be the greater man. He preferred the *Mariner* to anything Wordsworth had written. Wordsworth, he thought, is narrow and confined in his views compared with [Coleridge]. He does not, like Shakespeare, become everything he pleases, but forces the reader to submit to his individual feelings. This, I observed, lies very much in the lyrical character, and Lamb concluded by expressing high admiration of Wordsworth." [4] Partly in revolt against bleeding romanticism or what Empson calls "romanticism gone rotten," Rimbaud moved temporarily into his own version of empathy ("car *Je* est un autre"). But probably because he practiced it more seriously and severely than anyone had, Rimbaud had many more qualms than Keats did about what the process could do to him. The tradition carries clearly through Hopkins's conception of "inscape," another version of the penetrative imagination, and into Rilke's *Dinggedichte*, which, however much they owe to the French Parnassians, are surely the finest poems to come out of the latest stages of the romantic empathic tradition. The connection of empathy with Wilhelm Worringer, whom Stevens read seriously and profitably, draws us to the completion of a circle within which Wordsworth could never—and would never want to—step.

It is less that Wordsworth rejected identification or even that identification, were it possible, meant a loss of the self, a loss that his good memory would rapidly connect with the uncertainties of his most desperate period. The suspicion Keats

---

[4] *Henry Crabb Robinson on Books and Their Writers*, I, 17.

has in "Ode to a Nightingale," that the world of the bird is quite probably unassailable, comes closer to Wordsworth's sense of things than do the comments Keats makes elsewhere about the impingements of other selves upon his own. The "sole self" left looking and listening at the end of Keats's ode has more of Wordsworth in it than does the assailable selfhood easily lost at a crowded party or dropped for that of a sparrow. Self-consciousness eventually degenerated into a smug egocentricity for Wordsworth. It was not, however, always so complacent as a number of contemporary and subsequent comments would make it, e.g., Hazlitt's review of *The Excursion*. Wordsworth watches that which he can know best, the self which is most available to him experiencing the curious orders in the world outside. This is no complacency but a near fanatic regard for the truth and for what is possible. Lamb's remark that Wordsworth "does not, like Shakespeare, become everything he pleases" is accurate of course, but like most other contemporary comments about Wordsworth's contemplation of self, it misleads because it cannot seem to grasp that Wordsworth is doing only that which he knows can be done. He could never create a complete Imogen or Iago, much less be one. For him there are only the tensions of nearness and distance, what the coincidence of being can join together and what absolute unlikeness keeps forever asunder. Here, only, is the marriage, with all its difficult conditions indicating that whatever harmony mind and universe come to must be earned or given by luck. It is a dialectic like the marriage of heaven and hell or the conjunction of the worlds of innocence and experience, which can live together because they are complementary but which live successfully together only when there is a full recognition of all likeness and difference. Wordsworth's world fluctuates with an often savage tension between what he is and what the things outside are; thus, between his own possibilities and all that which he can never be. There is here no potential identification, obviously; there is only the chance of an occasional leap partway into the world of another. One leaps so that the moment of the acquisition of new knowledge—a moment that is imperfect and precarious, somewhat dangerous, and always quick—can happen and be gone, to be brought back again into the drama of consciousness that can unfold at the center of a romantic lyric. The drama is there in "Ode to a Nightingale," which shows all the labor of encounter and shows also, more gorgeously than any romantic poem, all the potential frustration in a situation of forced intimacy. But Keats never dies into another being in the ode: he never ceases being himself and, in fact, makes clear how in that situation he wants to hold onto what he is and at the same time share in the world—not, it should be noted, in the existence—of another. He wants not to be the nightingale but to be with it. Wordsworth would find even that secondary choice a most unlikely possibility.

To put it another way, those passages where Keats speaks of the empathic imagination show struggles only in holding onto one's self, not in getting to take part in the existence of another. The latter, indeed, seems very easy to do and may be difficult to avoid. But for Wordsworth and for Keats in "Ode to a Nightingale," awareness of another's being means awareness of its difference, whatever may be joining them, and it is only with recognition of the strangeness in the object out there that the knowledge in a Wordsworthian encounter can come to him. Otherwise there is opportunity only for identification, dazzling and unnerving perhaps, but still not truly dialectical because one pole in the scheme fades into and becomes another. Wordsworthian encounter needs partial contraries. Absolute ones would mean that the marvelous knowing in encounter could not come through because there would be no likeness or similitude to hold onto. Thorough identity, or anything very close to it, would mean the loss of idiosyncrasy and therefore a misrepresentation of the self that is doing the experiencing. Wordsworthian contraries necessarily hold onto their integrity and purity as they come to meet each other. But an aesthetics of pure empathy, where tension eases into fusion, can offer no such balance. And though it may unnerve, it does not usually raise any hairs. The empathic imagination, as Keats experiences it, does not hold Wordsworth's manifold terror of otherness. It was not, though, because of fear that identification was out of Wordsworth's bounds but because of what the fear pointed to, that kind of thing out there.

What Wordsworth tried to do, then, he did because it was

all that he felt able to accomplish, the only way he could discover whatever truth there was to be found. We remember that the truth about the object grows out of its situation during the process of encounter. Truth for Wordsworth was therefore multiple, often oppressively so. This is not to say that it is relative but, rather, many-faceted and multidimensional because the strange and familiar truths about all of the participants come together to make the whole new truth of that moment of encounter. Further, the local and individual truth of each experience was what it was because of the uniqueness of the meeting (which includes the idiosyncrasies of the participants), not because its truth shifted or became untrue somewhere else. There was no somewhere else for that truth or its experience to be. The difficulty here, then, is not in finding what will suffice, for the actors change but the play tells true things. Rather, it is in knowing exactly all the lineaments of the situation, all that he and his antagonist are (separately and together), all, finally, that the truth of this particular moment of encounter comes out to be. An aesthetics of empathy has to differ from an aesthetics of the meeting with strangeness because of the kinds of truth available to the participants in each. Wordsworth could never know of the cuckoo all that Keats could know of the sparrow. Empathy offers, theoretically, all the truth of another being, but the mode of encounter makes nothing like that claim. In fact, in a world peopled with otherness, truth is more difficult to find in another being than it is in the process by which one comes to contact the other. Any truths asserted about another ought, then, to be met with suspicions that are always acceptable and proper. Such recognition of difficulties—imaged, frequently, in fears of delusion—makes for a romantic dilemma as basic and prevalent as any. The problem drifted down to Arnold, who knew well what its face looked like:

> The grand power of poetry is its interpretative power; by which I mean, not a power of drawing out in black and white an explanation of the mystery of the universe, but the power of so dealing with things as to awaken in us a wonderfully full, new, and intimate sense of them, and of our relations with them. When this sense is awakened in us, as to objects without

us, we feel ourselves to be in contact with the essential nature of those objects, to be no longer bewildered and oppressed by them, but to have their secret, and to be in harmony with them; and this feeling calms and satisfies us as no other can. . . . I will not now inquire whether this sense is illusive, whether it can be proved not to be illusive, whether it does absolutely make us possess the real nature of things; all I say is, that poetry can awaken it in us, and that to awaken it is one of the highest powers of poetry.[5]

Wordsworth worried these matters through a number of great poems. His concern with the difficulties involved emerges, for example, in the regularity with which he refers to instances of potential self-deception. *The Prelude* is full of passages in which he peers, with a compassionate skepticism that seems quite unsure of itself, at his own thoughts about what and where he was. At times he sprinkles the appropriate qualifications, at others issues a simple statement that he once owned certain ideas but that those ideas were not necessarily absolutely accurate. (A fuller deception—or at least an abandonment of insoluble intricacies—was to be later enshrined in *The Excursion*.) The great poems, thus, tend to imitate the tension of a continual nervous dance around the areas of possible rebuff. The stress on the "human" soul in "Lines Written in Early Spring" makes one version of discontinuity, but he kept finding and pointing to other kinds everywhere. Wordsworth was usually too concerned with amplitude of valid knowledge to skirt around the facts of discontinuity, which were the facts of his life; and denying them was out of the question. Later he learned to ignore them. He saw that there were limitations even with a figure like the solitary reaper alone in her kind, which happened also to be his. What Wordsworth gave to himself he was too clear and too truth-bound not to give to others as well. And if about himself there were fewest hiding places, he knew that even his own past existence was not fully to be recovered: the child in the "Immortality" ode has about it a "self-presence" which he recognizes to be untouchable. The process of recovery had always been guided and hindered

[5] From Arnold's essay on Maurice de Guérin in *Essays in Criticism* (Boston: Fields, Osgood, 1869), p. 74.

by inherent limitations: "We see but darkly / Even when we look behind us" (*Prelude*, III, 482–483). It was for good reason that the image of the stranger, intrusive or diffident or merely unaware, haunted him even into those late days when distance was little more than a concept useful to glorify man.

So complex was this set of states and relationships, based partly on simultaneity and partly on succession, that Wordsworth's fullest understanding of it was earned only after a protracted, intricate learning experience. Ideas about the approximation of man and nature, therefore, are not so much wrong as insufficient. Approximation rests on the coincidence of being, which ensures by its existence that there are ties, and it implies for some—this follows much too easily—that there must be a bridge over separateness. Clearly, that which Wordsworth saw in the coincidence of being was permanent truth, but it was not all of the truth, and the coincidence left open as many puzzles as it completed. For the question is whether the bridge over separateness can be found; and if so, when, how often, and under what conditions. The recognition of the fact and the meaning of approximation is moving and perhaps even comforting, but the full situation Wordsworth saw with all the strength of his mature imagination did not ease him into comfort. Wordsworth had been startled too often to allow approximation more than its due place.

Far less successful in its depiction of what happens to some of Wordsworth's characters is the related idea of dehumanization, which argues that they go through a process removing from them most of what is characteristically human. His characters, it is asserted, fade so well into the natural that they come through very much like dehumanized objects in a landscape, objects which show little difference from any other kinds out there. Here, then, there would seem to be a real danger in Wordsworth's moves toward approximation. But to see dehumanization as anything more than a rare and quite special occurrence (it probably does happen in "The Old Cumberland Beggar") is surely inaccurate because it misses a radical play of tension within the contours of Wordsworth's world. It is not, for example, sufficient or even satisfactory to draw on a part of Wordsworth's familiar comments on an early version of "Resolution and Independence" when only the whole pattern of comment offers the full lineaments of his understanding of the old man he is looking at: "What is brought forward? 'A lonely place, a Pond' 'by which an old man *was*, far from all house or home'—not stood, not sat, but *'was'*—the figure presented in the most naked simplicity possible. This feeling of spirituality or supernaturalness is again referred to as being strong in my mind in this passage—*'How came he here* thought I or what can he be doing?' " [6] This man abides magnificently on the plane of being on which all absolute being has a place. But other passages in the letter show that this is not all there is to what Wordsworth saw: "But Good God! Such a figure, in such a place, a pious self-respecting, miserably infirm, and [ ] Old Man telling such a tale!" The figure who *was* was a man in his absolute humanness, and that was what Wordsworth understood there in one of his greatest moments, the absolute being of that man *as man*. For an instant he has a rare and tremendous knowledge of pure being, but it is the being of that particular man out there, the manifestation and incarnation in this human figure of the being shared by all. He *was*, but Wordsworth knew that he never ceased being a man or became less than one: "though I believe God has given me a strong imagination, I cannot conceive a figure more impressive than that of an old Man like this." The old man has moved toward the center of full humanness, and only at that point is the completeness of the experience achieved.

What this passage shows of a taut equalization, strained but not brittle, is far more typical of Wordsworth's figures as they face the natural than is any slip down the scale toward a complete leveling of all qualities. Whatever characteristics have been removed from the single girl reaping alone in the field cover only the idiosyncratic. The stranger who has just entered her world can meet her not only on the level of absolute being (he can meet all the birds there too) but on the plane of humanity as well. The point is in the balance between para-dimensional coincidence and unbridgeable diversity, not in approximation or dehumanization. It is this same balance which

[6] *Early Years*, p. 366.

keeps his figures human in a world that is not anthropocentric. "Composed upon Westminster Bridge," a poem about arti- facts in their context, pictures the city as an object in the natural world, that is, approximates them; but it never slips the city so completely into the natural world that the lines between their kinds blur. It is a poem of wholeness, not identity.[7] In Book One of *The Prelude* (88–89), when the wandering ob- server casts

> A backward glance upon the curling cloud
> Of city smoke, by distance ruralised

it is, again, wholeness. To be in the same world is not to be the same. This game is dangerous, obviously, but it has to be played. Wordsworth's clarity about the conditions involved is remarkable, but more remarkable are the skill and assurance with which he plays with approximation, bringing together what man creates and what he finds already created out there. In some cases he brings the human and the other which is not quite hostile so closely together that only a rare purity of vision and the deftest of hands can keep them just barely apart, just where he wants them to be. Dorothy's skill at the same game is often as impressive as his. This is from a letter she wrote in October 1804: "In Duddon vale Rocks, hills, bushes and trees are striving together for mastery, green fields and patches of green are to be spied wherever the eye turns with their snug cottages half-hidden by the rocks, or so like them in colour, that you hardly know rock from cottage."[8] The sentence should be compared with this passage from the Wordsworth of 1798:

> The day is come when I again repose
> Here, under this dark sycamore, and view
> These plots of cottage-ground, these orchard-tufts,
> Which at this season, with their unripe fruits,
> Are clad in one green hue, and lose themselves
> 'Mid groves and copses. Once again I see
> These hedge-rows, hardly hedge-rows, little lines

---

[7] Cf. *Journals*, I, 385.
[8] *Early Years*, p. 508.

Of sportive wood run wild: these pastoral farms,
Green to the very door; and wreaths of smoke
Sent up, in silence, from among the trees!

In both passages only a few qualifiers keep the different forms
of creation, the various sharers in order, apart: in the letter this
is done with the words "half-hidden" and "hardly," in the
poem with that point right at "the very door" where the en-
croaching greenness has to stop. Elsewhere, of course, Wordsworth does show so total an encroachment of the partly foreign that hierarchy (and therefore all difference) disappears
or will disappear. But these instances tend to image states of
decay, as in "The Ruined Cottage," and may have as mood an
irony that carries melancholy and rage for bitter companions:

No motion has she now, no force;
She neither hears nor sees;
Rolled round in earth's diurnal course,
With rocks, and stones, and trees.

In some moods, only death seems viable. But Wordsworth's
world is not entirely inhuman either. Man sinks into the natural
only when he begins to rot, and then only in order to do so
more conveniently. When man alive sinks in Wordsworth's
world, it is ordinarily not toward nature but away from it. To
be fully a man means, among other things, to know well what
there is out there of threat and bliss, what warms and surrounds,
and what is impenetrable. Least human for Wordsworth are
not figures like the old man who *was*, or even (in intention at
least) the old Cumberland beggar, but those who are willfully
ignorant, who, through the conceit of a sour anthropocentrism,
choose to ignore all that can be known of their potential relationships with things—even, ironically, all that they could
know of themselves. This paradoxical defeat of self is indulged
in by the characters in "A Poet's Epitaph" and by Peter Bell
before he fell into conversion. Levels of humanity and strata
of awareness rise concurrently for Wordsworth. For this,
therefore, if for no other reason, approximation and dehumanization, particularly when unqualified, are only rarely adequate
as ways of understanding fully what Wordsworth meant by

the cohabitation of the human and the nonhuman. To show man alive and sinking would be to make of him less than available order allows him to be, and only in his own moments of willful ignorance or in even rarer ones of savage irony did Wordsworth show this happening.

Yet if he was frequently far from Keats, Wordsworth was never close to Blake. He could never have accepted Blake's Swedenborgian vision of the universe as perceptible in the image of one great man, though he might have considered this kind of anthropocentrism as more humane than the other indulged in by the willfully ignorant. Further, Wordsworth's admiration of the imaginative force in myth did not preclude his uneasiness with its anthropomorphic forms. "The World Is Too Much with Us" and the corresponding passage from *The Excursion* show that myth should be turned to only in moments of emergency, and then with no serious credence. At every stage in his development, not just in *The Excursion*, he knew that myth made an image of the world which was not a world he could believe in. Wordsworth does not work with nature by making it into man or anything like man. If man can never be fully natural and is only occasionally approximately so, this difficult universe can never be entirely human. Nor should it be if both idiosyncrasy and the truth are precious. Wordsworth would, theoretically at least, accept devices including personification for only the most sparing and precise use, because personification does not bring man closer to nature but brings nature closer to man. It is not, then, an instrument of dehumanization, since it does not sink man but raises nature. The device is not, after all, naturification, and if Wordsworth rarely puts flesh on abstractions or forces of nature (or so he claims), he almost never pastes leaves on people. Wordsworth's sense of what he was did not come easily to him and was not always reliably there. But his sense of what he was *not* was usually reliable. It took full knowledge to see wholeness, a knowledge drawn out of the most tenuous and difficult balance. He achieved this fullness just often enough—we should never exaggerate its frequency—to articulate an order that dazzled even himself. Those poems which embody the order show him as discovering it anew each time. Even that order, precisely because it was full, had chill within it; the human kind of self-consciousness is bought at a terrible price. But the order was so whole that he could usually find within it a cure for chill which made joy more than an arrogant gesture.

CHAPTER SEVEN

The Universal Dance

WHEN the eighteenth-century nature poet reaches out to touch the universe, he can do so with delight, irony, and passion; even, perhaps, with a kind of love. But there are rarely the characteristic romantic tension of love and dread and the consciousness of the processes of experience. On the other hand, a poet like Gray at times saw some of the same things Wordsworth saw, and if they looked different to Gray, that should surprise less than that they sometimes looked alike:

> To Contemplation's sober eye
> Such is the race of Man:
> And they that creep, and they that fly,
> Shall end where they began.
> Alike the Busy and the Gay
> But flutter thro' life's little day,
> In fortune's varying colours drest:
> Brush'd by the hand of rough Mischance,
> Or chill'd by age, their airy dance
> They leave, in dust to rest.
>
> Methinks I hear in accents low
> The sportive kind reply:
> Poor moralist! and what art thou?
> A solitary fly!
> Thy joys no glittering female meets,
> No hive hast thou of hoarded sweets,

No painted plumage to display:
On hasty wings thy youth is flown;
Thy sun is set, thy spring is gone—
We frolick, while 'tis May.

These are the last two stanzas of Gray's "Ode to Spring," which bring fully into sight some curious uncertainties that had been hovering about the poem. Up to the last stanza, the poem had been above all a conventionally oriented monologue of commentary on the natural, in which "insect youth" and similar creatures had served primarily as objects from which metaphors could be drawn that would illustrate human experience. On one level the last stanza snaps this mode of metaphor back at the observer, aiming particularly at the enormity of that arrogant human egoism which uses the natural as a tool for man's private benefit: the observer had been interested less in the full reality of what he saw than in how it could offer imagery for human enlightenment. When the poem becomes dialogue (and this observer had never dreamed of an answer), irony sets in, for the natural understands the observer better than he understands the natural. He had been aware of analogies and had realized that the very fact that analogies could be used meant that man and the natural shared a context together. But if he had sensed difference, his terms would have defined it only in the light of a conventional view of the great chain and especially that aspect of the view which emphasized how all the creatures below man lead up to him, to some extent for his glory but ultimately for God's because he is the mortal image of God. If that is in the poem only by a clear implication, Gray's assertions could move in no other direction. What he learns—and nothing could surprise him more—is that a different direction is possible.

In other words, this very interesting poem works in a number of related areas simultaneously. In one, the poem brings the limitations of human perception clearly to the center and focuses also on a species of egoism that seems natural only to man. There is here the inchoate stage of a kind of candidness that was to unnerve and glorify much of romanticism. Yet the essay on human limitations is embodied in a verbal stratum which is an elaborate assertion of human artifice, and this stratum calls attention to man's ability to make a world of his own which is not only eminently but also exclusively human. This is the egoist as artificer. But the situation is defined fully only by its ambiguities. For if language as it is used here offers artifice as a conscious opposition to the natural, the poem also faces up to the insufficiency of those metaphors, which are simply too self-contemplating to take in all that is really there. The irony directed toward the inadequacies of the observer's vision also includes as object the imagery that his vision creates. Gray did not, however, build better than he knew: the uneasiness was there, and he had only to go just too far for it to emerge, briefly and lightly but definitely.

Gray and his surprising respondents speak, sometimes quite directly, about the continuum of life in time, of a movement which is necessarily a process. Further, they are profoundly aware that where they are now is one moment in the long experience of all creatures that undergo time. In this poem, then, the sense of continuum cuts across the hierarchy of nature and is acknowledged—naturally quite impossibly—by all stages on the great chain. Wordsworth was close enough to Gray's way of thinking for continua like this to have the most intense significance for him. Yet he was far enough away from Gray, deep into another mode of organizing things, so that he could occasionally deliberately block out continua because they distracted from experiences that he wanted to be absolutely immediate. Wordsworth could create a strange emphasis on temporal modes simply by claiming that he was ignoring or rejecting them. The outrageousness of this momentary repudiation brought the continuum of time more clearly into the center than it would have been otherwise:

> "Where are your books?—that light bequeathed
> To Beings else forlorn and blind!
> Up! up! and drink the spirit breathed
> From dead men to their kind.
>
> "You look round on your Mother Earth,
> As if she for no purpose bore you;
> As if you were her first-born birth,
> And none had lived before you!"

Here two kinds of continua have been rejected, the first enclosing the best embodiments of the unfolding history of the human mind, the second the continuity of time itself. Both disappear under the pressure of a desire for a complete immediacy which would be unhampered by any versions of temporal continua, for the latter would necessarily frame this virgin moment and thus, somehow, detract from its intensity. As it turns out, the purpose of this careful adoption of blinders is to make another kind of continuum more apparent because everything focuses on it: that, of course, is the continuum of man and the natural, which, through an amazing variety of images and phenomena in a number of poems, is seen persistently as an unbroken circuit of unhampered impulses of energy. "Lines Written in Early Spring" exhibits one version:

> To her fair works did Nature link
> The human soul that through me ran;
> And much it grieved my heart to think
> What man has made of man.

The structure of a continuous circuit reappears in "To My Sister":

> Love, now a universal birth,
> From heart to heart is stealing,
> From earth to man, from man to earth:
> —It is the hour of feeling.

In its own way the stance of the observer in "Expostulation and Reply" is a product of artifice quite as much as anything Gray chose to assert, though Wordsworth's is an artifice of exclusion, a position based mainly on the temporary rejection of what memory can bring into the making of order. From one point of view, this special trick (no other word is more accurate) is an induced regression into an earlier state, quite close to that of the child in the "Immortality" ode or in the earliest stages of personal development, when nothing exists except what is happening immediately in that place. Indeed, the maternal imagery in stanza three of "Expostulation and Reply" indicates Wordsworth's awareness that this position looks like a form of reversion. In another sense (Wordsworth's self-confidence is impressive here), the move out of the order shaped by memory drops the observer sharply down the hierarchy of being, down to where there would be nothing but immediacy; but he maintains the proper balance subtly, through the studied sophistication of his choice to limit his experience. He is neither child nor animal but an extraordinarily aware observer who chooses limitation in order to achieve a special, subtle intensity. Balancing of this sort is what pastoral always has done, though in pre-Wordsworthian pastoral the hierarchy was social rather than one of qualities of being. Wordsworth held on to some of the structure and even part of the content of the old pastoral, but the shifts in emphasis added up to a recognition that the world now looked quite different and was not altogether charming. Some of the shifting had begun with Gray. Yet the decision taken in "Expostulation and Reply" and its related lyrics, the decision to stand alone without any tie but the immediacy of this unrelated moment, has within it a level of courage and confidence, born out of a firm sureness of control, that would have been merely puzzling to Gray. Only a few years before, there had been no sureness for Wordsworth but only the untied order that he passed through in "Incipient Madness."

Though it offered a perfect image of seamless continuity, timeless immediacy (which is an aspect of the Faustian consciousness) was not usually Wordsworth's way, however much it helped as a rhetorical standpoint from which to debate some truths about the order of the experiencing self at its moments of pure receptiveness. In several of the early poems, Wordsworth had to work hard to argue the self out of time because his impulses always pulled him in the other direction, toward seeing what and where he was in the widest possible context. For Wordsworth object-consciousness was stereoscopic, that is, multidimensional as well as wide and intense. Further, at the beginning of his great decade, and of course all through it, he was concerned with the developmental elements of self and particularly with its movement through stages of consciousness which expanded in their capacity for awareness as they moved closer to his present position. Wordsworth began "Tintern Abbey" one month or at the most two after the composition of "Expostulation and Reply" and "The Tables Turned," both of which had come, as belated answers, out of a long walking conversation with Hazlitt in May 1798.[1] In "Tintern Abbey" he showed how, at certain remarkable moments, there emerged an awareness not only of the immediate, unhampered continuum of being that spread out spatially from this moment, but also of a movement through time so complex that its delicate intricacy spreads everywhere throughout the poem. "Tintern Abbey" ambles gracefully, though not in exact chronology, through time present, time immediately past, and time far past to a future of his own and eventually to another that continues beyond the point when he will cease to have any future. The pattern is elaborate but not willfully extravagant. Taken simultaneously with the continuity in immediacy, this web of time places the observer and his poem at the crossroads of two impulses that move tightly along recognizable paths, one of which is probably cyclical as well as immediate, rolling through all things and back, the other surely irrevocably linear. In both, though in different ways, the self seems to partake in endlessness. Both impulses are horizontal, or democratic, for no distinction is made among the creatures living within their dimensions. The taut pattern of continua that holds these impulses in order is basic to the early nature poems and to some sections of *The Prelude*, and it was apparently satisfactory as a framework for certain statements concerned with that most difficult fact about self, that it is personally continuous while changing in time through immutable succession. Wordsworth made clear that the continuity of self was in time only: it took more of a solipsist than he was to see it in any other continuum. But with that qualification made, and with the necessary control it pointed to, Wordsworth could yield to the impulse to expand context, whether of his self as central object or of the object outside of him. He pushed out the confines of his surroundings in an attempt to encompass all that his perspective would hold, and the success of the effort was measured by the breadth of the perspective it allowed. For such purposes any object would suffice, since every object was, eventually, surrounded by everything. Tours de force were frequent and were usually great poems.

[1] See Mark L. Reed, *Wordsworth. The Chronology of the Early Years*, p. 238. For an argument against the traditional association of these poems with Hazlitt, see the review of Reed by Jack Stillinger in *JEGP*, 66 (1967), 464.

One of the most intriguing of these, "I Wandered Lonely as a Cloud," is like many other of Wordsworth's poems in that it offers an interpretation of its own meaning that gives only an incomplete indication of what is actually going on within it. Most readers focus on the poem's own reading of itself, that is, on the uncomplicated relationship among sensuous stimulation, memory, and the bliss of sensation.[2] Yet the lyric on daffodils is not only about a process but also about something seen, and it is not merely in the quality of the observer's seeing but also in what he sees that the fuller import of the poem lies. Wordsworth, smarting from a particularly clumsy comment on it, said in a letter to Sir George Beaumont, "The very object of my poem is the trouble or agitation both of the flowers and the Water."[3] This comment offers a beginning toward what seems the proper direction, one from which we can come to a fuller understanding of the poem and the whole experience within it.

In 1815 Wordsworth added a note to "I Wandered Lonely as a Cloud" which, though few critics have accepted his own evaluation of the content of the poem, has its special pertinence: "the subject of these Stanzas is rather an elementary feeling and simple impression (approaching to the nature of an ocular spectrum) upon the imaginative faculty, than an *exertion* of it."[4] Ocular spectra consist of visions triggered into being when the

---

[2] Basic to any serious discussion of the poem is Frederick Pottle's analysis, "The Eye and the Object in the Poetry of Wordsworth," *Wordsworth: Centenary Studies Presented at Cornell and Princeton Universities*, ed. Gilbert Dunklin (1939; reprinted, New York: Russell and Russell, 1962), pp. 23–44. Nearly every book on Wordsworth mentions the poem, most comments differing little in substance and tone from Pater's remark that it is "prompted by a sort of half-playful mysticism!" Pater at least puts the poem in the same category as "The Two April Mornings," though this description stands for both; see *Appreciations* (New York: Macmillan, 1903), p. 58. Useful brief comments can be found in Ferry, *The Limits of Mortality*, p. 10: the poet's loneliness "is a separation from the harmony of things and the aspect of eternity." See also Perkins, *Wordsworth and the Poetry of Sincerity*, p. 198: the poem shows "the unity of all things in a bond of joy," though the unity Perkins speaks of is exclusively terrestrial, as in most other discussions of the poem. There are important comments in Hartman, *Wordsworth's Poetry*, pp. 3–5, 269-270.
[3] Letter of February 1808, in *Middle Years*, Part 1, p. 194.
[4] *Poetical Works*, II, 507.

perceiver is either especially tense or half dozing.[5] Their content is furnished by memory out of the storehouses of the mind. The visions themselves are intensely real to the perceiver through their effect of vivid immediacy. Like the half-dozing perceiver of an ocular spectrum, the observer in Wordsworth's poem begins in an odd state and within it receives "an elementary feeling and simple impression . . . upon the imaginative faculty." The impression, which Wordsworth carefully indicates is something like an ocular spectrum but not the same, shares with the spectrum in its qualities of vividness and depth. Yet the differences are very important: however simple the impression in the poem, the experience leads in toward the full meaning of the complex of activities at the center. Ocular spectra are, finally, the spawn of memory, however dazzling their immediacy: their life exists only as he sees them. But the events in the middle stanzas of "I Wandered Lonely as a Cloud" bring the suddenly awakened observer deep into the permanent reality of things, where, if he is not yet fully aware of all that he sees, he has at least seen. More than an ocular spectrum but somewhat like one in conditions and intensity, the experience in the poem (and this includes the recollection at the end) takes its essential character not from hallucinatory immediacy but from the paradoxical simplicity of its form, which leads to a vision of the grandest depth and fullness.

The fullest extent of what the observer sees begins to establish itself quietly but firmly with the first image in the poem, the cloud. This image does many things, serving not only to define the qualities of the observer's condition but also to sketch the larger dimensions in which what he experiences is taking place.

[5] The subject was dear to Coleridge; see, for example, his letter to Southey of 7 August 1803, *Collected Letters of Samuel Taylor Coleridge*, ed. Earl Leslie Griggs (Oxford: The Clarendon Press, 1956), II, 961. In his well-known criticism of the poem on daffodils in *Biographia Literaria*, Coleridge talks of a "vivid image or visual spectrum" (Shawcross edition, II, 190). Z. S. Fink, in *The Early Wordsworthian Milieu* (Oxford: The Clarendon Press, 1958), pp. 54–56, defines ocular spectra succinctly and points out an example of one in a rejected passage of *The Prelude*. In Chapter Twelve of Peacock's *Nightmare Abbey*, the character of Flosky, who represents Coleridge, is made to speak of a ghost as "a *deceptio visûs*, an ocular spectrum, an idea with the force of a sensation."

These dimensions emerge more clearly when the second stanza repeats a pattern that had been drawn in the first. The cloud, or rather the observer as cloud, is detached, not only alone but also lonely and drifting without purpose. Though not part of the earth, the cloud is still so close to it that a mental image can take in, within a single frame, the wandering of this piece of sky over part of the earth. The rest of the first stanza expands a series of details about the earth, drawing quite generally the shape of what could be seen from the cloud. The pattern in this stanza encloses a movement of perception from above to below and, further, shows by the single glance sweeping them all in that the things of earth and sky are unified, part of the same context. When this movement from high to low recurs in the second stanza, the repetition of the pattern reinforces the unity of above and below at the same time as it expands that unity into an awesome scope of vision. The range of his seeing, which has gained in detail about the earth, has come now to include the hemisphere of the heavens as well. Wordsworth pushes out the walls and draws in the cosmos over the scene, moving the poem from the beautiful to the sublime and giving to the observer's loneliness and his eventual understanding of relationship the framework of the whole universe itself.

Such a joining of earth and sky was hardly a new action for Wordsworth. Indeed, the movement in which the two come into unity appears very often in his poems, frequently in the early stanzas of a lyric or in a passage where part of its function is to place the events that follow in the grandest context man can comprehend, the universal scheme of things. In "Tintern Abbey," for example, earth and sky come together to show that what he sees does not stand alone in "absolute independent singleness" but stands as part of the wholeness which is the universe:

> Once again
> Do I behold these steep and lofty cliffs,
> That on a wild secluded scene impress
> Thoughts of more deep seclusion; and connect
> The landscape with the quiet of the sky.

And the green he talks of is a total, unified greenness, "one green hue." All of this implies that the events of his life do not stand alone either but are themselves part of a whole, the temporal continuum which affirms the unity of his own being. The three stages of his development echo in their own dimension the linking of all things which is the universal pattern. (The linking occurs whether we take "I" or "cliffs" to be the subject of "connect"; but the role of the poet as unifier makes "I" the much more likely possibility.) The pattern occurs again in "A Night-Piece," which shows a number of similarities to the lyric on daffodils, particularly in its awareness of how earth and sky, in certain situations, have to be perceived together. Here he brings them into relationship through negatives, by showing what they are not doing but soon will be when the moon breaks through:

> the Moon,
> Which through that veil is indistinctly seen,
> A dull, contracted circle, yielding light
> So feebly spread that not a shadow falls,
> Chequering the ground—from rock, plant, tree, or tower.

Another example, in Book Two of *The Prelude*, has particular importance because it details a childhood version of the experience and also because it shows heaven and earth united in one who was to be a poet, capable of seeing them as joined and of passing on his seeing to others:

> oh, then, the calm
> And dead still water lay upon my mind
> Even with a weight of pleasure, and the sky,
> Never before so beautiful, sank down
> Into my heart, and held me like a dream!
> (170–174)

With this recurrent trope of "a blended holiness of earth and sky" ("The Recluse," line 144), Wordsworth offers his own particular version of the holy marriage, the coming together of sky and earth in a union which, whatever the form it took, promised fruitfulness, often through an alliance of the divine and mortal (as it did in a range extending from vegetation myths to the imagery of adultery in Old Testament prophets like Hosea and the vision in the New Testament of the church as the bride of Christ). In the passage just quoted from *The Prelude*, water substitutes for earth, not so much in a variation based on the four elements (although that idea lingers in the background) as to draw in a new series of reverberations working toward an analogy with the functions of the imagination. A spectacular display of evening sun, repeated in the water "with unity sublime," occurs in *The Excursion*, IX, 590–613. Another example of the nuptial metaphor, with exactly these variations and implications concerning the imagination, is in "There Was a Boy" and the equivalent passage in *The Prelude*, V, 384–388:

> the visible scene
> Would enter unawares into his mind,
> With all its solemn imagery, its rocks,
> Its woods, and that uncertain heaven, received
> Into the bosom of the steady lake.

Indeed, the metaphor of the holy marriage does so much to signify the characteristics of this Wordsworthian mode that these last lines brought from Coleridge the remark that "had I met these lines running wild in the deserts of Arabia, I should have instantly screamed out 'Wordsworth!' " [6]

When a distinctly divine being and the natural creature unite in the trope, they ordinarily create a demi-god or demi-divine object.[7] Wordsworth uses the archetype of the hierogamy in part to create a frame of awesome dimensions that gives order and space to the world in which his objects move:

> A violet by a mossy stone
> Half hidden from the eye!
> —Fair as a star, when only one
> Is shining in the sky.

But he never really breaks with the spiritual implications present in the very nature of the trope: in harmony with these implications, but in his own carefully defined terms, he reworks the

[6] From a letter to Wordsworth, 10 December 1798, *Collected Letters of Samuel Taylor Coleridge*, I, 453.

[7] When the offspring is not demi-divine, there is frequently some reason for the exception. In Genesis 6:1–4 (Revised Standard Version), when "the sons of God saw that the daughters of men were fair; and they took to wife such of them as they chose," the usual kind of product would seem about to follow. But God says, "My spirit shall not abide in man for ever, for he is flesh, but his days shall be a hundred and twenty years." And the products,

archetype so as to suggest that divinity is not where the tradition had frequently asserted it to be, on only one side of the union. Such reworking emerges in poems like the lyric on daffodils, where the meaning of the holy marriage for the world Wordsworth creates takes significant form.

The speaker in "I Wandered Lonely as a Cloud" enters the poem so detached from everything as to seem not to touch anything. The focus of his attention must have been within, distracted from any precise perception of his surroundings, for his awareness of the daffodils is sudden and apparently quite surprising. Wordsworth, typically, points out through the language of the experience what the conditions were under which the experience came about at all. "Crowd" is the first word he uses about the flowers; this is, obviously, his initial, instantaneous, and generalized impression of a mass outside of him. And the famous rhythmic pattern in the last line of the first stanza—"Fluttering and dancing in the breeze"—reinforces the idea that what came through next was a vivid, rhythmic pulsation.[8] Mass and movement, then, initiate the experience for him, giving body and life to what he sees. He, too, has both body and life, the mass and movement of a cloud drifting purposelessly, and thus he can know that in an important sense he is like what he sees. But the second stanza details the consequences of his intense, concentrated gazing, and he comes to know just how different his situation really is.

The observer has begun to move out of his state of introspection, that kind of relaxed awareness, partly in and partly out of himself, which occurs so often in Wordsworth that it must be a precondition for experiences of the sort rendered in this poem. As he moves out, he learns more and more about what there is

when they do appear, are called gigantic men (the Nephilim). This ancient story inserted into Genesis by the writer(s) of the Yahwist strand had been an etiological myth designed to explain the existence of the race of aboriginal giants. But in the context, in this part of Genesis, of the increasing degradation of man (the Flood follows immediately after this passage), the myth points back to God's order in 3:22 to expel man from Eden "lest he put forth his hand and take also the tree of life, and eat, and live for ever." The products, therefore, are human and mortal.

[8] The 1807 version of the line has much less life to it: "Ten thousand dancing in the breeze." The "ten thousand" dropped out of the line and was picked up in the stanza added in 1815.

outside of him. The second stanza therefore offers considerably more detail about his surroundings, not only in specifics but also in scope and depth. As his consciousness expands and deepens, the scene thickens and extends, forcing his seeing to absorb most of his intellectual energy. The first and third stanzas are replete with self-reference (one of Wordsworth's favorite methods for setting up the relationships in an encounter), but the second has only one, enough to show that the object has a subject and therefore a perspective; but it shows no more than that, for he is too busy looking.

What he looks at indicates to him just how crowded is that scene of which he had been only partly aware as he came up to it. He is surrounded by groups (surrounded, it should be added, on the vertical and horizontal planes he has begun to see), collections of stars, flowers, and waves, all going through an experience very different from what he himself has been going through. Here one has to grasp all the import and force of those two movements of perception, identical in form and increasing in scope, which had opened up the cosmos for this wanderer and given to the actions of the poem the largest conceivable frame of reference. For what he sees is not only terrestrial but also cosmic: the dancing he comes upon takes place not only beside Ullswater but also upon it, and in the elements of the Milky Way as well. The elementary dichotomy of "single" and "crowd" has to be applied not only to himself in relation to the host of daffodils but also to his relation to all the large groups of things everywhere around him which are going through a similar motion. So much the more does his aloofness stand out, for of all the things he sees he is the only one that is alone in its kind, doing and being somewhat different.

In another context a situation of aloneness like this could be very bleak indeed. Two years earlier he had drawn such a context, in a poem he was to finish in the same year he wrote the lyric on daffodils:

> Now, while the birds thus sing a joyous song,
> And while the young lambs bound
> As to the tabor's sound,
> To me alone there came a thought of grief:

A timely utterance gave that thought relief,
And I again am strong.

If in "I Wandered Lonely as a Cloud" there is a very different version of the situation of communion, the difference comes not in the form of a conscious acceptance of the outsider (i.e., not "What, you are stepping westward?") but in his awareness, partial during the encounter and completed only later, of the full meaning of what he has seen. Here, again, the total range of what he sees contains and in an important sense *is* the basis of meaning.

The earliest published version of the lyric, in the *Poems in Two Volumes* of 1807, had what are now stanzas one, three, and four but not the second stanza (first published in 1815), in which the movement of perception is completed and encompasses the universe. Closely related to this addition is the replacement, also in 1815, of "dancing" in line four of the 1807 version with "golden," an image which is visual only, not both visual and kinetic as "dancing" is. Taken alone the change appears to mar the poem, since the color of these daffodils is not so rare a piece of information that it has to be substituted for a particularly lively image. But what Wordsworth now has, after all the additions and replacements, is a series of four grammatical variations on the most important word in the poem: "dancing," "dance," "danced," and "dances." None of these forms is repeated; all of them together ring the changes on the movement of energy that runs through the poem. Emphasis through grammatical variation, typical of Wordsworth's retreat from flashiness into a straightforward statement of immense richness, parallels the radical mode of a kind of poetry in which the literal, it becomes apparent very quickly, is also intensely symbolic.[9]

The variations, one of them in each stanza, spread the idea and image of dancing like a leaven through the whole poem. And because the poem holds the universe within it, they spread dancing through the universe as well. Further, because the variations are all different, the poem comes at dancing from different positions, as it were, catching it at different moments in time and in

[9] Cf. in "The Solitary Reaper" the series *singing, sings, strain,* and *sound.*

159

various forms, from a participle to a noun to past and present tenses. Dancing is everywhere and at all times in the universe the observer comes to see. It is, as I have said, beside the lake and upon it, but it is also in the stars themselves, whose twinkling echoes the rhythmic pulsation the observer becomes aware of here on this earth. There is a rhythm in the universe, a continuum that spreads through the things of this world but also swings up to the stars themselves. The imagery of the cosmos achieves its fullest effect, after the movements of opening, when it ends by providing the space and dimensions in which the universal rhythm can pulsate. The dance is, of course, Wordsworth's image of the One Life, whose mode is joy and whose movement is a vast rhythmic energy. If it may be too fanciful (I think it is not) to look upon this as a marriage dance, celebrating the nuptials of earth and sky, the image of dancing clearly draws its full import only when he sees earth and sky as joined together to form a single context.

If the dance seems tailor-made for Wordsworth's purposes, offering the effect he needed of a vibrant, joyously rhythmic life, it too comes out of an old tradition. The image of the universal dance, though surely not as ancient as that of the hierogamy, has its own dignified history, of parts of which Wordsworth was unquestionably aware. At the back of most uses of this figure is Plato's *Timaeus*, 40, where the heavenly bodies are spoken of as going through a form of dance: "To describe the evolutions in the dance of these same gods, their juxtapositions, the counterrevolutions of their circles relatively to one another, and their advances . . . to describe all this without visible models of these same would be labour spent in vain." [10] Eventually the image becomes a commonplace, associated usually with the music of the spheres, to which, it may be assumed, the stars did their dancing. Wordsworth could easily have picked up the image from its wide use in the Renaissance where it was a familiar topos, related to the concept of universal order and harmony and to the celebratory joy of a universe delighting, at this point in its

10 *Plato's Cosmology*, trans. Francis Cornford (1937; reprinted, New York: Liberal Arts Press, 1957), p. 135. The association of the soul with a harmony like that of music offers interesting relationships to Wordsworth's own preoccupations in the lyric on daffodils.

history, in its own coherence.[11] By then the dance had moved out from the stars to include all things in all places, pulsating happily to the harmony of universal order. Perhaps the most characteristic as well as one of the most interesting uses of the topos as a radical metaphor occurs in Sir John Davies's *Orchestra*, which Wordsworth may well have read though I can find no evidence that he did. The following, stanza fifty-five of *Orchestra*, bears a remarkable relationship to Wordsworth's poem, not least because it brings into the confines of a single stanza the two themes, the holy marriage and the universal dance, that Wordsworth made use of later:

> See how those flowers, that have sweet beauty too,
> (The only jewels that the earth doth wear,
> When the young sun in bravery her doth woo)
> As oft as they the whistling wind do hear,
> Do wave their tender bodies here and there;
> And though their dance no perfect measure is
> Yet oftentimes their music makes them kiss.[12]

(Here, surely, the dance is a love dance if not yet one of marriage.) Yet Wordsworth needed to go no further than *Paradise Lost*, always close to the center of his imaginative experience, to find a varied series of instances of the stellar dance; for example:

> the great Luminary
> Aloof the vulgar Constellations thick,
> That from his Lordly eye keep distance due,
> Dispenses Light from far; they as they move
> Their Starry dance in numbers that compute
> Days, months, and years, towards his all-cheering Lamp
> Turn swift their various motions, or are turn'd
> By his Magnetic beam.[13]

[11] The chapter "The Cosmic Dance," in E. M. W. Tillyard's *The Elizabethan World Picture* (1943; reprinted, London: Chatto and Windus, 1958), gives a useful summary of some of the issues involved.

[12] I quote from *Orchestra*, ed. E. M. W. Tillyard (London: Chatto and Windus, 1947), p. 28, but have added "is" in the next to last line, the word having been omitted from Tillyard's text.

[13] III, 576–583. Herbert Agar's *Milton and Plato* (1928; reprinted, Gloucester, Mass.: P. Smith, 1965) lists in the appendix a number of passages relevant to Milton's use of the image of the cosmic dance, though not the one I quote

But Milton, it should be noted, usually confines the dance to the stars themselves, keeping the image within the terms of Plato's use of it. There are a few exceptions though: *Comus* extends the pulsations down to the seas of the earth:

> We that are of purer fire
> Imitate the Starry Choir
> Who in their nightly watchful Spheres,
> Lead in swift round the Months and Years.
> The Sounds and Seas with all their finny drove
> Now to the Moon in wavering Morris move.
>
> (111–116)

The wordplay on "wavering" moves this version of the dance into line with what Davies had done and Wordsworth was to do. In "I Wandered Lonely as a Cloud" Wordsworth returned to the full Renaissance use of the image as a means of bringing into focus his sense of a universal delight that takes form in an ebullient pulsation of energy. But he does more, for if the delight is the self-contemplating joy of the One Life, and that Life is divine, then in this version of the holy marriage there is divinity on both sides of the union and not just on one. Wordsworth uses the trope to show that the meeting in this poem does not involve elements that have absolutely different modes of being. Here, if the marriage is holy, there is in it no wholly other. He recasts the archetype into a new setting in which mortal and terrestrial are not fully identical. Divinity rests equally in each member of the ceremony because the One Life that runs through all things is a leveling influence that spreads the essence of divinity through the cosmos and on earth. His shift in the traditional implications of the hierogamy always emphasized a completion, the coming together of two halves of a single whole, so that when he would "connect the landscape with the quiet of the sky," it could be seen that the halves were closely related in essence though each had a different sphere of action. The emphasis ultimately rests on variety in unity, the variety in the forms that the dance takes as well as in the elements that do the dancing, the unity not only in the unifying joy but also in the totality of the joyful elements.

---

here. Related to this context is the dance of Universal Pan in *Paradise Lost*, IV, 266–268.

No demi-god could come out of this union: its product had to be the wholeness in which all things have their being.

And it can be seen that the separate images of dance and marriage, however much they have their individual jobs to do, attain their fullest meaning only when seen in the light of each other. The idea of the marriage dance is perhaps not so fanciful after all. Each trope gives support to the other while they remain joined in a state of tension, themselves gaining in richness by the act of completion which puts them together into a single context. When the poem reaches the point at which temporal perspective comes into the picture, what the observer sees through time is another perspective, in other dimensions, created by the harmonious meeting of these images.

Only in the fullness of these dimensions does the observer learn that he can take part in the universal dance. Earlier, at the moment of the original event, his achieved gaiety was still surrounded by ignorance: the image is of a stranger at a show, a spectator on the sidelines, watching the spectacular dance with no awareness that he too has a right to be a participant. Given the conditions announced at the beginning, to cross from the sidelines to the center had to be an enormous step for him, one that he could not take in the "Immortality" ode (though in the lyric on daffodils there is no sense that he had any struggle in coming to learn what he did). When, in the lyric, he does take that step to the center, it is clear that he could have done so only by discovering in the fullness of time the meaning of the continua embodied in the juxtaposition of the holy marriage and the universal dance. His wealth takes the form of a communion, one that came with his recognition that if the dance were everywhere, he was no longer a lonely wanderer. This is not simply a case of delighting in dancing daffodils; nor is the poem only one more instance of the recollection in tranquillity of something as pretty as this scene of vivid joy beside a lake. When he joins in later (with the same blend of kinesis and insight held by the original event), the union means that his ignorance has been dissipated. The outsider comes to realize that he is no longer entirely a stranger and alone but another participant in an activity whose scope and stage are not only beside Ullswater but everywhere that anything can be. When he brings back the flowers, the cosmic fullness of their context comes with them. Neither his remembrance of an object, nor even his immediate perception of it, is ever of the object alone but always within the frame in which he first saw it. Thus, the emphasis in "I Wandered Lonely as a Cloud" is on a vision of wholeness achieved through the awareness of continua. Seeing through time, the kind of joining that the poet always does, brings actively into play the knowledge that there are wholenesses everywhere, groups of all sorts partaking in one idea and one movement. If it takes time for him to see that his strangeness has been partly overcome, that active seeing means also that there are links between then and now, that even in the dimension of time (and *because* it is a dimension) there is a kind of wholeness for him to perceive and to partake in.

At the beginning of the "Immortality" ode, the outsider's perception of joy offers no concomitant possibility that he can take part in what he sees. But the days of childhood, his own and those of the children he now perceives, work into harmony with his present state through Wordsworth's development of the metaphor of travel, which emerges now and then in the poem. For the metaphor implies a continuity in time and therefore parallels and reinforces the insistence of the headnote (which for this reason may well be the "timely utterance") on the child's fatherhood of the man: both note and metaphor stress the unity of being involved in the consistent, unbreaking movement of the temporal continuum. At this point the two poems finished in 1804 come together, for in "I Wandered Lonely as a Cloud" one of the last unities he becomes aware of, as we have seen, is that of time, through which the quality and substance of the whole have finally become apparent to him. But even the pleasures of time cannot gloss over the contextual differences between "I hear, I hear, with joy I hear!" and "A poet could not but be gay, / In such a jocund company": the ode, more doubting and frantic at that stage, has pain within it that the lyric never shows.

The ideas of loss, time, and the dance had come together five years earlier in "The Two April Mornings," which prefigures many of the preoccupations of each of these poems of 1804 as well as the juxtaposition of images in the lyric. Matthew, for whom the recollection of time can bring only a heavy sense of loss, refuses to accept the consolations available in the sight of "a blooming Girl," whose movements and joy are figured for him in the imagery of dance:

> No fountain from its rocky cave
> E'er tripped with foot so free.

Matthew's refusal to find room in the world of his loss for this image of dancing joy is probably a limitation on his part.[14] In the lyric on daffodils, though, the observer eventually recognizes the meaning of what has been offered to him, both meaning and recognition having much to do with what the lyric offers of a multidimensional world. The poems of hierogamy make clear that, for Wordsworth, a vision of the multiplicity of interlocked dimensions has a positive result, one that brings awe and joy along with a sense of omnipresent wholenesses. Both the "Immortality" ode and "The Two April Mornings" dwell obsessively on the dimension of time alone, which, quite possibly because it is by itself and therefore unidimensional, seems to offer only the most weighty sense of what time can take away. A comparison of "Simon Lee" and "Resolution and Independence" should make clear how temporal perspective has to function in harmony with other kinds to turn a feeling of what time takes away, in the person of characters such as Simon Lee, into the grand vision the leech-gatherer excites of what time in the present tense has to offer. The range of vision makes all the difference in "I Wandered Lonely as a Cloud" and in other poems in which Wordsworth shapes out a world like the one within that lyric. (That the range need not be perfectly visual is indicated in "Resolution and Independence," where the dimension of time crosses and meets joyfully with the hierarchy of the great chain of being.) Time by itself brings only the knowledge of thoughts beyond tears, but the range of vision, however awesome, brings into time an understanding of the joy the observer can know in his life and that of others. There are no other human beings in "I Wandered Lonely as a Cloud," and that may be *its* limitation. Perhaps the observer is most comfortable with joy in other than

---

[14] I am convinced here by the argument of Anne Kostelanetz, "Wordsworth's 'Conversations': A Reading of 'The Two April Mornings' and 'The Fountain,'" *ELH*, 33 (1966), 43–52.

human bodies. Certainly in "Resolution and Independence" his satisfaction is tinged with the sadness of human change. But the point is that he does experience the cosmic dance and its joy when, in the fullness of time, the total experience of which the daffodils are the center and synecdoche comes back to him. That, obviously, was a lesson sufficient for what this stranger needed to know.

Yet out of the relationship between the early and later experiences emerges a further, probably final perspective on all these activities. At the end, when the observer begins to understand what he has seen, the understanding comes to him under the impetus of a sudden, surely unexpected turn in the mode of his current state: there is clearly no conscious effort on his part to bring back the memory of the dance but, rather, the surprising reemergence up to the surface of an image unsummoned but cherished when it is known. He is, in other words, reliving the pattern of the whole early scenario. The pleasure that comes after his re-vision of the dance parallels the sudden gaiety he felt before, and each separate moment of delight follows and fills a state of spiritual vacuity, embodied, in the original scenario, in his lonely wandering and, in the subsequent repetition, in his inner emptiness as he lies on the couch. Between the vacancy and the joy come, at each time, the flowers.

This pattern of event and repetition clarifies, even as it embodies, the ground of the poem, the radical movement on which all the others are centered. The poem moves in a nearly complete cycle, from a partial absorption within self outward to an awareness of the whole universal context and then inward to a new absorption within self, one that seems total. That second movement within, however, carries something different with it, the universe that comes with the daffodils when they come back to him. At one end of the spectrum the poem holds the universe, and at the other the inner life of the self, the cosmos within that can contain very comfortably a vision of the whole universal context. Within itself the universe of the mind has its own spaces, in which a dance of cosmic dimensions can be experienced again and again because the microcosm has not only illimitable proportions but also the weird ability, active within those proportions, to bring back a moment in time.[15] And it exercises that ability so that the reliving of the moment, because it repeats and repeats, shows the microcosm as not, after all, really subject to the linear burden of the temporal dimension. The joy within the relived moment is lifted out of chronologically successive time into a different temporal scheme, in which events repeat themselves continually in a ritual reliving of an earlier revelation. This blend of the two universes, the paradoxical containment of the macrocosm by the microcosm, the ritual moment of time out of time—all this is what the heightening of consciousness brought about by a vision of the universal dance ultimately means.

Somewhere within the organization of its inner life, every major poem that Wordsworth wrote faces what he had to face in the encounter with the daffodils, which is not to say that he saw exactly the same thing everywhere. If such an encounter is never made with perfect equanimity, that indicates, among other things, what he had come to learn as well as what he had yet to absorb within the confines of his own being. Moments of unparalleled joy, which ranged from the cautiously subdued to some that were nearly hysterical, shared with the uneasy moments, and even with those that risked serious pain, a delicate and intense sense of context. Even during the period when he had quite nearly been broken, he characterized his state in terms of having no ties, no context in which he could look around and determine where he stood in relation to all the things that shared in it. We have noted at several points how any object Wordsworth could see (and that included himself) took significant elements of its definition from whatever surrounded it in place, from wherever it had come from in time, and finally, in the dimension which gave immense depth to his world, from its situation in the hierarchy of being. The encounter which is the meeting of contextual creatures is embodied in the dimensions in which every moment finds each creature. Even in poems in which encounter is not the matter at issue, the idea of context

15 There is much of interest on the idea of the inner spaces of the mind in Clarke, *Romantic Paradox*.

still comes through, sometimes melodramatically as in "The Thorn," at others with a subtle toying with aspects of context, aspects which turn out to be the critical structuring elements within the poem, as in "Composed upon Westminster Bridge." The fact that one of the central objects within an encounter can become a synecdoche for the entire experience can, if followed through to all its conclusions, point to a variety of dimensions of extraordinary complexity. For the encounter brings together a diversified series of objects, each with its own history and location and degree of spirituality. In the meeting the total context of each object manages to touch, at every available point (which means all points immediately there), the context of all the others. The creatures are, after all, impinging on each other's context while each is in his own. Wordsworth could never do more than indicate that this elaborate touching happened and show how a few of its aspects worked. The meeting brought clearly to him once more and in another way all of the difficult multiplicity of what he felt compelled to learn to every possible extent. If the multiplicity led him toward a kind of poem that anchored a central object as a pole of coherence, he saw simultaneously that the object itself (which must also have gotten there in some way, in travel through some set of dimensions) had a contextual multiplicity within itself as well as in the place where it sat. It too had a history within and without and was almost entirely dynamic, whatever its consistency of self. And it too was locked into the different kind of dynamism of the hierarchy of being, where the fixedness of each creature was paradoxically shot through with the vividness of a central being that moved up through a continuum of the variously changeable to the Unchanging.

The full comprehension of context came sporadically to Wordsworth because it was a total imaginative grasp possible nowhere but in those rare, unforeseeable glimpses that surprised him into a joy compatible with awe. Thoughts which can reach deeper than tears are too generally available to give so profound and comprehensive a view, and they usually say a good deal less about context than does his sudden recognition that he is in one. Ultimately the experience of context is formed by a sense of dimensions. It comes from a knowledge that he is at a point that can extend everywhere that anything is extensible. If the moments of awareness were painful partly because of their unusualness, they could achieve a kind of permanence in the shape of a poem that was itself a point which could hold within itself all those dimensions: we remember that the poem on daffodils shows an understanding of how the universe within the mind can hold the extent of the universe outside of it, and that the microcosm of mind is therefore somehow homologous with the other microcosm that is the poem. Form, content, and creator had never been so reflective of each other. Even a fragment of doggerel by Coleridge, from a notebook of 1803, has the same sense of coherent extensiveness seen to varying degrees in most of the great works:

> Happily disengaged & vacant never
> Look'd at the Sky & Clouds in every puddle,
> Along the Winter Road.[16]

Here is a joyful hierogamy, glimpsed at a point in seasonal time and along a simple image of travel through time and space. Wordsworth always made more of such moments (so too did Coleridge elsewhere), though his glimpses appear to have been more sudden in their onslaught and less persistent than what Coleridge does here. But there is no question that the joy comes from what Coleridge experiences of wholeness and of a negation of vacancy that recalls the recollection of daffodils. And thus he can well afford to be "disengaged"—that is, untied —because in the most basic sense he is full of the universe: its wholeness has filled him so that he is "vacant never." He is therefore a part of it in the deepest intimacy possible.

Clearly the recognition of dimensions has curative possibilities. Indeed, it is remarkable how frequently moments of sudden awareness come out of a context in which a wide and deep series of dimensions has been carefully drawn out, sometimes with the observer's comparative ignorance. In "Stepping Westward" he had opened up a large, stereoscopic world before and behind himself, and the voice that appears to come from another world pushes out the reach of context in a further and definitely surprising way. Here, and so frequently elsewhere, the metaphor is

16 *The Notebooks of Samuel Taylor Coleridge*, I, no. 1697.

of travel, which by its given structure sets up an order stressing extent of time and space as primary areas from which other kinds of extensiveness can be reached. (*The Prelude* as a whole works in this way, and so does most romantic travel literature.) The unlooked-for gift of awareness comes to be accepted, probably, without an initial understanding of all that it can mean and do. Experience had taught Wordsworth how forms could be drunk quite deliberately as medicinal potions ready to be produced later to forestall or repair an expectable drought; Wordsworth was always somewhat of a camel, storing up for the desert he had learned to foresee. But there was no preparing for this surprising welcome into a strange land or for an unexpected invitation to a universal dance. The gift spreads through his inner vacancy, filling every dimension and contour within it, and because it always brings surprises, the gift reveals other contours within the order of the self that had been unsuspected though perhaps secretly hoped for. In an encounter the observer learns of new dimensions within as well as without, and learns something, often not very much, of how those dimensions abut on each other. What he learns is not only imperfectly explicable but often no more than slightly clear. And that learning frequently has within it several kinds of unpleasantness that were themselves surprising when they appeared. None of these observable facts about encounter could lead to a facile assertion of unity. Self does not melt here, though it may warm slightly. The encounter asserts wholeness, unquestionably, but this assertion that has been earned with astonishing difficulty goes on to point out that there is more to be seen and known than it was comfortable to suspect. And, conversely, it indicates that much which was apparently available to be known is not really so. The assertion also insists, not quite in passing, that the order of the process of recognizing ties is shaped much like the order of the cosmoses within and without.

The vision on Mt. Snowdon, in Book Fourteen of *The Prelude*, goes over this latter point more extensively than do most other similar passages in Wordsworth's poetry. But it also shows, again extensively and with great clarity, how a surprised —perhaps even startled—recognition of the dimensions one has always been moving in can lead into an understanding of the wholeness and likeness of the inner and outer cosmoses. This sudden insight caught the introspecting observer on Mt. Snowdon with as much surprise as did the similarly abrupt influx of knowledge centering on the daffodils or (in a far less developed but still complete situation) the dropping of the moon onto the cottage in "Strange Fits of Passion." An inflow of light startles the observer on Snowdon into the cosmos:

> at my feet the ground appeared to brighten,
> And with a step or two seemed brighter still;
> Nor was time given to ask or learn the cause,
> For instantly a light upon the turf
> Fell like a flash, and lo! as I looked up,
> The Moon hung naked in a firmament
> Of azure without cloud, and at my feet
> Rested a silent sea of hoary mist.
>
> (35–42)

Here his awareness of dimensions apprehends a massive depth below him as well as that which holds the moon locked high and seemingly alone in a broad and endless extent of sky. The curious metamorphosis of the land into a sea studded with islands serves, among other things, to begin the extent of the sea just below him (rather than somewhere in the center of his sight) and, in stretching it out to the limits of what he can glimpse of the Atlantic, to give all that firmer an impression of another plane going out from where he stands to infinity.

Wordsworth's commentary on the scene builds from the likenesses of the cosmoses within and without and does so in an image which, at first, seems as violent a juxtaposition of the distant and different as any he had accomplished. But, in fact, the whole image of the mind feeding on infinity is a hall of mirrors in which content and creator continually merge with form in a most complex perfection. If mind as well as matter were spatialized, it would look like this, so the image implies; and, at the same time, the image also displays the mode of mind's action and the material that the majestic intellect feeds upon. Here, the image of a mind which is shaped and acts like the immense dimensionality of the external cosmos has itself been shaped by a mind, the poet's, on which the immensity of that cosmos had quite suddenly acted. Every aspect of the total experience reaches its full meaning only in the presence of all the other aspects, for the cosmoses not only intersect but also are part of each other in a wholeness beyond paradox. One of the more impressive aspects of the passage describing the vision on Mt. Snowdon is actually a kind of negative result, for nowhere within this battery of self-reflecting planes of order and creation, this vastly dimensioned organic whole, does Wordsworth slip into solipsism. The roar of waters mounting out of the abyss has, perhaps, spread over the cosmos; but Wordsworth's tactful control always intimates distance and doubt with just enough of a gentle touch to show that the world is never entirely his:

> through a rift—
> Not distant from the shore whereon we stood,
> A fixed, abysmal, gloomy, breathing-place—
> Mounted the roar of waters, torrents, streams
> Innumerable, roaring with one voice!
> Heard over earth and sea, and, in that hour,
> For so it seemed, felt by the starry heavens.
>
> (56–62)

A dozen heavier touches could do no more than does "seemed" here or than do the temporal limitations built into "in that hour." And if the Atlantic "appeared / To dwindle" (47–48), it did so in the form of something seen and also of something that might have been, the firm ambiguity of "appeared" holding comfortably all it is supposed to hold, which is very much indeed. Significantly, and quite possibly to offset solipsism by distinguishing as well as cohering, there is no movement toward hierogamy here. Somewhere on the sidelines of the passage stands the marriage of mind and universe, but Wordsworth holds it aside with care, for a less tricky context.

However much his poetry is celebratory of the sight of order, neither Wordsworth nor any other romantic could depend with unalleviated comfort on always being able to hold such a massive, endless intricacy in balance. The romantic sense of distinction and difference, of uniqueness, individuality, and concreteness, of the importance of specific points in space and time —ideas and language which were cant only in the third-rate— set up for them an organic world crammed with discrete individualities. It was a world they wanted and believed in, but it was also one that could too easily get beyond any but a control leaning more on luck than on strength. Sentimentalizing did odd things, such as juxtaposing uniqueness of response and painless unification, and it rarely felt the need to recognize, not to say deal with, such paradoxes. Wholenesses containing self and other not only involved the usual blended souls (the favorite stance for sentimentality) but, more seriously for poetry, postulated a world which moved graciously toward the perceiver, sharing its images with him for a common but never clearly specified purpose. The simplest level of this movement made trees weep. In a more subtle and potentially disturbing variation, a poem like "Le Lac" makes under its apparently necessary public rhetoric a plea that the wholeness which seems to be offered on the level of rhetoric should actually exist. Ultimately there is probably not a single major romantic figure, beginning and ending where one chooses to, who does not show at some point the simultaneous existence—buried deeply at the moments of the assertion of public dogma—of the opposite of warm, blanketing states and of the grand fanfare of public celebration. At some stage in every romantic experience, and certainly at most advanced stages, there is a lonely, bitter, or melancholy wrestling with an angel who may touch a thigh but will leave no names behind for himself *or* his antagonist. The point is not that there are Lamartines at one end and Leopardis at the other but, rather, that everywhere within the range of possibilities there are figures whose honesty gets in the way of what they would like to be true. Wordsworth was one of them.

All of the information left to us about the stage when contrarieties had wearied Wordsworth confines it to a brief period of obviously serious danger. On the other hand, even though he settled into a more or less generalized awareness of order, the sense of contrarieties, of the simultaneous presence of irreconcilable elements, never left him. Rather, it became part of a framework in which contrarieties were recognized as such, and there was usually little more that Wordsworth could do with them than that. In the high moments, though, which may have been implicit in the generalized order but were neither mandatory nor regular, he recognized and brought into a compelling version of coherence all of the various contrarieties of his organic yet always partly mysterious world. To do so—which meant to learn to live with the unassailable—he had to recognize that there was much that nature could not do. The mode of encounter may well have been inevitable, given the qualities of this observer and what there was out there for him to work on, but there was in the mode a built-in insufficiency grounded in the limitations of both the observer and his immediate material. Nature could not lead him where his compulsion for knowing wanted him to go, toward the *fullest* comprehension of all that was out there and beyond. Its opacity was inaccessible to recourse. If there were areas he could not enter into, the fault was, surely, due in part to inadequacies he could neither avoid nor control; but, then, the material was thick and stubborn and was manageable only by some method that defeated it by going beyond it. Here is another whole area of Wordsworthian ambivalence: if there was much that nature could not do or show, nature did have the concreteness which made for a kind of truth that he respected and that could be found nowhere else. The world was intractable and dense, resistant to penetration except at rare moments. But the world was dense *because* it was palpable. It gave and withstood at the same time, and the same qualities made it do both. When Wordsworth pushed at a gate to show Bonamy Price how to put a world out there to protect against solipsism, he was pushing at a density which reassured by the truth of its presence but tended to keep other dimensions closed off to him. To overleap it completely into a state beyond sense was to purchase another form of awareness at the expense of the guarantees in palpable presence. (A dilemma of similar proportions haunts the gorgeousness of Keats's "Ode on a Grecian Urn.") On the other hand, the truths about things were usually circumscribed, the areas they illumined were narrow, and the occasional push through offered by such as a disembodied voice or by his own removal from the senses was rare and in itself never more than a glance. The expansion urged by his compulsion for knowing would, at its most intense, settle for nothing less than whatever could overcome the subjection imposed by the natural. Still, Wordsworth was no Blake and no mystic: he always knew that the natural was less than all, but knew too that it was very much of what there was and was generally very good. But very much and very good turned out to be not enough, since he evidently realized later that he carried his limitations with him wherever he went. *The Excursion*, as such, was perhaps not inevitable, but its presence and nature should not be surprising, given the probable directions in which Wordsworth could have gone. It is equally unsurprising that the development of the Wordsworthian canon shows that the limitations of natural knowing vexed him into other ways of seeing. In those other ways there were new kinds of assertions about coherence which overcame what had bothered him previously by the simple expedient of ignoring it.

In "Yes, It Was the Mountain Echo," a poem of 1806, a group of curious ambiguities reveals the strain of change and the wrestling of Wordsworth's mind with the meaning of where he stands and of standing as such:

> Yes, it was the mountain Echo,
> Solitary, clear, profound,
> Answering to the shouting Cuckoo,
> Giving to her sound for sound!
>
> Unsolicited reply
> To a babbling wanderer sent;
> Like her ordinary cry,
> Like—but oh, how different!
>
> Hears not also mortal Life?
> Hear not we, unthinking Creatures!
> Slaves of folly, love, or strife—
> Voices of two different natures?
>
> Have not *we* too?—yes, we have
> Answers, and we know not whence;
> Echoes from beyond the grave,
> Recognised intelligence!
>
> Such rebounds our inward ear
> Catches sometimes from afar—
> Listen, ponder, hold them dear;
> For of God,—of God they are.

This is, of course, a variation on the theme of the disembodied voice, and it ignores none of the implications of that image.

Like "Stepping Westward," it talks of a voice that came when no voice was expected, here projected toward a wanderer (the cuckoo, his surrogate in the analogy) who is "babbling," which the wanderer in "Stepping Westward" most certainly was not doing. Sporadic contact with otherness has a different organization in this poem than it does in "Stepping Westward," and there is, therefore, a tone essentially different in kind, however clear the similarities. The voice from another dimension comes through nothing here, in this place, a situation opposed to that in "Stepping Westward" and all other similar poems. There is nothing here that is even apparently creaturely except the bird and the observer; but their creatureliness is so emphatically presented as one of the organic dimensions of the world within this microcosm that they appear grounded in the physical as though it were quicksand holding them fast. He, like the bird, is "unthinking," though obviously the two different voices he hears are not the same as those the bird hears. Hierarchy does not disappear in this experience; indeed, it does quite the opposite. Levels of hearing are naturally stages on the hierarchy of being. Further, though he and the bird are very different, they are together in a present in this place, which is unimaginably far from the source of the echoes the man hears (or at least the place from which they rebound). This long space bridged by an echo may enfold a coherent context, but there is in it no welcoming into a whole; rather, there is a division of parts, which, though they may all belong together in a context, are most certainly and emphatically divided. The most positive aspect of the physical in this poem is its usefulness as a source for metaphor. (For very good reasons Wordsworth is coming close here to the mode of Gray.) But even that aspect has an odd ring: somewhere deep in the analogy on which the poem turns is an irony which reveals an uneasiness, and the tone of that uneasiness recalls an earlier mode of encounter (or lack of it). For it is, after all, the bird's own voice that comes back to it, "Solitary, clear, profound," different and deeper in sound, a bit more awesome than its own babbling, but its own voice nevertheless. The poem asserts—it is its point and business to assert—that the echoes which come back to the human observer come from that mode of being which is highest and therefore absolutely other. If this is an assertion based on faith, the poem does not make that basis as clear as *The Excursion* was later to do. There is in the poem, however, a reiterated insistence on the source of what he hears that is reminiscent, in its somewhat flurried manner, not so much of what was to follow in *The Excursion* as of stanza four of the "Immortality" ode. Nor, on the other hand, does the poem dare to imply, except at the deepest level of analogy, that he may be hearing his own voice come back, though all consistency in the analogy pushes in that direction. The analogy is not slipshod. More significantly, the ambiguities buried within it are indicative of his difficulties in working out of one stance into another, difficulties so recalcitrant that there is even, very probably, a rise almost to the surface of a time when he could talk only to himself. Thus, there is that within the central analogy, a potential irony reiterated even in the "rebounds" of the assertive last stanza, which disturbs the balance of the assertiveness just enough to show its tenuous order. Wordsworth never works that disturbing element out of the situation. He would have had to draw limits around the analogy which would make it practically useless or call it a lie. He leaves the submerged ambiguity there, showing, if nothing else, the strain of what he was going through in saying what he did. The easier assertions of *The Excursion* have no comparable strains within them, but they have no difficulties of that sort to cope with either.

In "Yes, It Was the Mountain Echo" there is a rebalancing which reveals a shift in Wordsworth's perception of the relationships among the elements and dimensions of his world. In the apparently similar situation defined in "Stepping Westward," the voice comes out of, and is emphatically part of, a wholeness, and the fact of wholeness receives equal emphasis with the fact that there is a voice which offers a greeting. But the poem about echoes, though it nowhere denies wholeness or even context, stresses that the sound moves from one distant part of the situation to another, and it is the distance, not the wholeness, which receives equal emphasis with the fact of the voice. Further, though there is context and even hierarchy in "Yes, It Was the Mountain Echo," the idea of continuum gets no more emphasis than what there is in the fact that the voice comes down to him from a very distant place. Again it is the distance that matters, not the (comparatively quite weak) continuity. It is worth noting, too, that such distancing of parts makes for a context in which objects seem, inevitably, to take on a subsidiary role. In these cases, objects would tend to be drawn on primarily for what they can reveal about the relationships among the distant parts of the framework. When the objects are shown to have weight, it is usually the weight of flesh and mortality which is important in the context, and not the substantial presence of the thing. The result, then, is a poem like *The White Doe of Rylstone* or—in another category of quality —*The Excursion.*

In one way or another, every major work of Wordsworth's great decade and later has to do with wholeness or lack of it, and especially with a sense of dichotomies. The progress he mapped out (elaborately, though never in one place) starts from the child's mind, goes to that of the superstitious peasant, and moves finally to his own painstaking and pain-transforming awareness of distances within a context. The solipsism of the child in the great ode turns into the indivisible, externalized world of the child in "We Are Seven," who has no difficulty realizing that there is a world outside of herself but who also has no recognition of the boundaries of here and there or death and life. She has established a unity encompassing all things that have an intimate meaning for her life, but she carries them all within an eternal (or internal) present where there are none of the dichotomies that an adult would recognize. In "Lucy Gray" there is a meeting of sophistication and superstition, each with its own conception of dichotomy. On one side are the parents and the narrator, brutally aware of the division of death and life, and on the other are those who say that the child can still be heard skipping and singing. If it takes a comparatively unsophisticated mind to think that Lucy still bridges dichotomies in this way, it is only a most sophisticated one which can see how superstition is related to imagination because in both there is an impingement of areas which seemed forever absolutely separate. The kind of wholeness Wordsworth came to see always had within it the possibility of such impingement, though there was much less possibility in the later poems (almost none, from the evidence available) because his world had stiffened into a set of respectable dimensions. At some time, though, especially in his earlier, more flexible and fluent world, impingement could leap from potentiality into presence at any moment. As the wholeness he saw grew more distances within itself, and as long as the dimensions remained fluid and not frozen into orthodoxy, the parts of his world could reach out and touch each other in the most surprising ways. This touching, the impingement, was more than just a patching of breaks in the continua around him, for that patching, assertive as it was, was really all that superstition could do. And the patching would never confess what he was often moved to point out, that what he knew was never quite enough to unravel all that there was of the continua. The knowledge came to him out of a wholeness that was partly unexplained though still, he knew, coherent. When knowing and mystery coalesced with a stunning awareness of dimensions of being and, simultaneously and vividly, with the substantiality of a present world, there were poems of a kind that made his difficult cosmos click into place. Usually these were poems of encounter and an especially dramatic impingement. Some, like "Resolution and Independence," touch lightly upon a mode of personal myth which seemed always just ready for him to develop, though he never took it very far.

At the beginning of that poem, Wordsworth spreads out an elaborate groundwork of physicality, one of the points of which is to verify the substantial reality of what is about to happen to him by showing the palpable kind of world in which it did happen. What he is to see will seem odd, not so much because of the old man's difficulties or his own, not even because of the bleak surroundings—all of these are normal in the world his poems inhabited—but because of the complex strata of what he sees in the man or, conversely, what the man causes him to see. The first two stanzas are anchors, palpable points not only for the experience to start from but also for it to return to periodically. What he does in them is exactly parallel with the experience recorded by Bonamy Price: in one way or another he seemed always to be grasping at substance to convince himself that he stood among substantial things. The third stanza makes the transition into the poem proper, not so much by putting him within the frame of the scene (it does that very obviously) as by showing that he can slide out of it and into himself, or at least that he is on the verge of doing so. The stanza holds a flood of personal pronouns. At the same time, it carefully brings in a series of substantives that progresses up the ladder of abstraction as the nouns show increasingly less of the specificity of immediate perception. The changing level of these nouns, the push toward subjectivity indicated with the packing of personal pronouns, and the candid statement that he can easily shut out part of the external world if he chooses to—

> I heard the woods and distant waters roar;
> Or heard them not, as happy as a boy

—all prepare for the complete turn within that he makes with the abrupt, irrational, and bewildering shift in mood. After the shift, there comes in stanza five another rush of personal pronouns, again with a parallel series of generalized nouns, this time embedded in generalized situations. The point here is that the observer has moved away from the pressing, detailed immediacy of the outside world into the unphysical world within. When he comes out of it again (he had gone in very deeply), he has to do so slowly, to refocus his vision, as it were. For a time it appears that he is not quite certain of what he is seeing outside of himself, for as he is refocusing, he runs over several ways of defining what he sees, and those possibilities cover a large sweep of the great chain of being.

Whatever it is that he sees draws him out toward an awareness of external things but not, immediately at least, to those things directly external to him. What he sees is so unexpected, so little to be foreseen, that he first analyzes it, tentatively ("whether"), in terms of a gift. Obviously he has been surprised in his musing, surprised not only that something is out there but, further, by the nature of that which suddenly stands out there over against him. It is there and strange, so strange indeed that it could have come only from that which is foreign and most high. Or at least he chooses to talk about the highest first. (Hints of the later Wordsworth are here.) As his focus clears, he moves from the general area ("this lonely place") to something wide just near him ("beside a pool"), then up again, as if stretching his visual muscles into focus ("the eye of heaven"), and then finally to the central object, which, once it is defined and placed, is set up immediately in an extravagant hyperbole ("The oldest man he seemed that ever wore grey hairs") which takes the object at once out of the realm of the common and everyday; or, better, prevents him from ever considering it as being in that realm.

But there are kinds of strangeness other than that which is foreign and most high. The passage has moved along the hierarchy of being from the implied source of grace down through the man, but with a swift glance upward or backward to "the eye of heaven" to show both context and the place from which his vision had moved. Now suddenly settled to earth, the passage plummets against a huge stone, a hunk of the bottom of things, on which a very different kind of foreignness manages to crawl in order to indulge in a low form of hedonism. The crawling object is, perhaps, more obviously part of the everyday, but it is no less unlike him, though it is far on the other side of that spectrum from the source which, mysteriously, might have sent him a surprising gift. The man stands between the source and the beast, related to both though different from each. He is, further, between life and death ("not all alive nor dead"), and not at all coincidentally, considering the allegory that runs all through Wordsworth, he is a traveler. Wordsworth never lets go, in this poem, of the sense of the in-between. Just after the passage on the source and the beast, he talks of the man, first in terms of one end of the scale ("a more than human weight") and then in terms of the qualities associated with the far end of the other ("motionless as a cloud"). The old man is not so much on the edge of things as between them. And because he is the point through which the observer has seen all the levels and stages, he embodies them all as well.

The observer falls out of a thorough concern with himself and back into a world where the object on which he first focuses clearly is like and unlike himself, and it is the unlikeness which strikes him more at the beginning of his awareness of the old man. Later the likeness (which makes possible the didacticism of the ending) comes through more forcefully than it did at first, but the initial strangeness never disappears. Quite accidentally, Wordsworth has stumbled upon man in the universe —not universal man, although the leech-gatherer could be thought of in those terms if there were another kind of emphasis, but man as he stands in the cosmos, under the sky in a lonely place beside a bare pool on the moors, somewhere between heaven and a beast. Wordsworth's commentary on stanza nine in the 1815 Preface dwells on approximation and would seem, therefore, to collapse the great chain, but in actuality it has quite another effect:

> In these images, the conferring, the abstracting, and the modifying powers of the Imagination, immediately and mediately acting, are all brought into conjunction. The stone is endowed with something of the power of life to approximate it to the sea-beast; and the sea-beast stripped of some of its vital qualities to assimilate it to the stone; which intermediate image is thus treated for the purpose of bringing the original image, that of the stone, to a nearer resemblance to the figure and condition of the aged Man; who is divested of so much of the indications of life and motion as to bring him to the point where the two objects unite and coalesce in just comparison.[17]

Stanzas eight, nine, and ten make up a unified passage, the main action of which is exploration: Wordsworth is trying with precision to place the old man who stands there in front of him. The middle stanza, the one Wordsworth is primarily commenting on in the Preface, draws man, beast, and rock together, almost superimposing their outlines. What he talks about in his commentary is one kind of imaginative activity that stanza nine, taken by itself, illustrates. But the stanza is surrounded by two others, and exactly at the beginning of stanza eight and at the end of stanza ten, framing the coherent wholeness of the passage, are references to that which is more than human, not below it. The approximating in the middle stanza is thus balanced by the sundering in what surrounds it. In other words, the imagery of assimilation is only part of what Wordsworth sees in the old man and is not in itself sufficient to describe all that is there, for the passage lives on the delicate balance of the interplay of approximation and hierarchy that is imitated in the three stanzas. Within their context, Wordsworth explores and finds in the old man a myriad of varieties of strangeness, all kinds that are in a man and most of the kinds without.

[17] *Poetical Works*, II, 438.

Wordsworth's moral relationship to the leech-gatherer comes only after his initial shock of recognition over the being of the old man, which he draws near to seeing in its absoluteness: "the figure presented in the most naked simplicity possible," which Wordsworth goes on to say gave him a "feeling of spirituality or supernaturalness." [18] Certainly he sees that being as a presence. Further, and most significant, this kind of presence has a special relationship to all other potential presences. Wordsworth wakes suddenly and with surprise into a vision of cosmic wholeness, although the wholeness does not come immediately to him but only as he hunts for images to define all that he sees. What happens here happened elsewhere, for he had also stumbled into a sense of the totality of the cosmos with the daffodils, with his vision on Mt. Snowdon, and in "A Night-Piece," these poems among others. But there is a crucial difference between this poem and, say, the one on daffodils; and in the difference is that single step further which Wordsworth occasionally took and which might well have made this or a similar poem the "timely utterance" he needed at one point. "I Wandered Lonely as a Cloud" had shown the cosmic order with man as dancer within it, but he had been an undifferentiated member of the team. "The Solitary Reaper" had pointed out the difference of man, but the vision is essentially grounded in the things of this world. But in "Resolution and Independence" there is the whole hierarchy of the entire cosmos, not just the One Life within it, which Wordsworth dances with all other beings, but also the special place of man in that Life. And this observer, like the one in the great ode and "To the Cuckoo," has an intense awareness of himself at a stage in the development of his private segment of the earth's flight through time. The temporal unity of being that his personality moves in has its spatial counterpart in the coincidence of being in which he and all other creatures share at every point in time. What the observer sees through the person of the old man is, then, the variety of disparate wholenesses which meet in him. What he makes out of what he sees—the tag in the last stanza—is necessary for the moral dimension in the poem, but that dimension actually has nothing directly to do with what he stumbled upon, though the dimension and what he

[18] *Early Years*, p. 366.

sees work together elegantly. This is the curious split which haunts many poems of the great decade and is not observable later. It is not that the moral tag is an excrescence, since it follows inevitably from one level in the dramatic structure of the poem, which is, after all, about a moral crisis. Rather, it is that what he sees lives by itself and that the process of his seeing and the nature of what he sees are about matters different from those dealt with in the moral, self-referential dimension. It is Wordsworth's triumph that he can bring these very different matters, with their different areas of concern, into a magnificently ordered poem. In his best poems, such as "The Solitary Reaper," he performs that same feat time and again.

An earlier poem like "Lines Written in Early Spring" is worth looking at to see the meaning of the hookup into the cosmic hierarchy. In "Lines" there is a strong assertion of the separateness of man (even of this sympathetic observer tied into the continuum) and other natural beings, but that is as far as he takes unlikeness. The argument and interest rest principally on what man could do, not only for other men but also within the continuum, should he choose to see where he can find a place for himself within the totality. Man is the missing link here. A deep sense of harmony supports the belief that may have been sent by heaven (and it needs support, as he knows well), the faith that there is actually a feeling out there akin to his own joy but in a different version. Yet man is the disrupter of the order of nature here; or, to be more generous, man does not complete all the order potentially there. A poem like "The Poet's Epitaph" makes the same point in another way. One of the ironies of Wordsworth's early world is that the lowest have a better awareness of order (perhaps because their awareness is unthought) than do the highest, who are closed or smoothed or crusted.

Some of the man-centered concerns in the *Lyrical Ballads* ended up, eventually, in the quasi-religious humanism of *The Excursion*. Between the ballads and the long poem, however, there were moments of grand coalescence, one of which occurs in "Resolution and Independence." This is man not as a disrupter but as an object, a synecdoche surely, through which a glimpse of the whole organization can be reached. The observer in

"Resolution and Independence" begins a series of melancholy notes which are potentially disruptive of the joyful order into which he has walked. And this disruption, paradoxically, moves closer to actuality because he asserts his likeness to the creatures around him ("Even such a happy Child of earth am I"), a likeness which obviously disturbs him at a level of consciousness different from the one on which he had been working. At this point the moral dimension and the plane of objective seeing begin to work with and out of each other. To see similarities but no difference is, in the moral dimension, to do an injustice to one's full humanity. That is, to be human in terms of that dimension means to partake of the publicly recognized levels of responsibility in which all men, *as men,* should share. This whole pattern is clearly a development away from the situation of "Lines Written in Early Spring." It has a partial counterpart (though not on the plane of public morality) in the uneasy, false notes of the observer in stanza four of the "Immortality" ode, who is also a disrupter of the order of joy and has to learn all that his role calls for. (We remember how important role-playing is in stanza seven of the ode.) The man in the ode ended by asserting something he could not feel quite easy with, though its values are clear enough. But there is nothing of the *pis aller* about the shock of recognition in "Resolution and Independence." The old man comes through to the observer as the center through whom the whole can be seen, the individualized holder of most stages of being, with all the flesh of the sea-beast and with his own version of the higher spirit that moves up from him. Rather than disrupter, man is the embodiment (quite literally) of the order that is out there and that is also within those who can see beings like the old man and reach an encompassing knowledge of what they see. Deep within the poem is an area which absorbs and transcends the moral dimension because it is more aware of all that a man can be and do. In that area the moral dimension appears (in this poem full of paradoxes) as less irrelevant than if it is taken as his final assertion. For the morality is the public stance, the tag which ties the situation into the world which he can share with others. It is one way, a generally accepted one, in which the activity of being human can take shape; out of this aspect *The Excursion* developed its own mode of asserting. But on the level deep within the poem there is another assertion: what the observer sees here, it argues, is *also* what it means to be human, not in terms of agreement with others but in regard only to one's self and the orders within and without. At that level the leech-gatherer has nothing to do with moral dimensions. No public stance is available there, but only that which is most one's own, because all it can do for the observer is give him an exact sense of what he is.

This is a private dance, then, though its point is that Wordsworth is not dancing alone. The recognition of being can only be hinted at, through images which move downward toward the deep truth but cannot contain it. The more explicit phrasing of the earlier version ("by which an old man *was*, far from all house or home") fascinates by its directness, but it was apparently too flatly assertive, without getting at everything that the paraphrase in the letter gives. The latter ("not stood, not sat, but '*was*'—the figure presented in the most naked simplicity possible") moves further down than the earlier text does, but it has within it little of the awed recognition that the final passage holds. Wordsworth stands on the moors and stares at a man, but he is dancing nevertheless, with all the solemn joy of an encounter that leads him out into the center of the dancing circle. There he can dance only for himself, privately, without myth, but inside an order that contains all mysteries though it reveals none. This is Wordsworth's *Commedia*.

The Sense of Hierarchy

THIS STUDY BEGAN with a comment by Basil Willey to the effect that Wordsworth's poetry was an attempt to produce "a record of successes." The poetry was that and more, for it was certainly a record of surprises as well, and, with a muted passion that was never out of control, it was also a series of celebrations of the successes. We have seen something of what a Wordsworthian success looks like and how difficult it was for it to come about. There remained, of course, the uncertainty of how to talk about it. Wordsworth always asserted that he wanted to develop a usable public language for what he saw, and he went partway toward doing so, with a rhetoric that others drew on to make out of his own ways a familiar mode. But it was developed only in part, because there was little he could say about the private dance, or the private aspects of the dance. Where he stands single, he stands alone. Whether at the edge of joy or fully within it, the observer in a Wordsworthian encounter makes out of that moment something which others can see him going through but which remains, at some points and in some dimensions, beyond empathy. No one felt this more intensely than Francis Jeffrey, never negligible as a critic of Wordsworth. What Coleridge said of Wordsworth and Goethe, that each was somehow a "spectator *ab extra*," is to a degree true of the observer *of* a Wordsworthian encounter, but it is definitely not true of the observer *in* one, who (in a moment which is truly of encounter) is fully within all that happens.

Every romantic seems at some time to have felt this warring, ambivalent urge toward both prophecy and privacy. What Willey calls Wordsworth's rejection of available tradition, "his *deprivation* of mythology, his aloneness with the universe," [1] comes back to affect the modes and manner of Wordsworth's ways of knowing. The record of Blake's and Hölderlin's successes (tenuous only for their contemporaries) stands at one end of a spectrum of privacy, close to the cherished esoterica of some of Novalis and Hugo and of much of Nerval. Wordsworth works somewhere about the middle: his world had within it areas which were only deceptively available, as well as some which were genuinely so. Near the other end of the spectrum stands Scott, who translated a quite private sense of the rich presence of palpable things into a generally accessible fictional universe in which all times can be simultaneously present—their differences never chill—and in which a permanent moral order can be discovered. But strange knowledge, in one of the most bitter romantic puns, can lead without recourse to an estrangement from community, though it is more likely to do so to the poet who stands, at some point in his experience, near to Hölderlin's end of the spectrum:

> Weave a circle round him thrice,
> And close your eyes with holy dread,
> For he on honey-dew hath fed,
> And drunk the milk of Paradise.

The anguish can be compounded by the realization that one is also a stranger to the world from which the knowledge comes. This was Hölderlin's problem exactly, and in outline it was Wordsworth's too; but the difference in tone (i.e., the comparative presence of anguish) starts from a very different awareness on the part of each poet of his role in relation to community. My last comments on Wordsworth shall come out of this area.

Wordsworth accepts, with an almost audible sigh of relief, that much of what he sees is either beyond his ken and therefore beyond communication or else so private as in effect to be incommunicable. This is not to say that he was content with

---

[1] Willey, *The Seventeenth Century Background*, p. 295.

strangeness; he surely never was. But occasionally, in rare moments of an astonishing vision of order, he coped successfully with it. And, in turn, he knew that the strangeness was within and without, and that much of the strangeness without became —when he did cope with it successfully—part of that which was within. He slipped comfortably into a stance of partial privacy, the poet alone with a busy universe, because he had to and because he wanted to. (Eventually even that was not enough, probably because the rare moments came too rarely and then hardly at all.) Hölderlin, though, lives tensely his role as the poet in a dark time who sees dimly but at least sees, and has to tell of what he sees so that the festive meeting of god and man can take place again. (Analogously, Coleridge's Mariner corners his hearer and prevents him from going to the secular wedding echoing in the background.) Hölderlin's world was shot through with privacy primarily because others would not see what was in it; it *should* have been accessible. With Wordsworth, however, it could never have been; at bottom he was his own community.

What follows is that Wordsworth, when he talks about his experience, works with how and what he goes through as well as with the odd qualities in the things which go through it with him. Hölderlin, when he talks about himself, dwells on his role and on himself as actor of it, i.e., not so much on what he is doing in the experience (the process) as on what the experience is doing to him (the unheard seer as victim). To carry this somewhat further: for Wordsworth, as we know, the conditions of the barest solitude were the optimum ones, and only in those conditions could what happened to him happen at its most direct and forceful. But for Hölderlin poetry was a communal experience, the hymn of praise an aspect of community worship in which the seer, as priest, leads the choral song. When he was alone, he could not do what he was supposed to do. His loneliness was a road not to desired experience but away from it, a terrifying separation from god and man. His hymns were, in part, elegies; Valéry's characterization of biblical poems works for much of Hölderlin as well: "Les Psaumes, par exemple, participent de l'hymne et de l'élégie, combinaison qui accomplit une alliance remarquable des sentiments collectifs lyriquement

189

exprimés avec ceux qui procèdent du plus intime de la personne et de sa foi." [2] Even the dualism of mortality and divinity seemed to exclude Hölderlin: he was the poet isolated from other men and the man separated absolutely from divinity, with only a glimpse (but that is more than anyone else cares to have) of what and where divinity is. The biblical prophet, locked into much the same intermediate stance, at least spoke for God to man and for man to God. Hölderlin hopes that he does the former and cannot hope to do the latter.

At times, in poems like "Lines Written in Early Spring," Wordsworth offers an inchoate version of this multiple separation, but even though he stands apart from other men and, in certain respects, from nature, he knows that he can occasionally tie into continua that are only rarely there for Hölderlin and deadly when they are there. If Wordsworth ever thought of himself as a genuine public figure (and he does so far more in his letters and essays than in his poems), the title seems mainly honorific and more than slightly ironically bestowed: the drive toward a public voice which is at the center of the prophet's works is hardly observable in Wordsworth's best poems and rarely close to the living center of his most significant experiences. The public voice he developed eventually to work for *The Excursion* talks of public matters, but by that point there was little left of horror or glory or mystery for him to write about. Blake's complaints about those lines in *The Excursion* in which Wordsworth passes Jehovah and his choir unalarmed have their point.

This was not, however, the mode of public speech which Hölderlin tried to work out and which Wordsworth approached in some of his poems. In "Lines Written in Early Spring" it was a *belief* which may have been sent from heaven; in "Resolution and Independence" it was an old *man*. When Wordsworth stared at the old man, the man came alive as a center of energy and did so in a way which no object in *The Excursion* or its related lyrics could achieve. But that way was shared by "Resolution and Independence," the Lucy poems, "Lucy Gray," "The Solitary Reaper," and a number of pas-

[2] From Valéry's essay on the "Cantiques Spirituels," in *Variété V* (Paris: Gallimard, 1945), p. 171.

190

sages in *The Prelude* and its related lyrics. In a world where an observer can fall suddenly and disquietingly upon centers of energy and order such as this old man, no external source of symbols is really necessary. These centers, disarmingly familiar (thus the surprise of epiphany), open up suddenly to reveal within and through themselves not only the multiplicity of the cosmos but also all the mysteries of an otherness which touches, strangely, upon that which is not other but just like the observer. If the center of energy were a tree or a mountain, there would be even more mystery but less of the deceptive familiarity that comes through when the form is an old man or a young girl; less, then, of the observer's likeness out there. The egotistical sublime, which is an imposition of self upon that which is not self, is in part a protective gesture which makes familiar what is potentially dangerous. To that extent it borders in its effect upon the humanity in the human figures in his landscape but with the difference that their humanity never does what the egotistical sublime does, which is overwhelm the landscape into the suffocation of its integral being.

For a Wordsworth or a Hölderlin, outflashes of the energy of otherness were always potential, and they occurred often enough in a human form to shape the mysterious into a present reality that had areas of familiarity about it. Thus, if traditional myth was not usable, the world of Wordsworth's poems had most of the requisites for a contemporary private myth, though it never quite reached there. It was involved with an understanding, or at least an awareness, of dimensions of being, the kind of picture of things a field fertile for myth has to have. It lived, further, on a hierarchy where differentiation is as important as likeness but where the recognition of likeness is so intense that differentiation is all the more striking when it appears. Yet we have seen that Wordsworth, for the most profound reasons, was uneasy with anthropocentrism. Perhaps equally as important, the radical privacy of his experience ensured that the forms of even a personal myth were not among the choices available to his imaginative order. A writer like Camus lived in a world without hierarchy, or at least without one that he could sense. The world of Camus is a world of man, not myth, for if there is foreignness in it, there is no spectrum which reaches toward an otherness that is both strange and high. There are traces of that kind of world in Wordsworth, traces strong enough to shake him into an occasional uneasiness, but epiphanic moments could open up a sense of hierarchy which Camus recognized as lost to himself. Wordsworth stared, nervously and with excitement, at those moments when otherness entered in and at the places where it happened. But even when he was between those moments, the possibility of their reoccurrence gave every object within his sight the potential for a shining out of radiance which was only partly his own.

Index

II. WILLIAM WORDSWORTH: POETRY AND PROSE

Index

NOTE ON THE AUTHOR

FREDERICK GARBER is associate professor of comparative literature at the State University of New York at Binghamton. He
received his B.A. from Boston University in 1957 and attended
Yale University as a Woodrow Wilson Fellow in comparative
literature. He received his Ph.D. from Yale in 1963 and has
taught at the University of Washington. His interests range
from the eighteenth to the twentieth centuries, and he has written on various subjects, including Edwin Muir, Rilke, Thoreau,
Ann Radcliffe, the romantic hero, and the *mal du siècle*.

UNIVERSITY OF ILLINOIS PRESS